Ancient Bingley

or, Bingley, Its history and Scenery

J. Horsfall Turner

Alpha Editions

This edition published in 2019

ISBN : 9789353299316

Design and Setting By
Alpha Editions
email - alphaedis@gmail.com

This book is a reproduction of an important historical work. Alpha Editions uses the best technology to reproduce historical work in the same manner it was first published to preserve its original nature. Any marks or number seen are left intentionally to preserve its true form.

WILLIAM FERRAND, ESQ., J.P.

Ancient Bingley:

OR,

Bingley, Its History and Scenery.

By J. HORSFALL TURNER, J.P.,

IDEL, BRADFORD.

ONE HUNDRED AND EIGHTY ILLUSTRATIONS.

PRINTED FOR THE AUTHOR, BY
THOMAS HARRISON AND SONS, BINGLEY, YORKS.
1897.

TO
WILLIAM FERRAND, Esq., J.P.,
ST. IVES,
This Volume is Respectfully Inscribed
as a small recognition of the
assistance received from him, and from
his late Father's MSS.
The Author holds himself culpable if
any error of transcription be found,
and pleads his multifarious
engagements as some
extenuation.

PREFACE.

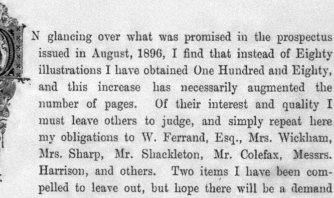

IN glancing over what was promised in the prospectus issued in August, 1896, I find that instead of Eighty illustrations I have obtained One Hundred and Eighty, and this increase has necessarily augmented the number of pages. Of their interest and quality I must leave others to judge, and simply repeat here my obligations to W. Ferrand, Esq., Mrs. Wickham, Mrs. Sharp, Mr. Shackleton, Mr. Colefax, Messrs. Harrison, and others. Two items I have been compelled to leave out, but hope there will be a demand for their publication in a separate volume, viz., The Parish Registers from 1577 to 1638, as copied by the late Mr. Hartley Hartley and myself; and the Churchwardens' Book, 1650 to 1694, copied entirely by him and carefully read over by us with the original. Though these are necessarily omitted much other matter has been inserted.

I have had such an abundance of material that I fear I shall be charged with condensing rather than elaborating. I have had neither time nor inclination to attempt "fine writing," and already have discovered the word "were" where "was" ought to have been used.

20th Nov., 1897.   J. HORSFALL TURNER.

CONTENTS.

———✦———

                                                                                                PAGES.

SITUATION.—Geology. Lake-dwellings. Pit-dwellers. Iberians. Aryans. BRITISH REMAINS.—Druids' Altar. Earthworks. Fire-worship. Cairns. Skirtfuls. Castlefield. British names. Roman occupation. Roads. Coins. Rumbles Law. Elam discovery - - - - - 17-29.

ANGLES.—Norse, Danes. Runic stone, cross, dip-stone or font, battle memorial. Pagan settlers. Chieftains. Courts and laws. Gods. Feasts. Kings. Social condition. Christianity introduced. Place-names. King Eadberht. King Ongus. Hewenden battle. Haigh, Fowler, Stephens and Vietor on Bingley runes. Etymology. Old maps - - - - - - - 30-53.

NORMANS.—Dr. Collyer's poem. Doomsday Book. Craven Survey. Norman owners. Gospatric. Lords of the Manor. Burun. Paynel. Gant. Market. Magna Charta. Cantilupe. Zouch. Harcourt. Astley, pedigrees and arms. Walker, Currer, Benson, Lane Fox - 54-69.

SUB-MANORS.—Cottingley. Hainworth. Halton. Harden. Riddlesden. Montalt or Mauds. Paslew. Freeholders. Paslew trial. Currer. Savile. Ferrand - - - 70-76.

OLD DEEDS.—1100-1500. Pedigrees of landowners. Montalts, Marleys, Fairfax, Kighleys, &c., &c. - - - 76-100.

THE PEOPLE IN THE DARK AGES.—Wars. Black Death. Lists of inhabitants, 1327, 1336, Poll Tax, 1379. Family names. Trades - - - - - - - 101-109.

POSSESSIONS OF RELIGIOUS ORDERS.—Knights of St. John. Templars. The Knights' Court Records. Wills proved. Rievaulx. Kirklees. Kirkstall. Fountains. Paslews, two abbots. Halton skirmish. Drax. Priest-thorp, *not* Snitterton. Slavery. Frank. Casteley. Villayn - 110-120.

BINGLEY CHURCH.—Vicars, 1275. Eltofts. Bishop Wylson. Sunderlands. Church terrier. Excommunications. Puritanism. Registers. Pews. List of inhabitants, 1634. Place-names. Bells. Burial-ground. Clock - - 121-138.

CONTENTS.

	PAGES.
NONCONFORMITY.—Puritanism. Bingley Exercises. Easter Sacraments. Eli Bentley. Oliver Heywood. His visits. Ferrands. Leach. Walker. Broadley. Decayed gentry. Fanatics. Sunderland's robbery. Heywood's Register of burials, &c. Meeting-houses	139-153.
Joseph Lister. Bradford Siege. Accepted Lister. Independent Ministers. Squabble	153-163.
Quakers. Register	163-166.
Baptists	166-169.
Primitive Methodists, Free Church, &c.	169-173.
CHRONOLOGICAL CHAPTER.—Flodden Field. Subsidy, 1524. Topography. Deeds, 1580-1636. Subsidy, 1621-7. Cottages built, 1639. Fairfax and the War. Treatment of the Poor, 1655. Hearth Tax, 1672. List of inhabitants. Sunderland's Robbery, 1674. Cottingley bridge. Bingley bridge. Marley bridge. Gilbeck bridge. Stock bridge. Beckfoot bridge. Assessments. Bingley token. Voters, 1742. Market	173-193.
FAMILIES.—Benson, Lord Bingley. Lane Fox. Ferrand. Busfeild. Atkinson. Stansfield. Twiss. Sunderland. Rishworth. Birkhead. Eltoft. Oldfield. Rawson. Kighley. Briggs. Hartley. Hudson. Greenwood. Starkie. Peile. Fell. Leach. Horsfall. Feather. Dobson—Lamplugh—Wickham. Morvell. Appleyard. Anderton. Hulbert. Beanlands. Nevile. Broadley. Murgatroyd. Shackleton. Quakerism. Co. Kildare. Parker. Paslew. Wills. Abbot of Whalley. Elland. Mawd or Montalt	194-252.
Thornton, the African Geologist	252-257.
W. Busfeild-Ferrand, Esq. Alfred Sharp, Esq. Joshua Briggs. Milner. Oldfield. Fell. Field. Riddlesden. Priesthorpe. Frank. Dobson. Slater. Savile. Paslew. Currer	257-265.
BIBLIOGRAPHY.— Nicholson. Ben and John Preston. Abraham Holroyd. Harrison's publications. General	266-285.
CHARITIES AND GRAMMAR SCHOOL	286-288.
METHODISM	289-296.
MODERN ANNALS	297-303.
TOPOGRAPHICAL NOTES	304-312.

ILLUSTRATIONS.

WHOLE PAGE PICTURES.

	FACE PAGE		FACE PAGE
Wm. Ferrand, Esq., J.P.†	*Frontispiece*	Rustic Bridge, The Grange*	186
J. Horsfall Turner, large paper copies.		Bingley Market, large paper copies	192
Emblazoned Arms, Lords of the Manor; Burun, Paynell, Gant, Cantilupe, Zouch, Harcourt, Astley, Walker	17	St. Ives, anciently Halton or Harden Grange*	192
		St. Ives' Lake	194
Emblazoned Arms, Lords and Gentry; Currer, Benson, Lane-Fox, Paslew, Marley, Eltoft, Copley, Rishworth	64	Wm. Wickham, Esq., M.P., 1896	232
		H. L. Wickham, Esq., b. 1789	232
		His wife, née Lucy Markham	232
Gawthorpe Hall	68	Hon. William Wickham, M.P., born 1761	232
Old Vicarage	118		
Emblazoned Arms, Gentry. Ward, Ward, Kighley, doubtful. Elland, Swyllington, Maude, Sunderland	121	Col. Henry Wickham, J.P., born 1731	232
		His wife, née Elizabeth Lamplugh	232
		Alfred Sharp, Esq., J.P.‡	259
West Riddlesden	150	Old Grammar School	288
Fairfax Table, St. Ives*	180		

OTHER ILLUSTRATIONS.

	PAGE		PAGE
Druids' Altar	20	Copley Crest	69
Tailpieces	25, 53, 138, 173	Lane Fox Crest	69
Runic Stone	26	Clapham Arms	71
,,	39	Tempest Arms	72
,,	41	,,	73
,,	42	Currer Arms	75
,,	43	Savile Arms	75
,,	43	Parker Arms	76
,,	44	Thornhill Arms	81
Speed's Map, 1610	47	,,	81
Morden's Map, 1680	48	Clifford Arms	82
Bowen's Map, 1695	48	Ylton Arms	82
Teesdale's Map, 1827	49	Mauliverer Arms	82
Busfeild Arms	55	Hawksworth Arms	82
Ferrand Arms	55	Baildon Hall	84
Doomsday Book, 1087	56	Hastings Arms	86
,,	56	Dodsworth Arms	86
,,	56	East Riddlesden Hall	88
,,	56	Rawdon-Hastings Arms	90
,,	57	Kighley, Keighley Arms	90
,,	57	,,	90
,,	57	Steveton Tomb, Steeton	93
Maude, Montalt Arms	66	East Riddlesden Hall¶	94
Copley Arms	69	Marley Hall¶	97

From photographs by *Mr. H. England. †Messrs. Elliot and Fry. ‡Mr. Appleton.
¶Lent by Bradford Historical Society.

ILLUSTRATIONS.

	PAGE		PAGE
Frank Arms	99	Elizabeth, wife of Dr. Busfeild	207
Arthington Arms	99	Ryshworth Hall	208
Fairfax Arms	100	Col. J. A. Busfeild	209
Rookes-Stansfield Arms	103	Upwood, 1790	210
Lister Arms	103	Upwood, 1874	211
Wade Arms	103	Thomas Busfeild, Esq.	212
Thornton Arms	104	General Twiss	215
,,	104	Myrtle Grove	216
Wood Arms	105	Briggs Arms	223
River and Church	109	Rev. Richard Hudson	224
Dixon Arms	114	Mr. Hartley Hartley	225
Gascoigne Arms	115	Leach Arms	227
Ferrand Arms	116	Calverley Arms	232
Bingley Church, S.	120	Appleyard Arms	234
,, N.E.	122	Hulbert Arms	236
Hoyle Arms	128	Richard Shackleton	240
Wickham Arms	135	Bingley	249
Duncombe Arms	136	Thornton's Autograph	252
Rev. Oliver Heywood	143	Cottingley Hall	253
Hudswell's Writing	160	Elm Tree Hill	258
Rev. E. S. Heron	162	Myrtle Grove	259
Baptist Church	168	Wesleyan Church, Board School	260
Primitive Methodist (Liberal Club)	169	Briggs' School, Rumbles Moor	262
,,	170	Field Arms	263
Rev. A. McKechnie	171	Stage Wagon	265
Morton Primitive Methodist	171	John Nicholson	266
Christian Brethren	172	Bingley in 1830	268
Castlefield Wesleyan	173	Benjamin Preston	272
Old St. Ives	176	John Preston	274
Rev. E. R. Lewis	183	Abraham Holroyd	275
Sunderland Chest	184	Cottage Hospital	280
Rev. J. Martin	185	Bingley Parish Church	280
Cottingley Bridge	187	Holy Trinity Church	283
Beckfoot Bridge	189	Greenhill Hall	288
Bingley, &c., Tokens	190	Old Market Place	289
Market and Stocks	192	Toils Farm	291
Grange Doorway, St. Ives	193	Eldwick Wesleyan Chapel	291
Lord Bingley	194	Toils Window	292
Rev. Bradgate Ferrand	197	Ancient Deed, 1357	296
Walker Ferrand, Esq.	198	Five Rise Locks	298
W. Busfeild Ferrand, Esq.	199	Eldwick Hall	307
J. A. Busfeild, Esq.	201	Eldwick Church	308
W. Busfeild, Esq., d. 1729	203	The Heron	310
Elizabeth, his wife	204	Goitstock	311
Rev. Dr. J. A. Busfeild	206		

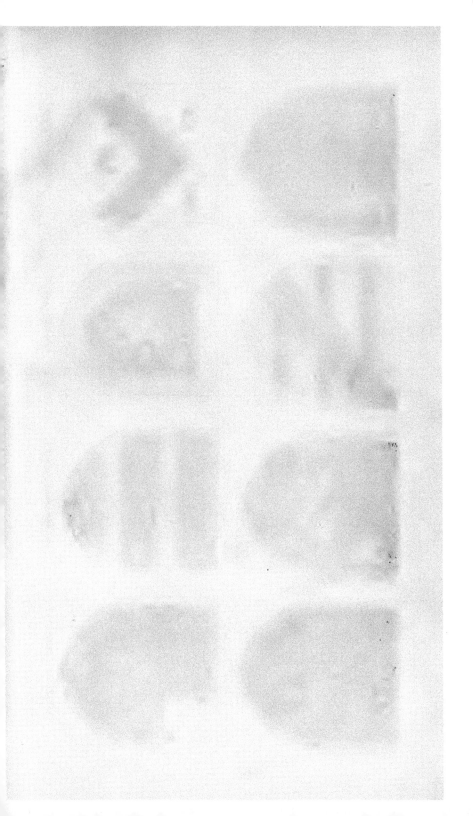

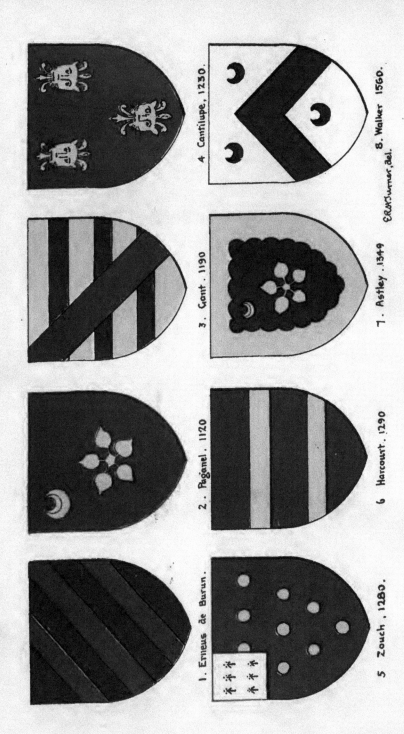

Bingley, West Riding of Yorkshire.

BINGLEY Town is situated on the banks of the River Aire, in the West Riding of Yorkshire. Its longitude is 1° 50' west of Greenwich, and its latitude stands at 53° 51'. A great peculiarity of the valley is noticed by all observant travellers by rail. This consists of extensive superficial beds of alluvial deposits, of immense boulder beds, and accumulation of Esker gravels. We are on the border of the limestone of the north, the coal of the east, and the millstone grits of the south and west. We have also the presence of a glacial drift. We have crow coal at Cottingley mixed with galliard, averaging 75 feet in thickness. At Morton Banks a seam of coal crops up. The accompanying table will give the reader a general idea of the geological formation of the district. On Gilstead Moor are well-developed flagstones. Fire-clay is found at Morton and Baildon. The Eskers are specially noticeable near Hawksworth, but mounds of water-worn gravel and sand enclosing hollows occur below Keighley, and the pebbles in them bear traces of ice-scratching.

The gravel mounds near Bingley have probably formed part of the moraine of a glacier which descended Airedale. They more or less fill the bottom of this valley between Bingley and Shipley, and also the tributary valley of Harden Beck. At Bingley the thickness of the gravel is over a hundred feet.* Here they form a barrier across the river, and the valley above this place formed the bed of a lake. Large quantities of decayed wood, nuts, &c., have been found in the alluvium hereabouts. Between Shipley and Bingley another barrier formed by these gravels completely dammed up the river, which afterwards cut a new channel for itself through the solid sandstone on the north. In some places terraces of sand, gravel and

Soils, sands, gravels, clay, building-stone.	Man, and present plants and animals. Mammals, anthropoid monkeys. Extinct animals. Subtropical plants.
Coalfields, millstone-grit, ironstone, lead.	Tree-ferns, coal-measures, club-mosses.
Sandstone, flagstone, limestone, metals.	Reptiles, amphibious.
Slates, metals, stratified rocks.	Fishes, shell-fishes, sea-weed.
Slates, limestone, metals.	Sea-weed, worms, shells, corals.
Unstratified rocks, granite.	No organic remains

---

* Geological Survey, 1879.

clay indicate former banks of the Aire. The Rough Rock of Keighley and Oakworth Moors is thrown out by a fault from Cullingworth to Oakworth. It is again thrown down by the fault through Cuckoo Park. It occurs as an outlier on Harden Moor. In the country lying south east of Harden Beck, the triangular space lying between two faults south of Wilsden, is occupied by Rough Rock, which finally runs down to the Aire valley to the north of Cottingley, whilst south of this village it is again overlaid by coal measures. The highest escarpments of Ilkley Moor and the surface rock of Baildon Moor are Rough Rock. Between Bingley and Baildon it forms the bold escarpments of Gilstead Moor and Baildon Bank.

From these introductory remarks it will be noticed that the ancient parish of Bingley was mainly a series of moors and fens in very primitive times. The marshes were preceded by a chain of lakes, but that period was probably long anterior to the appearance of the human species in Britain. I can quite conceive that the expansive beds of the Aire, and the security of the valley mounds already referred to, would be readily occupied by primitive man as he ventured further and further up the stream. I need not dilate on the Cave-dwellers, evidences of whom exist in several Craven caves, but of Pit-dwellings and Lake-dwellings we may be sure that this locality has had ample evidence. Of the three modes of primitive homes, the lake dwellings are the most difficult to discover, as might be expected by destruction of floods, the rotting by water, and the extra casualities incurred in valleys. Yet numerous remains have been found in Europe of pile-houses, built like Stockholm on the margins of lakes and streams, and Ulrome in East Yorkshire is only one of many found in fair preservation in the British Isles. These abodes have only been systematically studied and explored during the past fifty years, and the numerous stakes that have been pulled out of the beds of the Aire and Calder were probably relics of lake dwellings, had there been persons present to see them, able to identify them. These brushwood platforms and piles are invariably covered deeply with sediment and thus hid from view. In Venezuela, Africa, and other lands recently explored, such dwellings are still found inhabited. The crannoges of Ireland and Scotland have long been known, and the numerous lake dwellings have had scientific treatment in Dr. Keller's two volumes. Lieut. Boynton of Ulrome has been the pioneer in Yorkshire, and the result of investigations there and abroad shews us that these dwellings were placed near islands or peninsulas in the lakes and rivers for protection against unfriendly tribes and wild animals. The occupiers were a pastoral people, they tilled the ground, kept some domestic animals, and added fish to their daily diet, and nuts and fruits for dessert. The relics I saw at Ulrome, and the remains of the interlaced floors, shew that they had comfortable, dry, and well supplied homes. Their pottery was numerous though very crude; and the Romans had made their homes over the demolished abodes of the Britons, as was evident by finding all the Roman remains eighteen inches above the British ones. Flint, bone and horn were utilized for making knives and other domestic utensils, and for war implements. These were co-eval with and followed by stone and bronze. The piles were six to ten inches in diameter, and three feet long.

Unfortunately anthropology is a science of very recent date, or we should have heard more of the finding of canoes like the ones at Giggleswick, Stanley,* &c., and of lake-dwellings, like those I have seen at Ulrome in the East Riding. Anyone who has read the works that have appeared on Lake Dwellings in Switzerland, Ireland, Scotland, &c., would notice at a glance the special adaptability of the Aire basin for such homes.

From the remains of crannoges or stockaded islands found at Ulrome by Lieut. Boynton, by Keller and others in Switzerland, Sir W. R. Wilde in Co. Tyrone, I am convinced that the Iberians who first peopled Airedale had similar homes here. Near crannoges, raths or earthwork castles are often found. Cæsar, Dio Cassius and Severus had to take refuge in marshy raths. The travels of Livingstone shew similar conditions in Africa.

The Aryans or the Gallic, who followed quickly on the Iberian track, were a more active race, in this sense that hunting suited their tastes rather than fishing and trapping. Pit-dwellings or moor-land holes on the dry highlands, where natural caves did not exist, afforded them less troublesome homes. There were no wicker platforms to weave; no stakes to point and drive into the embankments; no flimsy structures to erect; and no dangers from flood. Their highland holes were dug at much less trouble, covered with branches and bracken, and considerably safer, and could be abandoned without much regret on emergencies. I doubt whether the Brythons or Welsh were numerous in these parts, but of the Iberians and Aryans the bones found on the Baildon, Ilkley and other local moors amply testify to their presence. Whilst the Aire valley at Bingley has been till recent times a swampy and marshy district, there were two extensive moorlands bordered close upon it, and on the two slopes, rather than on the hills or in the hollow, the homes of the succeeding inhabitants were first placed. Timber was to be found at that time on the moors, as well as dense jungles in the valley, and we need but see the museums at Giggleswick, Driffield, Leeds, &c., to be convinced that man had to fight his way against wolves, wild boars, the urus or wild bull, the reindeer, the bison, hyæna, and the cave lion; not to mention the beaver, fox, and smaller animals.

Traces of remains of ruminant and pachydermous animals, the elephant, hippopotamus, bear, small lion, elk and giant deer—probably of pre-glacial times, have been found in the gravel deposits. The remains of human handiwork of a later date may be grouped under two heads, (*a*) *weapons*, as stone hammers, arrow-points, axes, spear-heads; (*b*) *domestic* utensils, scrapers, saws, hatchets.

---

* Found in the Calder in 1818; from an oak tree,—burnt hollow.

We generally speak of our first inhabitants in West Yorkshire as
Brigantes, which indicate either highlanders or fire-worshippers, and
a hardy, fearless race they proved when the Roman legions attacked
them. We speak of their re-
ligion as Druidism, but we know
very little about it. On the
verge of Harden Moor, overlooking Bingley, is the Druids'
Altar, which Mr. James says
has been so known from time
immemorial. About half-a-mile
below, not far from Ryshworth
Hall, are two curious earthworks
of a conical form. Mr. James, describing
the earthwork at Flappit Springs, says it
is about fifty yards in diameter, with a
ditch two yards deep and three wide. This
"Castle Stead Ring" he conjectured was
one of a line of British forts, or an agrari-
an camp for guarding the cattle. It is

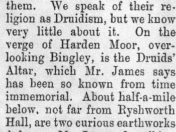

DRUIDS' ALTAR. quite likely that the Druid rocks are not
misnamed, considering the rock-markings, circles of stones, burial-
mounds, carneddes, ("skirtful or apronful of stones," a name given
to them not only on Burley and Harden Moors, but at Ecclesfield,
Pendle, and other places,) canoes, flints, hammer-heads, arrow-heads,
found in abundance on Ilkley, Baildon, Burley, Gilstead and other
West Riding Moors. My friends Mr. John E. Preston and his son
must have the credit of discovering the bulk of such British remains
as have been noted in this parish. Their collection from Gilstead
Moor should be secured for some local museum. Etymological
students trace fire-worshippers in the names Brigantes, Brigantium
in the Alps country, brigands, and even in the Irish name, St.
Bridget. Of course I need not remind most readers that the names
of our rivers—Aire, Wharfe, Calder, Don and Ouse are British.
The Aire was in name and character the clear stream, alas! how
inappropriate now. The hills, Pennine, Pendle, Chevin and Baildon,
have British names. Possibly Bailey hill, the site of Bingley Castle
is also British, from the Gaelic balla, a defence or rampart. A map
of Europe will shew how wide-spread are the names of these rivers
and hills.

I must refer the reader for further notices of such remains to
"Ilkley Ancient and Modern," and to "Wardell's Baildon Moors."
The Britons were nature worshippers, and as the word Druid indi-
cates, they specially honoured the oak and mistletoe. They were
undoubtedly sun-worshippers. The study of this creed, their phallic
cult, has been recently revived, but is far from being matured. On
Harden Moor is a cairn or "skirtful of stones." It is named Cat or
Scat stones, and like the notable Skirtful on Romalds Moor at

Burley, others at Pendle, indicates the burial place of a chieftain. Harden Cat Stones is enclosed on three sides by a considerable bank of earth and the ground bears traces of having been ploughed. This considerable entrenchment or camp is a marked feature of the map, but bears now a more modern name, Fairfax Entrenchment, though it is much more ancient than Fairfax's time. Opposite to it, near Flappit Springs, there remains about a fourth part of a considerable rampart, section of a circle of eighty yards' diameter. It is about three feet high from the inside, and as much as three to seven feet externally from the bottom of the ditch. It is known as Castlestead Ring. Similar earthworks and burghs are frequent in upper Calder valley as well as Airedale, and also bear the name castle. There is no doubt that many of them were utilized also for defensive purposes by the Romans, Danes and Angles. Castlefield in Bingley carries in its name the memory of one of these ancient fortifications, and it is noteworthy that the name Bailey Hill—commonly associated with British and Roman entrenchments—also survives to tell of the position of the Castle at Bingley. Bailey Hill, near Bradfield, Sheffield, and others of the name in Yorkshire, have earthworks remaining.

It is worthy of note, that British personal remains, celts, flints, arrow-heads, cinerary urns, calcined bones, charred wood, have been found mostly on the east or left bank of the Aire, probably because researches have not been carefully made on the right bank. About the year A.D. 70 the Brigantes yielded to the Romans, and Druidism lost its hold. Previous to this date the Druids had not only been the priests, but the physicians, astrologers, law-givers and clan-advisers. The terrible name of Agricola, the irresistible force of Roman arms, put an end to their influence, and stopped their abominable human sacrifices, A.D. 84. Hadrian in 120 and Severus, the old Emperor, in A.D. 210, fairly completed the subjugation of the British tribes, and the military occupation by the Romans, for they did not come to colonize, but to hold as we hold India, and let us hope to as good a purpose one as the other,—initiated the prosperity of this island. Substantial roads—such as have never been superseded, scarcely equalled—remain in this and neighbouring parishes to this day, testifying to the thorough workmanship of the invaders. The Roman roads have generally been the pioneers of our chief modern highways, a word that got its application from the high roads, raised by the Romans above the adjoining ground. For the first and best account of one of these roads we are indebted to the celebrated Dr. Richardson, of Bierley Hall, given in a letter to his friend Hearne, and printed in the second edition of Leland's Itinerary, (Vol. I., 143-6). "Meeting of late the Rev. Mr. Roberts, rector of Linton, in Craven, he told me he had observed a paved way of an unusual breadth, between Hainworth and Cullingworth, in the parish of Bingley, which must doubtless have been a Roman way. It appears there bare, being above twelve feet broad, and neatly set of such stones as the place afforded. Its stateliness shews its origin; and you may trace it where the ground is pretty hard, a ridge appearing higher than the surface of the earth, in some places being only covered with grass; though I have been informed that it is often met with at several feet deep upon the moors, in digging for peats.* It crosses the height of Harden Moor, where it is visible in several places, and points at a place called the Moor-house, above Morton; and appears again, as I have been told, upon Rombalds Moor and thence leads to Ilkley. Nigh this way, upon the moor before mentioned, [it should be the Burley section of the moor,] are two large heaps of stones, called Skirts of Stones; one of them still of a conical figure, but much the lesser. From the other have been removed vast quantities of stone employed in walling the neighbouring enclosures, within the memory of man. The remainder are now thrown abroad, and cover a considerable piece of ground. If these had been heaps of earth, or so much as covered with earth, being so nigh the [Roman] way, I should have believed them to be a *tumuli* of the Romans; but being only heaps of stones, I shall suspend my thoughts till I am informed that the Romans ever erected such monuments over their dead." . . . [As I have no better place of recording a few facts found since I published "Ilkley," I may be excused stating here that the Skirts still remain. The larger one has been nearly hollowed by the removal of the largest stones for repairing the road, and yet is a vast accumulation. In the centre is a fallen pillar used as a boundary mark, for here Menston, Burley, Hawksworth, and Ilkley sections of Rombalds Moor abut upon the ancient Roman and British road, in traversing which I have twice been challenged by gamekeepers, but persisted on following the well-defined road as the inhabitants have done for more than two thousand years. On the boundary pillar are also the words, "This is Rumbles Law," Few people now know the word 'law' for a hill or mound, as used in this case. In examining the manorial deeds at Burley Hall, by favour of Mrs. Crofton, I met with several perambulation accounts, wherein the great Skirtful is always mentioned as a conspicuous landmark and boundary, and a nominy was always recited there, 1600-1700, which ended with the words "This is Rumbles Law," yet however the people understood or misunderstood it, I believe the word means a *hill* and not a *regulation*. J. H. T.]

"Upon the top of Harden Moor, not far from the above mentioned way, was shewn me by Benjamin Ferrand, Esquire, another Skirt of Stones much less than the two former, and nigh it a row of stones placed in a line nigh two hundred paces in length, but few of them appear above two feet above the heath, and some lie hid under it. That these stones were placed here by design, no person can doubt; but for what end I cannot conjecture,

---

* This is interesting also as shewing that former inhabitants burnt turf in their house-fires.

having never seen anything of this kind before. There is no tradition of them, besides being out of all roads, they are known to few . . . . . Nigh Cullingworth before mentioned, there is a camp of a circular form now called Castle Steads, though I am convinced there was never any building there. There is one of this kind upon Thornton, and another upon Wike Moor of the same form." Such was Dr. Richardson's account two hundred years ago. Mr. John James was unable to find the Harden Skirtful fifty years ago, and rightly assumed most of the stones had been used for local purposes. An aged man told him that the Roman road had been dug up in the allotments from Upwood to Morton Moor, and the stone used for building the enclosure walls.

Leaving Harden Moor the Romans dropped down to the Aire near Marley where was an old ford, as indicated by the name Longland's ford, and the road mounted to Morton Moor, via Elam, Morton Bank and Morton Moorhouse. Whitaker of Manchester, 120 years ago, describes the road as overgrown with turf on Rombalds Moor, keeping upon the shelves of the hills to avoid the cliffs on one side and the morasses on the other, pointing directly to Ilkley, the Olicana of the Romans. At Black Knowle it appears as a paved way, and for some distance afterwards it coincides with the Morton and Ilkley road. I have not been able to see three plans which gave the course of the Roman road and indicated other antiquities of Bingley parish. They were lent by Miss Ellis to a temporary museum at York, when the British Archæological Society visited the city in 1846.

A great find of Roman coins by Simon Mitchell, contained in what may be assumed to be a military chest, at Elam Grange, near Longland's ford, must be told in the words of a gentleman whose antiquarian and genealogical labours must henceforth be ever associated with Bingley. I refer to the late Johnson Atkinson Busfeild, Esquire. The chest had most likely belonged to the paymaster of the Roman forces hereabouts, and had been buried on some sudden emergency. At Lightcliffe, fifty years after the Elam discovery, another large collection was found, and similar cases have occurred elsewhere, giving us the impression that the coffers have been hid during a skirmish, and left undiscovered. Further notes on the Elam hoard may be found in Whitaker's *Craven*, and *Gentleman's Magazine*, Vol. 75.

"With reference to the great discovery of Roman coins made in Morton Banks, Bingley, in 1775, it would be extremely interesting if something more was known really authentic, in regard to this remarkable discovery. Tradition would have us believe that the quantity was almost fabulous. Whitaker, in his "History of Craven," mentions it as "one of the most valuable deposits of Roman coins ever turned up in Britain. It consisted," he adds, "of a very large quantity of denarii, in excellent preservation, for the most part Septimus Severus, Julia Domna, Caracalla, and Geta contained in the remains of a brass chest, which had probably been the military chest of a Roman legion and buried upon some sudden alarm."

Again, in his edition of Thoresby's *Ducatus Leodiensis*, referring to discoveries of coins, he adds—"The next is, perhaps, the noblest discovery ever made in Roman Britain. March 7th, 1775, as a farmer was making a drain in a field at Morton Banks, near Bingley, he struck upon the remains of a copper chest about twenty inches beneath the surface, which contained nearly a hundredweight of Roman denarii. There was also in the chest a silver image about six inches long. They included every Emperor from Nero to Pupienus—Pertinax and Didius Julianus only excepted—together with many Empresses, and a great variety of reverses." Such are the terms in which a distinguished author and antiquary, writing when living testimony might easily have been obtained, describes this great discovery, but it must be confessed, without one reliable word to show either the actual extent of the treasure, or how or whence it had been dispersed! If there was any foundation for Dr. Whitaker's statement of the weight (one hundred pounds), we must assume that nearly twenty thousand coins were found, which is extremely improbable, and quite incompatible with the facts which follow.

On the 14th of March, 1775, within a very few days of the discovery, a short paragraph appeared in the *Leeds Mercury*, from a Keighley correspondent. announcing that a chest had been dug up in Morton Banks, containing a considerable quantity of Roman coins, and promising a more perfect account the following week. Accordingly, on the 21st of March there appeared a letter addressed "To the Printer of the Mercury," signed "A. B." The following (he writes) is a description of some of the Roman coins found on the 24th of February (Whitaker says March 7th), at Elam, near West Riddlesden, as mentioned in your last. The oldest that I have seen, Imp. Galva, the next T. Vespatianus, then Imp. Titus Cæsar, Augustus Vespatianus, Hadrianus Commodus, Antoninus Pius (numerous), Imp. Anton. Pius, Julia Augusta, Imp. Maximus Pius, Victoria Aug., Julia Pia, Felix Aug., Faustina Aug., Antoninus Augustus, and after describing many others, the writer adds, "As to the number it is uncertain, but there were many hundreds for they were neither numbered nor weighed. The box or chest of brass which contained them was locked, and carved on the lid. Some think it was a Roman military chest,".&c.

Thus we have the testimony of a gentleman evidently much interested in the discovery, writing upon the spot, and modestly speaking of "many hundreds," which he scarcely could have done had there been many thousands.

It also happened that my grandfather, then the principal land owner in Morton, purchased from tenants and others as many of these coins as he could. Among the farmers he was able to secure them in numbers varying from one to half a dozen, at 8d., 1s., and 2s. each; but when he got to the small shopkeepers in Keighley their value was better appreciated, and I find him paying 3s. 6d., 7s., and for a Vespasian, 10s. Altogether he secured 75, of which he appears to have given 25 to friends, the remainder being still preserved at Upwood.

I am not sufficiently versed in the science of ancient coins to venture upon a description of Roman denarii, but I may observe that they are in remarkable preservation. Many of the heads show the perfect expression of the face; the reverses of others are very curious, and the lettering on nearly all as easy to decipher as our own current coin. I should observe that Elam, where the box was found, is on the line of the ancient Roman road, passing over Harden Moor, Riddlesden, Morton Banks, and Rombald's Moor, to the Roman Camp at Ilkley.

Upwood, Bingley. J. A. BUSFEILD.

The Angles, Norse, Danes.

THOUGH the materials in Bingley parish do not afford scope for expatiating on the Roman occupation as those of the neighbouring parish of Ilkley did for "Ilkley, Ancient and Modern," we have ampler remains for the story of the Anglian history, a history that so seldom occupies much attention in a local work that I venture to enlarge somewhat at length upon it. The story of the Angles, though covering only six centuries, must be divided into two parts, Pagan and Christian. Of the Pagan history we have no contemporary records as they had no literature in Yorkshire; probably, they had not even brought with them the art of carving records on stones, in runic letters. So far as I know, all the runic remains that have been found in Yorkshire are of a Christian character. One of the earliest is the carved stone in Bingley Church. Those who get letters from France, Spain, Italy, &c., will know that they are always addressed to Angle-land (Angleterre), and we in the north are more nearly related to the Scandinavians, Icelanders, Jutes and Danes, Holsteiners and Frisians, than to the Saxons, whose descendants populated Es-sex, Middle*sex*, Sus*sex*, Wes-*sex*. But all these tribes had a common language originally, and as Pagans had similar manners and customs. The Angles were, when we first hear of them, fearless and active pirates, and marauders. They not only robbed, but massacred and burnt in wanton mischief. They were a physically powerful race, trained as athletes, and expert in using their clubs or hammers and sachs, (short daggers), from which possibly the name Saxon is derived.

Runic Stone.

"The Hardy Norseman's house of yore, was on the foaming wave." The dangers of mountain life and sea-roving trained our Anglian, Norse and Danish ancestors to vigorous activity, daring enterprise and presence of mind. The stern wildness of their barren hills, the exhilarating influence of the scenery, and the sombre effects of

Scandinavian pine-forests had much to do in preparing their piratical emigrants for the bravery and perseverance needed to subdue the country and the people they invaded. Fortunately they brought with them their free spirit. Servility they could never endure, and this high type of humanity has been manifest in these dales for a thousand years. It stands in high contrast to the mild character of the Saxon of Middle England and the cringing double-facedness ascribed to Celtic races. Retainers or slaves existed, but they were of British descent, and were not amenable to the tything. They were clan-governed, and paid greatest respect to the aged, or Aldermen. Elder was synonymous with greatest in their language. These Chieftains or Eldermen chose a leader or Cyning in time of war, but he relinquished his kingship when the war was over. It was these warlike clans that first left the eastern shores of the German or North-sea, but more peaceable Norse settlers soon followed as colonists, on hearing of the rich vales and dales of England, so that for four centuries a constant stream of settlers landed on the British shores, in much the same manner as we have sent emigrants to North America. Their condition in a strange land necessitated combination, and thus after a hundred years' unrest, wherein we find traces of Anglian, British, and Danish clans, mutually jealous of each other, struggling for self-defence, fortifying villages, making earthwork castles, erecting wooden ramparts, &c., the country settled under the rules of eight kings, and the contentions continued until about 827 when Egbert gained in a general sense, the supreme power in England. Bernicia, founded by Ide, was the name of the kingdom north of the Tees; Deira, established about A.D. 500, was about co-extensive with our present Yorkshire, but after fierce conflicts they were united under the name Northumbria (north of the Humber.) Their chiefs, like those of Northern Countries now, called their ealdermen, wisemen or witan together in cases of emergency. A peculiarity of their spoken laws was that payments were demanded in cases of injuries and criminal offences. Wealth was accumulating, and reckoned by the number of cattle rather than by extent of land. They were exceedingly vigorous in punishing cases of unchastity in men and women. The civilization and material remains, (houses, roads, &c.), left by the Romans had a beneficial effect on the Anglian settlers. It is almost certain that many large districts had been mapped out by name as Elmet, Rombles, before the formation of townships under the Angles, and some think that townships were first formed here in Roman times. Ten free families had a court of self-government, called a ty-thing. Ty means ten, and thing or ding means a court or moot, still preserved in the words hustings (house-courts), Dingwall, Tynwald, Storthing, Tinglaw (now Tingley), Headingley, where the Shireoak of Skirack (shire-ack) wapentake may still be seen. As these dings were also movable it is possible that the word Cottingley may have a reference to it, but of this anon. Folk-moots, or folk-meetings, is the old term for a town's meeting, and was used by Saxon and Norse. The Norman feudal system crippled the moots in some measure by coupling them with the Manor Court, which was followed by the older Court Leet, held on the same day and at the same place. Every wick, ham, stead or ton was largely self-governed, as the neighbours or nigh-bour, were mutually pledged; whilst under the Wapentake Court the privileged weapon-bearing men were in like manner brought under fealty. Blood-wite in case of injury was paid by the hamlet of the wrong-doer to the hamlet of the injured person in Anglian times, just as in later centuries—even two centuries ago, a highway robbery in any wapentake had to be recouped by the inhabitants of that wapentake. Then moots were held under a stately tree, like the one on Elm Tree Hill, on some rock or mound, but always in the open-air, possibly for fear of witchcraft as one reason. The Witan-moot was the national parliament. As special privileges, sanctuary was often granted to favoured or ecclesiastical properties, and doomed-crosses erected as boundary marks. The Shire-moot met in spring and autumn and all thanes—men who held 600 acres minimum—were required to attend.

The Norwegian parliament is named the Storthing, or great court; and our town courts for nominating Members of Parliament were called hus-tings, (house-court). The Tynwald (Thing-wald) Court is annually held near Peel for the Isle of Man.

Bingley is in Skirack Wapentake or hundred, which would originally have been formed of ten tythings. At the Wapentake Court the freemen had to attend with their weapons and *touch* or *tac*' the shire-reeve's weapon in *token* of fidelity to the king, whom the sheriff represented. We have the word still in the child's game, "tiggery, tiggery, touch wood." The great meeting place of Skirack hundred was probably at the shire-oak; that of Morley hundred at Thinglaw, now Tingley; of Agbrigg at the village of Agbrigg.

We have no need to advance further proof of the paganism of our ancestors than to remind the reader of the pagan names still given to our days, Sunnan dæg, Monan dæg, Tiwes dæg, Wodnes dæg, Thur* or Thunres dæg, Frigas dæg, Seternes dæg. The g is like y, as in yate for gate. Their name for idol was wig or wic, and, in passing, we may offer the suggestion that the modern spelling of Eldwick, which for many centuries was Helgewic, was probably a reference to a sacred or holy idol. Wig was also applied to a warrior. But we know such conjectures are dangerous, for the science of local etymology is in its infancy. From the great god Odin or Woden our lines of kings profess to be descended. The Anglian mythology also comprised beliefs in witchcrafts, oracles, holy-wells, and it is not difficult to produce many local evidences of the great impressions those made on the minds of our race, for a thousand years of Christianity have not removed the ingrained beliefs

---

* Thor was the god of war. Loki or Luck was a god of evil. They had gods for music, springs and rivers.

of paganism. Amongst the many Yorkshire incantations the following was a favourite one in this district; " From witches and wizards, and long-tailed buzzards, and creeping things that run in hedge-bottoms, good Lord deliver us." To this end they carried lucky stones, lucky bones, charms of various descriptions to protect themselves. A boy finding a white stone would spit on it, as many men do still on the first coin received in the first day's trading as indicating good luck. Perforated stones were specially endowed with blessings to the owner.

Our Folk-lore is mainly the un-written and un-scientific history of Anglian paganism. Our Christian Easter is the pagan Eostre; our Christmas is the pagan Yule, both of them relics of Sun or Baal worship. Their sacred stones, groves, fountains; their elf-rings and charms; their Ochy-pochy or Magician, their wicked Neccus or old Nick; their holy-trees and a score other superstitious notions have become part and parcel of to-day's creed.

Æfter Yule we now name January, but one name is as pagan as the other. February or Sol-monath is cake-month, the pancake being offered to Sol. Rehd monath corresponds with our March, and Rehda, or Ridda, became a family name, but I hardly think it has aught to do with Riddlesden. Eostur monath or April, was followed by Tri-milchi or three-milky month, May. Lida, first and second, and Wenden represent the mild months June, July and August. September was called Halig monath; or holy-month. Wyntyr filleth, preparing for winter, October; Bloth monath means the killing month for winter provisions, and blood was offered to the gods. Æra Yule, before Yule, was the great feast time of winter, as Bel was of midsummer, only the midsummer fires were lit on the prominent hills, whilst the Yule log was put on the manor-house fire. To let the fire go out on that eve was a sign of most disastrous consequences in the following year, and till recent times I have known cases where neighbours have refused to allow any fire to be taken out of one house to another on Christmas and New Year's mornings. I take the antipathy to a red-haired boy, or to any girl letting the "New Year in," called in Scotland the "first foot," to have originated in Saxon times, when the Danes were harassing the inhabitants. Many, if not all, of the Norse tribes had acquired the art of writing on books, or beech-bark (as the word book probably means), about the year 500, and they also scratched or carved these letters on stone or other hard materials. The letters are quite different from the Romans in shape, corresponding more with Greek forms. They are called Runes, but the word is used as we use the word letters, for learning as well as the alphabet. There are various alphabets of the Runæ, but the difference is only slight. The characters are called runa-staves, and like the Hebrew phylacteries, they were so scarce, wonderful and mysterious to the ignorant that they were treasured as charms. The heathen of South Africa held in veneration a chip of wood on which Dr. Moffatt had written a note to his wife. Our letters *th* and *w* (thorn and wen) are relics of Runes. The Angles used the word staef in preference to rune; thus 'staef be staef' means "letter by letter"; and the word write comes from writan, a stave or letter, or writ. After the introduction of Roman ecclesiasticism under Paulinus, the Roman forms were advocated and runes were deprecated as heathenish; but this prejudice cannot have been very great in Yorkshire for the few monuments of the period that still exist are in runes and not in Roman letters. They were used in the Isle of Man much later than in Yorkshire, and in Denmark and Iceland till after 1400.

Following upon the great influence exerted on the Angles by the Roman British who had learnt government, arts, comforts of home, food, clothing, health, &c., the introduction of Christianity and the Christianizing of heathenish worship, tended vastly to civilize the active settlers who had seized the land per-force, and made the few remaining aborigines into slaves. They followed the practice of farming and gardening which had been in vogue from Roman times; and regularly enjoyed hot-baths as the Romans had done before them. The Angles were not a literary people like the Romans, so their enthusiasm spent itself in athletic exercises, leaping, running, wrestling, and active games. They had no surnames, but gave their children such names as Ethelwulf, (noble wolf), Albert (all-bright), Egbert (eye-bright), Eadric (happy and rich), Edgiva (happy gift). When necessary the father's name was added Ælmer Ælfrices suna, that is Elmer son of Elfric, or Wulfrig Madding (son of Madd). Only a few of the wealthiest Angles were taught to read, and such generally became Monks. Boys and girls were of age at fifteen, but reverence for parents and seniority was a marked feature of their character. The food of the Anglo-Saxons comprised bread of wheat, oats, barley and rye; and the flesh of oxen, sheep, and particularly swine. Of fish, the eel was the most common. Eel dykes formed boundaries of their lands, and I take it that Elam gets its name from Eel-holme.

Under Alfwold of Northumbria, 785, horseflesh was prohibited as food for human beings. They ground their corn in handmills or querns, one of which may be seen in Bingley Free Library. Bread was mostly eaten fresh baked when warm from the bakestone. The floors were mostly of mud, a fire was placed on a stone, and there were no chimneys. Such cottages still exist in Sulby glen, Isle of Man, and I have often seen them in various parts of Ireland. The family name Baxter has come down to us from such primitive bakers. Orchards were fairly numerous, and honey was largely used. They also fed on herbs, beans, eggs, butter and cheese; and drank home-brewed beer from malt, mint, and sundry herbs. Salt meats were general from November to Spring. Meat was rigidly forbidden during fasts, and of course this rule was strictly observed during Lent not only in Roman Catholic times, but since, in order to encourage the fisheries. The father of Samuel Sunderland, of Harden, got leave from the Vicar of Halifax to have meat during Lent on account of illness. Wooden trenchers, made by the Turners, and drinking horns obtained from the horns of oxen, were, with coarse brown pottery, the chief domestic utensils. Forks were unknown, and knives were very rudely made, except for the wealthy. Ale-thelums or alehouses were not unknown in burghs or towns. Christian influence also modified the rude dress of the Angles. The women painted their faces and wore the hair in twisted locks. We read of their kirtles, gowns and mantles. These, like the clothing of men, were not confined to woollen materials, for flax and silk were obtained by the rich. The men bandaged their legs with leather and cloth strips. The style was nearer the Scotch kilts than our present fashion. A leather girdle, a cap, and rude shoes completed the outfit. The skins of wolves, lions, beavers and foxes served for linings. The household furniture, even of the yeomanry class, was heavy and inelegant; whilst a table, bed, stools, and a chest were the stock of the cottar. Hangings were necessary to shield from the storms in such ill-built dwellings; and rugs, straw, branches and rushes made up for the comfortless furniture.

Iron utensils were made at the charcoal furnaces both for home and agricultural purposes. They often made merry; sang wild war-songs, and supported the remnant of the Britons who played on rude harps and crowds. Our names Harper and Crowther indicate a descent from these harpers and crowders at a later date. Bear-baiting and bear-dancing were popular amusements. Hunting was a great diversion. Deer were common before and after wolves were extinct; and the wild boar was an object of chase. Hawks and falcons were a more genteel method of hunting in after-times.

The rights of a wife were carefully arranged before marriage, and women had such freedom as the Eastern nations never dreamt of. They frequently held lands and assembled at the Shire Moot debates. Still wives were considered to be purchased. A freeman was simply able to choose which master he would serve, and the king was his lord and patron. If by misfortune or misdeed the freeman fell into slavery he was called a wite theow, or penal slave. The theows and esnes were bought and sold like cattle, and we shall find some late instances from Mr. Ferrand's muniments. The sale of the Anglian boys at Rome in Gregory's time shews that they were even exported for sale. Exportation was afterwards forbidden. The bulk of the population down to the time of the Conquest was in real or semi-slavery, but manumissions in Christian times had augmented the freed class. The names often are given of men and women thus freed: Wulfware, Gerburg, Ælfsige and his wife, and eldest daughter, Ceolstane's wife, Pysus, Edwin, Wulflede and her daughter, Spror and his wife, Bicca's wife, Ethelgythe, Effa, Beda, Gurhan's wife, Bryhsig's wife, Wulfar's sister; Hagel, Hig, Dunna, Elfwig, Sewi Hagg, Egilsig, &c.

Of trades, smiths, woodworkers, shoemakers, salters, weavers, were the chief besides farming; markets were held at principal towns. Travellers were hospitably entertained for a night, but the host was held responsible if the stranger remained over two nights and did any wrong. If any wicca or horcwenan (witch or whorequeen) be known, they shall be driven out. All welworthunga (wellworshippers), licwiglunga (incantations of the dead), hwata (omens), frith plots and elm tree enchantings were discouraged by the Christian teachers. In the frequent cases of plagues, storms, &c., the Angles often resorted to pagan customs. Besides a strong faith in charms, they were much guided by prognostications, as to lucky and unlucky days. Nativities were specially believed in. They had even charms to find lost and stolen cattle, and for making fields fertile. Cremation was much in vogue till Christian times, when wooden coffins became common, but occasionally coffins were cut out of the solid rock. It is possible the large coffin in the rock near St. Ives, Harden, was made in Anglian times. Burials in towns and in and near churches were practised after the introduction of Christianity. A soul-shot was generally paid to the priest at the death of freemen. A gibbet was generally maintained in each manor.

The Angles held lands in freehold, and carefully describe the boundaries. Amongst the commonest words in these land marks we find Hlidegate, the Lidgate that swung like a lid between the enclosed lands and the commons, sheep-lea, hence Shipley; the military ways or forths, fyrds, as Bradforth, Horsforth, &c.; the Stocks of the high-ford, from which we may obtain a correct etymology of Stocks, near Keighley. Their chief land measure was the hide, or 120 acres. Their kings were elected, but nearly always from the royal family. This custom fell with the fall of the Witenagemote after the Conquest.

The Ealderman was a member of the national witan, or wise council. He was the Sheriff, (shire-reeve); afterwards named Earl, but the office was given to lesser landholders. The greaves or townreeves were annually elected from the local landowners, and were men of great responsibility. They assisted in the folk-moots, courtleets, halmoots, &c., to dispense justice. They had to secure robbers, see that the gates to the village were repaired (not only to keep cattle from wandering into the place from the unenclosed lands—but for defence of the inhabitants), and execute by their servants punishments, even death, on delinquents. Their chief assistants were the constable, pinder, &c. One unfair regulation was that men were valued according to rank,—each having his "were" or price, in case of injury, or manslaughter, or murder. It was eventually settled that no one should be gibbeted for stealing unless the value exceeded 12d. (say £1 of present money). See "Halifax Gibbet Law." Nighbors or neighbours were personally responsible for each other as pledges or bonds, or bail; so every man had to belong to a tything. "Every man shall have borh and the borh shall produce him to every legal charge." A most unsatisfactory mode of trial was by ordeal—by hot water or hot iron; and these were ecclesiastical rather than civil methods. Trial by jury was only partially developed.

On the removal of the Roman Soldiers, the country in the northern parts particularly was over-run by Scottish hordes, chiefly the Picts, and meanwhile gangs of emigrants were arriving on the east-coast. These were mostly marauders from Denmark, Jutland, Anglia, and North Germany. They were not savages, for there is evidence that they had been long accustomed to trade with tribes and nations along the north and centre of Europe to the Asiatic borders. Of course, they were heathens. The first great leader that touched our country was Horsa, about 457, he having brought his disciplined followers from the south, (where Hengist had been settled as king of Kent), to assist the Brigantes in repelling the incursions of the Picts. He is said to have been slain at Conisborough. From this time a continuous stream,—many of the vessels being loaded with colonists rather than pirates and soldiers—poured into the island, and Northumbria (the land north of the Humber) was chiefly peopled by Anglian settlers. They pushed their way up the river Humber, and thence up the Yorkshire streams, "winning by inches."

Tradition relates us wondrous stories of desperate struggles with the remaining British tribes, headed by King Arthur of Richmond Castle, where he and his Knights of the Round Table are said to sleep. The desperate struggles and lawless period of ninety years passed by, when an Anglian named Ida or Ide, more powerful or more favoured than his precursors, subdued the territory of Northumbria and reigned as King from 547 to 560. His kinsman Ella, wrenched the Yorkshire or southern part of the kingdom from him, and became King of Deira, whilst Ida was ruler of Bernicia, (from the Tees northwards). Ide and Ella were favourite Anglian names, and places such as Ide-hill, Idil, Kirkella, are memorials of Anglian foundations, whilst Deira forms part of the name Driffield, it is thought. The names of one or two chieftains who tried to sustain the British power against Ide and Ella have come down to us. Urien son of Guvare, Owen son of Brian, are mentioned for their prowess by Cymryc Bards. Ide the Anglian, of Schlesvig, was the son of Eoppa, and like monarchs the world-over claimed to be descended from a god. Bealdeag, fifth son of Woden, was his reputed ancestor. Our Wednesday—the day for worshipping Woden—reminds us of this powerful deity. Ida's praise is duly chronicled by William of Malmesbury, and his fame led other Anglians to emulate his example. Adda (after whom, or another of the same name, Adel is called), and Gloppa or Ellapa, succeeded their father Ida, as King of Bernicia. Ella held Deira from 560 to 588, reigning at Elloughton and York. He was son of Yffa, and of course, claimed Woden as progenitor. The beautiful story of Pope Gregory and the little Anglian slaves from Deira, stolen from Ella's kingdom to be sold in

c

Rome, most probably is true in the main, and led to the re-introduction of Christianity to Deira.

Ethelfrith son of Ethelric, fourth son of Ide, had married Acca the daughter of Ella, and succeeded to Deira in 589 and to Northumbria in 593. He was slain in 617 by Eadwine, his wife's brother, who after attaining his majority, was assisted by Redwald of East Anglia to gain Deira. Ethelfrith had the reputation of being an able monarch, but stained his laurels by the massacre of the Monks of Bangor. He bore a bear as his cognizance on the standard, and it was impressed on coins by other kings afterwards. His sons Eanfrith, Oswald and Oswy fled when he was slain. Eadwine or Edwin, the Martyr, ruled Northumbria from 617-633. Whilst an exile, he married Quenburga, daughter of Ceorl, King of Mercia, and had two sons, Osfrid and Eadfrid; and had issue by his second wife Ethelburga—daughter of Ethelbert, King of Kent,—Etheline, Uskfrea, Eanfleda, and Ethelreda. He founded Edinburgh and in 624, when Redwald his friend died, he was acknowledged as Bretwalda, or chief king in Britain. The British kingdom of Elmet, with Leeds as its capital, had with varying vicissitudes kept fairly compact till Edwin ended the guerilla warfare by subjugating Ceretic, the Elmet King, about 616. Edwin had a glorious reign, adopted Christianity, encouraged Paulinus to preach the Gospel throughout our Yorkshire dales. Coifi, the high-priest at Godmundham, led the way to desecrate the heathen temples, and on their sites were erected our first churches. This was in 627, and at York, Dewsbury, Whalley and other Christian centres began the diffusion of the new tenets that year. Penda, the old pagan king of Mercia, swore to root out the new faith, and, joined by Cadwallon of North Wales, he encountered Edwin at Hatfield near Doncaster, 633, and Edwin the Martyr and Osfrid his son were slain, the whole territory was ravaged, and Cadwallon became ruler. Ethelburga the Queen fled to Kent with Paulinus, where she died and was canonized. Eadfrid fled to Mercia, and his grand-daughter Hilda became Abbess of Whitby. Osric was ruler of Deira 633-4, Eanfrid of Bernicia, the same year. They were grandsons of Ella, but relapsed into paganism. Osric's son Oswin became King of Deira 644-651. Meanwhile, Oswald the Saint ruled Northumbria from 634 to 642. He was son of Ethelfrith and Acca, Ella's daughter. He adopted Christianity at Iona—where the new faith had been introduced from Ireland some time before any Roman influence was known. He led an army against Cadwallon at Heavenfeld, and there the Cymric king fell. Oswald founded Lindisfarne, completed the York Minster of that day, and several churches are still dedicated to his memory. Oswald was slain in fighting against old Penda at Masserfield. Oswy succeeded his half-brother Oswald, 642-670. He married Enfleda, daughter of king Edwin and had issue Eagfrid and Alfred, both kings of Northumbria, and three daughters, one of whom, Elfleda became second Abbess at Whitby, which abbey her father had founded. Oswin son of Osric regained Deira

644-651, and when he was murdered, the Deirians elected Ethelwald, son of St. Oswald, as their ruler. When Oswy gained the famous battle of Winwidfield, near Leeds, 642, where old Penda and Ethelbert fell, he seized Deira, and again united Northumbria. Ethelwald died soon after the great battle, so there was little obstacle in the way to the unity. The synod of Whitby, 664, was presided over by Oswy, when the two rival sections of Christians—the British and the Roman—had disputations, and the supremacy of Rome began to prevail. Oswy was buried at Whitby, and his son Ecgfrid succeeded to the Northumbrian throne 670-686, a period of wars and intrigues. In 675 he fought the Picts, and drove them back, but the Redshanks returned often, and he fell in Scotland whilst fighting them. Alfred, king of Northumbria, 686-705, was son of Oswy. He was a very learned man for his time, like his future namesake Alfred the Great. He was mortally wounded near Pickering in a Pictish battle, and was buried at Little Driffield. His son Osred, aged eight years, under Brithric's protectorship became king, 705. His rebellion ensued and he was slain, when Keoured, son of Kuthwyne, a descendant of Ida, ascended the Northumbrian throne in 716, his kinsman Osric II succeeded in 718, and in 730 he was followed by his cousin Keonwulf, brother of Keonred. He had a peaceful reign of eight years, and then assumed the cowl and died in Lindisfarne Abbey. These two Keons were brothers of Egbert the Archbishop of York and of Eata, whose name along with his son will always be coupled with notices of Bingley. Eata's son Eadberht, sometimes written Egbert, became king of Northumbria in 738. Soon after his accession, he led an army across to Scotland in repelling an invasion of the Redshanks or Picts. During his absence the Mercians entered his dominions and carried off a great quantity of plunder. He enlarged the boundaries of his kingdom, and so managed with the troublesome king of the Picts as to make friends with him, and thus secure on the whole a prosperous and peaceful reign until 757, when he imitated his uncle, King Keonwulf, by resigning the crown and entering a monastery where the remainder of his life was spent. One authority says Eadberht received the kingdom of Northumbria from his cousin Ceolwulf. On runic stones at Dewsbury and Thornhill are the names of Ethilberht and Osberht respectively. Here our Bingley runic stone has its story to unfold. The Rev. Daniel H. Haigh had his attention called to it by Mr. Ainley, but he could then only make out six runic signs. The stone had been used as a step for the Grammar School entrance. In 1863 he took further casts, and assisted by the Rev. J. T. Fowler, he concluded that the inscription recorded:—

+ Eadbert Eatting cy | ning Rehte Geban Œste Nys | ode Ongus Bingaleahes.

In an article on Runic Monuments (Yorks. Archæo. Journal, Vol. 2.), Father Haigh thus writes of the Bingley relic:—

"The inscription on a stone, which I believe was once the socket in which a memorial cross stood, at Bingley, demands particular attention. During the course of the past winter [c. 1871], I took up the photograph of this inscription one day, and was very much surprised to find that the sixth rune in the third line, which I had read E, was certainly U, and that it was followed by S, not by N. This discovery, most unexpected, throws new light upon the whole. I had identified *Ouama* or *Ouoma*, the place whence Eadberht led his army to the aid of Oengus, king of the Picts, A.D. 756, with Hewenden near Bingley, and supposed that the assembling of his forces there might be the occasion of Eadberht's visit.* The identification is now confirmed: the army really assembled at Hewenden, but the person whose visit to Bingley is recorded, was not Eadberht, but his ally Oengus,† whose name is here spelled Augus or Ongus, (for *as* and *os* differ but in a single stroke, and I cannot be sure which letter is here.)

I give a tracing from the photograph (by Mr. Holgate, of Bingley,) collated with the cast. My reading now is

+ EADBERHTEATTINGCY   + Eadberht Eatting Cy
NINGRIHTEGIBANŒSTENYS ning rihte giban œste Nys-
ODEONGYSBINGALEAHES | ode Ongus Bingaleahes

+ Eadberht, son of Eatta, King, uttered a gracious ban. Ongus visited Bingley.

It is but part of a longer record. The 'gracious ban' no doubt resulted in the alliance between Eadberht and Oengus, previously enemies, and at Bingley, we may believe, that alliance was cemented."

Father Haigh ascribes the erection of the Collingham cross, near Wetherby, to Queen Eanfleda, though called King Oswin's. The Leeds cross bears the name of King Onlaf. Guiseley church is dedicated to St. Oswald. These and numerous other items shew the identity of this immediate locality as a chief centre in the melancholy story of Saxon, or rather Anglian, wars and bloodshed. At Thornhill, Dewsbury, are fragments of runic inscriptions referring to Ethelbert, Osbert, and one to Eadred who set up a cross to Eata, a hermit.

+ EADRED ISETE ÆFTE EATE INNE.

---

* Father Haigh's reference is to the following from *Sim. Dunelm. et Rog. Houeden*, (Simeon of Durham and Roger Howden, the early chroniclers). "Eadberht rex, xviii. anno regni sui, et Unust rex Pictorum duxerunt exercitum ad urbem Alcwith [or Alclut,] ibique Brittones in conditionem receperunt, prima die mensis Augusti. Decima autem die eiusdem mensis interiit exercitus pene omnis quem duxit de Onama (or Ouana) ad Niwanbirig, id est ad novam civitatem. "*Ouamdene* would become Ouandene, *m* changing to *n* before *d*.

† This form of the name is given by the continuator of Ven. Bede's Chronology (to A.D. 766). Aongus, in the "Duan Albanach," more nearly represents the name on this monument. Onuis, in the "Chronicon Pictorum," gives initial *o*. Miscellanea Picta: the History of the Picts, with a Catalogue of their Kings and of the Roman Governors who fought against them and the Scots. Maule, 1818.

The omission of the usual asking prayer for the deceased is very remarkable at Thornhill. Simeon of Durham records that Eata the hermit died at Craic near York, about 752, and in another place at Cric, ten miles from York. A hermit at that time was not a Job Senior of Rombalds Moor, but one of the most noble and powerful souls of the period, a man of wealth and dignity, and the veneration he was held in accounts probably for the preservation of the cross at Thornhill. To further shew the importance of the district at the period, it is known that most of the coins of Cnut, or Guthrum, were minted at York. Regnald son of Guthfrith and grandson of Ivar reigned at York 919-923, and issued coins bearing his name Rahenalt and Racnolt. Eric, son of Harold Harfager ruled at York under Athelstan, 937. He fell in battle in 940, and Olaf son of Sihtric became king, and issued coins at York. Nigel or Neil, Earl, coined at Leeds, judging by the superscription Leiade. He was slain in 918 by his brother Sihtric, who claimed the greater title of king.

Yorkshire sundials exist that were erected at this period, the finest, at Kirkdale, bearing the name of Orm son of Gamel son of Orm, each great landowners in East Yorkshire particularly.

In 1846, Father Haigh found at Wensley a gravestone, the top of which was broken off, and had probably borne the words ORATE PRO, EAT-BER-EHT ET ARUINI, carved about the head of a cross, both cross and lettering being in relief. From the "Historia Ecclesiastica" and Simeon of Durham, we get the date, "A.D. 740, Aruwini et Eadberctus interempti." 23 Dec., 741, the same year that St. Acca went to heaven, Arwine son of Eadulf was killed. The coins of king Eadberht have the same spelling as this stone; as also, Eadberehtus and Eotberehtus.

Prof. G. Stephens, Copenhagen, from rubbings and photographs sent by Rev. J. T. Fowler, Durham, writes:

If my reader will kindly go back to my Vol. I, p. 485, he will see what was then known about this runish lave. [Bingley.] He will perceive that Mr. Haigh had done what he could but that the times were unpropitious. Since then circumstances have altered. Fresh materials have been placed at my service. The same energies and opportunities which have enabled my noble countryman Mr. Fowler, to restore to us the Crowle Runic Cross, have also permitted him to do what can be done for the Bingley Font. *To do what can be done*, for this precious relic, hundreds of years neglected, is now so shattered and worn as almost to make us despair. The staves are so faint and broken, the stone has so many false jags and cruel scratches, that the risting is almost unreadable. The best men may differ, and widely differ as to its meaning. And this difficulty is largely increased because it is not yet commonly agreed what this piece was intended for. I look upon it as a FONT, Mr. Haigh thought it the SOCKET OF A CROSS. But to understand this better let us describe it, using the details kindly given me by Mr. Fowler and Mr. Haigh. This piece, years ago, was found turned upside down, doing duty as a step to the entrance of the Grammar School at Bingley. When the said school was rebuilt this stone was taken to the church-yard, where it was for no-body knows how long. I now follow Mr. Fowler: "*Material*—The ordinary strong gritstone of the district. *General Form*—Irregularly four-sided, the inscribed side being longer than the opposite side. The under part is quite rough, as if it had never been workt. The sides are very thick, and the cavity accordingly small in proportion, especially at the bottom. *Dimensions*—About $2\frac{1}{4}$ feet square by $1\frac{1}{4}$ high, and 10 inches deep. *Details*—The ornamentation is confined to the four sides. These appear to have had a cable-moulding running all round the upper margin, which may perhaps have been continuous with the interlaced patterns on the sides. These are different on all the three sides which bear them, and are rude and irregular in character. The runic inscription is in three lines occupying what appears to have been the front side. There is a shallow rebate all round the brim of the cavity as if for the reception of a cover, but there are no traces of fastenings. The aperture is roughly made in one cover, and the stone so much broken away from it all round on the outside, as if driven off from within at some later period. *Present condition*—The under part is very rough as above stated, and perhaps it has never been otherwise. This condition may however be the result of the action of the frost or of mechanical violence. It is so much weathered all over that none of the original surface remains, and little hard points stand up, having resisted corrosion longer than the rest. It must have been in the open air for a long time, but of late years it has been kept in the church. *Similar remains in the neighbourhood*—UNINSCRIBED runic stones have often been found in South Yorkshire and in North Lincolnshire as shewn by my brother and myself in "Proc. Soc. Ant."

The hole or aperture above spoken of is cut horizontally in the corner as described. This being so, and without reference to the inscription, what would the piece seem to have been made for? I think undoubtedly for a church FONT. And this for three reasons, its general appearance, the rebate all round the brim of the cavity as if for the reception of a cover, and the HOLE to let out the water. Certainly it is large enough, for the hollow basin is about 1 foot 9 inches square at the top and about 10 inches deep, besides which baptism *by sprinkling* was not uncommon from the *very oldest times*. But general objections—smallness of the water cavity, barbarism of the work, &c., are quite inapplicable here. What do we know about Baptismal Fonts anywhere in the 8th century? How many have we left to us from that early date? In a rude neighbourhood and a half-heathen period, we must expect helpless workmanship. And this piece is very rude indeed. Perhaps its want of proportion was partly owing to the shape of the original block, while its unfinisht base was to spare labor. But both its rough ornamentation and its careless runes show the hand of an unskilled workman. True, and how many skilled workmen-carvers of stone should we expect to find in a small, poor, out-of-the-way hamlet in Yorkshire even now? And a thousand years back, I trow *none*. We know that all the earliest skilled workmen in whatever was not *wood* were brought over by the early Christian clergy about this time from the Continent, chiefly from Italy. *Native* village stone-cutting from the 8th year-hundred is scarce enough, and barbarous enough. A Font so old I have never seen. But I have examined, particularly in Scandinavia, some very old *native-cut* Fonts, as old as the 11th and 12th and 13th centuries, and I can testify that several of these are *as rude* and helplessly fashioned—tho' not perhaps so much ruined by time and brutality, which is quite another thing—as this piece at Bingley. And several of them have a water-basin even *much smaller* than the Bingley one. In plans and drawings of Fonts, sizes of top and bowls, &c.. (measured inside from rim to rim and the depth) are seldom given, else it would be easy to refer to scores of publisht instances. And many of these oldest fonts have the drain (water hole) not in the middle, but, as at Bingley, *at one corner* below, while others have no drain at all! These old Fonts are often square, as well as round, and this applies to the Bowl also. If we now turn to the runes we shall see that apart from all wearing and damage—they have never been so even and regular as on many other laves. It is also clear that the staves in the lower line have been purposely spread, partly to fill up the space and partly perhaps from the stone being unsmooth at parts. At p. 486 in Vol. I. of this work Mr. Haigh tells us that the first line began ... ...

EA D B E R H T C Ū N I NG.

that the second ended

and that the third commences with ... ...

(SIGEB ...... NŪS ODEO*N*GEN).

In 1869-70, Mr. Fowler generously and enthusiastically rusht into the field. At great expense both of time and money he lavished favour on favour upon me—details of every kind, drawings, rubbings, photographs, and at last a cast of the runic side. For all this labour of love I and the whole Republic of Letters offer him our hearty thanks. At this time a letter reached me from Mr. Haigh, dated 9th March, 1870, which contained the passage: "I have thought that the first line may be (see block—fourth line) **EADBERHT CVNING**. As my materials came in I began to work upon them,

and at last—after some few gradual ameliorations—have come to my
present text. Should I be right in this, of course we are sure that
the stone trough was made for a Font. Mr. Haigh has come to a
different conclusion. He rejects both my opinion that it was a Font
and also my reading of the runes. He insists that it was the socket
of a Cross, and has gradually decided that the stone bears *(besides at
least one other line)*:

"EADBERHT EATTING KY-
NING REHTE GIBAN ŒSTE NYS-
ODE ONGEN BINGALÆHES."

This he translates: "Eadberht Eatting, King, published a good
ban, visited again Bingley." [In the Runic Monuments of Northumbria, 1870, p. 29, my late accomplisht friend has modified this
to EADBERHT EATTING CYNING REHTE GEBAN ŒSTE NYSODE ONGEN
BINGALEAHES. Eadberht son of Eatta, King, uttered a gracious ban,
visited again Bingley. But the appended plate gives GIBAN as before].
To this I answer that—however much the stone has suffered, still
enough is left for us to see (at least in my opinion) that the above
runes have *never been there*. Minor points, as to the strangeness of
some things in the words as given and the—to say the least—unlikely
and meaningless character of this whole inscription on a public
monument, we can pass by. I now come to my own reading, to
which men able to judge will perhaps object as strongly as I have
done to that of my learned friend. After numberless and patient
examinations of all my materials, in all lights, and guided by the
faint traces still left, and avoiding what I conceive to be accidental
dints and jags, and partly holpen by the dividing dots which I think
here and there exist, I make out that the letters were as below, *complete in three lines*, no more; *my* fancy may have misled *me* as I think
his has misled Mr. Haigh, but still I submit my text for comparison.
The reader will then judge for himselᶠ. Font as I see it from cast
and light bild, &c. Runes as I see them, some more or less plain,
others partly or nearly worn away. As the whole surface has suffered
so much, it was impossible to engrave it otherwise. No photograph
could bring out the details of so excessively worn a stone; besides
which, to give a Sunbild to every copy of this work would have been
very expensive, and *no* artist can engrave such a photograph without
himself FIXING THE SHAPE OF EVERY LETTER.

In the last line, in the word GIBID parts of only two of the upper
strokes of the G are left, all the rest is broken away. Thus my
reading and version will be:

EADBIERHT CUNUNG   Eadbierht, King,
HET HIEAWAN DŒP-STAN US   Hote (ordered) to hew
GIBID FVR HIS SAULE   the dipstone (font)
                                              for us
                                      Bid (pray) for his soul

I need not remark that the longer and oftener we look at the light-build of the runes, the more will the at first so indistinct staves gather shape and look into our eyes. Should the above reading be accepted as substantially correct, the next question is the age of this font. Putting together, in short, the notices of EADBERT EATING (Eata's son), King of Northumberland, given in the Old English Chronicle, the addition to Beda, Florence of Worcester, Simeon of Durham, &c., we find that in 737 Ceolwulf, in the 9th year of his reign, takes St. Peter's tonsure (becomes a monk) at Lindisfarn (Holy Island) and gives up his sceptre to Eadbert (spelt in the skinbooks Eadberht, Eadbert, Eadberth, Eadbryht, Eatbert, Eathbert, Edberht, Edbrict, &c.), *fœderan sunu*, his uncle's son. In 740 Eadbert wars against the Picts. In 750 he adds the district of Cyil, in Ayrshire, to his dominions. In 756 he fights against the Britons, and loses most part of his army. In 757 he takes St. Peter's tonsure (is shorn as a clerk), gives up his kingdom to his son Oswulf, and becomes a Canon in York under his brother Archbishop Ecgbert. In 768, on the 20th August, Eadbert dies at York after ten years of private life, and he and the Archbishop both rest entombed in the same porch in the city of York.

BINGLEY RUNIC STONE (2).

Eadberht may have ordered this font for the church in Bingley while yet king, but the prayer for his soul makes it more likely that he did this when *near death*, in the usual way, by this oral or written *will*, by which doubtless many pious gifts were made to monasteries and churches near him for the good of his soul. A year or two would be sufficient for so simple a font, and therefore its date will probably be between 768 and 770. Perhaps the church at Bingley was first built or restored in his reign, or a *stone* church may have been raised instead of a ruined *wooden* one. Bingley is *nowhere* spoken of in our *oldest* books, and must have been in the 8th century an obscure hamlet with some scores or perhaps a hundred souls.*

---

*Of course, this is a great mistake on the part of Prof. Stephens.—J.H.T.

[So late as 1284 the Bingelei of the Domesday Book and the Byngeley, Bingeley, Byngley (of Kirkby) was but a single manor of fourteen carucates of land, making only one Knight's fee, (Kirkby's Inquest or Survey of Yorkshire, Surtees Society, 1867.) Even now it has only one church (?) So much the more extraordinary would it have been to raise a monument with a formal inscription to commemorate a first or second casual visit thither of a local king.]

Anxious to do full justice to this valuable relic, and wishful to give every view respecting it fair play, I now add that I have just (Oct. 1872), received my deceased friend's paper on "Yorkshire Runic Monuments." Mr. Haigh here partly abandons his former readings and gives a third or fourth, as follows, "During the course . . . cemented." See page 36.

BINGLEY RUNIC STONE (3)

With these words Mr. Haigh passes to the Frank's casket. Thus for the last: KYNING, REHTE, ONGEN, BINGALÆHES we have now CYNING, RIHTE, ONGUS, BINGALEAHESI.

I can as little see this inscription on the stone as Mr. Haigh's former ones, and look upon this *gracious ban* and *Ongus* as equally improbable on a Runic Cross at Bingley with the *good ban* and *again*. At all events these frequent alterations show—what we must all admit—that the block is too much damaged to justify us in looking for any historical names whatsoever, other than the first plain EADBIERHT. Whether the reader agrees generally with Mr. Haigh or with myself, he will equally remember that he has to thank the indomitable zeal of Mr. Haigh for first drawing attention to the pieces, and the noble labors of Mr. Fowler for the careful materials and trustworthy information here laid before him. We can now proceed to show the other sides of the Font which I here give photoxylograpbt by Herr Rosenstand but on a very reduced scale, from Mr. Fowler's excellent Rubbings, taken by him in February 1870. As has been said, the Runish side is the longest. The opposite or back is the shortest. Figure (4). The right side is still more simply ornamented. We can here see the water-hole in the right corner below. Figure (5). The left is the most graceful of them all. Figure (6).

BINGLEY RUNIC STONE (4.)

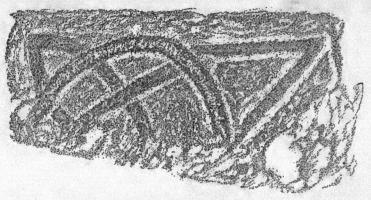

BINGLEY RUNIC STONE (5.)

This rude and undevellopt and backward decoration not only points to an early date, for art was not so low and helpless as this in the 8th century, either in Great Britain and Ireland, or on the Continent, still less in Scandinavia, (of course I here speak of Barbarian art)— but conclusively suggests a poor village in an outlandish part of the country, and no workmen at hand but the honest stone-smith of the hamlet.*   Thus far Prof. Stephens' account.

---

* A very ungrounded surmise.—J.H.T.

BINGLEY RUNIC STONE (6).

Although, from the little knowledge I have by personally inspecting the runic remains of Yorkshire and the Isle of Man and a large collection of runic photographs, I lean to Father Haigh's final rendering, it is but fair to add the only other great authority who has written on the Bingley stone. When spending an evening with Professor Armitage, I was shewn a German work entitled "Die Northumbrischen Runensteine" by Professor Victor, of Marburg, from pages 20 and 21 of which, the following extract respecting Bingley stone, kindly translated by Mrs. Armitage, has been taken.

"This stone, 'a square basin with a hole in the corner,' as Haigh describes it, with an inscription about 2 ft. 5 in. in length by 1 ft. 2 in. in height, is now in the church at Bingley. Haigh regarded it at one time as a baptismal stone, at another time he thought it the socket of a cross, and gave an interpretation of it! Before it was placed in its present position it served a very profane purpose in the Grammar School of the place, as I was informed by the photographer Mr. Holgate. I made squeezes of the inscription, and have also received from Mr. Holgate two new prints of the negative taken by him some time ago. One of these prints I reproduce here, by Mr. Holgate's kind permission.

Unfortunately I can contribute little to the elucidation of this enigmatical text. Haigh's different readings (compare Stephens, I. and III.) are so different one from another that in the remarks which I have to offer I shall not assume any fixed interpretation.

First line. The sign + at the beginning seems certain. Next to this Haigh reads SIGEB (Stephens I.) and I read SI; but the traces which follow will hardly fit with G. The next letters might perhaps be EB, or even ER, but the form of the latter letter is more like Œ: I do not profess to be able to read them. In the middle of the line and one or two letters further on the photograph shews forms very like the runic S, but in the paper squeeze these are much less marked. The sign + in the middle of the parts of the line which yet remain appears in the squeeze, but all the rest is indistinct.

Second line. The second stroke, under the questionable G E of the first line looks in the squeeze like an A. The sign standing under the R ? (Œ ?) looks like the runic N. Of the NUS or NYS which Haigh read from here to the end of the line, I cannot see the S ; Y (with a cross stroke) is possible ; N is clearer in the squeeze than in the photograph. The down-strokes which are visible before this appear in the squeeze to be N I C : the sign before, which looks like S in the photograph, is indistinct,

Third line. The word *Saule,* which Haigh read at the end of this line is contradicted by the letters, even although they are much injured. At the beginning of the line, where Haigh and others read GIBID, might very well be DDÆD. The space left between would be too large for the remains of the usual formula (pray for his soul) even with a much longer pronoun."

Our prejudices are likely to be more in favour of making 'something' of this rare relic than Prof. Vietor's "nothing," and I think the care bestowed by Messrs. Stephens, Haigh and Fowler entitle them to have given the general tenour of the reading until an equal authority not only disproves certain runes but substitutes a more reasonable consecutive reading. Whether a font or a cross, it is equally interesting. In one case the church dip-stone will satisfy us of an unexpected proof of the antiquity of the Church ; in the other we have a King's Cross that puts to the shade the antiquity of any other in England. In both cases we have evidences of the great antiquity of Bingley, and more interesting still, the residence—permanent or temporary—of a King ; for the names Angus, Eatta, and Eadberht are no inventions, they are well-known names in Saxon history. It is amusing to read how our Danish friend belittles Bingley. If it had been found at Bradford he could have found in the directories that Bradford was an important place, but Professor Stephens had no one to tell him that Bingley was formerly a larger village than Bradford, and had a market and castle, when its big neighbour was but an insignificant township.

Runes have been clearly traced to a Greek and Phœnician source, namely the Thracian or second Ionian alphabet, which through the intercourse of Greek colonists at the mouth of the Danube with the Goths south of the Baltic was introduced in a modified form into Northern Europe before the Christian era. There are three forms, the Gothic, Anglian and Scandinavian ; so that even the stones indicate by the style of rune which tribe settled in these parts. The Scandinavian type is largely found in the Isle of Man, but they are of a later date by several centuries than our West Yorkshire runes.

Continuing our Anglian history, from which we may gather some notion of the calamities that harassed the inhabitants of Bingley parish at that period, we find that good king Eadberht, (the friend of Ongus,) was succeeded by Oswulf, his son, on the Northumbrian throne in 757, but he only reigned one year, being assassinated at Machel Waytone (Market Weighton, or Mickel-wayte?) by nobles, and no successor was found for twelve months. Moll Eadilwold, a brave but common soldier, had gained great influence over the nobles, and led the rebellion against Oswulf, and managed to become king in 759. He slew Oswin, a noble who revolted, in 761. Ailred, a descendant of Ida, conspired against Eadilwold, and the plebeian king lost his life in 765. His son Ethelred escaped, but secured the throne in 774, was deposed in 778, restored in 789, slain by his subjects at Ripon in 794. He had married the daughter of King Offa of Mercia.

Ailred, son of Tanwise, the conspirator just named, ruled from 765 to 774 in a most tyrannical manner. Alfwold his brother ruled from 778 to 788, when he was murdered. Osric II.. son of Ailred, enjoyed the Northumbrian kingship in 789, but fled to the Isle of Man from the revolt of his nobles, and Ethelred resumed his mad career till 794. Under all this ghastly misrule, the Danes had made constant incursions, and had securely established themselves at thorpes and bys throughout our Yorkshire dales as may be traced in our place-name chapter.

Osbald, the son of Ethelred the cruel. held the sceptre of Northumbria twenty-eight days, when he was deposed, 794. Eardulf, an Anglian noble, had a troubled reign from 794 to 808. Even Archbishop Eanbald led a rebellion against him, and the king fled. Complete anarchy reigned; sanguinary conflicts with Picts and Danes were the regular duties of the Anglians. Rival factions made things worse; rival kings reigned in divers localities. Amongst these we can only stop to name Eardulf's sons, Alfwold II., 808-810; and Eanred, 810-833, latterly as sub-king under Egbert of Wessex. Osbert held Deira, 850-867. Rayner Lodbrog the Dane—the hero of Scandinavian Sagas—having died in Creyke dungeon, his sons Hinguar and Hubba joined Earl Bruern against Osbert in 867, and the Danes gained York, and Hinguar became Danish King of Northumbria, 867-872. Angles and Danes had intermarried in the north, and made the Danish rule easy. When Hinguar died, fighting and assassination became the normal condition. Halfden, Guttman, Guthrum, Ochta, Other, Egberht, Regnald, Nigel or Neal, Sytric, Rigridge a Dane, won and failed, ruled and fled or fell till 910. Sytric the Dane, brother of Nigel and Regnald, sons of Hinguar, got permanent hold from 910 to 927. Eric and Anlaf reigned 934 to 948, off and on. Athelstan fought the great battle of Brunanburg, the site of which is claimed by both Yorkshire and Lancashire. Anlaf fled at Brunanburg but returned in 904, and ejected Earl Eric after battles at Ripon and Castleford. At Anlaf's death in 948, Northumbria became a province of England, and was ruled over by Yarls or Earls until the conquest.

Danish Coins were issued from the York Mint bearing the impresses of Halfden, 875; Cnut, alias Guthrum, 877; Siefred, 895;

ANCIENT BINGLEY.

Alwald, 901; Regnald, 923; Sitric, 925; Eric, 927; Anlaf II., 943; Anlaf III., 949. It will thus be seen that Yorkshire was more under the rule of the Danes than under the greater kings, Alfred the Great, &c., of the south. Amongst the York Moneyers (Mint-masters) were Rafen, Stirc, Odin, Ketel, Grim, Ulfgrim, Ulfketel, &c.† These issued coins under Cnut the Great, who died Nov. 11. 1035. The York Mint was in operation also under the mightier monarchs of the south from Edward the Elder, 901, to Edward the 6th, 1533. From the thousands of York coins, ante the Conquest, about fifty names of moneyers have been secured. We thus find that the people were not the barbarians sometimes assigned.

Place-names were once as readily understood by all the people as West-wood and Salt-aire are to us. They are generally descriptive of their situation and surroundings, or they indicate their Anglian owner, just as in after-times many new fields bear the names of the men who ridded the wood from the ground, and thus formed a riding, or field. We have shewn already most peculiar names held by the Danes and Angles, but such works as Vigfusson's *Icelandic Dictionary* and Worsaae's *Danes and Norwegians in England* will have to be examined before reliable etymologies are advanced for many of our place-names.

Speed's Map, (1610).

Ton—*Mortune, *Sutun, *Middletune, *Dentune, *Cliftun, *Bichertun, *Ectone, *Mensintone, *Hateltun, (*Halton, not Harden as given by Bawdwen's translation of Domesday, and so followed by others), *Heldetone, Snitterton now Priest-thorpe (?), Heaton, Allerton, Thornton, Skipton.

Den—*Redelesden, *Wilseden, Harden, Hewenden, Silsden. Arden is Celtic for a wood.

Ley—*Cutnelai (Cononley), *Bradelei, *Vtelai, *Chichela (Keighley), *Othelei, *Fernelai, *Gisle, *Burghelai, *Scipeleia, *Bingheleia, *Cotingelei, *Mardelei (Marley), Bailey, Crossley, Dowley. There is a Bingfield in Berkshire. The likeliest etymology

---

† It will readily be recognized that these personal names are incorporated in such places as Ravenroyd, Grimshaw, Kettlewell; and Stirk is still a local family name.

* Mentioned in Domesday Book. See next Chapter.

Morden's Map, 1680.

is from Bing, an Anglian owner. Bingham is another instance of the name.

Hill—*Fernehil, *Timbe(hill).
Done—Don a hill, *Beldone, *Beldune.
Wick—*Childeuuic, *Helguic, *Heluuic now Eldwick, *Barnoldswick.
Burn—*Esebrune.

Worth—*Acurde (Oak-worth), *Henochesuurde, *other Hawksuurde, (Hauoceford), *Colingauuorde, *Hageneuuorde (Hainworth).
Thorp—Gawthorpe, Priesthorpe, Leventhorp, Laythorp. Gawthorpes, Goldthorpes are numerous and probably named after some such owner as Galme.
Stead—Stead near Ilkley, Gilstead, homestead.
House—*Neuhuse.

Bowen's Map, 1695.

Thwaite—*Muceltuoit (Micklethwaite), *Muceltuit, Braithwaite, Thwaites.
Forth—A road, not necessarily a ford, Bradforth, Horsforth, Rushforth, (Rushworth), Scotforth.
Cock—(? little, or ock-oak), *Lacoc.
Ham—*Stubham. A homestead or village, as in the word hamlet.

---

* Mentioned in Domesday Book. See next Chapter.

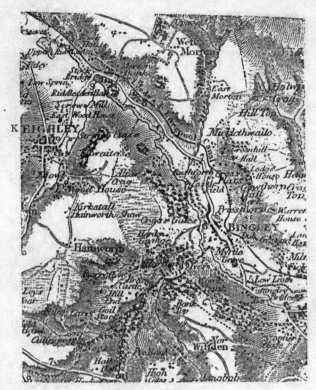

TEESDALE'S MAP, 1827.

All the place-names in and about Bingley shew that the Angles dominated the locality.

A *thorp* is Danish for a village, and is common in Denmark, and softened to *dorf* in German. There are no fewer than 55 Thorpes in the East Riding of Yorkshire, and 47 in the North and West Ridings, and 63 in Lincolnshire. These figures are considerably under the mark when combinations are considered, as in Priest-thorpe. How it got its name *Priest*—will afterwards appear. Its former name is stated to have been Snitterton, but I dispute this.

Ton, a town, tun, village fenced or staked in, is found in Snitterton, Morton, Halton. The name is common in Scandinavian countries. Morton is a common name for towns on the borders of moors. We find moor joined with wick, thorpe, gate, house, grange. Halton appears as Hadelton in Doomsday Book, on which we shall have more to write. Hadelsey, near Selby, like Hadelton, was probably named after an Anglian owner.

Vik, *wick*, was Scandinavian and Danish for a creek on the shore, (Schleswick), or a dam inland. Some think it may be a Roman relic, from the Latin, vicus, and we have seen the possibility of another derivation, from wic, a god or warrior. We have the word in Kildwick, berewick, and Eldwick. The latter looks like *old wick*, but it is quite a modern mode of spelling the place-name. In Doomsday, and for centuries afterwards it was written Helgewick, Holy-wick. Hell also means a grave. The syllable is also found in Helthwaite.

Thwaite is Norse or Scandinavian for a clearing of wood, and exists in Thwaites, Micklethwaite. Mickle (Norse) means great and is conjoined with fell, field, ton, how, by. That Bingley parish was formerly even more extensively sylvan than now is shewn by such place-names as toft, plantation, coppy, coppice, Elm-close-wood, Small-tail wood, Cophirst (from hirst—a wood), Hirst-wood (a redundancy), Roundhill-wood, Blakeyhouse-wood, Hollin-wood, Altar-wood, Ravenroyd (from royd a ridding, or essart, clearing or stubbing of tree-roots), Whitecote (cote—a wood), Woodbank, Carr-wood, Caw-wood, Bank-woods; Fell-wood, Maud-wood, Milner-springs, (Spring is dialect word for plantation), Crosley-wood, (woods named after four local families); and Crag-wood. Crag is a Scandinavian word, and is used in the Manx Testament in the passage "On this creg I will build my church."

Gap is rather a rare word in place-names, but is common as implying a breach in a hedge or wall. Dowley gap, Stone-gappe, and one or two more are found in this district, and indicate breaks in the natural features.

Ley, meaning a field or enclosure, is one of the commonest terminations of Airedale nomenclature. Running up the valley we have Armley, Bramley, Farsley, Calverley, Rodley, [Newlay is from New Laithe,] Apperley, Thackley, Shipley, Dowley, Bingley, Cottingley, Marley, Keighley, Bradley and many others. They are nearly always found in the valley. They are much rarer in Wharfedale and Calderdale.

Den, a dean or valley, is not so numerous in Airedale as in Calderdale.

Worth is a frequent ending for village names, and indicates a farm or hamlet warded or defended, Robinson Crusoe-like. The Worth valley has its Haworth and Oakworth. Rishworth, Hainworth, Cullingworth retain this Anglian word, and it is etymologically a word of some *worth*, (value.) It is worth noticing that the Danish ending *by* for a dwelling, so common in Lincolnshire (212 in number), East and North Yorkshire (135 in number), and only a sprinkling in the West Riding, is wanting here.

On the other hand *beck*, Eldwick beck, Harden beck, Beckfoot, rather than brook, is the usual name for a small stream, and *syke* rather than dyke for a ditch, and *dubb* rather than pond for a pool, all of which tell the story of Anglian rather than Saxon ancestry. But beck is both Danish, Swedish, Icelandic and Anglian.

Holme, water-bordering meadows, will be found on the maps of Sweden, Norway and Denmark in profusion; no wonder that our valleys have echoed the word; and some are on high lands, as Denholme, Hipperholme.

Lands, as in Longlands, are relics of land being held, as in the common field still at Haworth, as parts of village community possessions.

There are a few local names that may be mentioned though the history conveyed in them is comparatively modern. Jackfields, from being the possession of "Jack;" Milkinghill sounds pleasantly rustic; Currer-Laith was once the barn occupied by the Currer family; Ewehills may be either ewe or yew-hills, the latter more plausibly; Ravenroyd was probably a clearing made by a Dane or Anglian of the name Raven; Catstones hill indicates steps or footpath through a wood; cad, cote, cat implying a wood; and near is an ancient remain called Catstones Ring, evidently British. Fairfax Coppy (Fairfax-wood) is popularly attributed to the presence here of the great Parliamentary general, but the long series of entrenchments from Harden to Harden Moor are of far more ancient date than Fairfax after whom they are now named. That he was a visitor to Harden we shall afterwards give further evidence; and the soldiers' graves will also be referred to. Higher and Lower Heights remind us that the bonny moorlands rear to a height of 958 feet near Hainworth and Heather-glen; yet such names as Hainworth *Shaw* [shay, a wood,] tell us that timber grew on these heights in former times. Indications of rugged scenery may be assumed by the names Cradle Edge, Deep Cliff, Deep-cliff-flat, Spring-head-height, Midgeham quarries, Grinning stone, Druids' Altar, Hutler hill. Some of these words seem of capricious rather than scientific origin. Ryecroft, with its malt-house, is a very old place. The Rycroft family takes its name from the place-name Rycroft, but whether this one or not I cannot definitely state. Race-course and Race-course hill remind us where the famous Harden races were run. Adjoining is the extensive Harden Grange Park with its extensive lake and swamp, and peat-dykes and earth-work entrenchments, and Panhole. The two names Harden Grange and St. Ives have been interchanged during this century, and old St. Ives was in the valley at Harden whilst the Grange was on the site of the present St. Ives. The word grange tells of the time when the priestly orders held much property hereabouts, and I think St. Ives is named from a holy well dedicated to the Saint, Iva, who was a 7th century abbess. St. Ives' well, Pontefract, is another instance. There is a St. Anthony's well in Harden, a name indicative of ancient well-worship. Near Harden village is a castellated house of small dimensions named Brass Castle, said to indicate a Roman origin. No satisfactory meaning has yet been assigned, but the few Brass Castles that exist are near Roman roads. Midgram beck, like Midgeham quarries, has a puzzling name. Leaving the place-names at Cullingworth at present, on passing through Harden village we meet with Cockcroft fold (a yard where Cockcroft family lived), the kennels, new and old, where the packs of hounds were formerly kept, Cuckoo Nest, a quaint old home-stead in Harden wood, with a small lake near, the Low Park, Birkey bank wood, with its birch groves, Hesphill (another puzzling name), Beckfoot, of which full notice will afterwards appear, Bell-bank wood up which the bell-horses formerly carried their loads, and the Old Hills. This simple name is one of the most puzzling, for we have it again repeated twice across the river in a line with this one, (1) at Beckfoot, (2) south of Myrtle Park, (3) near Holy Trinity Church. Much mischief has been done by surface guesses at etymology or we might conjecture as to the cause of these names. Suffice it to note that the persons who originally gave all place-names had definite reasons, even captious ones, that the people well understood, and we must find the earliest mention to get nearest the true meaning. Harden is often printed Harding and several fanciful etymologies may be advanced. It will be found in our next chapter that the name Harden does not appear in Doomsday Book, it is called Hadelton, and Halton Grange the old name for the present St. Ives lingered on till recent times. Halton would indicate the *hall-tun*, hall enclosure, but the spelling in Doomsday, like the word Hadelsey, near Selby, implies that it was Hadel's tun. Harden, the valley name, has absorbed Halton, the hill name; and the case of the change from Snitterton to Priest-thorpe (if correct,) gives a second instance in this limited area. It has generally been asserted that *ing* in the middle of a place-name is proof of an Anglian clan settlement, but I am far from thinking the statement proven. Cottingley, Cottingham, Cottingwith, Cullingworth, Cordingley, are quite as likely to mean a meadow or ing; thus Cot-ing would be wood-field, and ley added though meaning much the same as ing. We have hirst-wood, and many similar duplications. Some of the tings and dings I have ventured to hint may have been derived from "ding," a moot or court. Even greater difficulty sometimes arises with the first syllable of a name, for the Angles and their kinsfolk had peculiar names, many now completely lost. There was a Fek owning land at Giggleswick in 1085, and Fixby is named after another Fek. If we rob Harden of its initial letter we get the poetical Arden, and unbridled conjecture would find the Knights of St. John, and foreign monks introducing the word. If we take off the *en* or *ing* we get the common root Hard, as in Hardcastle, Hardwick, Hardraw, Hardisty, Hardgate, Hardacre, &c., but this may be as foolish as finding *thumbs* in Nor*thum*berland.

Coming down stream from Keighley parish we have a few place-names of interest. Near Elam (eel-holme) the Roman road crossed the Aire, and the Ford is marked on the Ordnance Map. The country bordering on the river is liable to floods. A little lower down we reach Castlefield and Bailey hill, names that record a time when the Britons and Romans had fortifications for the defence of the trajectus across the river. For some time I thought that Ryshworth Hall got its name from the family who owned it, but an early deed seems to give it a place-name origin. The first two syllables of Riddlesden are past authentic etymology now. It is given as a distinct manor from Morton in Doomsday Book. On the Morton side of the town we find a Deer park, Walsh lane, Sty lane (probably stile-lane), Limefield, Greenhill, Lady house, Lime works; and, lower down—Gilstead, Little beck, Sparable lane (Sparables are small headless nails!), Sheriff house, Warren park, Moulding mill, Dunnock (dunnock, a wren), Tewet house, Myrtle park, Maud bridge, Healey lane, Bull Coppy wood, Milner field, Eldwick grange.

We may trace the spirit of our Anglian ancestors in the strong ties of home, family, and friends, and particularly in maintaining the dignity of woman. They sneer at the Celtic position of women, toiling and drudging whilst the men lounge about home, and nothing rouses their ire more than the exhibition of the Celtic hot-blood. This difference in the races manifests itself in the skill and cleanliness of the Anglian workman and his wife. The darker complexion of the Celt has had some effect in cross marriages in adding a dark-brown colour to the Anglian's eyes and hair, but, as Kombst observes, the fairer Teuton predominates over the Celt so far as frame of body, and—to a large extent—temperament is concerned. On the whole, the poet's description is still true:
"By the tall form, blue eyes, proportion fair;
The limbs athletic, and the long light hair."

I have a notion, however, that the strong antipathy still entertained against red-hair, especially lest a red-haired boy 'lets the Christmas or New Year in' and brings bad luck for the next twelve months, has arisen against the Danish descendants, owing to the sufferings caused by the Danish intruders.

The Norseman has none of the fiery impulsiveness of the Celt, but he has indomitable, plodding perseverance, sturdy independence, and it must be said intemperance in drinks, but not the gluttony of some Saxon tribes. Ecclesiastical and Civil dignitaries, of the highest as well as lowest degrees, scarcely call forth sufficient reverence from the Norseman, especially if the man is not equal to the office he holds.

The Norman Period.

Worn with the battle by Stamford town,
Fighting the Normans by Hasting's Bay;
Harold, the Saxon's sun went down,
While the acorns were falling one autumn day.
Then the Norman said, "I am Lord of the land,
By tenure of conquest here I sit;
I will rule you now with the iron hand;"
But he had not thought of the Saxon grit.

He took the land, and he took the men,
And burnt the homesteads from Humber to Tyne,
Made the freemen serfs by the stroke of his pen,
Eat up the corn, and drank the wine;
And said to the maiden pure and fair,
"Thou shalt be my leman, as is most fit,
Your Saxon churl may rot in his lair;"
But he had not measured the Saxon grit.

To the merry green-wood went bold Robin Hood,
With his strong-hearted yeomanry ripe for the fray,
Driving the arrow into the marrow
Of all the proud Normans who came in his way:
Scorning the fetter, fearless and free,
Winning by valour, or foiling by wit,
Dear to our Saxon folk ever is he,
That jolly old rogue with the Saxon grit.

And Kett the tanner whipt out his knife,
And Wat the Tyler his hammer brought down,
For ruth of the maid he loved better than life,
And by breaking a head made a hole in the crown.
From the Saxon heart rose a mighty roar,
"Our life shall not be by the King's permit;
We will fight for the right—we want no more!"
Then the Norman found out the Saxon grit.

For slow and sure as the oaks had grown,
From the acorns falling that autumn day,
So this Saxon manhood in thorpe and town
To a nobler stature grew alway.
Winning by inches, holding by clinches,
Standing by law and the human right,
Many times failing, never once quailing,
So the new day came out of the night.*

[* The author, Rev. Robert Collyer, D.D., New York, was born at Keighley, and fetched his first wife from Bingley. In Bingley Church Register, we have, "1847, May 25, Robert Collyer, of full age, batchelor, blacksmith, Ilkley, son of Samuel Collyer, blacksmith, to Harriet Watson, of full age, spinster, straw-bonnet maker, Bingley, daughter of Elisha Watson: married by J. Cheadle, vicar, in presence of Thomas Stephenson and John Walker."]

ANCIENT BINGLEY.

THE Normans, as the name implies, were offshoots of the Norsemen, but their contact with the Franks had considerably modified their language, manners, customs, and laws. Every schoolboy knows the story of the conflict at Hastings, when William, the Norman Duke, won the title of Conqueror, by subduing the English army under Harold the Saxon King. The English of Yorkshire rebelled against the rapacious Normans, and the result was that the old Anglian aristocracy and large land-holders were still further dispossessed and expatriated. The Normans introduced the Feudal System, whereby the King nominally held the whole country, and shared it out mainly to those Norman captains who had supported him in 1066, in his invasion. The old squirearchy were

BUSFEILD ARMS.   FERRAND ARMS.

generally demeaned into sub-tenants, and every tenant was responsible according to the amount of his possessions to supply men and arms to the King as required. This regulation necessitated that a correct record of the extent and value of all the estates throughout the country should be taken. This was completed about 1085, and the volume, known as DOOMSDAY BOOK, may still be seen in London, and by means of photozincography, I am enabled to give facsimiles from seven pages that bear on this locality. On the first plate are copies of extracts from Sir H. James' reproductions, pp. xli., lxii, (bis), lxxxi. On the second plate, from pp. viii., vii., xii.

In Scipeleia. ħb Rauenchil. iii. car' t'ŕa ad gld
ubi. ii. car' poss. ḗ. Ibo͞ ħ⁊ ⁊ Wast. ē. T.R.E. ual
x. sol. Silua past'. i. leu lg. ⁊ dimid lat.

TERRA ERNEIS DE BURUN
WESTREDING: SIRAC-ES W̄AP

In Bingheleia. ħb Gospatric. iii. car' t'ŕa
ad gld. t'ra. ē ad. ii. car'. Ernegis de burun m̄.
⁊ Wast. ē. T.R.E. ual. iiij. lb. Silua past'. ii. leu
lg. ⁊ i. leu. To͞ c̄ō. iiij. leu lg. ⁊ ii. lat.
Infra hanc met'á, continen' h soca. Beldune.
Coangeleí. helguic. Mucetune. Mardeleí. ha
rethun. Simul ad gld. viii. caruc. t'ra. ē ad. iiij. car'.
Waste sunt om's.

sol. m. v. sot.   In CRAVE
In Merdeleí. heldetone. Coangeleí. Colinga
uuorde. hageneuuorde. Simul ad gld. vi. car' ⁊ dim
t'c̄. t'ra ad. iii. car'. Ernegis ħ⁊. ⁊ Wasta sunt.

In horseford. vi. car'. In Roudun. iii. car'. In ladun. iii. car'
In Bingelei ⁊ Beldun. heluuic. Mardelei. Coangelei. harlton.
Mucetun. xii. car'. In Illidei. iii. car'. In adelei. i. car' ⁊ dim.
In Ardinton. iii. car' ⁊ ii. bo' dim. In Cucheric. iii. car'.

FOUR FACSIMILES FROM DOOMSDAY.

[Facsimile of Domesday Book entries — Latin manuscript, partially legible:]

m̄ In Cumelai. Torchil. ii. car' ad g̃ld
m̄ In Bugdela. Archil Torchil 7 Gamel. v. car' ad g̃ld
m̄ In Fornehil. Gamel. ii. car' ad g̃ld
m̄ In Childewic. Archil. ii. car' ad g̃ld. 7 i. scot'a
m̄ In Esebrune. Gamelbar 7 ii. bou' ad g̃ld
m̄ In Vdelu. Wills. i. car' ad g̃ld. [.vi. car' ad g̃ld
m̄ In Chicheta. Vichel 7 Tode 7 Rauenfuar 7 Wills
m̄ In Willedone. Gamelbarn i. car' 7 . . . i. ad g̃ld.
+ m̄ In Acurde. Gamelbar 7 Wills. i. car' ad g̃ld.
B In Newhufe. Wills. i. car' ad g̃ld.
m̄ In Lacoc. Rauenſuard. ii. car' ad g̃ld
m̄ In Sicun. Rauenchil. ii. car' ad g̃ld

m̄ In Morainc. Ardulf. iiii. car' ad g̃ld. t'ra ad ii. car'. xxx s'
m̄ In Rodelefdon. Ardulf. i. car' ad g̃ld. t'ra ad dim' car'. xxv s'
m̄ In Scadauuelle. Cheel. vi. car' ad g̃ld. t'ra ad iii. car'. xl s' +
m̄ In Morainc. Archel. iii. car' ad g̃ld. t'ra ad ii. car'. x s' +
m̄ In hareuuode. tor. Spuet 7 brim. x. car' ad g̃ld. t'ra ad v. car'. d s'

In rabelai. cu Berew' bis Stube Middeltune. Den
aine. Clifuin Bichertun ternelai. Timbe. Ectone.
pouele. Cifele. henochefuurde. alia henochefuurde.
Beldone Merfintone Bungheleu. Stecliue.
I'm omīs sum ad g̃ld lx. carucate. 7 vi. bouate.
in quib; poſſunt. ee. xxx v. car'. hoc habuit Eldred.

THREE FACSIMILES FROM DOOMSDAY.

M̄ In Scipeleia lib. Ravenchil iii. car'. tre ad gld
ubi ii car' poss ẽi Ilbt' h't & Wast' e T.R.E. val
x Sol. Silva past'. 1 lev'. l'g. & dimid' lat.'

TERRA ERNEIS DE BVRVN*
WEST RIDING : SIRACHES WAP'.

---

* His other Manors are given on the same page, and all are in the West Riding, save two in the East.

ⱮIn Bingheleia hb. Gospatric iiij car' tre
ad gld. tra ad ii car' Ernegis de Burun h't.
& Wast' e'. T.R.E. val. iiij lib'. Silva past' ii leu'
lg' & i lat'. Tot' m' e iiij leu' lg' & ii lat'.
Infra hanc meta continet h' soca Beldune ii c'
Cotingelei ii c' Helguic* i c' Muceltuoit i c' Mardelei i c' Ha
teltun i c' Simul ad gld' viii caruc' tre' e'
ad iiij car' Waste sunt om's.

In CRAVE.

iii Ⱶ In Merdelai i c.' Heldetone ii c'. Cotingelei ii c. Colinga'
& B. uuorde ii c' Hageneuuorde dim c' Simul ad gld
vi car' & dim' tre. T'ra ad iii car' Ernegis h't & wasta sunt.

Siraches Wapentac [Index.]

In Otelai (Arch*bishop*), Pouele, Gisele, Hauoceforde
& alia Hauocheford, Beldone Mersintone, Burgelei
Illeclive lx car' & vi bo'.
In Redelesdene (Rex) 1 car'
In Bingelei & Beldun† Heluuic Mardelei Cotingelei, Hatelton,
Muceltuit (Erneis) xii car'. In Illiclei (W. Prci) iii car'.
Ⱶ In Cntnelai, Torchil ij car' ad gld.
iij Ⱶ In Bradelei, Archil Torchil & Gamel vij car ad gld.
Ⱶ In Fernehil, Gamel. ii car' ad gld.
Ⱶ In Childeuuic, Archil ii car' ad gld & i eccl'a (church).
Ⱶ In Esebrune, Gamelbar & Carvetor ii bov. ad gld.
Ⱶ In Vtelai, Wills i car. ad gld.
ii Ⱶ In Chichelai, Vlchel & Thole & Ravensuer & Wills ii car' ad gld.
Ⱶ In Wilsedene, Gamelbar & Wills, i car' ad gld.
Ⱶ In Acurde, Gamelbar & Wills, i car' ad gld.
B In Neuhuse, Wills i car' ad gld.
Ⱶ In Lacoc, Ravensuard, ii car' ad gld.
Ⱶ In Sutun, Ravenchil, ii car' ad gld.
Ⱶ In Mortune, Ardulf, iiij car' ad gld. T'ra ad ii car'. xxs'
Ⱶ In Redelesden, Ardulf, i car' ad gld. T'ra ad dim' car'. xvis'
Another Morton follows after Shadwell.
In Othelei cu' Berew' his Stube', Middeltune, Dentune, Cliftun,
Bichertun, Fernelai, Timbe, Ectone. Pouele, Gisele, Henochesuurde,
alia Henochesuurde, Beldone, Mensintone, Burghelai, Ileclive.

Roughly translated, Domesday's account of this district is as follows:

In SHIPLEY, Ravenchil had a manor, three carucates of land to be taxed where there may be two ploughs. Ilbert [de Lacy] has it and it is waste. In the time of King Edward it was valued at ten shillings. Wood pasture one league long and half broad.

---

*Helgwic. Hellifield occurs as Helgefelt.

†This is not likely to be Baildon which appears under Otley, as above. It may be a mistake for Morton. The Archbishop, the King (Rex), Erneis, and Percy held those manors.

ANCIENT BINGLEY. 59

LANDS OF ERNEST DE BURUN, WEST RIDING, SKIRACK WAPENTAKE.

In BINGLEY Gospatric had a manor of four carucates of land to be taxed (Danegeld), land for two ploughs. Ernegis de Burun has it and it is waste. In the time of King Edward the Confessor it was valued at four pounds. Wood pasture two leagues long and one broad. All the manor is four long and two broad. In these boundaries are contained the soke of Beldune* two carucates, Cotinglei two carucates, Helwick one carucate, Micklethwaite one carucate, Marley one carucate, Hateltun (Halton, now Harden) one carucate. The whole to be taxed is eight carucates of land and there are four ploughs. All are waste.

In CRAVEN, held by E. de Burun. Three manors and a berewick. In Marley one carucate, Halton (now Harden) two carucates, Cottingley two carucates, Cullingworth two carucates, Hainworth† half-carucate. The whole to be taxed is six carucates and a half of land. [It will be noticed that there are 7½ carucates recorded.] Land for three ploughs. Ernegis has them and they are waste.

SKIRACK WAPENTAKE. Index.

In Otley (under the Archbishop of York), Pool, Guiseley, Hawksworth, the other Hawksworth (possibly Esholt), Baildon, Menston, Burley, Ilkley, 60 carucates and 6 bovates (oxgangs.)

In Riddlesden the King held one carucate.

In Bingley and Beldun, Helwick, Marley, Cottingley, Halton, Micklethwaite, Erneis held 12 carucates.

In Ilkley, W. de Percy held three carucates.

Under the King:—

In Cutnelai (Cononley) Torchil had a manor, two carucates.

In Bradley, three manors held by Archil, Torchil and Gamel, seven carucates to be taxed.

In Farnhill, manor held by Gamel, two carucates.

In Kildwick, manor held by Archil, two carucates and a church.

In *East*burn, manor held by Gamelbar and Carvetor, 2 bovates.

In Utley, manor held by William, one carucate.

In Keighley, two manors held by Ulchel and Thole, and Ravensuer and William two carucates.

In Wilsden, a manor held by Gamelbar of 3½ carucates.

In Acurde (Oakworth) a manor held by Gamelbar and William, one carucate to be taxed.

In Newhouse (Newsholme) a berewick held by William, one carucate.

In Lacock, a manor held by Ravensward, two carucates.

In Sutton, a manor held by Ravenchil, two carucates.

---

* I doubt Bawdwen's rendering of this place as Baildon; and prefer Bell-bank, Bailey Hill, or even Gilstead.

† Bawdwen gives Haworth,—but the spelling is decidedly in favour of Hainworth.

Under the King:—

In MORTON, Ardulf formerly held a manor of four carucates to be taxed. Land for two ploughs, value 20s.*

In Riddlesden, Ardulf had a manor, one carucate to be taxed. Land for half a plough. Value 16s.

The Archbishop held:—

In Otley with its berewicks [small manor, parcel of a larger one,] are Stubham (now included with Middleton, but Stubham Wood is still known,) Middleton, Denton, Clifton, Bickerton(?), Farnley, Timble, Ecton(?), Pool, Guiseley, Hawksworth, the other Hawksworth (unidentified), Baildon, Menston, Burley, Ilkley.

On page xxxv., under the properties of Ilbert de Lacy will be found Snitterton, 8 carucates formerly held by Nivelin, Maban, Morfare and Vctred. It seems to me certain that this is not Priest-thorpe.

Snitterton.—The author of an article on Holy Trinity Priory, York, says that "the two carucates of land in Snitterton are apparently identical with a township in Bingley, which by reason of this donation acquired the name of Priest-thorpe, and where canons from Drax occasionally resided. It is thus mentioned in Domesday as land of Ilbert de Lacy. Four manors, in Snitterton, Nivelin, Maban, Morfare, and Uctred had eight carucates of land subject to Danegeld, and six ploughs may be there. Now Ilbert has it and it is waste. In the time of King Edward it was worth sixty shillings. Two acres of meadow are there. In the index under Skyrack Wapentake the King is put down as having four carucates in Morton, [but not the township in Bingley], and next is the entry of the eight carucates in Snitterton, belonging to Ilbert de Lacy. Fawcather upon Rumblesmoor is also a hamlet in the township and parish of Bingley."

I have found no proof of the identity of Priest-thorpe with Snitterton, and in fact dispute it because the area, 8 carucates, is too extensive, and the Domesday record would indicate another locality in its arrangement, and the second Morton is a place near Leeds.

A carucate varied in different districts owing to the nature of the country, but principally because some localities had the three-fold system and some two-fold; leaving the half or the third fallow in succession. If two-field system obtained here we may estimate 160 acres to the carucate, but it is generally estimated at 120 acres. Fifteen acres made a bovate or oxgang, and 8 bovates a carucate. Again, only arable land, meadow and wood-pasture are recorded; moorland and waste having no report because producing no tax. The moor of Moortown (Morton) came down to the two villages till quite recent times as may be noticed by the long wall that skirts the road from Morton Banks, West and East Morton, and Moorhouse farm.

---

*It will be noticed that both Bawdwen and Skaife in their translations are in error in giving the value at 30s. It will also be noticed that Riddlesden land was of much higher value than the Morton land. It is probably correct to state that the 20s. would be equal to £100 at the present day.

The terra of Domesday corresponds undoubtedly with the campus or townfields of earlier and later dates, when the common-field system was followed in primitive style. I am not sure that the word leu' is properly translated by the word mile, even if the length of the old English mile be meant. It is given as *league* by some and *mile* by others.

Our earliest local landholders under the Normans were probably descendants of the men who were owners in the days of the Confessor, but it is impossible to trace direct genealogies, except in the very rare cases where title deeds have been preserved for the eleventh century. We are not always sure that Gamel who held land in one place was the same Gamel who held land in an adjoining district. So, all that we can do for these Anglian owners is to leave their solitary names on record.

The word "waste" tells of the devastation and cruelty that the Conqueror inflicted on these districts after the rebellion of 1070.

Ardulf, of Riddlesden and Morton, it is presumed was the Hardulf who retained Burnsall, and possibly of the same family as Glonieorn fitz Heardulf who, with other thanes, revenged the murder of Gospatric, Gamel and Ulf at York in 1065.

Archil was an Anglian or Englishman. There were more than one evidently. One was son of Ulf, and held lands under William de Percy. Barnoldswick is named Bernulfswic in the survey from its former owner. Whether Gamel of Bradley and Farnhill was the great Gamel, under-lord of Bradford, does not appear. He or another Gamel held Arkendale under Ernegis de Burun. Gamelbar may be Gamel-bairn or son. Ravenward, Ravenchil and Ravensuer bear Danish names, preserved in the place-name Ravenroyd. There were several Torchils in Yorkshire. Ulchil of Keighley, of Bramhope, of Kiddal and of Barnby-dun were probably divers Anglians.

Gospatric, third son of Uchtred, and Earl of Northumberland, was murdered by order of Queen Eadgith in 1065, for her brother Tostig's sake. He had two kinsmen, cousins, of the same name but exact relationship unknown. One made peace with the Conqueror, but had to withdraw to Scotland for safety, and became ancestor of the Earls of Dunbar. He was buried at Durham. The other cousin, Gospatric, son of Arkill, a thane or noble, held properties in Domesday Survey. His aged father, the thane, made a treaty of peace with the Conqueror in 1068, but joined his relative Earl Gospatric, Merlesweyn, Edgar Atheling, and others, at York in rebellion, 1069. Arkill fled to Scotland, and his son Gospatric would have been slain had not the King, who had had him as hostage some time, formed an attachment to him. He was the only Anglian who retained any of his possessions in Yorkshire. His mother was Sigfrida, daughter of the Yorkshire thane Kilvert son of Ligulf. Gospatric fitz Arkill married a daughter of Dolfin son of Thorfin, and had sons, Gospatric, Thurstan, Dolfin, Uctred, and Thorfin, all great men in after date, and progenitors of landed proprietors in a smaller degree.

Under the notices of the Mawdes it will be found that the Riddlesden branch claim to be direct heirs and descendants of Gospatric, but I have not much faith in it as corroborative deeds are wanting.

Gospatric held also the manors of Copemanthorp, Dunesford, Brantune, Graftune, Cathale, Hulsingoure, Copegrave, Birnebyham, Wipelei, Bemeslai, Beurelei, Dacre, Litelbran, and Michelbran, all of which became Erneis de Burun's manors.

THE DESCENT OF BINGLEY MANORS.

(1)—Gospatric (son of Arkil.)
(2)—Ernest de Burun.
(3)—Paynel, 1120.
(4)—Gant, 1190.
(5)—Cantilupe, 1230.
(6)—Zouch, 1280.
(7)—Harcourt, 1290.
(8)—Astley, 1349.
(9)—Walker, 1560.
(10)—Currer, 1600.
(11)—Benson, 1668.
(12)—Lane-Fox.

ERNEIS DE BURUN and Ralph de Burun were brothers, and greatly benefited by accompanying William the Conqueror. They derived their surname from Buron, near Cinglais Forest. Some Norman Burons in the 12th century were benefactors of Ardennes Abbey, (the Ardennes of Waterloo fame.) Bingley was one of the best of the twenty-two manors he got in Yorkshire. He had four houses in York, and half his Yorkshire property was in Burghshire, now Claro Wapentake. He also held twenty-eight manors in Lincolnshire. Though he does not seem to have founded any religious house, he lent 100 marks* to Benedict, the monk of Selby, who gave him for security the finger (relic) of St. German in a shrine. Erneis kept two lamps always burning before it, and allowed it to be exhibited without fee. His son Hugh, subject to epilepsy, being desired to watch it with prayer during the night, was thereby completely cured. Fear or faith may have been of service to Hugh. Erneis or Ernest was Sheriff of Yorkshire about 1086 when Domesday was finished, and he was succeeded by Ralph Paynel about 1087. He probably took sides with Duke Robert against the King, and thus forfeited his estates, which, with the exception of Bingley, were given to the Earl of Chester. Some Buruns and Fitz Erneis occur at Goxhill, in the East Riding, down to 1335. Henry I. granted Bingley to William Paynel.

PAGANELL, 1120. Arms; gules, a cinquefoil, ermine, a crescent for difference. Banks's *Dormant Peerage*, I., 153. The earliest Paynells bore also two lions passant.

---

* A mark was 13s. 4d.; a great sum in those days.

ANCIENT BINGLEY.

Ralph Paynel, of Leeds, Arthington, &c.
= (1) probably a Lacy. = (2) Matilda, dau. (co)heiress of Richd. de Sourdeval, of Adel, Ecup, Cookridge, and Hardinctone (Arthington)

Children of (1):
- **William**,
  - **Julian**, d. & heiress of Robert de Bahuntune
  - **Willm.** who obtained Bingley Manor in 1120 or thereabouts. He founded the Priory of Drax, in Yorkshire, and gave Bingley Church to it in the time of Archbishop Thurstan, 1119-1147, and two carucates at Snitterton (not our Priest-thorpe) and a bovate at Faucather (Faweather.)
    = **Avicia**, one of three daughters and co-heiresses of Meschines, of the Earl of Chester's family. Her mother was Cecilia, only daughter of Robert de Romilly, lord of Skipton, from whom the popular opinion is that Rombles Moor takes its name, but this is doubtful. Avicia de Rumilly had previously married Robert de Courcy, and had issue William de Courcy.
- **Jordan**, died without issue
- **Elias**, a soldier, aft. Abbot of Selby, 1153. = **Agnes**
  - Robert de Brus, head of Yorks. and Scotch Bruces.
    - Fulk, issue male failed.
    - Hugh.
    - Adam.

Children of (2):
- **Alexander**, died c. 1154.
  - **William**, of Hooton Pagnell,
    - **Jordan**, ancestor of the Paynells of Notts.
    - **William**, died 1200, refers to a charter made at Wapentake (court) at Horsford in 1162.

Alice Paynell, only child, = (1) Richard de Courcy.
= (2) Robert, son of Walter de Gaunt or Gant, who thus became lord of Bingley Manor.

ANCIENT BINGLEY.

Ralph Paynel, Pagenel, Paynell, from the word pagan, which meant a ruler of a country district, was a native of Normandy. His name first appears in England in Domesday Survey. He held many manors that had belonged to Merlesweyn the Dane, in Lincolnshire and Yorkshire. Drax, Armyn, Ribstain, Goldsborough, Dighton, Ripley, and four other Yorkshire manors thus came to him, and at Drax he fixed his Yorkshire abode. He also held Steeton, Leeds, and Headingley in Skyrack Wapentake from Ilbert de Lacy, and it is supposed that he erected a castle or fortified a manor-house at Leeds. He refounded the Priory of Holy Trinity, in Micklegate, York, by consent of his wife and four sons; and gave to Selby Abbey a meadow called Nesse, at the bend of the Aire, in Drax manor. In 1088 he was Sheriff of Yorkshire.

GAUNT, OR GANT, 1190. Arms; Barry of six, or and azure, a bend gules. Banks' *Dormant Peerage*, I., 313.

Another great Domesday owner in Yorkshire was Gilbert or Gislebertus de Gand of Ghent and Alost. He also claims descent from our Alfred the Great. He got the manors held by Ulf of Folkingham, near Grantham, who held also Hunmanby, in Yorkshire. To these he added Bridlington.

| Gilbert, Earl of Lincoln. | Hugh | Walter, | Robert inherited the English estates, and founded Bridlington Priory. | Ralph |

Robert de Gaunt of Folkingham, died 1192. He married before 1152, Alice Paynell, and acquired Bingley thereby. For the redemption of his soul and that of his wife Alice, and of his heirs and kindred, he granted and confirmed in perpetual frankalmoigne to God and St. Mary and to the monks of Kirkstall two carucates in Kikeleia (Keighley,) &c. Adam of Keighley and his children, Juliana and others, had given the said lands to Haverholme convent; afterwards transferred to Kirkstall. Adam's father, Peter son of Essolf, had also been a monastic benefactor. Robert and Alice de Gaunt had an only daughter, Avicia, but Robert having married secondly, Gunnora d' Aubigne, had further issue four sons, Stephen, Gilbert, Geoffrey and Reginald. Avicia (mistakenly called Alice in some pedigrees and in the record of an ancient lawsuit,) married Robert,—son of Robert fitz Harding, progenitor of the Lords Berkeley,—and the husband assumed the name of Gant at the marriage. Their only son Maurice de Gant, alias Maurice Paynell was a most notable baron. His father having married a second time, Maurice had a half-sister Eve de Gournay, who married Thomas, son of William de Harpetre. On her brother's death without issue, Eve or Eva laid an unsuccessful claim to most of his possessions.

Bingley can boast of having been a market town forty years before Bradford. The charter, Inquis. q. ad damnum, dated 14 King John,

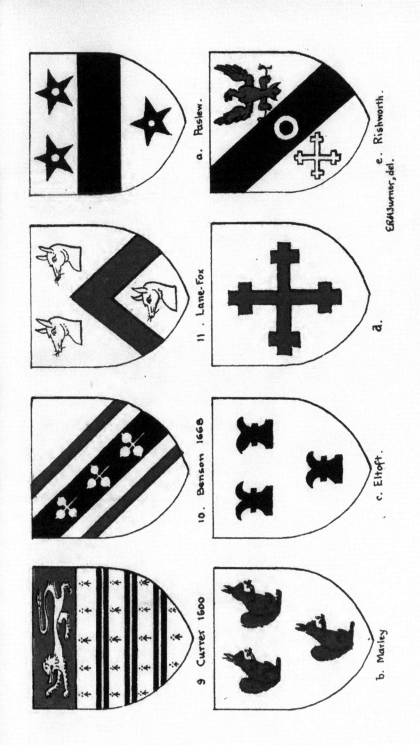

1212, will be found on the Rolls of Charters. "John by the grace of God, King of England, &c. Know ye that we have granted, and by our charter confirmed to Maurice de Gaunt that he may have a market at his manor of Bingley each week on Sunday, so nevertheless that that market be not to the injury of the neighbouring markets. Wherefore we will and strictly enjoin that the said Maurice and his heirs have the aforesaid market in the aforesaid manor of Bingley for ever, well and in peace, freely and quietly, with all liberties and free customs belonging to a market of this sort, as is aforesaid. Witnesses, the Lord Peter, bishop of Winchester, William earl of Salisbury my brother, William earl of Arundel, William Briwerre, Hugh de Nevill, John fitz Hugh. Given by the hand of Master Richard du Marais, archdeacon of Northumberland, at the Tower of London, 19th day of May, 14th year of our reign."

About 1251, a market was obtained for Bradford, and as certain taxes and tolls were easier than the charter gave to Bingley, the odds were against the Bingley market. Dortol and Huctol obtained till modern times at Lancaster. The door or gate toll was paid by a purchaser when carrying his parcel out of the town; the huc-toll was a hawker's licence, hence our word huckster. As there were few or no shops, pedlars and merchants passed from fair to fair, as the caterers for pleasure do still at country feasts. The great fair was held on the day of the Saint to whom the church was dedicated, and the market was held often on the Sunday. The inhabitants of Bingley were then styled Burgenses, or burgesses, on account of being within the district of a burgh or castle. They lived mostly in mud and clay huts, and wattled cottages; but timber houses were becoming more favoured; whilst the freemen built stone dwellings. There were still four classes, the slaves, tenants at will, freemen and freeholders.

In Testa de Nevill, 3 Henry III., 1219, the King had 18¼ bovates of land in Goulthorpe, Billingley, and in Swinton, which were escheats to him, and he gave them to Daniel the Butler by service of one sextary (three half-pints) or measure of wine to be rendered at London; value five marks (66/8d.) Blount's Jocular Tenures, p. 208. I do not think this has reference to our Gawthorpe and Bingley, though it has been so presumed.

Maurice de Gaunt was one of the chief barons, with Nicholas de Stuteville, Gilbert de Gaunt (son of Robert and Gunnora,) and Stephen Langton, archbishop of Canterbury, and others, who assembled an army at Stamford, Northampton and London, and proceeded to Runnimede, where on the 15th of June, 1216, Magna Carta and the Charter of Forests were granted by King John. King John shortly retaliated, and Maurice de Gaunt's possessions in various counties were given to several men, but chiefly to Philip d'Aubiny (Albinia,) who got promise of Leeds, &c., in Yorkshire, dated by the King at Doncaster. Although Maurice was one of the excommunicated under the pope's authority, the King tried to win his

E

allegiance twice. On the Patent Rolls, 17 King John, we find, "Of land given; It is commanded to the knights and free tenants of the fief of Maurice de Gaunt in Bingel' that they may be in all things obedient and answerable to Philip d' Aubigné, to whom he gave the land, which had been his, with all its appurtenances. At Yarm, 31 Jan." The barons, however, invited Prince Lewis of France to claim the throne in right of his wife Blanche of Castile, King John's niece, and he landed, but John dying at Newark, Oct. 19, 1216, his son Henry was crowned at Gloucester on the 28th. Lewis continued the struggle till May, 1217, when he and the barons supporting him were defeated. Maurice de Gaunt was one of the captives, and ceded to Rannulph earl of Chester for his ransom the capital manors of Leeds and Bingley. In the 14th year of Henry III., William de Cantilupe received a confirmation from the crown of the vill, market, and manor of Bingley of the gift and feoffment of Rannulph, earl of Chester and Lincoln, to be held of him by the service of half a fief of one knight. I have not been able to discover the family of Philip d'Aubigne, but it does not matter much for this history as his tenure was short and precarious.

Maurice de Gaunt, of Beverston castle, Gloucester, died 1230. } =

(1) Matilda dau. Henry d'Oylly, no issue.

(2) Margaret widow of Ralph de Sumery, no issue.

Maurice became a great man under Henry III. at his castles in Glo'stershire and Somerset, his possessions being granted at his death in 1230, to his nephew Robert de Gurnay, son of his half sister Eva.

CANTILUPE, 1230. Arms, gules, three leopards' heads inverted jessant, three fleur de lis, or.

Henry III. granted the Manor of Bingley in 1230 to William de Cantilupe, who had been Sheriff of Leicestershire, Worcestershire, and

MAWD ARMS.

Herefordshire in the reign of King John, and who was chief councillor of that King and his son Henry III. Cantilupe died in 1239, leaving five sons; William, the eldest; was steward to the king, like his father. He died in 1251 leaving two sons, Thomas, the younger, being Bishop of Hereford, and canonized as a Saint, (see Campbell's Lives of Lord Chancellors, Vol. I.) and the elder William married Eve dau. and co-h. of William Broase, lord of Brecknock and Abergavenny. William de Cantilupe was a powerful man in his day. He died in 1254 leaving two daughters and a son, George, aged 3, who lived to marry the daughter of the Earl of Lincoln, but died without issue. His sisters were *Milicent* who married (1) John de Montalt or Mawd, who left no issue, and (2) Eudo la Zouch; and *Joan* the wife of Henry Lord Hastings. Milicent la Zouch by charter, sans date, in her widowhood granted Bingley Manor to her daughter Ellen or Alianore. The mother died about 1280, and an inquis. post mortem records a son and heir William la Zouch, but the MS. at St. Ives mentions no son. Calendar Inquisition post mortem, Edw. I., George de Cantilupe held lands in Bingley. The Calendar Rolls of Patents, 26 Henry VI., the King confirmed to Thomas Astley, Esq., the grant made to Wm. de Cantilupe, 1240.

ZOUCH, 1280. Arms, gules, ten bezants or, a canton ermine, Banks, Vol. II., 620.

Eudo la Zouch sat in Parliament as Lord Zouch. Their only daughter Ellen married John de Harcourt, and carried Bingley manor to her children. In the Hundred Rolls there is an Inquisition of King Edward I., 1276, when the Jury found that Eudo la Zouch held pleas of illegal distress at Bingley. Also Eudo and the Archbishop of York have not permitted the officers of our Lord the King to enter Bingley for thirty years, nor Otley for four years, and Eudo holds the Sheriff's tourn at the time before mentioned; also that Robert Villein, while he was bailiff of Bingley, took Blithe (now indicted) p. priam 10s. for his liberty, and seized the whole of his land in Riseford (Rishworth) and as yet holds the same, and they say that the said Robert took of many persons much money for their concealed felonies as appears in the inquisition. They say that Hugo of St. Oswald, the sequestrator of the Lord Archbishop, took two marks at the execution of the will of Robert son of Syerith, two marks at the execution of the will of Simon Capellan of Bingley, before execution was allowed, and of others. They say the abbot of Fountains held Halton, Faweather and Cullingworth.

HARCOURT, 1290. Arms, Gules, two bars or.

John de Harcourt was knighted in 1306 along with the Prince of Wales, (Bridges' Collins, Vol. 4, 435.) He also fought in Scotland, and died in 1330, leaving an only son Sir William Harcourt, who married Jane daughter of Richard, Lord Grey of Codnor. Sir William died in 1349, leaving two sons, Sir Richard and Sir Thomas. The former died in his father's life-time, having married Joan, dau. and heiress of Sir William Skareshull, Lord Chief Justice, and their only issue was Elizabeth. By Inquis. post mortem, 8 Edw. II., Robert de Clifford had held three carucates in Riddlesden: and 11 Edw. II. (1318,) Henry, son of Nicholas de Preesthorpe had held a messuage and a cultura of land (20 acres) in Preesthorpe hamlet, with suit to Bingley court. William, son of John de Harcourt, had an inquiry respecting Bingley manor, and he had to pay 10 marks for pardon.

The Hundred Rolls of Edw, I. record the grants of Bingley and Ryshworth.

In 1316 (9 Edward II.), John de Harcourt was lord of Bingley and of Hellifield. In the same year Peter de Martheley of Marley and Ralph de Ilketon were lords of Morton. Ten years later William de Harcourt held Byngley.

From an undated deed we learn that Jordan de Risford (Rishworth) gave four acres of land in Helwick to Arthington Priory.

ASTLEY, 1349. Arms, azure, a cinquefoil ermine, within a bordure engrailed or, a crescent for difference.

Elizabeth Harcourt married Sir Thomas Astley, of Nelston, Leicestershire, second son of Thomas, Lord Astley by Elizabeth dau. of Guy, Earl of Warwick. Sir Thomas, lord of Bingley by right of marriage, sat in Parliament for Warwickshire during the troubled Wat Tyler's days, time of Richard II. His sons were Sir Thomas and Sir John. The elder, who was heir to Bingley, lived at Patshull in Staffordshire, and married Jane dau. of Sir Thomas Griesley, and had issue an only son Thomas Astley, Esquire, who married Margaret dau. of Sir William Boteler. Richard son of Thomas Astley, of Patshull, inherited the manor, and married Jane dau. of Thomas Oteley, Esquire, of Pitchford, Salop, and died in 1532. His son, Thomas Astley, Esq., married Mary dau. and co-h. of Sir Gilbert Talbot. Gilbert Astley, the oldest son by this marriage, married Dorothy dau. of Sir Thomas Giffard, Knight, and had an only son Thomas Astley, Esq., who had issue, but they died in their father's lifetime. Bingley probably never came to the last Thomas, for Gilbert Astley, Esq., sold divers farms in Bingley parish as attested by deeds bearing his autograph, 1562, and disposed of the manor to the Walkers. (Whitaker, p. 153.)

By Inquisition post mortem, 41 Edw. III., John de Dynelay had held lands and tenements at Bingley, and similar Inquisition 43 Edw. III., 1370, Johana wife of William de Harcourt had held the manor of Bingley. On 7 Richard II., 1384, John de Drax and John Balkok for the prior and convent of Drax held a messuage, two tofts, three acres of land near York and in Bingley. Eight years later, Thomas de Clifford, knt., and Elizabeth his wife, held a quarter of the fee of Morton and Riddlesden. An Inquisition post mortem, taken 1422, proved that William Gascoigne had held land at Torpark, Shipley and Cottingley; and at a similar Inquisition, 1483, it was found that the late Bryan Thornhill, of Fixby, had held lands at Fixby, Hyperum, Shibden, Northowram, Bradford, Byngeley, Haworth, &c.

GAWTHORPE HALL.

A Bill was filed in Chancery in 1573, between Gilbert Astley, of Patshill, Esq., v. Robert Whytley, respecting a messuage called Greenhill and a thousand acres on Bingley moor. Humphrey Hartley and John Campyntt had enclosed twenty acres of moor with a well and spring unlawfully. Whytley when required to answer refused.

WALKER, 1560. Arms, a chevron between three crescents azure. Crest, a moorcock treading a hen, proper, (Thoresby, p. 152.)

Walkers were an old family at Gawthorpe, near Bingley. John Walker, recorder of Leeds, 1710, was of this family. Thoresby writes from hearsay probably, when he states that the family at Gawthorpe Hall had held the manor for 250 or 300 years, unless they held a manor within a manor, of which there is no proof.

As notices of the Walkers, Currers, Bensons and Foxes occur afterwards they are briefly passed over here.

CURRER, 1600. Arms, Ermine three bars gemelles sable, on a chief azure, a lion passant, guardant ar.

Hugh Currer, Esq., Marley Hall, purchased Bingley manor from the Walkers. His grandson, Henry Currer, Esq., of Gawthorpe Hall, sold it to the Bensons, 1668.

LANE FOX CREST.

COPLEY ARMS.

COPLEY CREST.

BENSON, 1668. Arms, Argent, three trefoils in bend sa. cotissed gu.

Robert Benson, the purchaser of Bingley, was father of the first Lord Bingley.

LANE-FOX. Arms, argent, a chevron between three foxes' heads erased, gules.

Married Harriet, dau. and heiress of Robert Benson, Lord Bingley, 1731.

Although Bingley Manor Court had been held more than 600 years, Mr. Gray of York, the steward of George Lane Fox, Esq., informed the late J. A. Busfeild, Esq., in 1846, that the only rolls in existence are those written since 1708.

In very early times, and probably tending greatly to the prosperity of ancient Bingley, the parish was subdivided into five manors, namely :

(1) Bingley, including Gilstead, Helwick, Faweather, Micklethwaite with Rishworth and Priestthorpe.

(2) Cottingley Manor, held by the Copleys, then Sunderlands, and now the Ferrands.

(3) Hainworth Manor, held by the heirs of Sir George Cooke, Bart.

(4) Harden Manor, with Marley, Cullingworth, and Cowhouse, bought by the Ferrands from the Parkers of Alcancotes, Lancashire.

(5) Riddlesden, east and west, containing Morton and Morton Banks.

Morton was held, 9 Edw. II., by Peter de Marthley and Ralph de Ilketon.

Simon de Montalt was lord of Riddlesden in 1160. Thence it passed to Paslews. Francis Paslew died in 1603 and his sister and co-h., Ellen, married John Rishworth, Esq. Their son John and grandson Richard Rishworth, sold Riddlesden to the Murgatroyds. About 1692 it fell to the Starkeys.

Harden Manor.—The first manor roll given up to Mrs. Ferrand and her son when they purchased the manorial rights in 1841, only extended back to a court held Oct. 16, 1781. Probably no court had been held between that date and the possession by the monks of Rievaulx.

From a manuscript belonging to Mr. Robert Parker, of Marley, we learn that Thomas de Birkin gave to the monks at Rivalle the lands and woods called Harden, between Hadeltona (Halton) and Cullingworth, and between Hadeltona and Harden on the King's highway from Haworth to Bingley, bounded by Harden head, Harden brook falling into Wilsden brook, and Wilsden brook to Cullingworth brook to the pond of the mill, and thence to Hainworth Shaw. The witnesses were John, abbot of Fountains (1203-1209,) Stephen, abbot of Saleia (Salley 1210,) Richard, abbot of Selby (1194-1214,) John, parson of Birkin, Roger de Birkin, Roger de Kickel', Jordan de Haworth, Jordan de Hagenworth.

Another manuscript, dated 14 Queen Elizabeth, records that Robert Laycock and his ancestors of Whitecoate in Harden were, for fifty years before, owners of Whitecote, Bellbank and Butler's farm, then called Laycock's wood, now Mr. Ferrand's, and other woody grounds late Abraham Rawson's, and Milner Springs. Robert was drowned in Bingley mill-dam and left an only daughter heiress, who married Mr. Emmot of Wycollar, who in her right had all Laycock lands and woods and afterwards sold them by parcels.

Mr. Birkhead (J.P. in 1584,) purchased of Paslews, the Grange, Cross-gates, &c., in Harden, with the manor of Harden, and not long afterwards sold the Grange to Robert Ferrand, and other lands to Edward Brooksbank, with half of the manor of Harden and the rest of his farms in Harden to others.

In 1572, John Mylner of Harden Grange, husbandman, had a dispute with Robert Laycock respecting the road through Bellbank wood, which was referred for arbitration to Francis Paslew of East Riddlesden, Esquire, Thomas Mawde of West Riddlesden, gent., William Currer of Marley, yeoman, and others.

Edmond Watson of Ravenroyd who married Fether's widow there, and had a considerable fortune by her, purchased from Mr. Birkhead the Crossgates farm, adjacent to Milner Spring and Holling; one Edward Miller being then tenant at Crossgates at £8 per annum. Watson rebuilded it.

A Chancery suit between Paslew and the Freeholders of Bingley acquaints us with the chief tenants of the time and their properties:

William Clapham, John Rushford, Edwd. Brooksbank, Walter Ailmer, Francis Wilkinson, Thomas Lister, George Beanlands, Thomas Clapham of Morton, Anthony Whittingham, Thomas Fell, Thomas Clapham of Exley, George Clapham, Mary Rawson, Elizabeth Rawson, Isabel Rawson, Nathaniel Birkhead, Esq., Robert Ferrand, Stephen Ferrand, Jo. Millner, Mary ffeather, Jo. Shackleton, Thomas Blaykey, Jo. Rawson, Walter Thomas, Robert Emott, James Emott and Elizabeth his wife, Anthony Fell, Rodger Shackleton, Thomas Milner, Francis Lister, Brian Lister, Edward Ferrand, Thomas Fell, John Dobson, &c., complainants, and Henry Paslew elder, and Henry Paslew younger, defendants: Whereas by Inquisition taken at Wakefield in 1637 after the death of Francis Paslew it was found that Walter Paslew,

CLAPHAM ARMS.

LOYWF AS THOW FYNDS
TEMPEST ARMS.

grandfather of said Francis was seized of the Manor of Riddlesden and one water corn mill, one fulling mill, 103 acres of land, meadows, pastures and wood in Riddlesden, and a capital messuage and 160 acres of lands, pastures, &c., in Marley in the tenure of George Paslew brother of the said Walter, and a messuage in Marley called Thwaites, and 110 acres of land, &c., in Marley in the tenure of Henry Wilkinson, and of three messuages and 200 acres of lands, pastures, &c., in Morley (sic), and seven messuages and 400 acres of land, &c., in East Morton, and fifteen messuages and 500 acres, lands, pastures, woods, in West Morton, and a capital messuage called Ekisley (Exley) and 130 acres of land, &c., in Ekisley in Keighley in the tenure of Thomas Clapham, and a messuage called Horle House in Keighley and 86 acres in the tenure of Robert Sugden, and messuage and 40 acres in Keighley, &c.,. . . . and a messuage and 109 acres of land, meadow, pasture, and wood at Harden Grange in the tenure of John Long, and a messuage and 170 acres of land, &c., at Harden in the tenure of Robert Laycock, and a messuage and 19 acres in Harden in the tenure of Thomas Firth, and a messuage and 168 acres in Harden in the tenure of Sir John Tempest, and a messuage and 22 acres in Harden in the tenure of —— Glover, and twenty-three messuages, one water mill, one fulling mill and 315 acres in Harden in the tenure of Walter Paslew, and three messuages and 60 acres of land, meadow, pasture and wood in Bingley in the tenure of Walter Paslew, and two messuages and 70 acres in Scoles in the tenure of Walter Paslew, a messuage and 19 acres in Priestthorpe in the tenure of Margaret Rycroft, widow, and a messuage and 20 acres in Priestthorpe, six messuages and 20 acres in Oakworth in the tenure of Walter Paslew, and two messuages and 66 acres in Haineworth and Lees in the tenure of Walter Paslew.

He, in 1544, did enfeoffe Richard Paslew his second son of a messuage in Marley called Thwaites, with lands there, and Chatterford in Keighley for life. To his son Alexander, Marley &c., for life. To Thomas Mawde, gent.. and Miles Hartley, clerk, the Manor of Riddlesden, &c., to reinfeoffe the said Walter for life, with remainder to Francis his son, and remainder to the heirs male of Alexander his father for ever.

The said Walter died in 1545 leaving three sons, Francis, Richard & Alexander. Francis the eldest had issue Walter, Edmund, Alexander and William. Walter died in Dec. 1573, before his father, leaving issue by Helen his wife Francis, aged 5, Francis the father died in Sept. 1582, and Edmund the second son died April 1595 without issue, and Alexander died before his father, Feb. 1571 without issue, and William died Oct. 1596 without male issue, and Alexander the third son of Walter, (the grandfather,) had issue Francis and Henry Paslew.

TEMPEST ARMS.

Richard the second son of Walter (the grandfather) dyed in 1604 without male issue. Francis son and heir of Walter son of Francis son of Walter (the grandfather), dyed in August, 1603, without issue, at Bordeaux in France. The Francis of the writ returned to England in 1631, and Helen his mother having died in April 1617, he inherited the property. He died October, 1631, and Henry Paslew, second son of Alexander, third son of Walter the grandfather, was his brother and heir, aged 50. The messuages in Harden were held of his Majesty by Knight Service and were worth £6 yearly to the King.

This great trial and inquisition was said to be untruly found; they denied that Walter the grandfather had a third son named Alexander, and other points, and demanded an answer. The answer, a very long one, follows, amongst the depositions being the following:

THOMAS CORBOLD had known Henry Paslew the elder 55 years, Henry the younger 25 years.

ISABEL PASLEW knew Alexander Paslew 58 years since.

GREGORY SEAVEN, minister at Glemham, Suffolk, for twenty years, had known Richard Paslew, who lived there, twenty years.

MARY CULLAM swore that Alexander Paslew was minister of Glemham and son of Walter Paslew of Riddlesden, and died at Glemham an ould man.

JAMES POTTLE, rector of Glemham testified that Francis son of Alexander and Margery Paslew was baptized at Glemham in Feb. 1573, and Henry, another son, was baptized Sep. 14, 1578.

THOMAS CORBOLD swore that Francis Paslew of Glemham went to Bordeaux about 37 years since, and after returning died about 7 years since.

MARGARET CULLAM deposed that Richard Paslew had no issue, for at his going away he left his wife (deponent's grandmother) in Suffolk.

STEPHEN PASLEW declared that the complainants had made a common purse against him.

CHRISTOPHER WELBURN deposed that he had heard Isabel Paslew, say that Alexander Paslew, being a kinsman to her father whose name was Rawson, came often to his house at Shipley.

In 1658, Henry Paslew (son of Henry, son of Alexander, of Glemham,) having gained the victory, re-leased the estates of several persons in Bingley, and recited his descent on the deeds. To John Dobson he re-leased a messuage and 20 acres of land, 5 acres of meadow and 5 acres of pasture in Marley and Harden. To William Currer he leased a messuage, 30 acres of land, 5 acres of meadow, 10 acres of pasture in Marley and Harden. To Isabel Parker, a messuage with 20 acres of land, 5 acres of meadow, 5 acres of pasture in Marley and Harden. Crossgates, with a cottage, 20 acres of land, 5 acres of meadow, 10 acres of pasture in Marley and Harden to Edward Watson. To Robert Savile a messuage and 40 acres of land, 10 acres of meadow, 30 acres of pasture, and 100 acres of heath in Marley and Harden, and to the following he released houses and lands from four to 12 acres,—John Milner, John Furness, Robert Scott, Richard Driver, Alice Pighills, Thomas Blaykey, Thos. Milner, John Illingworth, Josh. Bayley, John Michael, John Murgatroyd, John Bynnes, Samuel Waddington, Anthony Fell, Anthony Hickhornegill, William Butterfield, Christopher Calverley, John Leach, Thomas Crossley, John Rogers, Henry Philips, John Philips, Christopher Berry, George Beanlands, Edmund Jennings, William Rushworth, Abraham Leach, John Wood, Francis Berry, Brian Lister, Thomas Lister, John Lister, John Walters, Edmund Turner, Walter Butler, Wm. Wood, Christopher Beanlands, Henry Turner, George Turner, Thomas Bradley, Anthony Fell, Joseph Hill, Joseph Angram.

In 1759 the boundaries of Harden manor are thus defined. Begin at Broad Oak in Unkram, Thwaites Lane, Wray Close, Coat Brow, Jackfields, Jackfield-house, stone on Royd Knowle marked RP (after Robert Parker), south to Fairfax Stone, then east to Farnley Cragg, marked SP,AB,IF, then south to Sunderland Stoup marked SP (for

Stephen Paslew perhaps), then south-west to Cullingworth brook called Ellar car or Threaproyd, then east down the brook to Cowhouse and Beckfoot, and north to Beckmouth on Aire, and up mid-river to Broad Oak in Unkram.

Walter Paslew of Riddlesden, son of Francis, by deed, 11 Elizabeth, demised to William Currer the capital messuage called Marley Hall and lands and Middleton wood reserving £4 13s. 4d. yearly and three boone henns, and the lessee covenanted to grind his corn at the lord's milne at Riddlesden. William Currer afterwards attended the Court

CURRER ARMS.

SAVILE ARMS.

of St. John of Jerusalem when Robert Dean the steward entered a memorandum as under—"Wm. Currer deposed that there ys paid forth of the premises to her Majestie as due to St. John of Jerusalem yearly, the scme of xviijd. as a free rent, and doth acknowledge suit at her Majestie's Court."

Wm. Currer occupied Marley Hall, and afterwards his son William Currer. In 1623, John Rishworth, Esq., of Riddlesden, succeded Paslew, and sold Marley Hall and lands for £700 to John Savile, Esq.,

PARKER ARMS.

of Halifax, whose arms yet remain over the porch and also in the hall window. In 1651, Robert Savile, of Marley Hall, mortgaged the estate to Samuel Sunderland, Esq., of Harden, for £100, and in 1665 Mr. Sunderland purchased the fee for £944 9s. 0d. In 1675, he settled the estate upon his nephew Robert Parker, Esq., who then resided at Marley Hall, and in the Parker family it remained until 1843, when the manor of Harden and Marley Hall, with nearly 400 acres of land and wood were purchased for £17300, by Mrs. Sarah Ferrand and her son Wm. Busfeild, Esq., M.P., from Thomas Goulborne Parker, Esq., of Browsholme.

On the Dissolution of the Priory of Drax, the King, Hy. VIII., seized the property and manor of Harden, and granted the same to Walter Paslew.

MISCELLANEOUS OLD DEEDS.

Amongst the Harleian MSS. (Randle Holmes') 2117, fol. 266-7, are eight deeds of local interest.

(1) Agnes, relict of John of Casteley in her widowhood, quit claimed to God and the church of St. Nicholas at Drax, and the canons there, all right and claim as dower in a toft with buildings near the church of Bingley, viz. the one which Richard of Shepley and Matilda his wife, formerly held of the gift of William of Casteley. Witnesses,—Hugemond of Leeds, William clerk of Bingley, John Villayn of Gilstead, and others. The seal was broken. These Casteleys, of Casteley near Leathley, were an important family about Otley and Harrogate from 1100 to 1350.

(2) I, Hugh, son of Robert de Newall, give to the Prior and Convent of Drax the right I hold in 18 acres of land with appurtenances, of the Lord of Prestorp (Priest-thorp). Witnesses,—Simon de Mahant, Peter of Anterne, Henry Barrat, Jernegan of Bingley, Galfrid clerk of Drax, Robert of Fulais, Roland of Hersewell and others.

(3) Richard, son of Roger of Neuhall, by the instruction of divine charity, and for the health of my soul and that of my predecessors and successors, have given to God and the church of St. Nicholas of Drax and the canons there serving God, in pure and perpetual alms (frankalmoigne) four oxgangs and four tofts with appurtenances in Priest-thorpe, and an annual rent of 3s. to be received from Robert, son of William of Alwaldeley for one oxgang and one toft, &c., to be

held as absolutely free from all secular service. Witnesses,—Robert Villans the bailiff of Bingley, William le Gentil, Maud of Matheley, Richard his brother, Nicolas of Barkeston, William of the Beck of Harewood, John of Casteley, and others. Seal gone.

(4) To all of Holy Mother Church, William of Casteley, greeting; know that I have given to God and the church of the Blessed Nicholas of Drax for my soul's health at the same time with the burial of my body at the same place, one toft in the vill of Bingley with croft and all buildings held of Anthony of Altaripa. Witnesses,—Robert de Montealto, Hugo de Montealto, Robert Villeyn, Henry of Risford, Robert of Greenhill, William Gentil, Adam Crone, and others. Seal, a fleur-de-lys.

(5) Brother John of Lincoln, Prior of Drax, gift to William the Fuller of Bingley, son of Henry of Shipley, and to Marjory his wife and their heirs, one toft, croft, and buildings which Adam de Laycock formerly held of us in the vill of Bingley between the toft which William the clerk holds of us and the toft of Cecily Tanatricer, for the sum of money they paid to us,—to hold the same, rendering 3s. at Penticost and St. Martins in winter by equal proportions. Witnesses,—John of Martheley, John Villayn, William of Ackworth (Oakworth?), William of Friston, John son of Simon Villayne, Adam of Leeds, William Clerk, &c.

(6) Robert of Baius from an affection for religion and for my soul's health and the health of the souls of my predecessors, give to God and St. Nicholas' Church in Drax, three acres in Bingley in Micklethwaite; namely two acres adjoining the land of Norman de Risseford on the east, one acre adjoining the land of Gilbert of Greenhill on the north, in pure and perpetual eleemosiny. Witnesses, —Hugo Capellanus (chaplain) of Bingley, Galfri of Eleas, Richard of Bingley, clerk, [Richard was Vicar of Bingley in 1369], William of Castelay, Hugo Gentil, William Ruffus and others.

(7) Osbert of Bahius, not risking his soul by witholding just dues to God and the church, confirmed grants made by his ancestors to God and the church of St. Nicholas of Drax, a carucate in the territory of Bingley, viz., the whole vill of Priest-thorpe (Prestorp) from the road leading to Gilstead, with marsh, meadow, wood from Dunpel stream and Merstall, with wood to burn, and build, and make hedges reasonably under the inspection of my foresters, and pannage for pigs and the food of the men in the Court of Prestrop, to hold for the redemption of my soul and the souls of my ancestors; and all quit-rents which William Paganel gave them. Witnesses,—Adam son of Peter of Altefane, Roger of Fodounghes, Ganger of Stivetona (Steeton), Villayn Adam of Clayton, Roger of Rigtona, Symon of Barkeston, and others.

(8) Indenture at Bingelay, 20 Sept., 1537, between Sir John Long, Vicar of Bingley, and George Passlow of Marlow, gent., that he hath demised to the said George the church of Bingley for three years next ensuing with all tythes, profits, &c., paying yearly to the said

vicar £10 at Martinmas in Winter and St. Marks by even portions, and the vicar had to pay all duties to the church of York and the King, and to discharge the cure as he will answer to God and man, and the said George shall lay no claim to the vicarage house nor the ground thereto belonging, with six acres of land in Bingley feild and Micklethwaite feild. Witnesses,—Walter Passlew Squire, Miles Hertley, prest, Jo. Dobson and others. A round seal bearing the impression of a heart under a five-pointed coronet.

To these I may add a ninth deed that I found loosely placed in the oldest church register over twenty years ago, which had been handed to the Rev. A. P. Irwine, Vicar, as a curiosity. It bears the date 1357. "Sciant p'sentes et futur' q^d ego Simon Mohaud fil Ade Mohaud dedi concessi & hac p'senti carta mea confirmam Dno Ade Leuanbred & Thome Mohaud de Morton mannr meii in Redelysdeyne, Morton Bank, Kesewyk, Ouer Yedon, Netheryedon, & unu' annual redditum in Halton, vid-unus libre piperis & aliu' annual redditu' de p'cella de Redelysdene vid.' octodecim denar' et totu' ius & clamem' quod h'm hes vel asigne modo here pot's in futur' in Bradeley & Skypton cum t'rio p'tis pasturis boscis vijs semilis sepibz stagn' aquis cum eor sectis homag' redittibz consuetidbz et cum omb. alijs p'tm suis hend' & tenend' p'dcm man' rum cum ombz rebz p'nstat a combz alijs man'io p'dco p'tinent prdc. Dno. Ade Leuanbrede capello & Thome Mohaud her' & assign copem libe bene & in pate imprpr' de caput d'mo feodor suor pmt inde debit et de iure consuet et ego vero p'dictis. Simon & her' mei p'dt mannerm. cu' om'ibz suis prtin' p'nstat prdc Dno Ade & Thome Mohaud her' & assign' eordn com' om'es gentes warantizab' inprp'm & defendem. In cuj' rei testi'm huis p'senti carte mee sigillum meu' apposui. Dat. apud Redelysdeyne die Marcur' psc post festum Apostolor' Petri & Pauli Anno Dm millo ccc^{mo} quinquagesimo septio hiis testibz Willo de Eltofte, Nicho de Ylton, Johe Locok & mult' alijs."

Briefly translated it runs: "Know present and future that I Simon son of Adam Mohaud give concede and by this my present charter confirm to Sir Adam Levenbred and Thomas Mawd of Morton my manor in Riddlesden, Morton Bank, Keswick, Over Yeadon, Nether Yeadon, and an annual rent in Halton [named now Harden], namely a pound of pepper and another annual rent from the parcel of Riddlesden, namely eighteen pence, and all rights and claims which I or my heirs and assigns have now or in future in Bradley and Skipton, with lands, pastures, woods, ways, bounds, pools, watercourses, homages, rents, customs, &c., to have and to hold the same to Sir Adam Levanbred, chaplain, and Thomas Mawd, their heirs and assigns, under the Capital Fee, owing all rights and customs thereto, and I the said Simon warrant them to hold the same against all people. In testimony whereunto I place my seal. Dated at Redelysdeyne, Wednesday next after the feast of Saints Peter and Paul, 1357, these being witnesses, William of Eltofte, Nicholas of Ylton, John Locok and many others."

Although I have copies of many of Dodsworth's notes taken from the Harleian MSS. at Oxford, by my friends Messrs. Carter of Birmingham, and Lister of Shibden, when students there, and have copied many from the British Museum MSS. it is just to acknowledge that the most popular transcription of the Bingley notes is the one in the Thoresby Society's publication, 1890, as follows :—

Bingley:

FINES. A° 10 Jo.

NNN. 98. Between Mauritius de Gaunt, demant, & Anthony de Alta Ripa, tenent, of one acre of land with the appurtnances in Norwod, & of 6 bovates of land with the appurtnances in Bingeley. The right of Mauritius. And he granted to the foresaid Anthony the foresaid six bovates of land in Bingeley forever, doeing therefore forinsecall service as much as belongeth to 6 bovates of land, whereof 12 Carucates of land make one K$^{t's}$ fee.

FINES. 10 JOHN.

NNN. 98. Between Mauritius de Gaunt, demant, & Robert de Hugate, tent, of one Carucate of Land with the appurtnances in Bingeley, whereof the said Robert called to warrant Peter de Alta Ripa in the said Court, who comes, &c. The foresaid Peter and Richard (sic) acknowledged all the foresaid Land with the appurtnances to be the right of the said Mauritius & his heires.

FINES. A° 11 JOHN.

NNN. 118. Between Mauritius de Gaunt, complt, & Mathew de Haneworth, tent, of one carucate of Land with the appurtnances in Haneworth, & of one bovate of land with the appurtnances in Bingl. The right of Mauritius &c. And Maur' granted to the foresaid Mathew all the Carucate of Land with the appurtnances in Haneworth, to be holden of William de Stiveton & his heirs for ever, by the service which belongeth to the foresaid Carucate. And the foresaid bovaie of Land with the appurtnances remaine to the foresaid Maur' & his heirs for ever.

FINES. A° 11 JOHN.

NNN. 119. Between Maur' de Gant, Complt, & Thomas de Mohaut, tent, of 6 Bovates of Land with the appurtnances in Mordele, & of 2 bovates of Land with the appurtnances in Binggeleia. Maur' acknowledged the foresaid 6 bovates of land with the appurtnances in Merdele to be the right of the said Thomas for ever, by the service belonging to that land. And the foresaid Thomas remitted, &c., to the foresaid Maur' & his heirs all the right & claime which he had in ye foresaid 2 bovates of land with the appurtenances in Bingeleia.

FINES. 13 JOHN.

NNN 121. Between Maur' de Gant, demandᵗ, and Alice de Bingel, tenᵗ, for William son of Osbert, of 40 Acres of Land, with the appurtnances in Bingel. The right of Maur' & his heirs. And the said Maur' gave and granted to God, & St. Mary & "fratribus milit' templi" those 40 acres of Land with the appurtnances in pure & perpetuall Almes. Allso the said Maur' granted for him & his heirs that the foresaid friers may have pasture in the said Towne of Bingel for 40 sheep & for 14 averias & to 6 hoggs & to 2 (?averes).

BINGLEY CHURCH, LAST OF MAY, 1621, QUIER WINDOW.

M. 168. Orate pro bono statu reverendi in Christo Patris Ricardi Wilson ingoponte* Episcopi Ebor ac prioris de Drax et pro animabus parentum cius, qui istum Chorum & fenestram fieri fecit. A° Di M° ccccc° octodecimo et die mensis Martii xxvi°.

IN SEVERAEL WINDOWS ABOUT YE CHURCH.

Ar. on a ∧ b a mullet of 6 poynts of ye first.
a | | | | | g.
Ward.   B. a fleur-de-lis or.
Kighley.   Ar. a fesse, sa.
At. 3 squerrells seient g. cracking nuts or.
A parke at Bingley (blank), at Hamlet Cottingley.
A Castle at Bingley nere the Church on a hill called Baley Hill.
It hath been a Market & Borogh Towne.

ESCHAETS 19 ED. 2.

AA. 117. The Jurors say it is not to the dammage of yᵉ Lord yₑ King if he grant to William sonne of John Harcourt & Jone his wife that they may hold the mannor of Bingley in the County of Yorke to them & the heirs of the bodies of the said William & Jone &c.

ESCHAETS 43 ED. III.

AA. 118. The Jurors say that Jone late wife of William de Harcourt held the mannor of Bingley and Heliaghfeild with the appurtnances of the guift of John Harcourt of Bosworth &c. of which William & Jone issued Richard first borne, now deceased, from Richard issued Elizabeth daughter & heire of the foresaid Richard, and so the said Elizabeth is

---

* This is marked (?) Negroponte.

ANCIENT BINGLEY.

heire of the foresaid William & Jone &c. And the foresaid mannor of Bingley (is held) of the Lord Zouche by homage, & the mannor of Helingfield is holden of the Lord Clifford by knight's service. This Elizabeth was the wife of Thomas Atley (? Astley), knight, who died 2 H. 4.

THORNHILL ARMS.   THORNHILL ARMS.

IN THE WRITEINGS OF THOMAS THORNHILL OF FEKESBY ESQ. 24 FEB. 1629.

K. 97. Richard de Thornhill demised to William Smith of Bingley for terme of his life all his lands & Tenements in the parish of Bingley, sct. in Presthorp, with the Burgage in Bingley, & in Grenhill. Dated at ffekisby, 1369. Witnesses, Henry Sayvill, William Bradley. 43 Ed. 3.

ibm. 97. Richard le proud souter of Bingley gave & granted to Thomas de Thornhill & Margret his wife, & Richard son of the foresaid Thomas & Margret, all those Tenem[ts] which he had of the guift of John de Ledes in Binglay. Witnesse, Thomas Mohaut, Ralfe de Hilton. Dated at Bingley 1330. 4 ED. III.

F

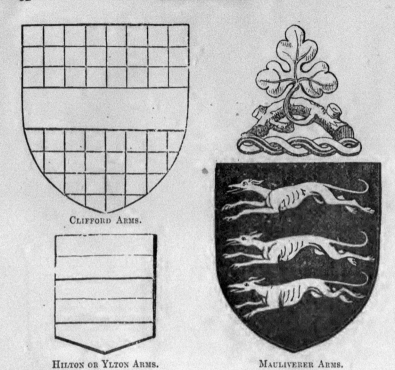

CLIFFORD ARMS.

HILTON OR YLTON ARMS.

MAULIVERER ARMS.

IN THE COLLECTIONS OF C. FAIRFAX OF MENSTON ESQ. 2 No. (? 2nd Nov.), 1629.

V. 110. Nicholas Bayldon confirmed to Robert Passelowe, Thomas de Hawkesworth, Jo. Mohaud & Walter Grauer all yᵉ Lands &c in the Townes of Bayldon, Bingley & Menston. Wittnesse, John Ward Kt, John Scot, Robert Maliuerer, John de Rawdon. Dat. die dominica, after the feast of St. Andrew, 4 Hen. 4.

HAWKSWORTH ARMS.

ANCIENT BINGLEY. 83

OUT OF DRAX COUCHER. 2 VOL.

AAA. 48. To all the sons of the holy mother the Church as well p'sent as to come Osbert de Bayons greeting. Know ye that I have given and granted & by this my p'sent Charter confirmed to God & the friers of the Holy Hospitall of Jerusalem one Toft in Bingley &c & Common of pasture & other easements which belong to the foresaid Towne in pure & p'petuall Almes. Wittnesse &c. fo. 44.

ibm.

ibm 48. To all &c Robert de Bayons greeting. Know ye that I haue given & granted & by this my psent charter confirmed to God & the church of St. Nicholas of Drax & the monkes there serueing God 3 acres of Land in the territory of Bingeley in [Michechuayt] sct, 2 acres of Land next the Land of Nor^{m}an de [Risseford] towards the East & one acre of Land towards the land of Gilbert de Grenehill towards the North in pure & ppetuall Almes &c. fo. 44.

ibm.

AAA. 48. Know all &c psent & to come that I William de Canteluy (? Cantelupe) haue granted to God & St. Nicholas of Drax & the monkes there &c, in the wood of Byngley for burning & building in the same place & all liberties of the same place which they were wont to have since the time of William Paganoll who gave that church to God & St. Nicholas freely & quietly without Impediment. fo. 44.

ibm. 49.

AAA. 49. The Charter of William de Cantulupo of the Church of Bingley.

OUT OF GREENFELD'S REGISTER, ARCH^P OF YORK.

B. 57. The Church of Drax & Bingley appropriated to the use of the Prior of Bolton.

OUT OF MELTON'S REGISTER.

B. 115. A Certificate of the Churches wasted & destroyed by the Scotts that paid the tythes undermentioned, *inter alia*.

117d. The Church of Bingley, xxij markes.

OUT OF THORESBY REGISTER.

B. 142. The Prior of Drax psents to y^e Vicariage of Bingley 1362. fo. 120.

IN KIRKBY'S INQUEST TAKEN 13 ED. I.

W. 164. Stephen Walleis holds 3 Carucates of Land in Bingley of Robert Eueringham whereof 14 Carucates make one K^{ts} fee.

84   ANCIENT BINGLEY.

Baildon Hall.

OUT OF DRAX COUCHER. 2 VOL., IN THE CUSTODY OF MARMADUKE CONSTABLE OF EUERINGHAM, ESQ.

AAA. 24. The Charter of William Paganell ye ffounder.
To all the sonnes of the holy mother the Church as well present as to come, William Paganell greeting. Know ye that I have given & granted & by this my present charter confirmed to God & St. Nicholas, & the monks serveing God & St. Nicholas in the territory of Drax, the Isle which is called Holinhom & Middelhom where the Church of St. Nicholas of ye Priory of Drax is founded, & the Land Horm & the Land Hadde &c. And the parochiall Church of Drax, and the Church of Bingley, and the Church of Roxby, & the Church of Media Rasa, & the Church of Hyrnesham, & the Church of Swinhamstode, & the Church of Salteby, with all their appurtnances and liberties. And 2 Carucates of land in Snyterton &c. All these I have given to God & the Church of St. Nicholas, & the monks there serving God, by the advice & consent of Thurston, Archbishop of Yorke, with Soch & Sach & Tol & Thom & Ingfangethefe, with all other liberties & Commodities, &c. Witnesse, Ralfe Paganall, Peter son of Essolf, Adam & Tho. his sonnes, Warinus de Scto Patricio, William de Stanegret, William de Alta ripa, &c. fo. 1.

ibm.

ibm. 28. The charter of Roger Archbishop of Yorke of ye appropriation of the Churches of Bingley & ffoston. fo. 2.

OUT OF DRAX COUCHER. 2 vol.

AAA. 48. To all the sonnes of the holy mother the Church as well p'sent as to come Osbert de Bayion greeting. Know ye that I have granted & by this my p'sent Charter confirmed to God & the Church of St. Nicholas of Drax & the monkes there seruing God one Carucate of Land in y Territory of Bingley wch William Paganell my Ancestor gave to the foresaid monkes & the Church of Bingley, viz.: all ye town of Presthorp with all the appurtnaunces, viz.: all the arable Lands which is between the said Towne and the wood towards the North & all the Land between the wood and the way which goeth from Presthorp to Gildestede towards the East from that place which is called Dimple. On the other pt of the Towne towards the West and South all the Land with the marsh meadow & wood the brooke which goeth from Dimple to the *vinyard* (? vinarium) encompaseth "*usqz ad terreium pontem*" and from there all the land betwixt the forementioned Towne of Presthorp and Maresall by the Circuit to the foresaid way which goeth from Presthorp to Gildestede towards the East. These foresaid Lands I have granted & confirmed by this p'sent Charter to the foresaid monkes in pure and p'petuall Almes freely & quietly to be holden for the redemption of my Soule & of all my Ancestors with all easements &c which William Paganell gave and confirmed to them. Witnesse &c. fol. 44.

Esch. 1 Ed. I. n° 16.

E. 3. The Jurors say that George de Cantilupo held the third part of the Burgage of Colne in Com Wilt &c & of Bingley in the County of Yorke, and they say that Milisanda wife of Eudo la Zouch who is of full age & John son of Henry & Jone de Hastings who is under age & in the Custody of the Lord the King are next heires of the said George.

There is here the extent of Bingley & *Baseford* (? Bradford) in the County of Yorke &c which were George de Cantelupes aforesaid.

Hastings Arms.

Dodsworth Arms.

The Jurors say that there is not there a Capitall mess. They say there is there a water mill, which is worth p annum viij^{li} & 30 Acres of land in demeasne which is lett to farme & worth yearly with meadow 36^s, "Tollinium cum furno" worth yearly 15/-^{s} & there are 21 free tenants which pay yearly iiij^{li} of which 8 doe service at the Court of Bingley from 3 weekes to 3 weekes &c. And they say that Milisanda wife of Eudo la Zouch & John son of Henry de Hastings are next heires of the said George. There is not the advouson of the Church there because the Prior of Drax hath the Church in his p'per use &c. Milescent daughter of Hugh Baron of Gornaier & Julian his wife, sister of Reginald E. of Bullen, married to

ANCIENT BINGLEY. 87

Americus E. of Euereux & Glocester. 5 Jo., was after married to William de Cantilupo who had issue Thomas Bishop of Hereford & Julian wife of Robert Tregoze. Cat. Hon^r. 367.

Esch. 41 Ed. 3 N° 20.

E. 162. The Jurors say that John de Dyneley held the day that he died joyntly with Isabell his wife yet liueing 1 Mess & 16 Acres of Land in Gerford by knight's service of Robert de Swillington & 4 Acres of Land & one wind mill in ye said Towne of the Abbot of St. Mary of Yorke by the service of 4^s yearly, he allso held one Carucate of Land and 5 markes rent in Mikelfeld of William de Raygate &c. he allso held one Mess & one Carucate of Land in Bingeley of Sr Ralfe de ffurrars by the service of 12^d yearly &c. Richard de Dyneley is son & heire & of the* age of 48 years.

Ffines. 13 Ed. I.

GG. 14. Between Alianor la Zouch comp^{lt} & Milesenta de Montalt defor^t, of the Mann^r of Bingel, the right of Alianor & the heires of her body & for defect &c to return to the foresaid Milisenta & her heires.

Recoueries. Mich. Term. 9 H. 7. rot. 323.

GG. 44. William Wymesbury, Richard Littilton, & William Wylkes complaine ag^t Humphrey Peschale Esqr & Margret his wife. The mann^r of Bingley with ye appurtnances, & calls to warrant William de Astele Esqr.

Clausæ. 14 H. 3. m. 11.

GG. 45. The King &c. We have seen the Charter of Ralfe E. of Chester & Linc. in these words,

Ralphe E. of Chester & Linc. to all that shall see or hear this writeing psent & to come. Know ye that I have given granted & by this my psent Charter confirmed to William de Cantilupo Juniori for his homage & service all the towne of Bingley with all the appurtnances in demeasne & service &c. To have & hold of me & my heires to him & his heires as freely as I euer had the same &c.

F. 149. [*Note.*—Nothing is given under this reference.]

Out of the Leiger of St. Leonard's, of York.

CC. 75. I, Anthony de Alta ripa have receiued of Mr R. Rector & the ffriers of the Hospitall of St. Peter of Yorke all the Land which they had of the guift of Gilbert de Arches in Binglei to have & hold of them in fee & Inheritance & paying yearly 2^s to the foresaid Hosp. Wittnesse Willm de Nottingham, Clerke, Peter de Alta ripa. fo. 108.

[*I am inclined to think that two or three of these extracts from our worthy Yorkshire antiquary, Dodsworth, refer to another Bingley.]

East Riddlesden Hall.

From General Harrison's MSS.; xviii., p. 981. Fine at Westminster, 10 Hy. III., 1225, between William de Muhaut and his son Simon de Muhaut, of the whole of the manor of Redlesden, the said William gave to Simon all the manor except six acres of land which he gave to James and Simon, sons of the said Simon.

(2) xx., p. 687. Quo Warranto Roll. 30 Henry III., Simon de Monte Alto versus Walter de Scoteny and Alicia his wife and Matilda her sister, two bovates of land, except 1 ac. 1 rood in Kesewic; and versus Rombald de Montibus and Margery his wife, two bovates of land in Keswic as his right; and he said that one Simon his ancestor was seized in his own right as of fee, &c., time of King Richard.

Simon de Monte Alto, 1189-1199,

William, Alicia = Ralph Mauleverer, who enfeoffed her
  | husband's brothers Hugh and Richard
Simon, plaintif. Mauleverer after her husband's death.

The defendants said that Simon had a daughter Alicia with whom he gave said land in marriage, and at her husband's death, she gave the land to her husband's brothers, and the said Alice, Matilda and Margery are their descendants.

(3) xxi., p. 1110. De Banco Roll, 27 Edw. I., 1298, William le Waleys at the suit of Robert de Monte Alto the custody of William, s. & h. of Godfrey de Neville.

Hugh de Neville held land of Cecilia   Cecilia de Monte Alto =
  | de Montalt. |
Godfrey   John, ob. s. p.   Robert
  | |
William
                   Roger, ob. s. p.   Robert de
                                      MonteAlto.

(4) feet of Fines, several counties, 1 Edw. III., 1327. Between Robert de Monte Alto and Emma his wife *versus* Mr. Henry de Clyf, clerk, deforciant, the castle, town and manor of Monte Alto, &c., in Keswyk East, to the heirs of said Robert and Emma, with remainder to Queen Isabella, mother of King Ed. III.

(5) Quo Warranto Rolls: 1267 and 1278.

Simon de Monte Alto
  |
William de Monte Alto and Alice his wife

Simon de
Monte Alto = Sarra, (2ndly) William fil Wm. Russell.   Adam

Alicia	Isabella	Sarra	Matilda	Elizabeth	Ismania,	Johanna,
=	= Thos.	=	=	=	under age,	under age,
John	de	Thos.	Nicholas	Wm. de	in custody	in custody
de	Eyvil	de	de	Lang-	of Adam	of Sarra
Mathe-	John	Eltoft	Aketon	feld	de Monte	her sister
ley	de		(Ilketon)		Alto	=
	Mohaut.				= (seeNo.6)	(seeNo.6)

Sarra and Matilda *versus* Galfri de Montealto, about the Manor of
Est Keswyk. The coheiresses and their husbands, as above, were
summoned to answer the King as to by whose right they claim free
warren in Riddlesden and East Morton, and West Morton, and they
say that Johanna is under age, and the king gave the said free
warren to their father Simon de Montealto, by charter 23 Jan. 38
Hy. III., 1253.

(6) Quo Warranto, 21 Edw. I., respecting the Manor of Redleston,
Kesewyk, Ackeworth and Hahgenworth.

The coheiresses of Simon de Montalt are named in the following
order, Alicia, Elizabeth, a daughter deceased (Isabella) wife of
Thomas de Ayville, leaving a son and heir John de Ayville, Sarra,
Matilda de Ilketon, Ismania married Gerard de Collum, and Johanna
married Henry de Ecckesley.

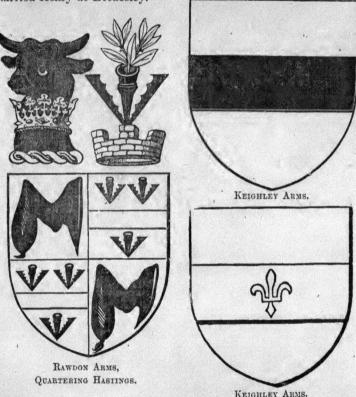

KEIGHLEY ARMS.

RAWDON ARMS,
QUARTERING HASTINGS.

KEIGHLEY ARMS.

(7) Hugh de Haltetleworth held two parts of the Manor of Haltetleworth from Simon de Monte Alto, father of the co-heiresses, and
the jury found that William his son and heir was under age ; 1278.

(8) De Banco Roll, 19 Ric. II., 1395. John Sayvill, of Eland, senior, knight, and Thomas Maude, of Morton, Henry fil Thomas de Raudon, John del More de Bailedon; plea of debt.

(9) Quo Warranto, 10 Ric. II., 1386. John de Draghton and Anabilla his wife, William Neleson and Margaret his wife, John Mohaud and Juliana his wife, Adam de Menwyth and Agnes his wife, and Alicia filia Jordan de Kyghley, heiresses of Jordan, on behalf of John, deceased s.p., son of Richard de Kyghley, who (Richd) was brother of Jordan, *versus* William de Langbergh, taillour, and Amicia his wife of a messuage and 12 acres in Ilkelay and Wodhous.

From Dodsworth's MSS.

(1) From Mr. Fairfax of Menston's Booke, (I give a brief translation rather than the Latin as copied by Dodsworth, J.H.T.) Know present and future that we Christofer Ward, knight, and William Maud, gent., give to John Greene, Laurence Kighley, Arthur Mawd, Robert Dyneley, Michael Rawdon, gents., and Bernard Maud, chaplain, messuages, &c., in Otteley, Gyseley, Carleton, Yedon, Rawdon and Mensington, which we had of the gift of Thomas Haukesworth & John Green, Esquires, and Richard Browne, chaplain, to hold for the sustenance of a chaplain to celebrate mass at the altar of the Blessed Mary in Gyseley Church. Witnesses, Tho. Mawd, Jas. Hardwicke, John Hollins, & Thos. Browne, 12 Hy. VIII.

(2) Wills at York. Arthur Mawde, of Bynglay, 11 May, 1534, desired that his body should be buried in the church of All Saints at Bynglay. To the church of the Blessed Andrew the Apostle, Kighley, 20s. for a bell. John Mawde, his brother, named. That Laurence Kighley & Thomas Mawde his son receive from Stephen Tempest de Broughton, Esq., forty marks which he owes; to the use of Stephen Paslewe his heirs and assigns. His wife Johanna Mawde, Thomas his son and Stephen Paslew, to be executors. Witness, Walter Paslew of Riddilsden, Esq. Proved July 31, 1534.

John Carr, Knt. = Margaret, dau. Thos. Lord Clifford

| John | Anna = Roger, son of John s. Wm. s. Roger Tempest, of Broughton, 7 Hy. IV. |

| Several other children | Katherine Tempest = Thos. Mawde |

Arthur Sister married Thomas s. Stephen s. Edwd. s. John s. Wm. s. Roger Tempest, of Broughton, 7 Hen. IV.

(3) Grant from Edwd. son of John Passelawe, Esq., to John Neville, Esq., and others of lands, &c., in Presthorpe and Bynglay.

(4) Vol. 83. (Translated and abridged, J.H.T.) Know present & future that I Milisenta de Monte Alto, in my pure and legitimate widowhood, give &c, to Alianore la Zuche my daughter and the heirs of her body lawfully begotten, my manor of Byngele with all edifices, knight's fees, homages, free services, villeinages, lands, meadows, pastures, mills, waters, burgages, market, fishing, ways, woods,

moors, marshes, &c., to pay to the said Mileisenta for life 40 marks of silver, at Pascha (or Easter) and St. Michael's in equal portions, and after her decease a penny for all services (except foreign) to the King. Witnesses, Sir Robert de Everingham, Sir Stephen de Waleis, Sir Simon Ward, Sir Richard de Thornhill, Sir Hugh de Swyllington, Sir Robert de Styvton, knights, Walter de Hawksworth, John de Mardele, Robert Vileyn, Hugh de Ledes, John de Feyernes, William de Byngele, clerk, Peter de Wakvile, John de Casterton, Roger la Zuche, & many others. A long Latin deed without date.

(5). Dodsworth MSS. "Monasticon Boreale,"* Vol. 2.
fo. 52b.   [Ex autographis in Turri beatæ Mariæ Ebor.]
S. fo.   Charter of Adelize de Rumelli to the Canons of St. Mary and St. Cuthbert, of Embesey, co York, temp. Hen. 2. "Simone Muhaut" among witnesses.

Carta Simonis de Montealto.

Notum sit Sancte Matris ecclesie filijs tam presentibus quam futuris quod ego Simon de Montealto, pro salute anime mee et uxoris mee et heredum nostrorum, pro animabus patris et matris mee et omnium Antecessorum meorum: dedi et concessi et hac mea carta confirmavi, deo et Sancte Marie de Kirkestal et Monachis ibidem deo servientibus, quatuor acras terre cum bosco iuxta decem acras quas eis dederam antea in bosco meo de Ridlesdene iuxta Merecloch ad caput Essorti Thoret, ex parte Aquilonali illarum decem acrarum. Dedi eis has quatuor acras tenendas de me et heredibus meis in puram et perpetuam elemosinam, liberam et quietam ab omni terreno seruitio et seculari exactione, sicut aliqua elemosina liberius datur vel tenetur. Et ego et heredes mei predictam elemosinam cum omni reliqua elemosina quam tenent de me warantizabimus prefatis monachis et adquietabimus ubique et erga omnes homines. Huius rei testes sunt, Nicholaus de Erdeslau, Willelmus de Montealto, filius meus, et Ricardus nepos meus, Ricardus De la lunde, Rogerus de Hillum, Willelmus frater Nicholai de Erdell.

Carta Simonis de Mohaut.

S. fo. 53b. Sciant omnes presentes et futuri Quod ego Simon de
)6). Mohaut, pro amore dei et pro salute anime mee et anime vxoris mee et heredum et omnium Antecessorum meorum, dedi et concessi et hac mea carta confirmavi deo et Sancte Marie et Monachis de Kirkestal communem pasturam ducentis onibus in Ridelsdene et in Mortona, in puram et perpetuam elemosinam, liberam et quietam ab omni seruitio et demanda. Ita tamen quod non transibunt uersus de Air Chyminum altum quod tendit

---

* This is Dodsworth's own title to these Charters he copied from the originals in the Tower of St. Mary, York.

de domo Roberti de Mohaut ad villam de Biugeleia. Et sciendum quod predicti Monachi habebunt in predicta pastura mares ones uel feminas prout voluerint. Si uero predicti Monachi ibidem habuerint matres oues, Agni earundem remanebunt donec a lactere separentur. Et tunc omnes Agni amonebuntur exceptis quadraginta qui ibi per annum integrum remanebunt ultra predictum numerium ducentarum ovium. Ego vero Simon et heredes mei predictam pasturam prefatis Monachis warantizabimus, adquietabimus et defendemus vbique contra omnes homines imperpetuum. Hijs testibus, Willelmo de Stineton, Reinero fratre eius, Thoma de Mohaut Rogero de Kichelueia, Gernagot de Bingeleia, Alexandro Clerico de Bingeleia, Stephano Cunel, et multis alijs.

S. f. 53. (7). Carta Ricardi filii Simonis de Mohaut Sciant omnes presentes et futuri quod ego Ricardus de Mohaut, pro amore dei et salute anime mee et ad peticionem domini et patris mei Symonis de Mohaut, concessi et hac mea carta confirmaui deo et Monachis Sancte Marie de Kirkestal, quatuor acras terre cum bosco quas pater meus eis dederat, que, scilicet, iacent ex parte Aquilonali decem acrarum quas eis pater meus prius dederat in bosco suo de Ridelesdene iuxta Merecloch tenendas et habendas eisdem monachis de me et heredibus meis in puram et perpetuam elemosinam, liberam et quietam ab omni seculari seruitio et demanda, sicut carta patris mei quam inde habent testatur. Et ego et heredes mei predictam elemosinam prefatis Monachis warantizabimus et defendemus ubique et contra omnes homines. Hijs Testibus, Willelmo de Stiueton, Willelmo de Mohaut, Rogero de

TOMB OF
SIR ROBERT DE STIVETON,
AT STEETON.

East Riddlesden Hall.

Kikel', Roberto de Mohaut, Nicholas de Barkeston, Hugone filio Hugonis de Lelay, et multis alijs.

(8). Charter of Eudo la Zouche to the Canons and Church of St. Nicholas of Drax, n.d. Among witnesses, "Domino Ada de Montealto, Ricardo de Montealto, Johanne de Montealto."

(9). Charter of Sir Helias de Stiveton (Steeton) to the Monks of St. Mary of Kirkestall, n.d. Among witnesses, "Roberto de Montealto."

(10). Charter of Hugh fitz Wathef de Yadun to the Nuns and Church of St. Mary and St. Leonard of Eshold, n.d. Among witnesses, "Ricardo de Montealto."

(11). Finis inter Monachos de Kirkestall et Robertum de Montealto.

S. f. 54. Hec est finalis concordia facta inter Monachos de Kirkestal et Robertum de Montelto apud Eboracum, Anno primo Regni Regis Ricardi, quando Willelmus Eliensis Episcopus, Cancellarius Domini Regis, uenit Eboracum de controuersia que erat inter eos de domibus edificatis ab eodem Roberto in communi pastura Monachorum apud Aeldefeld, scilicet, quod idem Robertus domos easdem remoueri faciet ab eadem pastura nec in ea ulterius aliquod edificium faciet nec fieri permittet, poterit tamen predictus Robertus reedificare easdem domos, si noluit, ex parte orientali de Spinkeswellesic infra essartum Martini per cilium montis qui est ultra domum Jordani hominis sui. Terra uero de qua predictus Robertus facit domos illas remoueri remanebit eidem Roberto essartanda et colenda si noluerit, et Monachi habebunt communem pasturam in ea sicut carta Simonis de Montealto testatur. His testibus, Ada filio Petri, Ada filio Normanni, Willelmo [blank,] Hugone filio Roberti, Toma Pictauiensi, Waltero filio Hugonis, Henrico clerico de Kelinton, Hugone filio Walteri, Hugone de Cresseld, Ada de Wirkeleia, Hugone de Litheleia, Roberto fratre eius, Ricardo de Montealto.

Seal of Robert Montalt or Mawd, a lion passant to the dexter side.

S. f. 56. Carta Ricardi filij Ade filij Gospatrich de Muhaut.
[RICHARD SON OF ADAM SON OF GOSPATRIC DE MAHAWD.]

(12). Notum sit omnibus sancte Ecclesie filijs tam presentibus quam futuris quod ego Ricardus filius Ade filij Gospatrick, dono et concedo et hac mea carta confirmo in puram et perpetuam elemosinam deo et Abbatie Sancte Marie de Kirkestal et Monachis ibidem deo seruientibus, totam terram que de feudo meo est, sicut carta patris mei eis testatur scilicet, in bosco et plano ab orientali parte fontis

qui vocatur Morekelde et sicut Morekeld . . . uadit
vsque ad Cilicium montis qui vocatur Brocholeclif super
quem Grangia eorum sita est, et totam terram in bosco
et plano inter Oust-clumbec et Vtteleiebec a pede montis
qui uocatur Hiwclif usque in magnam aquam qui vocatur
Air, cum pertiuenciis suis in bosco et plano in pratis et
pasturis et aquis, et communem pasturam totius terre
mee et liberos exitus et introitus in bosco et plano, et
sufficientiam ad omnia necessaria sua in bosco meo. Hec
omnia eis concedo et dono et hac mea .. concedo in puram
et perpetuam elemosinam pro salute anime mee et patris
mei et omnium parentum meorum, liberam et quietam ab
omni terreno seruitio quod ad me vel heredes meos
nel dominos meos et heredes eorum pertinet. His testibus
Ricardo filio Aluer, Ada nepote, Ricardo, Sijmone filijs
Willelmi, Hugone fratre Simonis, Willelmo de Castelei,
Waltero le Tanur, Hugone de Snitale.
In dorso confirmacio Ricardi de Muhaut de terra de
Ridelesdene et de Aldfeld.

f. 139b. Carta Simundi de Montealto.

(13). Notum sit omnibus tam presentibus quam futuris quod
ego Simundus de Montealto dono et concedo sanctimoni-
alibus de Saingwait terram de Hossehirst cum omnibus
appenticiis suis in bosco et in plano, in aquis et in prato,
et in omnibus locis, in liberam et perpetuam elemosinam.
Teste, Willelmo de Harawda, Adam de Monte alto,
Johanne de Harawda, Serlone le Redlesden, Yuone de
Bradelai, Thoma de Saltebi.
In dorso, Carta Simonis de Montalto de Horsist.

Carta Simonis de Montealto.

(14). Omnibus Sancte Matris ecclesie filijs ad quos presens
scriptum pervenerint, Simon de Montealto, salutem.
Nouerit uniuersitas vestra me diuine pietatis intuitu et
pro saluacione anime mee et predecessorum et successor-
um meorum, dedisse et concessisse et hac presenti carta
mea confirmasse deo et ecclesie omnium Sanctorum de
Bingeleia totam decimam molendini mei de Ridelesdene,
et decimam pratorum meorum atque uirgultorum et etiam
apum mearum manerei mee (sic) de Ridelisdene prefate
ecclesie de Bingele temporibus suis annuatim Imperpetuum soluendam. Vt autem hec donacio ista rata et incon-
cussa in posteris permaneat presens scriptum in testi-
monio sigilli mei apposicione robaraui. Hijs Testibus,
Domino Willelmo de Montealto, filio meo, et domino
Henrico, filio meo, Domino Willelmo de Stiueton,
Roberto de Montealto, fratre meo, Adam de Montealto,
Nicholas de Barkeston, Roberto le Vilan, Geruegan de
Bingele, Roberto le Gentill, et alijs.

ANCIENT BINGLEY.

(16). KIRKBY'S INQUEST, 1284, RECORDS OF BYNGELEY.—Stephanus le Waleys tenet iii car. terræ unde xiiii. car. faciunt feod. milit. de Roberto de Everyngham, et idem Roberto de Alianora la Zusche, et eadem Alianora de Milicenta de rege in capite. Item, Johannes de Martylay tenet in eadem iii partes unius car. terræ de eodem feodo de prædicto Roberto de Everyngham ut supra. Et totum residuum manerii tenet prædicta Alianora pro di. feodo milit. de prædicta Milicenta et eadem Milicenta de rege in capite et nihil redd. ad wap. prædictum. The meaning of this is that Stephen le Waleys (or Foreigner) holds three carucates of land where fourteen carucates make a knight's fee from Robert de Everyngham and the said Robert from Eleanor la Zouche, and the said Eleanor from Milicent de Mawd (eldest daughter of William de Cantilupe, co-heir to her brother

MARLEY HALL.

George, married (1) John de Montealto (Mawd) who died s.p., and (2) Eudo la Zouch of Ashby-de-la-Zouch; her inquest post mortem was taken in 1292, when Wm. la Zouch was found to be her son and heir;) and the said Milicent held of the King in chief. Also John de Marley (married Alice, dau. and co-heir of Simon de Montealto,) holds in the same three parts of a carucate of land of the same fee from the aforesaid Robert de Everyngham as above. And all the rest of the manor the aforesaid Eleanor holds for half a knight's fee of the aforesaid Milicent, and the said Milicent from the King in chief, and pays no rent to the aforesaid wapontake.

The heirs of Symon de Montealto hold Morton for two and a half carucates of land where xiiij carucates of land make a knight's fee of the Honor of Skypton by knight service and pay to the wapontake of Skyrake annually xijd.

It is evident from this and other charters that Dr. Whitaker was in error in stating that "ten carucates only make a knight's fee, a proof of the warmer climate and richer soil for corn than that of upper Craven."

(18). Out of the Kirkstall book in the Duchy of Lancaster records at Grays Inn.

Notum sit omnibus, &c., quod ego Adam filius Gospatrick concessi Abbatie Sancte Marie de Kirkstall, &c., totam terram que de feode meo est in bosco et plano ab orientali fontis qui vocatur Morekeld et sicut Morekeld sita vadit usque ad Cicilium montis qui vocatur Brochole cliffe, &c., et terram inter Oustelumbec et Vtlelcibec a pede montis qui vocatur Hiwcliffe usque in magnam aquam que vocatur Ayr, etc. Huius rei testes sunt, Outi (?) sacerdos de Bingley, Willelmus de Hedyngley, Ketell de Moretuna, &c.

Endorsed—Adam de Muhand de Riddlesden et Aldfeld.

(19) Symon de Montealto, for the souls of his father and mother, gave to the abbot of Kirkstall all the lands of his fee of Riddlesden which Adam son of Gospatrick his uncle (avunculus), gave. Witnesses, Bertram de Stiveton, Ralph de Folifot, Alan son of Elie, Thomas Pictavensis, Ralph son of Baldwin, William de Ryder and William! his brother, Richard de Rupe, Peter de Ardington, Ralph Vilain, Adam Pictavensis, Robert son of Roceselin, William de Letheley.

(20) From Drax book in the custody of Marmaduke Constable of Everingham, Esquire. Charter of Isabella daughter of Sir Simon de Monteult of a plot of land lying in the field of Morton. To all the sons of holy mother church to whom the present writing shall come Isabella daughter of Sir Simon de Montealto, health; know all men that I, with the assent of William le Gentill my husband, for the salvation of my soul and the souls of my ancestors and successors, give, &c., to God and the church of St. Nicholas of Drax and the canons there serving God in pure and perpetual elemosinam a plot of land in the field of Morton with a barn between the land of lady Clarice de Ridelesdene my mother, called Silkeriding of the one part,

Frank Arms.

Arthington Arms.

and the lands of Richard son of Hawyse de Morton of the other part and butting on a way called Milnegate, to have and to hold the same for ever.

(21) Charter of John de Montealto de Marthelay of a toft called Baldwincroft, with the assent of Alice his wife, giving to God and the church of St. Nicholas of Drax the said toft lying beyond his garden, between the king's highway of one part and a stream of water called Milnesike on the other and a barn thereon.

(22) Quit claim of Peter de Marthelay, grandson of John de Marthelay alias Monte Alto and Alice wife of John, of a Messuage called Baldwyncroft to the prior of Drax.

(23) From the Evidences of Thomas Fairfax of Denton Knight. I Symon Mohaut of Riddlesden give to John my son and Alice his wife a messuage and building in Est Keswyke in Harwood. Witnesses, Wm. Ryther, Richard Redman, Knights, Nicholas Frank, Robert Mauley, Thomas Thwaites and others. Dated at Est Keswyk 2 Henry IV.

(24) In the charters of Stephen Tempest of Broughton, Esquire. I Arthur Mawhaut give to Thomas my son and heir apparent and Katherine his wife daughter of Roger Tempest a messuage &c. in

Yeadon called Dibbehouses of the annual value of 20s. Dated at West Riddlesden, 1 Sept., 25 Henry VIII.

(25) From the charters of Thomas Lord Fairfax, Baron Cameron. Charter of John Judson of Gilsted to Thomas de Hawkesworth, 20 Feb., 1419. Witnesses, Thomas Mowhaud and others.

(26) Amongst the Bundles of Fines at York, 10 Henry III., 1226, between William de Mahaut and Simon de Mahaut of all the manor of Riddlesden. James and Symon sons of Simon re-lease for their father's lifetime.

(27) Burton's Monasticon gives a composition made in 1312 between the abbot and monks of Rieval, and the prior and convent of Drax about certain tithes in this parish, by which we learn the names of certain cultivated lands, viz., Dakhus-flat, Netherstayn flat, Lang-flat, the field about Belted-banks, Cherry-tree-butts, Oxhus-flat, Overstayn-flat, Cayselflat, Moreflat, and Huhil, all being cultivated and tithable. The following places were uncultivated: Tomrode, Broadenge *alias* Intak or Munkery, Wilimotrode, the Wynhowe, Overpark, Ryecroft, Coll-

FAIRFAX ARMS.

ingworth-rode, Smythrode, Oxpark, and Hustubbing. Belonging to the grange of Fawdre (Faweather), uncultivated, were,—Moreflat, Langmoreflat, Hallested, Lamblegh, Wale, Driflat, Olnescastle-flat, Pine-flat, Lang-flat, Hucroft, Pighelees, Cayles-flat, Cote-flat, and Calve-park.

The People in the Dark Ages.

PERHAPS no period of English History has been so much neglected as the 13th and 14th centuries, yet I venture to assert that the prosperity of England commercially, socially, and intellectually commences from those so-called dark days, but dark mostly because historians have overlooked them except to record the national wars and kingly intrigues. The distresses of the period, the wars, famines, and pestilences, tended to give the populace greater freedom. It is true, even as we shall find in Bingley parish, that slavery existed; and those who were free from abject serfdom, the villains, bondsmen, and cottars, were only a trifle more contented than the serfs. From 1311, the Northern counties were greatly harassed by Scottish incursions, wars, and plagues. All the immediate neighbourhood from Skipton to Bradford was ransacked in 1316 by bands of red-shanked robbers from Scotland, who not content with robbing and murdering the inhabitants, maliciously burnt what they could not carry away. In that year a soldier had to be provided by each township to join the army against Scotland, but the failure at Bannockburn was but the beginning of distress. Repeated depredations were followed by a great famine, when children were kidnapped and eaten. In 1332 one of the most disastrous Scotch incursions to this district took place, and the scarcity of labourers added to the scarcity of money, led to a general depreciation in land. Labourers were not to be obtained, so wages became higher; and serfs absconded to become free men. The most disastrous plague that history ever recorded, scourged the countries from Asia right across Europe and reached England in 1349. It spread desolation everywhere. Consternation reigned for some months; rents were uncollected; courts suspended in several Yorkshire manors; half the priests died; the poorest suffered more severely. This terrible Black Death was succeeded in 1379 by another plague in Airedale. Population was never lower in number or prosperity than at this time, and the subsidies imposed by the king and his parliaments were outrageously heavy. We are able to give two of these, and thus discover the names of the wealthier men residing here in those dark days, but the most interesting list is afforded by the Poll Tax fifty years later. These heavy burdens were then extended to every householder and person of sixteen years of age, except the clergy and slaves. The insolent and exacting manner in which they were collected roused Wat Tyler and others to rebellion. A silver groat (4d.) was equal to 10s. of our money probably, and where there were two or three children over 16 also to pay for, it was insupportable.

The Thoresby Society have printed some valuable Subsidy Rolls from which we may gather the names of our chief landholders, in 1327, the first year of Edward III. In these subsidies granted by parliament to help the king in his foreign wars, the chief men were taxed to the extent of a twentieth. In the succeeding one here given it was a fifteenth. The second roll is undated but may be fixed for 1332, 1334, 1336, 1337, 1340 or 1344 in which years subsidies were laid. Probably 1336 was the one.

1327.   [1336.]
ILKELEY. Robt. ....   Will. de Grantham ijs.
          Will ....   Thos. de Calvirley ijs. vd. ob.
          Will ....   Robt. fil. Simon ijs. ixd. ob.
          John ....   John Crokebarn xxd. qa.
          Adam Ulf ....   Adam Wolf xxijd. ob.
          Robt. Wod ....   Robt. Gydicok xvjd.
              Sum xjs............   Sum xijs. ijd. qa. pa.

BINGGELAY.
Hug. de Colingworth iiijs.   Hug' de Cullingworth vs.
Hug. Wode*cok* iijs.   John Heir ijs.
Will. fil ijs. viijd.   Hug' Wodcock iijs.
John de Ledes ijs. ixd.   Will. Carpenter ijs.
Will. fil Richard iijs. xd.   Walter atte halle ijs.
Will. de Hagen*worth* ijs. xjd.   Ralph del Legh iijs.
John Carpenter ijs. viijd. ob.   John de Dyk vs.
Robt. fil John iijs.   John atte Kirke iijs.
Ralph de Leges ijs. ixd.   John de Long ijs.
Adam de Ilkelay ijs. ijd.   John de Ledes iiijs.
Will. Carpenter xxjd.   Adam le long iijs.
Henry Forestar xxd.   Rich. p'po (greave) iijs. iiijd.
John del Dik xixd.   Will. le hyne iijs.
Richd. p'po. (the greave) xvjd.
    Sum xxxvjs. jd. ob.   Sum. xls. iiijd. pa.

BAILDON.
Henry de Baildon ijs. vjd.   John de Hope ijs
Will. de Baildon xviijd.   Will. Morevill ijs.
Richd. del Rodes xviijd.   Richd. del Rodes iiijd.
Will. fil Elie xviijd.   John fil Walter
Henry fil Ralph xijd.   Will. fill John
    Sum viijs.   Mat......... Katrine
                                            Sum ixs. viijd. qa.

OTLEY. Sum xvijs. ijd.   Sum xixs. viijd.

MORTON. [No list.]   Peter de ......holm
                                        ....*Ilketon*
                                        Adam de Oldfeld
                                        John le Mohaud xvd.
                                        Robt. fill Will. xijd.
                                            Sum ixs. xjd.

LEEDS. [No list.]

William Passelewe
Robert Paslew
Thomas le Wayt
Richd. le Wayt
Sir Roger de Ledes, &c.

Total for Skyrack £40 6s. 8d. Sum lvijs.

It will be noted that Bingley runs next to Leeds and Barwick, in Skyrack Wapontake.

POLL TAX, 1379.
BYNGLAY.

Nicholaus de Stansfield, ffranklan, & ux' iijs. iiijd.
Johannes Lowcok, Hostiler, & ux' [uxor=wife] xijd.
Johannes Chartres, Hostiler, & ux' xijd.
Thomas Collyngworth, Talour, & ux' vjd.
Willelmus de Wyke, Carpenter, & ux' vjd.
Thomas Rosell, Sutor, & ux' vjd.
Nicholaus de Ilton, Talour, & ux' [de=of] vjd.
Ricardus del Grange & ux' [del=of the] iiijd.

LISTER ARMS.

ROOKES-STANSFIELD ARMS.
[1, 4, Stansfield; 2, Crompton;
3, Rookes.]

WADE ARMS.

Johannes Coke & ux' iiijd.
Willelmus Lyster & ux' iiijd.
Willelmus de Rowlay & ux' iiijd.
Johannes Kytson & ux' iiijd.
Adam Wade & ux' iiijd.
Johannes de Ledes & ux' iiijd.
Ricardus Walker & ux' iiijd.
Adam Wilson & ux' iiijd.
Jordanus Thorneton & ux' iiijd.
Willelmus Turnour & ux' iiijd.
Hugo filius Hugonis & ux' iiijd.
Adam Balle & ux' iiijd.
Johannes de Collyng & ux' iiijd.
Johannes de Newerke & ux' iiijd.
Ricardus Talour & ux' iiijd.
Henricus Sutor & ux' iiijd.
Johannes Smyth & ux' iiijd.
Johannes Mylner & ux' iiijd.
Johannes Vylan & ux' iiijd.
Johannes Yole & ux' iiijd.
Ricardus Lang & ux' iiijd.
Willelmus de Ilkelay & ux' iiijd.
Johannes Judson & ux' iiijd.
Johannes Hnetson & ux' iiijd.
Johannes Wade & ux' iiijd.
Johannes Curtays & ux' iiijd.
Henricus Couper & ux' iiijd.
Henricus de Stubbyng & ux' iiijd.
Thomas de Parys & ux' iiijd.
Johannes ffouler & ux' iiijd.
Ricardus Wyn & ux' iiijd.
Johannes Ilkelay & ux, iiijd.
Johannes de Bowland & ux' iiijd.
Petrus Studehird & ux' iiijd.

Thornton Arms.

Thornton Arms.

ANCIENT BINGLEY.

Thomas Grenehill & ux' iiijd.
Thomas de Brunlay & ux' iiijd.
Johannes Yarkar & ux' iiijd.
Symon del Wode & ux' iiijd.

Wood Arms.

Johannes Dykehouse & ux' iiijd.
Adam Myryman & ux' iiijd.
Johannes Diconson & ux' iiijd.
Johannes Hanneson & ux' iiijd.
Robertus Ibbotson & ux' iiijd.
Willelmus Dyconson & ux' iiijd.
Adam ffydcok & ux' iiijd.
Johannes ffydcok & ux' iiijd.
Henricus Capiman & ux' iiijd.
Rogerus Webster & ux' iiijd.
Johannes Collyngworth & ux' iiijd.
Thomas ftlecher & ux' iiijd.
Robertus Gybson & ux' iiijd.
Johannes Elysson & ux' iiijd.
Ricardus Milner & ux' iiijd.
Willelmus Turnour & ux' iiijd.
Johan. filius [son] Rogeri & ux' iiijd.
Willelmus ffrerson & ux' iiijd.

Adam del Wode & ux' iiijd.
Johannes fflecher & ux' iiijd.
Ricardus Hunt & ux' iiijd.
Johannes Kytson & ux' iiijd.
Thomas de Crosselay & ux' iiijd.
Willelmus Sugden & ux' iiijd.
Johannes del Rodes & ux' iiijd.
Johannes del Syke & ux' iiijd.
Willelmus Wyllesden & ux' iiijd.
Thomas de Rode & ux' iiijd.
Johannes Couper & ux' iiijd.
Johannes Dobson & ux' iiijd.
Adam de Ravenrod' & ux' iiijd.
Nicholaus de Cottynglay & ux' iiijd.
Johannes de Parys & ux' iiijd.
Henricus del Cote & ux' iiijd.
Anabilla Collyng iiijd.
Matilda Blawer iiijd.
Matilda Costyne iiijd.
Isabella Balle iiijd.
Johannes Wade iiijd.
Cecilia filia [dau.] Johannis iiijd.
Johannes Huetson iiijd.
Matilda Cosyn iiijd.
Margaret Newark iiijd.
Matilda filia Johannis iiijd.
Cecilia Milner iiijd.
Johannes serviens [servant] Johannes iiijd.
Isabella serviens Thome iiijd.
Johanna de Scheplay iiijd.
Matilda Vylan (Villain) iiijd.
Agnes del Wode iiijd.
Alicia de Northall iiijd.
Alicia ffouler iiijd.
Johannes ffouler iiijd.
Matilda de Ilkelay iiijd.
Matilda de Parys iiijd.
Juliana Bonet iiijd.
Ricardus Wyndhill iiijd.
Rogerus Wade iiijd.
Hugo Rylyng iiijd.
Agnes Couper iiijd.
Willelmus Diconson iiijd.
Johannes Symson iiijd.
Willelmus de Pillesworth iiijd.
Ricardus serviens Vicarii iiijd.
Alicia de Preston iiijd.

ANCIENT BINGLEY.

Thomas serviens Vicarii iiijd. Willelmus filius Willelmi iiijd.
Alicia de Wyndhill iiijd. Adam filius Ade iiijd.
Rogerus serviens Johannis iiijd. Johannes filius Willelmi iiijd.
Johannes filius Willelmi iiijd. Juliana de Haworth iiijd.
Johanna de Helwyk iiijd. Agnes del Syke iiijd.
Agnes de Claton iiijd. Matilda Milner iiijd.
Anabilla Blolk iiijd. Cecilia de Parys iiijd.
Elisabet de Knapton iiijd. Summa xlvijs.

We here get a most interesting census of Bingley township (including Harden, Cullingworth, Cottingley, Gilstead,) and find a franklain or gentleman who paid 3s. 4d. tax, two hotel keepers at 1s. each, two tailors at 6d. each, a carpenter at 6d., and a shoemaker at 6d.; these seven paying 7s. 4d., or as much as twenty-two ordinary families. Then we have 73 married couples, and 46 single men and women, or 119 payments of a groat each. I believe the largest landowners and the clergy (which not only included the vicar but the representatives of Drax Abbey and the Knights of St. John) were taxed on another list, so that we may add possibly ten to the eighty householders given above; and as there were a few serfs and aged poor the population would not be less than five hundred. Young people under 16 years of age were exempt from taxation.

MORTON.

Ricardus de Morton & ux' iiijd. Magota del Gylle iiijd.
Willelmus filius Stephani & ux'iiijd. Willelmus Thomson iiijd.
Thomas Hird & ux' iiijd. Thomas Wodehouse iiijd.
Johannes Wodhouse & ux' iiijd. Agnes filia Rogeri iiijd.
Johannes Skynner & ux' iiijd. Johanna Raudoghter iiijd.
Robertus Wade & ux' iiijd. Johannes de Lokwode iiijd.
Adam Wade & ux' iiijd. Radulfus del Halle iiijd.
Robertus Ryder & ux' iiijd. Johannes Alcok iiijd.
Johannes de Cave & ux' iiijd. Willelmus Hunt iiijd.
Rogerus filius Rogeri & ux' iiijd. Johannes de Manne iiijd.
Radulfus Smyth & ux' iiijd. Matilda Wade iiijd.
Ricardus Aldfeld & ux' iiijd. Thomas Ryder iiijd.
Johannes filius Mathei & ux' iiijd. Emma Ryder iiijd.
Ricardus de Weston & ux' iiijd. Matilda filia Roberti iiijd.
Matheus Lynthawith & ux' iiijd. Isabella filia Ricardi iiijd.
Thomas Mohaut & ux' iiijd. Willelmus Badger iiijd.
Thomas ffouler & ux' iiijd. Summa xjs. viijd.
Thomas Wilson iiijd.

Here we have 18 married couples and 17 single men and women over sixteen years of age; no one paying more than a groat. I estimate the population at about 140, making from 650 to 700 for the whole parish. How does this compare with neighbouring townships?

Otley had a franklain, four tradesmen at 6d., 38 married couples, and 25 single taxed persons, half the population of Bingley township.

Hawksworth had Symon Warde, knight, at xxs., 17 married couples, 11 single persons taxed; amongst the married ones was

John de Byngley. Bayldon had William de Bayldon, a franklain, John Smyth, a faber or smith, and John Lyster a tinctor or dyer, (as both names would indicate even if the trades had not been mentioned,) at 6d. each, 13 married couples, 11 single: or five times less than Bingley. The Morvills afterwards of Bingley, were then living at Baildon. Yeadon had 22 married and 12 single taxations at a groat each; amongst the single women was Johanna de Ridelsden.

Ilkelay had Squire Methelay's widow at 3s. 4d., a hostler at 1s., two Walkers who were walkers, that is fulling millers, a Tailor who was a tailor, a Ward who was a marshall, and a souter or shoemaker, all at 6d.; and 19 other married couples, with 17 single. Leeds, always regarded as the head of Skyrack Wapontake, had Roger Leeds, Esquire at xxs., John Passelew, hostiler, at 1s., Ralph Passelew, a barker or tanner at 6d., Symon Passelewman, a bocher (butcher) at 1s., a smith and a merchant at 1s. each; a Lyster, two smyths, a shoemaker, two taylors, a mason, each at 6d., another hostiler at 1s.; 37 other married couples; 57 single, many of them described as servants. Thus Leeds township was at this time rather less than Bingley.

Bradforth township had hostilers at 1s. each, two shoemakers (considered the staple trade at Bradford at one time), two tailors, a fuller or walker, and a mason at 6d. each; also 17 married couples, 34 unmarried; thus Bradford township had not half the population of Bingley township. Johanna de Bingley was one of the Bradford list of unmarried tax-payers. Shipley had only 16 married couples and 12 unmarried tax-payers; total 9s. 4d. Amongst them were John of Cullingworth and John Byngley, both married. Haworth had a merchant at 1s., 23 married couples, 16 single. Bolton near Bradford has a melancholy record:—Quia nemo est manens in eadem Villa-nichil inde-nec fuit a tempore concessionis predicte, nec huc usque: [None remaining since the plague.] Halifax township had only 25 married couples at 4d., and 13 single. Kyghlay had Nicholas de Kyghlay, armatus, at 3s. 4d., a lady hosteler at 2s., a marshall at 1s., a smith, a webster or weaver, a Taylor who was a tailor, a Walker who was a fuller, a Wryght who was a carpenter, and another carpenter, each at 6d., giving 48 married couples, and 14 unmarried people taxed. The Benelands, Sugdens, Cloughs, Howsons, Greenwoods, Lacocks, Saltonstalls, Thwayts, and Eloms are amongst the Keighley inhabitants. Under Addingham we find William Mann, the fuller, at 6d., and all the rest (28) are entered as married. The "de Eloms" occur at Addingham, Steeton, &c. Skypton had a draper and a spicer at 2s. each, a merchant, a harbeiour named Rayner of Silsden, a fuller called Walker, a shoemaker, a spycer named Spycer, a roper named Roper, a webster named Webster, each 1s. Three tailors, a textor or weaver named Thorbrand, a fuller named Lamb, a carnifex, flesh-dealer, two other tailors called Taylor, another Webster called like his father Peter Brabant (shewing they had been fetched from the continent), a mason named Mason, a smith, a glover, these with the rest of married couples total 54, and there were 17 unmarried. Castle influence will account for the extra number of trades there; yet it does not equal Bingley in population.

It seems from this comparison that Bingley had not suffered much from the fearful Black Death; and it is certain that it was then one of the most populous townships of the North-west Riding.

Very briefly we may now consider how the surnames originated. Many of them, especially sirenames, were not perfectly settled on families before 1400. It will be readily noticed that there are three main classes;

I. Those derived from *places* where the people lived, or whence they had come: of Stansfield, Collyngworth, Wyke, Ilton, Grange, (either Harden or one of the other Granges in the parish), Rowlay, Leeds, Thornton, Collyng, Newark, Ilkley, Stubbyng, Paris, Bowland, Grenehill (in Bingley), Burnley, the Wood, Dykehouse, Crossley, Sugden, Rodes (or clearing), Syke (or ditch), Wilsden, Ravenroyd (in Bingley), Cottyngley, Cote (or wood), Shipley, North-hill, Windhill, Rylyng, Pillesworth (a mistake for Rillesworth or some such name), Preston, Helwick (now Eldwick), Clayton, Knapton, Haworth.

In the Morton list we start with Morton, Woodhouse, Cave, Oldfield, Weston, Linthwaite, Maud or Mont-alt, Gill, Lockwood, the Hall, Manne [? stone].

II. From *trades* we obtain Lyster, Coke (probably), Walker, Turner, Taylor, Sutor, Smith, Milner, Couper, Fowler, Studehird, Yarkar (probably), Blawer.

In the Morton list—Hird, Skynner, Ryder, Smith, Fowler, Hunt, and probably Badger.

III. From *patronymics* or sirenames,—Wilson, Lowcock (possibly), Kytson, Wade (probably), Hughes, Hughson, Judson, Huetson, Diconson, Hanneson, Ibbotson, Fydcok (possibly), Gybson, Elysson, Rogers, Rogerson, Friarson, Dobson, Costyne.

In the Morton list, Stephenson, Wade, Rogers, Matthews, Alcock (little Alexander).

We cannot vouch for the sirenames in the unmarried lists because they were not intended as sirenames by the writer. They can fairly well be identified with the married people before mentioned, being sons, daughters or servants of persons previously mentioned. Thus Robert Ryder of Morton, would be father of Thomas and Emma Ryder without much fear of a doubt. John Symson was likely to have been Symon of the Wood's son, and Joan Raw-daughter, or Rawson as we should foolishly write it,—the daughter of Ralph Smith. The rest of the surnames may be headed, IV. *Capricious* or descriptive; including — Chartres, Rosell, Balle, Vilan simply means villeyn or villager, Yole, Long, Curtays, Wyn, Myryman, Capiman, Bonet, Blolk (wrongly copied probably). Finally we notice that the vicar had two male servants,—Richard and Thomas, whose descendants could have taken the surname, Vicars or Vicarman.

We have already seen that there were several families of the name Bingley in different West Riding villages, and there is no need to assume that they were all of one family named Bingley of Bingley, for the probabilities are altogether against it. There was an important family named Bingley from at latest 1240 about Arthington, one of whom was prioress of Arthington in 1349. If we desire to claim this family name as from our Bingley we ought in justice to admit John son of Alan de Bingley, who was probably the John de Bingley who paid the poll tax at Bradford in 1379. Yet, tell the truth, he was a thief in 1354, having stolen a bow and fifty arrows from the lord Duke of Bradford Manor, but as they could not get butter out of a dog's throat, he was let off, having nothing to distrain upon. In Kirkburton district there has been for over three centuries, probably very much longer, a family named Bingley, but I believe it is from a village of the same name in South-west Yorkshire. There is more probability that the wide-spread but not numerous family of Riddlesden have taken their name from the Bingley Riddlesden.

RIVER AIRE, BINGLEY.

Possessions of Religious Orders.

THE TEMPLARS.—The chief homes of the Templars in West Yorkshire were at Temple Newsam, Temple Hurst, (near Drax and Selby), and Ribston; but Thirsk, Beverley and Newland were their chief Yorkshire centres. The Templars originated in 1119, by nine Christian Knights resolving to protect pilgrims on their visits to the Holy Sepulchre at Jerusalem. These knights had a house on the east side of the Temple ruins. In 1146, the then pope appointed the Templars to wear a red cross on the breast of their white mantles. This suggested, the martyrdom to which they stood exposed.

Spencer's *Fairie Queen* probably gives the true origin of the *red cross*:—

"And on his brest a bloodie crosse he bore,
The deare remembrance of his dying Lord."

The knights of St. John of Jerusalem wore a white cross on their black mantles. [See Dugdale, Tanner, Burton.]

In 1172 the Order had greatly increased in numbers and wealth, and before 1200 numerous possessions had been granted them in Yorkshire. Like other religious orders they began well, and probably did not end so badly as they have been represented. They vowed to fight in God's name under the Red Cross Banner, against the infidel, but never to strike a Christian; never to swear nor behave discourteously to any Christian man; to allow no woman to wait upon him, nor even to kiss his mother or his sister; to attend divine service regularly; to be frugal at meals, and to become a devout priest as well as a sincere soldier. Where they had properties at a distance they built a grange or farm-house for storing their goods and housing their steward; and from this custom, in common with other religious orders, we have many old homesteads still named Grange, as at Harden. By 1185 they held lands at Newsam, Hurst, Ribstan, Skelton, Pannel, Leventhorpe, Crossley in Thornton-dale, Skipton, Bingley, &c. By the gift of Osbert de Baines, archdeacon of West Yorkshire, 1150-74, they held an assart, or wood-clearing, which Aliz of Bingeleia held for 2s., and all service. Edward I. found in 1275 that they claimed in Skyrack free warren in Halton, Newsam, &c., but this "Halghton" may have been the village near Leeds and not the one at Harden. He charged them also with keeping and hunting with hawks, which was strictly forbidden to them. In 1308 the Templars of Yorkshire were seized and their possessions taken by the king; the pope was induced to denounce the order; twenty-five chief Templars were confined in York Castle for over two years and then condemned at a trial, but justified by the common people and the knights' servants, so were eventually set free. They entered

ANCIENT BINGLEY.

Selby, Kirkstall and other abbeys, in 1319-20. (Kenrick's *Knights Templars in Yorkshire*.)

The knights of the Hospital of St. John of Jerusalem, the white-cross Hospitallers—obtained the possessions of their rival Order before 1324.

The Royal Charter of Henry, king of England and France, and Lord of Ireland, to Thomas Dockwra prior of the Priory or Hospital of St. John of Jerusalem, confirmed by kings Edward and Richard, grant the privileges of holding lands, mills, &c., &c., with soc, sac, tol, infangtheif, outfangtheif, hamsoc, grithbreach, bloodwitt, sichwitt, slotwitt, sledwitt, hangwitt, lotherwitt, slomeswitt, murther, larcenie, forestall, oredelf, orefrid, &c., and acquit from all amerciaments, they and all their men free from scott and guild and aids, hidage, cornage, Danegeld, hornegeld, armies, wapentakes, scutage, tollage, lastage, stallage, shires and hundreds, wards and ward-pennies, averpennie, hundred pennie, lithingpennies, castleworks, parks, bridges, carriages, building of king's houses; also their woods were not to be taken, &c. Dated at Tunstall, Nov. 15, xi Henry III. The powers thus profusely bestowed were unusually liberal, for it will be seen that not only freedom from all kinds of taxes, tolls, market charges, military dues, and other national and local impositions was granted, but they had the proving of wills, the fining of culprits, and could hang at their own gallows such miscreants as fell within their clutches. The town's miller was not allowed to take his usual measure out of their sacks when they brought their corn to be ground. It was an imperative order that on all their lands and buildings there should be the double cross erected or carved on a stone, and nearly a score of these memorials still remain in Harden, Bingley, Beckfoot, Cuckoo-nest farm (dog-kennel), Cottingley, Crossley Hall, Shuttleworth Hall near Bradford; all subject to the Manor Court of Crossley, Bingley and Pudsey, which represented the dissolved Priory or Hospital of St. John of Jerusalem. At Beckfoot also we shall notice, as an ornament on the house, what are called The Templars' Lanterns. At the charge of the Court Leet and Court Baron, the steward called out, "Oyez Oyez, Oyez;* Gentlemen, all you that are sworn of the Court Leet and Court Baron draw near and hear your charge. What you are to enquire into are of such things as are here inquirable and presentable only and not punishable, or else of such things as are both presentable and punishable in these Courts which I shall reduce in two heads.

(1) includes capital offences as petit treason, felonies and accessaries therein, not punishable here;

(2) presentable and punishable, as blood-sheds.

Also, whether the constable hath discharged his duty in arresting felons, pursuing hue and cry, apprehending rogues and vagabonds.

---

* French word meaning, "Listen, attend, hear."

112 ANCIENT BINGLEY.

Also, if the stocks are in repair for securing idle and disorderly persons, or the village shall be amerced. Also, enquiry shall be made into all manner of affrays and breaches of the peace, riots, routs, and unlawful assemblies. Also, if any person hath false weights or false measures, or double weights or double measures, a great one to buy with and a small one to sell by, so as to deceive. Also, if any freeholder be dead or hath alienated his estate, who is the next tenant. Also, what advantages have happened to the Lord by escheat or forfeiture; as, if any freeholder hath committed felony. Also, if the several tenants be present and do suit and service at this court, and amerce all in default; or any dispute between tenant and tenant. Proclamation—If any man can inform this Court Leet or Inquest of any treasons, felonies, blood-sheds,—let him come into Court and he shall be heard.

God save the King and the Lord of this Manor."

Court Records.

The following record of courts held here will shew how order was maintained in feudal days.

1338. Court held at Bingley on Wednesday after the feast of St. Matthew the Apostle.

Distress—Distraint, John son of William the Scot for fealty, and shew by what he holds his tenement of the Rodes and by what service.

Distress—the Prior of Drax, ditto.

Rent—John Heyr acknowledged 4d., rent per annum, with arrears for two years in Greenhill, therefore levy.

Rent—the same John Heyr acknowledged rent, 2d. for a tenement which belonged to Alice who was wife of John Millison in Greenhill, and arrears for five years.

Ralph son of Symon, clerk, came here and showed a certain charter by which he purchased under the court of St. John of Jerusalem his tenement in the Leyes, namely Hospital-rode, six acres of land from Hugh le Marshall.

Amerciament—Inquisition taken by Robert le Longe, William son of Hugh, Walter of Ravenrode, William son of John of the Leyes—jurors—who say upon their oath that John of Paris brews contrary to the assize, therefore amerced vjd.

Item, William atte Kyrksteyel brews and bakes contrary to the assizes therefore amerced vd.

[We have here an old authority for the couplet:
> Where God erects a house of prayer
> The Devil builds a temple there.]

Item, William son of Allan Barkar (shepherd) brews contrary to assize and is a rogue, therefore amerced vd.

Item, Roger son of Richard of Stanbyry struck and other enormities committed on Ralph son of Symon, clerk, tenant of the Hospital, therefore summoned by letter of citation.

1345, 20 Edward III. post conquest, Court of Bingley, the day next after the Feast of Easter.

Amerciament—The Prior of Drax for not erecting a cross on the property he holds, fined iijs. iiijd.

Amerc.—The Prior of Drax for not coming to the Court as a suitor, fined xijd.

Amerc.—William atte Kyrkestele is a rogue and sells contrary to the assize and custom of the manor, therefore fined iiijd.

Amerc.—Said William and his wife, brew and sell contrary to the assize therefore fined iiijd.

Amerc.—William of Paris and his wife brew and sell; fined vjd.

John Hair enters plea against Adam le Grayve.

Distrained,—John son of same, did not appear; fined iiijd.

William son of Hugh of the Thwaites surrendered a messuage and eight acres with appurtenances in Rodes which is entrusted to William Page for eight years, fine for entry iiijd.

The day is given to Constance Mohaud who complains of John son of John Hair of plea holden.

Alice of Bayldon is distrained to answer two charges which were existing from last court. Court Receipts vs. xd.

1347. 21 Edward III. Court at Bingley, the Monday next before the Feast of St. Michael.

Amerciament—Ralph of the Lee because he came not, ijd.

William atte Kyrkesteyl because he brewed and baked contrary to assize, viijd.

John of Paris for the same, fined iiijd. Total xivd.

1350. Court at Bingley the Friday next before the Feast of St. Wilfrid.

Amerciament—William son of Hugh of the Thwaites because he came not to court, vd.

Ralph of the Lee, for the same, iijd.

John of Bayldon for the same, (came later.)

Ralph son of William son of Richard, for the same, jd. Total ixd.

1482. 22 Edward IV. Court of Bingley of the Commandery of Newland, Thursday next before the Feast of St. Luke the Evangelist.

Inquisition taken there on the oaths of Walter Bayldon, Robert Wodde, John Wodde, and Robert Champynot, jurors, who say that William Stede (ijd.), Richard Wilkinson (ijd.), Richard Rawson (ijd.), John Heton (ijd.), Christopher Morevill (ijd.), and Thomas Cromoke (ijd.), owe suit to the Court and came not, therefore fined.

Item, it is remarked that each tenant erect a cross upon their holdings under pain for each cross not erected of vjs. viijd.

1486, 1 Henry VII. Court of the Prior of the Hospital of St. John of Jerusalem in England of the Commandery of Newland, July 4th. Inquisition on the oaths of Walter Bayldon, John Wade, (Wodde?) Richard Wade, Robert Champynot, Thomas Morville, John Stede, Richard Wilkinson, Richard Rawson, John Heton, Richard Cave, Robert Stede son of John aforesaid, who say upon oath that Walter

H

Bayldon, Richard Wilkinson, and Richard Cave owe suit and came not, therefore each was fined ijd. The word sworn is written over all the jurors except those renamed.

1600, 42 Elizabeth, August 26.

The Jury found that probate of all testaments and granting and administration of all dying under the cross [house bearing the Templars' cross], or upon any lands belonging to the Hospital of St. John of Jerusalem doth belong to Her Majesty, and her steward hath proved the wills, and it appears that William Webster, vicar of Calverley church (including Pudsey township), had proved divers wills of tenants of St. John, and got promises of money, as namely the will of one Jeremiah Fletcher, and others belonging to this manor and persisted in doing so. They found also that Her Majesty ought to have, after the death or change of every of her free tenants a releyf certayne which is two years' rent, and called Lord's rent.

A payne was laid that every tenant of the Manor of Cottingley, do henceforth grynde all their corne at Her Majestie's millne in Cottingley growing upon his grounde in his occupation, on payne of vjs.

Thomas Dixon and Walter Kighley shall bring in their milner at the next court to be sworne, and also his moulter dish to be tryed on pain of 20s.

That everie man that holdeth any land of this manor shall sett a double crosse on his house or ground before the 25th of March next, in most viewe to be seen that hath not one already, on pain of 40/- everie man.

1616, April 3rd, Court held at Cottingley.

Proving wills. The administrators or executors of the will of Richard Jowet of Helwick, deceased, who died under the crosse at Helwicke, shall make their appearance here at the next court, and prove the will of deceased on pain of 30s.

Assize of ale. That William Longe, Edmund Fairburne, William Scott, William Wright, and John Symson are common typlers and alehouse keepers, and that they have not kept the assize of ale, but sould the same contrary to the statute, therefore they are amerced as in the statute.

Dixon Arms.

1617, April 21. Court at Cottingley, William Bayldon, foreman juror.

Affrays. We find that William francke made affray and drew blood upon William Lange of Cottingley, and we amerce him 6s. 8d.

for the blood and 3s. 4d. for the fray. William Franke made affray upon Steven Franke his father; fined 10s.

Sabbath desecration. Abraham Willman for playing at football upon the Sabbath, fined 3s. 4d.

1617, Sept. 29. Court at Cottingley.

Right of way. Robert Breare is to suffer and allow the inhabitants of Nether Helwicke a sufficient and lawful way for cart and carriage through his ground to the common as hath been accustomed, upon every default of 3s. 4d., and the jury lay in paine that no manner of persons use the footway over a certain close called Nunynge in Helwicke upon every default, 12d.; and they find that certain inhabitants of Cottingley have suffered their swine to goe unyoked as it is presented to them, namely, Stephen Franke, three, Robert Lister, four, William Long, two, and John Wright, one; amerced 6d. for every swine.

1620, Oct. 20th. Court at Cottingley.

Recovery of debt. Samuel Longbothom is indebted to Isabel Paslew 4s. 8d., and he must also pay her for charge, 12d.

1621, April 6th. Court at Cottingley.

Stephen Frank, gent., late of Cottingley Hall, deceased, died there since last court, and his executors ought to prove his will at this court and pay to the lord 5s., and ought also to compound with the lord of the manor for the bed wherein he dyed (deodand) or deliver ye same to ye sayd lord as by ancient composition, if the same composition is in force and effectual. That Peter Mitchell, of Pudsey, and John his son, make their fences betwixt Stephen fetters and Rollingrood before May on pain of 10s., and set fences according to the ancient standing, on pain of 10s.

The prior and convent of St. John of Jerusalem had held Shipley. By an Inquisition, 1 Henry VI., 1422, William Gascoigne, gent., of Milford, had died seized of the manors of Thorparch, Shipley and Cottingley.

Cottingley he had held of Thomas de Ashley, knight, and Shipley of the Knights of St. John, and it was found that William Gascoigne was his son and heir, aged 18. Agnes, daughter and heir of William Gascoigne, of Milford, married in the reign of Elizabeth, William Rawson, of Shipley. Their son Laurence married Mary dau. of

GASCOIGNE ARMS.

William Hawksworth. Their son William Rawson, who held Shipley manor, married Martha, dau. of Richard Pollard of Tong. Their son William, married Mary dau. John Lister of Manningham. Their son was William Rawson, the father of William Rawson, who died in 1745.

Under Farnhill Manor, Edward Jackson, of Lane End, Colling, was one of the Brethren having local charge.

It has been stated that a large chest full of wills may be seen at St. Ives, as proved under the Manor Court of Bingley, Crossley Hall and Pudsey, ranging in dates from 1610 to 1795. This collection has been sent by Mr. Ferrand to Wakefield, and instead of being a large chest full, only numbers 160, including a few that have been discovered recently. An alphabetical list is kept in the family record-book at St. Ives.

———

1267. RIEVAULX ABBEY. Jury present that Robert de Ripariis, steward of Alesia de Lacy, sent Adam son of Thomas de Manningham

FERRAND ARMS.

and others to impound the abbot's cattle in the Grange of Halton (Harden), Skyrack Wapentake, because the cattle were feeding in a pasture belonging to the vill of Bradeford in which the Abbot had no common. And William Chirichek (?Cherry-cheek), Adam, son of Roger de Gildestedis, Henry his brother, Louecok of Bingley, Yvo le Mouner (Miller) of the same, Adam de Wadewrthe, forester of Halton (Harden), Robert son of Simon the Reeve of Mickeltweyt, Richard son of Thomas Lamb of Prestesthorp, Richard Wodecok of Bingley, and many others coming from the said grange and wishing to rescue the cattle, a medley arose among them; and William

Chirichek shot at Adam with his bow and wounded him in the left side, so that he died within six weeks. William Chirichek went to the house of John Bullok in Gildestedis, and when he had notice of Adam's death he went away; and he is suspected. Therefore let him be put in exigent and outlawed. The others were all acquitted.

FOUNTAINS ABBEY, founded 1132, sent an off-shoot to Barnoldswick in 1147, afterwards removed to Kirkstall. To Fountains, Simon de Montealto gave lands in West Morton, before 1200. In the next century, Galfrid Haget gave lands at Elwick, possibly the Elwick in Bingley, to Fountains.

Thomas Paslew, said to have been one of the Riddlesden family, became Abbot of Fountains, March 26, 1435. He is spoken of as a handsome person, of a soul devout, and countenance serene, pious among his brethren, and kind to all around him. He was seized with a severe palsy, Sept. 8th, 1442, and in consequence resigned his office of abbot. He died on the 21st of November following, and was buried in the nave of Fountains, near the choir entrance.

In 1540, at the dissolution, Fountains property at Morton Banks was valued at 13s. 4d. yearly.

KIRKLEES NUNNERY. At the Dissolution of the smallest Monasteries it was found that 17s. 7d. yearly was paid to Kirklees out of lands at Cullingworth.

KIRKSTALL ABBEY. 1299. The Abbot of Kirkstall charged Adam son of John Maud with committing waste in the land, houses and gardens in Mickelthweyt.

Symon de Mohaut gave pasture for 200 sheep in Morton and Riddlesden, date not given.

Simon de Montalt gave besides this pasturage, fourteen acres of wood near Meredock at the head of Thoret assart in Riddlesden.

Elias de Stiveton, knight, gave lands in Riddlesden to the monks at Kirkstall in exchange for two oxgangs at Eastburn. Robert de Mohaut confirmed the gift of fourteen acres of land and wood nigh to Meredock.

Henry II., by the evil counsel of Roger de Mowbray, disseised the brethren of Kirkstall of their best estate the Grange of Micklethwaite. This occasioned great murmurs; and the Monks imputed to their Abbot, not only the loss of the estate, but of some sacred utensils and ornaments which he had disposed of; for, in order to conciliate the King's favour, he had presented him with a gold chalice, and a MS. of the Gospels. At length the convent was broken up for a time, and the brethren were dispersed in other houses of their order; partly on account of real distress, but principally for the purpose of moving the King to compassion. But this expedient failed in its effect. Henry's heart was obdurate, and death at length cut off from the monks all hope of recovering their grange, and "from the monarch of redeeming his soul."

DRAX PRIORY. In the Pleas of Edward I. the Prior of Drax was summoned to answer by what right he held soc, tol, and assize of ale in Drax and Bingley, and he shewed his authority from King Richard and William Paganel the founder, and Robert de Gaunt and Alice his wife and Avicia de Romelli. The Prior of Drax claimed compensation for assize of ale taken away.

The canons of Drax held Priest-thorpe and other possessions in Bingley. A small amount of their Bingley lands was held under the Knights Hospitallers of St. John of Jerusalem. They got a toft on the south side of Bingley Church, between the road and the river Ayre by gift from Richard de Castlehay (probably de Casteley in Wharfedale), on condition they paid xijd. yearly rent to the Knights as he had done previously. Bingley Church was given, in the reign of Henry I., by William Paynell to the canons of St. Austin and Drax, at the instance of Archbishop Thurstan, and the canons gave three marks annually out of the profits to the Knights of St. John. These grants were confirmed by Archbishop Roger and Archbishop Geoffrey Plantagenet, and by Pope Celestine in 1194. An enquiry in 1315 resulted in a further confirmation by Archbishop William de Grenefield. In 1312 a composition was made between the abbot and monks of Rievaux and the prior and convent of Drax about some tythes in Bingley, when it was agreed that the convent of Drax should receive tythe of all corn growing upon the premises belonging to the grange of Halton [now called Harden], which had been given to the monks of Rievaux, namely on Dakhusflat, Netherstaynflat, Langflat, in all the fields about Belled Bank, Cherrytree-butts, Oxhusflat, Overstaynflat, Cayseeflat, Moreflat, and Huhill, all which at that time were cultivated and titheable. The Canons of Drax were to have tithes of places now uncultivated, viz., Tomrode, Townrode, Johnland, Ranrode in the upper part of the close at Whitecote in Ravenrode, Broadinge alias Intak or Munkery, Willimtrode, and Wynhouse; of Over-park and Ryecroft (except two acres of new broken ground, and Ox-park and Hus-stubbings, Colynworth rode, four acres in Smythrode new broken ground, which shall not pay tithes), and the monks of Rievaux shall also be exempt from payment of tythes for all their lands in Halton Grange hereafter to be broken up. The canons of Drax shall also have tithes of all the now cultivated lands of the said abbot and monks of Rievaux belonging to the grange of Fawdre (Faweather near Rombles-moor), namely, Moreflat, Langemore flat, Hallsted, Lamblegh wall, Driflat, Olnevcastleflat, Piniflat, Longflat, Hucroft, Pigheless, Caylesflat, Castleflat, Coteflat, Calve-park, and whenever any of the following lands now uncultivated shall be tilled the said canons of Drax shall have tythes thereof, namely, Cotepark, Ald Fawdre, with circumjacent crofts, but Kilnecroft and Lathegarth and all other places belonging

The Old Vicarage, Bingley.

to Rievaux Abbey shall be exempt from payment of tythes; the monks of Rievaux paying only a composition of 10s. yearly.

The founder of Drax convent, William Paynell, gave also a carucate (about 120 acres) of land in Bingley, namely the whole township *(sic)* of Priest-thorpe which Osbert de Baixis confirmed; all the arable lands between the said town and the wood towards the north, and all the land between the wood and the road from Priest-thorpe to Gilstead towards the east, from a place called Dimple, to the said canons of Drax, and also all the land with marsh, meadow and woodland from the other part of the town to the west and south, as the rivulet which descends Del Dimple into the pool, to the bridge, and thence all the land between Priest-thorpe and the marsh by the circuit to the road aforesaid from Priest-thorpe to Gilstead.

Robert de Baixis gave to Drax three acres of land in Micklethwaite, confirmed by William de Cantilupe, with the grant of the church, and wood out of his grove of Bingley, as William Paynell had done before.

Eudo de la Zouch. with the consent of his wife Milisant, (who died c. 1281), gave three assarts (clearings or rodes) at the Rodes of the fee of Bingley, called Lillemandrode, Emmotrode, and Cotecroft. Hugh son of Robert of Newhill, quit-claimed to them also 18 acres in Priest-thorpe, and Richard son of Roger of Newhall quit-claimed four oxgangs and four tofts in Priest-thorpe, and an oxgang of land with toft there to be paid by Robert son of William de Alwodeley. Anthony D'Autrey (de Alta ripa) quit-claimed the service of THOMAS DE OXNOPE WITH HIS CATTLE AND FAMILY. William de Casteley, with his corps, gave them a toft and croft in Bingley, and Richard de Castlay gave to William his brother, the toft before mentioned on the south side of the church between the road and the Ayre, the canons; out of the profit therefrom paying 12d. yearly to the Brethren of St. John of Jerusalem, which John son of the said William confirmed.

Peter d'Autrey also gave ten acres in Northwode for the said canons of Drax to maintain three lamps with oil to burn on festivals in Bingley church.

John de Montealto de Matherley (Marley), with the consent of Alice his wife, gave them a toft called Baldwincroft lying between the Highroad and the course of water called Milnesich which Peter de Matherley their grandson confirmed.

John, son of Hugh de Matherley, gave to them William, son of Robert de Wayles WITH ALL HIS FAMILY AND CATTLE. [Serfdom.]

Robert, son of Robert, gave them a toft, an oxgang and an acre of land in Bingley field. Osbert de Howard gave them an oxgang in Micklethwaite. Robert son of Ralph (?Robert) Villayne of Bingley confirmed the gift of toft, oxgang and acre which his father had granted. The said Robert gave also, with his body to be buried in the priory, to the canons residing at Priest-thorpe, two acres of arable land in the territory of Bingley, one abutting on Brigflat and

Bretilands, and the other acre in Northfield, all of which Simeon his son confirmed.

On the Monday after St. Luke, 1317, 11 Edw. II., the Prior of Drax was called before Thomas de Montealto, steward or bailiff of Bingley, to shew what exemption he had from all secular services, and he produced several charters with confirmations thereof by Richard I. and Edward II. The last, made in 1311, exempted them from all manner of courts, and granted them toll, team, sac, soc and infangtheof. Isabel, daughter of Sir Simon de Monte Alto, with the consent of William Gentile her husband, gave a piece of land in Morton Fields abutting on the road called Milnegate, near the land of Lady Clarisa her mother. Simon de Monte Alt gave to Bingley Church all the tithe of his milne at Riddlesden, with the tithe of his meadow and springwood, and also of the bees throughout this manor.

The gifts confirmed by Richard I., Robert de Gant and Alice his wife, and others were confirmed by Alice de Romelli and Walter de Scoteni.

The Baius, Bavis, Baixis (from Bayeux in Normandy), were a family that gave lands in various parts of Yorkshire to Drax, to Fountains, and to Whitby Abbey. In 1234, Thomas de Bingel' held lands under Drax convent.

At the Dissolution, 1538, Drax was granted to Sir Marmaduke Constable of Everingham. The list of the priors of Drax, 1178-1530, appears in Burton's *Monasticon*, p. 114, but Mr. Paley Baildon has recently printed a revised list (*Yorks. Archæol.* Soc.) The 22nd prior was Richard Wilson, the Bingley Church benefactor.

BINGLEY PARISH CHURCH, FROM THE SOUTH.

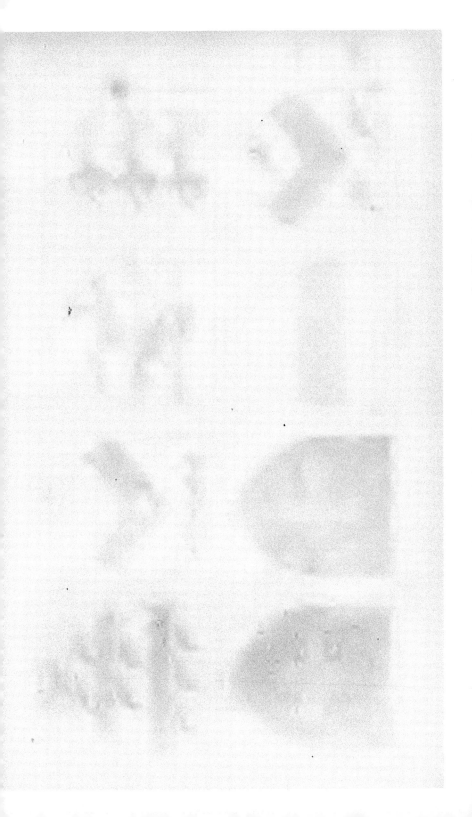

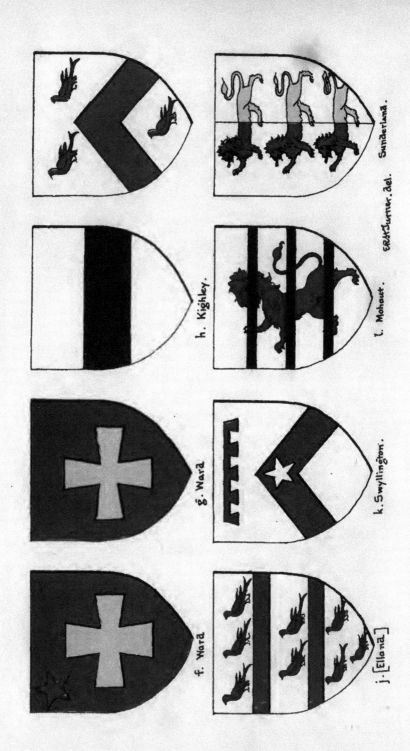

Bingley Church.

THE Church of Bingley, or as the place is often spelt in old deeds, Byngelay, Byngele, Bingeleia, Bungelai, Bingelay, Bingheleia, Bingelai, Bynglay, &c., &c., is undoubtedly the place around which most of the history of the parish clusters. It is in the southern division of the deanery of Craven. There is every probability that a church was erected here before 700. We have seen in our last chapter that the church and its possessions were given to the priory of Drax by William Paynell, the founder of Drax Convent, between 1119-1147. Up to 1197 it continued to be rectorial, but in that year Pope Celestine III. appropriated Bingley church to Drax, but the names of the rectors and vicars before 1275 have not been preserved. Like many other very ancient churches, it is dedicated to All Souls or All Saints. That it is of Saxon foundation there can be no doubt, though the many restorations, and notably the great rebuilding in the time of Henry VII. and Henry VIII. have destroyed the architectural proofs. The choir is said by tradition, and the presence of Wylson's arms, to have been rebuilt by Richard Wylson, Prior of Drax and Archbishop of Negropont *(in partibus)*, afterwards Bishop of Meath in Ireland. Wylson is recorded to have been a native of Bingley, and Dr. Whitaker gives us the astonishing observation that he did not know that the deanery of Craven had given birth to any other bishop, Catholic or Protestant. It would be extremely interesting to learn the story of Christianity in Bingley for the six hundred years before 1275, when Richard of Pontefract became Vicar, but the records at York only begin about the latter period, and one line each has to suffice at present in recording the life-work of many of the following vicars. When the valuable series of manuscripts at York have been either printed or placed more freely at the services of antiquaries, we shall be able to trace the parentage and work of the clergy of this country. It is high time that such rich collections should be garnered in a Yorkshire Public Record Office.

The Vicars of Bingley since 1275.

Instituted

4 ides Oct. 1275. Fr. (brother) Richard of Pontefract, a canon of Drax, presented to the living by the Prior and convent of Drax. The same words may be written against all the names down to 1504, when Fr. John Long was instituted, for they were all canons of Drax, and thus presented.

16 kal. August 1291. Fr. William of Roteholm. He resigned.
2 kal. Dec. 1299. Fr. William of Wylmeley.
2 id. July 1323. Fr. Nigel or Niel of Abthorp. Resigned.
13 kal. Mar. 1339. Fr. John of Ledes. He resigned.

Bingley Parish Church, North-East view.

16 Aug. 1348. Fr. John of Wyghton. He resigned.
24 Sep. 1354. Dominus John of Ousthorp. He resigned.
19 Jan. 1362. Fr. Thomas of Berewyk, who died whilst in possession.
6 Sep. 1369. Fr. Richard of Ledes. He resigned.
10 Oct. 1391. Fr. John of Usflet.
- . . . Dominus Laurence Dawtre, died whilst in possession.
28 July 1399. Fr. Robert of Emesay.
19 Oct. 1417. Fr. John of Usflet: probably the same person who was vicar for a short time in 1391-2. To this time it will be noticed that the vicars are always named by place-surnames, and whilst refraining from asserting that it was an absolute rule, I have frequently noticed in the Archbishop's books of that time that when an acolyte proceeded to the office of deacon or priest he assumed a place-surname indicating the place of his birth, in preference to his former sire-name. Also at this period, 1400, "de" (or "of" as I have preferred to translate it,) is left off the manuscripts.

11 Feb. 1420. Fr. Thomas Frost, canon of Drax, was presented by the Prior and Convent of Drax to Bingley Church, which he held until his death.

8 Mar. 1428. Fr. William Chippindale, resigned next year.

19 Nov. 1429. Fr. John Hunt followed, but whether he died in possession or resigned has not been ascertained. It is also likely that his successor's name is lost.

26 November, 1464. Fr. Richard Swillington. He resigned. He was a younger son of the Lowther Swillingtons. Arms, argent, a chevron azure, a label gules, mullet for difference.

13 Oct. 1473. Fr. John Byngley who held it until his death.

13 April, 1504. Fr. John Long who died whilst in possession.

15 June, 1536. Dominus John Scholay, priest, was presented by King Henry VIII., and from this time we only find three resigning. The patronage vested in the Royal family until the present reign when it was given to the Bishops of Ripon. Sir John Scholay, the priest, died within a year of his appointment.

26 July, 1537. Dominus Alexander Jennyns was instituted on the nomination of Henry VIII. Whether he resigned does not appear, as probably another name is missed in the list of vicars of this period.

3 Aug. 1572. Robert Wood, clerk, was presented by Queen Elizabeth, but had only a short tenure, being followed on his death about 1576, old style, by a vicar whose name will often be found in the Registers and Warden's Book. Parish Registers were ordered to be kept in 1538, but few of the earliest books have been preserved. Had they been written on parchment, as in after years, they would probably have been more valued and better cared for. Meantime, by a slow process of evolution, rather than revolution, the Reformation of Religion in England had taken place, and in common with

many parts of the West Riding, Bingley became decidedly Puritan, more advanced than kings and parliaments have even yet become.

15 Jan. 1576. Samuel Oley, clerk, was presented by Queen Elizabeth. After 42 years' tenure he died, and was succeeded,

5 Dec. 1618, by Thomas Howgill, clerk, Master of Arts, on the presentation of King James I. He held the living 44 years.

The will of Vicar Oley was proved at the Cottingley Court, and was preserved at St. Ives until Mr. Ferrand transmitted the Wills of this peculiar to Wakefield. It may be noted that the vicar was buried 18 Nov. 1618, two days after the will was made. It reads briefly as follows,

In the name of God, amen, November 16, 1618, I, Samuel Oley, clerk, give my soul to God Almighty my Creator, trusting to be saved by the death and passion of Christ Jesus my only Saviour. I hereby direct that the tithes, &c., be paid to William Shepherd, Bradford, Francis Oley, clerk, my brother, John Midgley of Headley in Thornton, and Thomas Hudson of Bingley for specified uses. To the poor 40s. due from the town to be paid within three months after my decease to the School and Poor Fund. To Daniel Oley my grand-child, a noble (6s. 8d.), to his brother and sister 5s. To Samuel Oley, my son, the use of my Latin books for life, and a silver spoone and a bedd with clothes, and all my apparell, if he will be ruled and governed by Stephen Wright my son-in-law, and Rebecka Whitley my daughter, but if not, only one-fifth part of my apparell. The rest I give to Sarah wife of Edw. Shakleton of Morton Banks, Jane wife of Stephen Wright and Rebecka Whitley my daughters equally, and I make the said Edward, Stephen and Rebecka executors. He was evidently at death's door for he signs with a cross, Saml. Oley X marke. Witnesses, Thomas Hudson, George Whitley, James X Utley, Anthony X Whitley, Robert Illingworth.

17 June 1662, Jonathan Fairbank, clerk, Master of Arts, on the presentation of King Charles II. He came here from Luddenden in Halifax parish, where he was curate from 1652 to 1662. Oliver Heywood has an unfavourable reflection on his character.

10 May 1687, James Roberts, clerk, presented by King James II. on the death of Mr. Fairbank. He resigned, as did also his next successor.

7 Sep. 1710. Gervas Neville, M.A. who was presented by William III. In one manuscript I have seen the induction of Vicar Ferrand given Aug. 17, 1714, but Whitaker gives 1718.

25 April 1718. Thomas Ferrand was instituted vicar by George I. and held the living until his death.

2 Jan. 1740. Richard Hartley, A.B., was nominated by George II. On his death, George III. presented Samuel Clapham, Master of Arts, 26 May 1791. He resigned.

28 June 1797, Richard Hartley, D.D., on the presentation of George III., succeeded.

8 Feb. 1837, the Rev. James Cheadle was appointed under the patronage of the Bishop of Ripon. At his death he was followed by the Rev. Arthur Parke Irwine, M.A., March 15, 1862, presented by the Bishop of Ripon. On Mr. Irwine's death he was succeeded by the Rev. Canon Charles Edwards, M.A., in 1890. At Canon Edwards' death in 1892, the Bishop presented the Rev. F. C. Kilner, M.A., now Archdeacon of Craven.

Pope Innocent XXII. gave the first fruits and tenths in 1253, to Henry III. for three years, and Bingley contributed to this taxation. In 1288 Pope Nicholas granted the tenths to Edward I. for six years to aid in the expedition to the Holy Land. In this taxation Bingley is valued at £30, and in his new taxation at £14 13s. 11d. The third taxation was in 1318 as the border counties had suffered so much by the Scots' invasions that they were not able to pay the former taxes. All taxation was regulated by Pope Nicholas' document until 26 Henry VIII., when the King's Book was compiled. In the King's Book, Bingley Church is set down at £7 6s. 8d. In the time of the Commonwealth a Parliamentary Survey of Churches was taken, when it was found that Bingley Vicarage (Vol. 18, p. 343, Lambeth Library), was worth £26 per annum. There were a thousand communicants. This included all the inhabitants over 15.

The record runs as follows:

"Wee finde belonginge to the parish church of Bingley a viccaridge presentative with cure of Soules, the proffitte thereof worth about £26 which is received by Mr. Thomas Howgill a preaching Mynister (this definition betokens a puritan community,) and viccar there who performs the cure. The Rectorie is impropriate. Wee finde the parish greate consisting of about one thousand communicants who may conveniently resorte to theire parish church everye Lord's daye. York, 25 May, 1650."

In Lawton's Yorkshire Churches the Rev. W. Penny is given as the impropriator and the Lord Chancellor (for the king) as patron. In 1585 there was a decree in the Exchequer between Wm. Ball and the parishioners of Bingley by which we find that the great and small tythes of the parish belonged to the priory of Drax originally, but came to the crown at the Dissolution of the Priories and Queen Elizabeth demised the said Rectory unto William, Richard and Thomas Ball reserving a rent of £24 yearly. In 1525 it had been granted for £20 yearly rent for twelve years, by Richard (Wylson), Bishop of Meath and Prior of St. Nicholas at Drax to Anthony Eltoft, Esquire, of Rushforth, with all tithe corn and wool, except tithe corn of a parcel in trust between the abbot and convent of Rivallx and the yearly rent of 10s. by the said prior and convent of Drax. Several leases had been made in the time of Henry and Edward to parishioners of tythe corn in kind by Sir John Scoley the priest and one Wood successively farmers of the said rectory or parsonage, and in Elizabeth's time by William Bourley (? Ball) the farmer, to sundry inhabitants upon which leases, fines were paid to the farmers on granting them. It was decided that the defendants and the rest of the parishioners should peaceably pay to William Ball, his executors, &c., upon demand all arrears of rent for tithes, a copy of which decree is preserved amongst the Harden Manor Rolls. By deed, Oct. 15, 1608, between Richard Sunderland of Coley Hall, gent., and John Shakleton of Newsome, yeoman, and Richard Shakleton his brother, reciting that Sir Thomas Sherley the elder of Wiston, Sussex, knight, Gyles Sympson of London, goldsmith, Sir Thomas Peyton, Anthony Crewe of London, and William Starkye of London, gent., by indenture of bargain and sale. 3 James I., to Richard Sunderland, Anthony Wade of King Cross, Halifax, Wm. Currer of Marley, Abraham Byns of Rishworth and John Oldfield of Gilstead and their heirs, the Rectory of Bingley with all rights, &c., &c., and the annuity or pension of 10s. which the abbot of Ryvalls was accustomed to pay to the Rector, being a total value of £22 belonging formerly to Drax, and also messuages, lands, tenements, pastures, feedings, commons, woods, underwoods, tythe of sheafs, grain, grass, wool, flax, hemp, lambs, and all other tythes, profits, commodities, advantages, emoluments, &c., in the townfields, hamlets, and parish of Bingley to hold the same of the King as of his Manor of East Greenwich by fealty only in free and common socage, and not in capite or by Knight's service, being a yearly rent of £22 reserved to the crown and payable at Lady Day and Michaelmas. Reciting further that John Shakleton was lawfully interested to him for divers years upon one messuage in Harden being the inheritance of Richard Shakleton, then occupied by Bryan Illingworth and Richard Shakleton, and was also lawfully seized of a messuage in Harden in the occupation of John Hayley, the tithes of both being parcel of the Rectory; also that the said Richard Sunderland had obtained the rights of the four others, and that Richard Sunderland for £12-14-8 had granted and sold to John and Richard Shakleton all tythes, &c., on the said messuages, (where ten carucates make a Knight's fee?), reserving 5s. 10d. yearly rent to the said Richard Sunderland.

It has been said that John Sunderland, gent., of Purston, descendant of Richard Sunderland of Coley, conveyed, about 1712, all the unsold tythes of Bingley and the modus or rents reserved, to James Roberts, clerk, vicar of Bingley, and that vicar Roberts conveyed them to Thomas Fell, Esq., Nov. 1721, under which title Mr. Solomon Fell, as his heir, has claimed tythes and modus out of several estates. This is stated on the authority of a paper belonging to Mr. Currer of Kildwick, April 1772.

Amongst the Lambeth Palace records is one bearing the name of Gervas Nevile, A.M., vicar, [1705], *Notitia Parochialis*, vol. 4, p. 783, and stating that the great tithes, corn, wool and hay are impropriated and every freeholder reaps yt advantage, only a reserved free rent is paid to Bryan Sunderland, Esq. The church is endowed with ye small tythes and a small modus wch is paid throughout ye parish. About 45 years ago, John Bynnes, Esq., of Rushworth, charged his whole estate with ye payment of £2 yearly to ye vicar, and also Samuel Sunderland, Esq., about 30 years ago, left houses and lands to ye Church of Bingley, amounting to £22 yearly. His charity to the church, school and poor and to other small chapels and schools is £100 yearly. The church was dedicated to St. Lawrence long before the Reformation. [He is evidently in error, but a private chapel or altar may have had this dedication.] There is no union or dismembering; no salary settled. The yearly value is about £30. The advowson belongs to ye Queen, and is within ye commission of ye Lord Keeper. It is not canonical with any other place. See *Valor Beneficiorum.*

In the handwriting of the Rev. T. Ferrand, vicar, 1714, a terrier records the church possessions as follows:—

(1) One house, two cottages, one large barn, one old barn on the backside. one garden, one orchard, one meadow about an acre, all north of Bingley street the gift of Mr. Sunderland to Bingley Church.

(2) One small house with garden or backside opposite the house named, on the south side of the street the gift of Mr. Sunderland.

(3) One rent of £4 per annum, exempt from all taxes, except the land or king's tax payable out of a farm called Royd House in Haworth chapelry, the gift of Mr. Sunderland to Bingley Church.

(4) One quit-rent of £6 per annum, exempt from all taxes out of an estate called Sugden House in this parish given by Mr. Sunderland to the Church for ever.

(5) The fields called Snapes near Great Horton near Gilbert Brooksbank's house containing about 6 acres, the gift of Mr. Sunderland.

(6) A clear annual rent of £2 out of the estate of Mr. Leach at Micklethwaite, the gift of Mr. John Binns to the Vicar of Bingley for ever in lieu of Easter Offerings, &c., due from Rishworth.

(7) The small tithes of eggs, geese, foals, milk, calves, bees, and pigs within the parish.

(8) Easter Offerings due at Easter, a modus or composition for hay, composition for plough, 1d., house, 2d., and a modus for mill, 10s. (*unjustly detained by Lord Bingley*: these words are deleted.)

(9) Surplice dues of churchings, 6d., marriages, 2s. 6d., and burials, 1s.

In another hand is added, (10), a farm called Brackenbed in Kighley, viz., one large house and large barn and eleven enclosures called Shuttle Ing, Middle Ing, Far Ing, Mousedale, Oaks Close, two Corner Leys, Wheat Close, Long Close, two rough woods, purchased by £200 from ye Governors of Queen Anne's Bounty, £100 given by the Rev. Mr. Robinson of Leeds, and the fourth £100 raised by the gentlemen of this parish.

There is also an account of the Common Plate belonging to Bingley in the writing of Vicar Ferrand, and this too is dated 1714 in the copy I have seen.

(1) Two chalices and two pattens bought for £20 the gift of Mr. Henry Hoyle late Schoolmaster.

(2) One flaggon bought by the contributions of the people and the price received for the small old plate then sold.

(3) One flaggon given by Elizabeth wife of William Busfeild of Ryshworth, Esq., to this church; cost £20.

HOYLE ARMS.

As explaining number 6 in the above terrier, I find that on Sept. 25, 1673, Abraham Bynnes of Ryshworth, gent., sold the manor and estate of Ryshworth to William Busfeild, Esq., and the deed recites that John Bynnes, father of Abraham, had by will given 40s. yearly to the Minister of the Parish Church, the said Abraham in order to save Mr. Busfeild harmless, devised two closes, wet acre, longlands, bottoms and water-ends, for a thousand years by way of indemnity.

In a Puritan district, like Bingley, we may expect to find that the morals of the people were duly, perhaps over-duly, inspected by the Vicar. In 1639 we find the names of twenty who were excommunicated. After the Restoration, those who left the Church were added to the lists though far from being immoral, so we have no scruples in recording the full list of those who were excommunicated at ye Archdeacon's Visitation, Jan. 23, 1664: viz., James Walton, Jane Keighley, George Wilkinson, Mary Wood, Peter Taylor and his wife, David Boococke, Anthony Utley, William Pighells, Anne Kellett, John Wright, James Hustler, Joshua Dawson, Simeon Butler and his wife, Anthony Illingworth and his wife, William Phillip, Edward Pighells, William Mawde, Thomas Morvel, William Kighley, Edmund Clarke, James Hall, James Woodhead.

In 1666,—Richard Lister, Mary Illingworth, James Willman and his wife Mary.

In Sept. 1682,—Richard Shackleton, John Eastburn, John Naylor, Anthony Whitley, Jonathan Bailey, William Holmes, Cornelius Laycock, William Frankland, Jeremy Hillhouse, Jonas Murgatroyd, James Willman, Richard Walker, John Milner, Thomas Pighells, Elizabeth Hosfold, Isack Gott, Ann Illingworth, Anthony Bentley, Isabel Hartley and Mercy Rigge.

Excommunicated at the Archdeacon's Visitation, no date recorded,—Richard Baldwin, Ann Bullock, Robert Gomersall, Diana Claiton, Thomas Thackerow, Marie Illingworth, Robert Howgate and Ann his wife, Francis Greenwood and his wife, James Utley, junr., George

Newell, Gabriel Lea, Richard Barraclough, Hugh Butler, William Wilkinson, William Holdroid.

The alternate names of men and women very likely indicate immoral conduct, for bastardy was very common as the parish registers will shew.

The Registers have been fairly well kept, though, as is very frequent, the one that should record the names from 1538 to 1577 is wanting. The first book was generally of paper, and when parchment books were ordered in Elizabeth's reign, the paper ones were put aside and lost or destroyed. The first book in existence at Bingley dates from 1577 to 1637; the second from 1638 to 1686, but defective 1653-1663; the third from 1687 to 1740; the fourth from 1741 to 1753; the fifth from 1754 to 1780; the 6th—of baptisms and burials, from 1779 to 1792; the seventh—marriage banns, 1780 to 1799; the eighth—baptisms and burials, 1793 to 1801. The New Registration Act since 1813 has elaborated all entries, and the books are far more numerous.

In the first book is a Register of Stalls or Pews in the church, which is of great interest in shewing the actual number of families and houses in the whole parish, and also the names of the families, and the manner in which pews were built and allotted. Until recent times pews and sittings were often sold by auction along with the farm or house to which they had been allotted. Churchwardens had no easy work in avoiding friction and partiality in this as in many other of their duties, and the old Churchwarden's Oath was possibly not too strong for the times.

Cherchye Wardenys, thys shal be youre charge, to bee true to God and to the cherche but to resseve the dettys to hyt belongythe or ellys to goo to the devell.

Before the Reformation there were no seats generally speaking; then people began to take their stools, like Jenny Geddes.

July 23, 1634, Register shewinge what Pewes or Stalls every householder hath his seate, ancient and new.

1. John Walker, Gawthorpe, gent., pew next the great quire or chancell, under the pew (pulpit) where the vicar doth read Divine Service, south side of middle alley.

2. Thomas Mawde, gent., north side of middle alley, next the pew wherein the clarke sitteth in tyme of Divine Service; for West Riddlesden.

3. Robert Farrand of Harding Grange, gent., next to No. 2, close to the great north pillar of the chancell.

4. Robert Blaykey for Marley Bank house, next to No. 1, close to the great south pillar of the chancell.

5. James Emmott, at the little south church dore right hand going in.

[Abraham Bynnes, Esq., hath his pew adjoining No. 3, and Thomas Fell, gent., hath his pew adjoining A. Bynnes pew; confirmed by the Archbishop Dec. 10, 1668.]

Antient Seats.

1. Stephen Slater, Cottingley, John Houldroyd, Gilstead, William Leach, Bingley, William Midgley, Marchcote, paid 4s. for mending the seats.

2. Robert Feather, Ravenroyd, Stephen Slater, Cottingley, Thomas Hudson, Cottingley, James ———, Whytecoat, Henry Rawson, Lees, antient seats and paid for mending them, and Richard Hudson of Cottingley has one new seat and paid for it.

3. Third stall; Thomas Howgill, vicar, for his house in Priest-thorpe (probably the one now known as the Old Vicarage), Robert Hall of Roydfield, John Rogers of Woodhouse, William Leach of Bingley, ancient seats, paid for them, and Henry Beanlands of Rycroft hath a new increased seat and paid for it.

4. Edward Skirrow, Thomas Green of Priesthorpe, John Morvell of Bingley, Jonas Lister of Lees, John Rawson for John Illingworth in Bingley, antient seats in the north stall, and Symon Collier a new seat there.

5. William Rawson of Stubbinge, George Farrand of Bingley, William Lister of Cottingley, Walter Taylor of Beckfoot, William Leach of Bingley, antient seats, paid for mending them.

6. John Fairbarne, Gilstead, John Whitley, Edmund Farrand, Bingley, Thomas Ellison, Cullingworth, John Shackleton, Harden, antient seats, paid for mending them.

7th stall. William Walters, William Rawson of Stubb house, George Farrand, Bingley, Thomas Milner, Harden, new seat, paid for it.

8th stall. Thomas Howgill, vicar, for house in Priest-thorpe, John Rogers of Woodhouse, Robert Hall, Roydfield, James Emmott, Whitecote, paid 4s. for mending, and John Milner, junior, Harden, for a new one and paid for it.

9th stall. Robert Blaykey of Marley Bank two ancient seats, John Illingworth, Richard Walker, Richard Walker for John Long's house, Jonas Utley, Bingley; antient, paid for.

10. Edward Skirrow of Priesthorpe, John Morvell, Bingley, Thomas Thomas of Priesthorpe, Jonas Lister of Lees, paid 4s. for mending; Stephen Tennant, (Farrant?) of Hellwicke a new one.

11. Robert Illingworth, Edward Brooksbank, of Harden, Walter Taylor of Beckfoot, Edm. Illingworth, Bingley, 4s. mending; Thomas Milner of Harden a new one.

12. Thomas Ellison, John Ellison of Cullingworth, John Whitley, Iysacke Drake, Bingley, John Rawson of Greenhill for house in Bingley, paid 5s. mending, and Christr. Leach, Cullingworth, for a new seat.

1. Thomas Dobson, Priesthorpe, Henry Johnson of Gilstead, Samuel Wilkinson, Faweather, John Hollingrake, Cullingworth,

William Midgley, Marshcote, Robert Wilkinson of Thwayts, Thomas Fowler of Riddlesden Bank and Christopher Smith of Haneworth, ancient.

2nd stall. John Dobson, Marley, Jane widow of Stephen Wright, Alexander Woodd of East Morton, Daniel Broadley, West Morton, for Butler's farm, Richard Sugden of Haneworth, Christopher Waynman, of Priesthorp, ancient.

3rd. Thomas Ellison, Cullingworth, Jane widow of Stephen Wright, John Turner of East Morton, Richard Driver of Cowhouse, ancient.

4. Widow Waddington, Cullingworth, John Brigg, Sugden House, John Hustler, Cottingley, James Slater, Gilstead, for Bland's house, John Cockcroft, Hardinge, William Wright, Bingley, the stall under the pulpit.

5th stall. John Milner of Crossgate, Bryan Lister of Cottingley, Thomas Smith, Woodhouse, Mr. Sunderland for his house at Cottingley Bridge, John Illingworth, Christopher Armitstead of Haneworth, William Hollingrake of Gilstead, antient.

6. Thomas Rawson, Priestthorpe, Richard Walker, Bingley, Bryan Lister, East Morton, Richard Hargreaves, Haynworth, Francis Wilkinson, Gilstead, for John Long's house in Bingley, William Leach, Isake Drake, Bingley, Thomas Shaw, West Morton, antient seat.

7. John Rawson, Greenhill, two seats, ffrancis Wilkinson, Gilstead, for Beeston farm there two seats, Isacke Drake, Bingley, John Rawson, Beckfoot, antient, and Thomas Rigg for a house in Bingley, bought of Mr. Bynnes, a new seat.

8. John Dobson, Marley, Edward Brooksbank for his house in Harden, Alexander Woodde of East Morton, Richard Sugden of Hayneworth, Nicholas Hudson, Harden Grange, Christopher Waynman, Priestthorpe, Daniel Broadley, West Morton, antient seats, and John Dobson, junior, Marley, and Thomas Milner, Harden, an odd seat, paid 8d. for it on the piller end.

9. Robert ffether of Ravenroyd, Thomas Ellison of Cullingworth, Robert Farrand of Harden Grange, Richard Driver of Cowhouse, Walter Midgley, John Cockcroft of Harden, Widow Waddington, antient.

10. Stephen Wright, Bingley, John Milner, John Fairbarne, James Slater.

11. New erected stall, Martyn Lister, Richard Birktwizle of Knaple Ing, Samuel Catlow, Isack Wilkinson, Christopher Sugden, Thomas Howgill for a house in Bingley, Stephen Farrand.

In the Long Stalls on the North side of Bingley Church.

1. New made, Henry Butler of Micklethwaite, Isabel Walker, widow, for Birkclose, Stephen ffarrand for Harden, Thomas Rogerson of West Morton, John Rawson, Beckfoot, Thomas Hudson, Cottingley, Thomas Ellison, junr., Cullingworth, settled by Dr. Easdell, Chancellor of Yorke, August 1635, by the Commissioner, Thomas Howgill and Churchwardens.

2. William Franke of Cottingley, John Walker of Gawthorpe for Marshhouse, John Bynnes of Rishworth for his house in Gilstead which was bought of John Leach, William Clapham of Beckfoot for John Morvell's house there, James Murgatrood for his house at Elom, Thomas Midgley of Rycroft, antient seats.

3. Thomas ffell of East Morton, Gyles Beane of Gilstead, John Murgatroyd of Lees, Michael Driver of Cowhouse, antient.

4. Edward Butler, Jonas Barker of Micklethwaite, George Beanlands, Anthony ffell, Walter Philipp of West Morton.

5. Thomas Watters, Francis Lister of East Morton, Anthony Whittingham, William Rogerson of West Morton, John Walker of Gawthorpe for a house in Priesthorpe, Robert ffarrand for Kighley mill, Thomas Kighley of Micklethwaite, antient seats.

6. William Frank of Cottingley, John Walker, Gawthorpe, Mr. Sunderland for his house at Cottingley Bridge, John Rawson of Beckfoot, Edward Butler of Micklethwaite, James Stead, Gilstead, Thomas Hudson, Cottingley, John Binnes, Rishworth, for a house at Gilstead bought of John Leach, antient.

7. New erected and increased stall. Joshua Bayley two, Thomas Leach, Harden, two, Thomas Binnes, Bingley two, Thomas Watters, Morton, one.

8. Henry Butler, Micklethwaite, George Walker, Bingley, John Ellison, Cullingworth, Abraham Butler, Height, Edmund ffarrand, Bingley, John Rawson, Greenhill, antient.

9. William Midgley of Marshcoate, Bryan Lister, Cottingley, James Murgatroyd for his house at Elom, Robert Wilkinson of Thwayts, John Walker of Gawthorpe for Marshhouse, Samuel Wilkinson, ffawether, Thomas Illingworth, Bingley; antient. Henry Beanland and Thomas Midgley of Rycroft join at another antient seat.

10. Gyles Beane, James Beane, Gilstead, Thomas ffell, East Morton, John Murgatroyd, Lees, Michael Driver, Cowhouse, Thomas Turner, East Morton, antient.

11. George Beanlands, Walter Phillips, West Morton, Edward Butler, Jonas Parker, Micklethwaite, Anthony ffell, of Heights, John Illingworth, Harden, antient.

12. Thomas Walters, Francis Lister, Bryan Lister, East Morton.

13. John Turner, East Morton, George Nutter, Priestthorpe, two, Robert ffarrand for Keighley mill farm, Walter Thomas, Beckfoot, George Bean, Helwick, for John Brier's farm; antient.

14. New and increased. William Leach of Moorhouse, four, William Drake of West Morton, John Wood of Helwick for John Crabtree's tenement.

Antient Seats in the Short Stalls in the North side of the Church.

1 and 2. Samuel Longbothome and Richard Longbothome have right antient seats and paid for mendinge, 8s. Izabel Walker, widow, hath one of the new seates there for her house at Birkclose and Edward Wood of Helwicke hath the other new seat.

3. Robert Butler, Micklethwaite, Thomas Illingworth, Bingley, John Houlroyde and James Stead of Gilstead, have one each, antient and paid 4s. mending. Richard Waugh of Gilstead has a new seat paid for.

4. Anthony Whitley of Greenhill, Thomas Kighley and William Smith of Micklethwaite, Thomas Beane of Gilstead, Samuel Dobson of East Morton, antient, paid 4s. for mending. John Kighley of Micklethwaite, junior, has a new seat there, paid for it.

5. John Oldfield, Gilstead, Robert Leach, Micklethwaite, Thomas Shaw, West Morton, Edmund Turner, East Morton, Christopher Beanlands, East Morton, antient, paid 4s. mending. John Thompson, Knaple Inge, new seat, paid.

6. William Haneworth, Robert Rogerson, Walter Phillip, West Morton, John Wood of Ebridge, antient, paid 4s. mending. Christopher Hall of Height, new seat, paid for it.

7. John Shackleton of Banks, John Oldfield, Gilstead, Christopher Beanlands, East Morton, William Hollingdrake, Gilstead, antient, paid 4s. mending. John Ickhornegill, Riddlesden Bank, new seat, paid.

8. Henry Johnson, James Slater, Thomas Wilkinson, Gilstead, John Shackleton, Riddlesden Bank, antient, paid 4s. John Ickhornegill, Riddlesden Bank, new seat, paid.

9. Edward Shackleton, Riddlesden Banks, two antient seats. Edward Brooksbank for house at Harden, John Rawson, Beckfoot, paid 4s. Richard Hogg, Helwick, new seat.

10. Thomas Dobson, Priest-thorpe, Walter Milner, Thomas Wood, East Morton, Thomas Whitley, Bingley, Henry Johnson, Gilstead, antient seats, paid 4s. mending, Walter Milner a new seat.

11. James Beane, Gilstead, John Hustler, Cottingley, John Brigg, Sugden House, John Hollingrake, Cullingworth, antient, paid 4s. mending. Isack Hollings, Cottingley, new seat.

12. Richard Waugh, Gilstead, William Smith, Thomas Kighley, Micklethwaite, Anthony ———, Greenhill, Samuel Dobson, West Morton, antient, paid 4s. mending. Isack Hollings, Cottingley, new.

13. Robert Leach, Micklethwaite, two seats, John Kighley, Robert Smyth, Micklethwaite, antient seats, paid 4s. mending. Thomas Turner, East Morton, new seat.

14. William Haneworth, Robert Rogerson, West Morton, Richard Ellison, Cullingworth, William Butler, Thomas Butler, Marley, antient seats, paid 4s. Walter Phillip, West Morton, antient. Christopher Hall, Height, new seat, paid 2s. 9d. for it.

15. James Slater, Gilstead, Anthony Whitley, Bingley for Lady house, Nicholas Wilkinson, Cragg, John Thompson, Knaple Ing, antient seats, paid.

16. William Skirrow. Priest-thorpe, John Morvell, Bingley, Edmund Illingworth, Bingley, William Wood, East Morton, antient seats, paid 4s. Stephen Dobson, Hellwicke for John Crabtree house, new.

17. Robert Hardcastle of Greenhill gate, William Skirrow, Priestthorpe, Robert Leach, Beckfoot, Widdow Tennant of Helwicke, antient seat, paid mending.

In Stalls behind the great South door.

John Taylor, an odd seat.
1st Stall. Henry Slater of Rycroft, Anthony Illingworth, Harden, Walter Milner, John Fairbarne, Gilstead.
2. Richard Sugden, Haneworth, Thomas Milner, Harding, Walter Blaykey for a house at Beckfoot, John Brigg of Haneworth, George Beane of Bingley.
3. Richard Hudson of Cottingley.
Stall next beneath the ffunt; blank.
Longstall beneath the ffunt north of middle alley.
1. William Skirrow of Priestthorpe, Thomas Butler, Marley, Henry Slater, Rycroft, Richard Dickinson, Cottingley, John Kighley, senr., Micklethwaite, Richard Longbothom, Helwick, Thomas Phillip for house in West Morton, Laurence ffarra, Cottingley, each antient seat.
2. John Whittaker of Ellar Carr, two, Thomas Howgill, vicar, for a house in Bingley, John Taylor, butcher, of Bingley, George Beeston, Bingley, John Ickhorngill, Riddlesden Bank, Richard Dickinson and Laurence ffarra, of Cottingley, John Taylor of Bingley, tanner, every one an ancyent seate.
3. James Utley of Bingley, Thomas Whitley.
[4. William Rishworth of Morton for his house he dwells in being without ease in the church the whole stall is allotted to him: Jonathan ffairebanke, Vicar de Bingley, Matthew Ackroyd, his mark, James Kighley, William Rishworth, Robert Lister, witnesses, after 1662.]
Seats behind the north church door: blank.
1668, Dec. 10. Faculty from Richard (Sterne) Archbishop of York to Abraham Binns of Rishworth, gent., and Thomas Fell, yeoman, for pews at Bingley.
1695, June 20. Faculty from John (Sharp) Archbishop, to Thomas Fell and Thomas Dobson, gents., for pews.
18 Charles II., 20 March, Mem. that John Murgatroyd of Riddlesden, gent., by deed gave & granted to Thomas Murgatroyd his uncle of Greenhill one pew two yards long five feet broad in Mr. Murgatroyd's Quire upon a piller upon the north side of the Quire. True copy by W. Wiglesworth.
Seats that Mr. Sunderland hath for his several houses—
(1) In the long stall in the sune side of the church one seate in 5th stall for his house at Woodhouse.
(2) In the long stall, north side, two new seats for the house at Harden where Thomas Leach dwelled, in 7th stall.
(3) In ditto, one seat for the house where Christopher Armistead of Haneworth dwelleth, in 5th stall.
(4) In ditto, one seat for the house where Richard Hargreaves of Haneworth dwelleth, in 5th stall.

ANCIENT BINGLEY.

(5) In the front stalls, sun syde, one seat for the house which he bought of Henry Rawson, late of Lees, in 2nd stall.

(6) In long stalls, sun syde, one seat for the house of Christopher Smith of Hayneworth, and one other there for the house of George Sugden, both in 1st stall.

Copied from the original given up by Mr. Parker of Browsholme with the title deeds to Harden Manor.

1679, Oct. 7. Faculty for St. Ives and Harden Grange Pews at Bingley, by Richard, Archbishop of York to Robert Ferrand, gent., greeting, whereas a vacant place between two pillars at the lower part, second and third from the belfry, five yards by three yards one foot, convenient for erecting a loft there for sitting, kneeling, praying, speaking, and hearing Divine Service, we therefore assign the said vacant place, &c., so long as you dwell in the said parish and frequent the church.

On July 4, 1671, Toby Wickham, Prof. Theol., Dean, to our dearly beloved in Christ Robert Ferrand of Rushworth, Esquire,—assigned some benches at the west end on the north side of the middle aisle, now used in common, for a stall for your family and tenants.

1724, April 10. Thomas Fell conveyed to Thomas his eldest son and heir, the moiety of the Quire of Bingley Church and seats therein, except one belonging to Mr. Parker and another to Mr. Dobson.

WICKHAM ARMS.

Lawton (1840) gives very few particulars respecting Bingley Church, except that the area was 13180 acres, the population 9256,* church-room 500, in 1818 returned at 1000, and net value of the living £233. Samuel Sunderland, Esq., by will gave £22 to the Vicars of this parish for ever. In 1730 the Vicarage was augmented with £200 to meet the benefaction of £200 from William Busfeild, Esquire, Benjamin Ferrand, Esquire, and Thos. Dobson, gent., and in 1818 with £300 from the Parliamentary Grant to meet a benefaction of £200 from the Rev. Dr. R. Hartley and Mrs. Duncombe's trustees.

Archbishop Sharp's MSS., I. 120, mentions an augmentation to this Vicarage of a house and lands to the value of £16 per annum. Inclosure Acts for parish common lands for Riddlesden with Morton, 28 Geo. III., and for Cullingworth, 49 Geo. III.

In 1739, Bingley Church Tower was raised, and in 1773 a peal of bells placed therein. The inscriptions on the six bells were as follows:

> 1st. Although I am but slight and small
> I will be heard above you all.

---

* Bingley and Micklethwaite, 8037; East and West Morton, 1219; an increase of 1861 persons in ten years.

2nd. If you have a judicious ear
you'll own my voice is sweet and clear.
3rd. At proper times our voices we will raise
to our Benefactor's praise.
4th. Such wondrous power's to music given
it elevates the soul to heaven.
5th. Ye Ringers all, that prize your
health and happiness
Be sober, merry, wise, and you'll
the same possess.
6th. "This Peal was raised in 1773
Johnson Atkinson Busfeild, Esqr.
was the principal benefactor."

TENOR BELL. This bell was cracked in 1827 and replaced by a new one without this inscription, in 1828, with the names of the Vicar and Churchwardens recorded upon it. One of the other bells was renewed the same year.

In July, 1873, Mr. Walter Dunlop of Harden Grange (the old St. Ives) added two bells, (making now a peal of eight), by Messrs. Mears & Stainbank, at a cost of £360. On one is the legend—RING OUT THE DARKNESS OF THE LAND, RING IN THE CHRIST THAT IS TO BE.

An additional burial ground was consecrated July 2nd, 1781. After abandoning the Old Vicarage in Priestthorpe, there was no glebe house until modern times, unless "a good house attached to the school" may be regarded as one.

Mr. F. Butterfield, in May, 1856, issued an amusing circular, in which he makes the church clock record its petition to retire, especially as it was sickly two hundred years ago. In the first list of subscriptions, Nov. 1856, the promises amounted to £188 towards a new clock, with three dials. Amongst this list appear the following sums,—William Ferrand, Esq., Harden Grange, £10; Hon. Mrs. Ferrand, £5; Alfred Harris, junr., Esq., £5; F. Butterfield, churchwarden and old clock's friend, Beck-house. £10; G. Lane Fox, Esq., Bramham Park, £5; W. R. C. Stansfield, Esq., £5; Mrs. E. Hailstone, £5; F. S. Powell, Esq., £5; Mrs. Ferrand and Mrs. Amphlett, London, £5;

DUNCOMBE ARMS.

W. Murgatroyd, Esq., Bankfield-house, £5; J. A. Busfeild, Esq., Upwood, £5; A. England, Esq., £5; Mrs. R. Tolson, £5; Hon. Capt. Duncombe, £2; W. Horsfall, Esq., Calverley, £6 6s. 0d.; J. Horsfall, Esq., Thirsk, £3; W. Horsfall, junr., Esq., Oak-house, £2; F. Greenwood, Esq., Norton Conyers, £3; B. B. Popplewell, junr., Esq., Milner-field, £3 3s. 0d.; Dr. Outhwaite, £2 2s. 0d.; Edward Townend, Esq. Bent-house, Cullingworth, £2 10s. 0d.; Rev. G. Wright, Bilham, £2; Thomas Walker, Esq., Gilstead, £3; Matthew Walker, Esq., Dowley-gapp, £2 10s. 0d.; James Hulbert, Esq., Old Vicarage, £2; Rev. T. Dixon, £2; Messrs. Ellis, Castlefield, £2; Rev. J. Cheadle, Vicarage, £2; Benjamin Broadbent, Esq., £2; Messrs. Jonas Sharp & Sons, £4 4s. 0d.; J. B. Greenwood, Esq., Morton, £2, &c.

In 1870, July 31, the Bingley Burial Grounds, (Church, Independent and Wesleyan), were closed for interments, except for those who owned vaults under certain conditions.

In this year and 1871 the church was restored, but with the exception of a vestry built out from the north aisle, it retains its original character. In 1877 I accompanied Mr. Morant to inspect the edifice, and the following paragraph gives his description at that time:

The Church consists of nave, with clerestory of four squareheaded, three-light windows, and two aisles opening from the nave by four arches, the octagonal; chancel arch, and arches dividing the nave aisles from the chapel or chancel aisles, a south porch, and west tower. The plaster has been removed from the walls, and some relics of the former Norman church discovered. The seats, font, pulpit, &c., are all modern. The tower is good, and in its original state; it has a curious west window. At the apex is a shield charged with the arms of Paslew, a fess between three pierced mullets, and at the termination of the hood mould are other shields, one defaced, the other also much defaced, but apparently, A lion rampant debruised by three bars. At the sides of these shields are two others, one, Three birds; the other, A double-headed eagle. In the east wall of the north chancel aisle is a shield, Three chess rooks, for Eltoft, and another bearing a chevron between three fleurs-de-lis, for Busfeild. The east window is of five lights, and beneath the sill is a short buttress, a most unusual position for such a support; it may possibly originally have been carried up between two lancet windows. There is a small two light window at the south-east end of the chancel. The east window of the south chancel is original, and of five lights. The chancel is supposed to have been rebuilt by Richard Wylson, Bishop of Negropont, Suffragan of York, and Prior of Drax in 1518. The north chancel aisle, or Ryshworth Chapel, was rebuilt at the cost of Mr. J. A. Busfeild, and on the richly-carved cornice of the oak screen which divides the chapel from the chancel is the following inscription:

"In Pious remembrance of his ancestors this Chapel was restored by Johnson Atkinson Busfeild in A.D. 1870."

This chapel formerly belonged to the Eltoft family, but in 1591 it was purchased, with the manor and estate, by Edward Bynns. In 1672 Abraham Bynns, of Ryshworth Hall, sold the property to William Busfeild, Esq., of Leeds. The chapel on the south side of the chancel was known as the Riddlesden Chapel. During the restoration of the church great care was taken to preserve the tablets and slabs with inscriptions, and many which were removed from their original positions are now fixed to the walls of the tower. [I am sorry to add that two or three are placed too high to be read, and that recently two of the finest carved ones, including Sunderland's, have been boarded over to accommodate the choir surplices. J.H.T.] In the west window of the tower are the following shields, with the names in old English beneath:—1, Argent, a fess between three pierced mullets sable; Paslew. 2, Argent, three chess rooks sable; Eltoft. 3, Argent, a lion rampant gules, over all two bars sable; Mohaut. 4, Argent three squirrels sejant gules; Martheley of Marley. 5, Sable on a plate or, between two goats' heads erased argent a leopard's face between two annulets azure. The shield is surmounted by a mitre, and beneath is this inscription—" REVERENDUS IN CHRISTO PATER RICARDUS WYLSONNE NEGROPONTE | Ebor. Suffragan ac Prior de Drax | istam chorum et fenestram | fieri fecit Anno Dom. MCCCCCXVJJJ | et die Mensis Martii xxvj."| 6, shield baron and femme, dexter, quarterly—1 and 4, sable a chevron between three fleurs-de-lis or, Busfeild; 2 and 3, gules a double-headed eagle displayed or, on a chief of the last a rose gules between two martlets sable, Atkinson; a martlet on a mullet for difference; impaling gules on a chevron argent between three towers of the second, from which issue demilions rampant or, as many grappling-irons sable; Priestley. Inscribed beneath: "THIS WINDOW, DESCRIBED BY DODSWORTH IN THE ACCOUNT OF HIS VISIT IN 1621, BUT SUBSEQUENTLY DESTROYED, WAS RESTORED BY JOHNSON ATKINSON BUSFEILD, ESQ., ANNO DOMINI MDCCCXLVII." (Craven, 3rd edition, Morant; and also the MSS. at St. Ives.)

The monumental tablets will be given in the chapter on Bingley families.

Whitaker says the fabric of the church, a plain and decent structure, was probably restored in the earlier part of Henry VIII.'s reign.

Nonconformity.*

"THE Puritans were men whose minds had derived a peculiar character from the daily contemplation of superior beings and eternal interests. Not content with acknowledging in general terms an over-ruling Providence, they habitually ascribed every event to the will of the Great Being for whose power nothing was too vast, for whose inspection nothing was too minute." Such are the just words of Lord Macaulay in his essay on Milton, the Puritan Poet.

John Wickliffe, the Yorkshireman, a century and a half before Luther, made England ring with the true key-note of the Reformation by denouncing priestly autocracy and by translating the Scriptures, but he was, like other great leaders, doomed to sow rather than reap; and it took several generations to prepare for the Reformation, which when it came was more of a civil than a religious movement, and consequently the seed of religious freedom had still to germinate till the heart of England was thoroughly Puritan. Had the rulers at the Court been of the same mould, or had they wisely foreseen the result of thwarting popular conviction, the great disasters of the Stuart dynasty would never have happened, neither the political nor the religious eruptions. Though the word Puritan did not come into use until the reign of Elizabeth, 1564, the principles had been working silently amongst clergy and laity. This was particularly the case in Yorkshire, and William Sautre, a Yorkshireman, became the proto-martyr of Protestantism in England.

There were many men who objected to the union of Church and State, but those objections were but trivial in consequences, compared with the disasters wrought by demanding the full "assent and consent" forced by civil rulers on religious creed and church polity. Two thousand clergymen—the best in the country—who would never have left the establishment on matters of religious belief, were driven by this intolerance from the pale of the church. Nobler men never lived in England, and amongst the noblest was the Rev. Oliver Heywood, of Coley, near Brighouse, who was the instrument in founding Bingley Nonconformity. He was indeed the Bishop of the West Riding of Yorkshire and South Lancashire. He deplored the forced work that had imposed hard and fast rituals on the century then passed; and fearlessly, but with inexpressible sorrow, he maintained for fifty active years the right of private judgment as against the domineering spirit at the head quarters of London and Canterbury. As an instance of puritan custom, the episcopal chapel at Idel, built by the freeholders in 1630, was not consecrated till sixty years

---

* The first portion of this chapter was delivered as a lecture at Eldwick, in Oct., 1891, by J. Horsfall Turner.

afterwards. Perhaps nothing strengthened the puritan principles more than the "Religious Exercises" which obtained at many Yorkshire towns, notably Halifax, and to a lesser degree Bingley and Bradford. Before the Civil Wars, persecution had driven staunch puritans to seek freedom on the New England shores, and the descendants of Broadley, Parker, and other Bingley emigrants still remain in America, and write to enquire after their English ancestry. Whilst the bishops and lay-leaders in parliament were strengthening the stakes of the Established Church, they shortened the cords they might have lengthened, which would have kept the bulk of the puritans within the fold. Harsh tyrannical means followed quickly on thoughtless, selfish, intolerant laws, and many in the establishment denounced the severity, though not puritans themselves. As Lord Macaulay puts it, the party in the church in 1564 became by expulsion the anti-church party in 1662. The Church of England to-day would not (if they could) have thus spited their face by cutting off their nose.

Long before the Reformation, even from Wickliffe's days, the Archdeacon's Visitations shew that there was a struggle for ecclesiastical freedom amongst the Catholic clergy, and had the Reformation been kept free from state influence, and royal dictation, the church in England would have taken a Puritan basis. There was hardly any middle party between Roman Catholics and Puritans, until the Stuarts ascended the throne. Amongst the several notable centres in Yorkshire where the Puritan element was specially maintained was Bingley. Here the religious services known as EXERCISES were held monthly, on a fixed week-day when the religiously disposed from far and near met for worship, and to hear one of the many able divines of the period expound the scriptures in a sermon of two to three hours' duration. At that time there was a frequent exchange of pulpits and we gather from such churchwarden's books as have been preserved the names of the Exercise preachers, most of whom became founders of Nonconformist causes. The Bingley book shews that, though Craven hardly gives us any instance of a clergyman leaving his church under the Uniformity Act of 1662, puritan teaching had up to a recent date obtained in this parish. From the Bingley Churchwarden's Book we learn:—

1651. April 13. For meate and drinke when Mr. Town preached, 4s. Robert Town, was ejected from Haworth in 1662. He had previously been at Elland. He died in 1663, aged 70. Robert Town, junr., was ejected in Lancashire.

1651. To Martha Wallis for 19 quarts 1 pint of wyne for two first communions at Whitsonday 17s. 10d.

Bread the same, 9d.

Twenty quarts of wyne for Christmas communion £1.

Twenty gallons of wyne at Easter, £4.

We may be tempted to think this indicates extensive wine-bibbing, but it must be remembered that every inhabitant who had reached his or her teens was compelled to resort to the Easter Sacrament on pain of a heavy fine.

To Mr. Howgill for the releife of a poor minister, 18d.
To Mr. Johnson the minister, 8d.
To Jane Wright for meat and drinke when Mr. Town and Mr. Taylor preacht, 6s. 6d.
Mr. Eagland preacht, 28 July, 4s.
Mr. Coare and Mr. Eagland 17 August, 5s.
Both Mr. Townes 5s. 8d.
Mr. Smyth, 19 Oct., preached, 3s. 4d.
Mr. Thompson, 26 Oct,, 5s. 6d. Mr. Moore, 2s. 6d.

Thomas Johnson, Vicar of Sherburn, preached after his ejectment at Sandal, Idle, &c. Mr. Taylor may have been Thomas or Christopher, both of whom became leading Quakers or Friends. Richard Coore was a curate in Halifax parish, but was ejected from Tong, near Birstall. He was author of Antinomian works. On his expulsion he practised physic. He died at Leeds, Dec., 1687, aged 71. Mr. Smyth was possibly Joshua Smyth, a noted Leeds man, ejected in 1662 from Kirby Hall, in which year he died. Mr. Moore had been curate of Coley, Haworth, and Baildon. He conformed.

1652. Ministers' dinners this year £1 9s. 6d.
A pottle of sache sent to Mr. ffetherston for bestowinge his paynes in preachinge, 2s. 8d.
To Mr. John Ellis about the Commonwealth's Arms setting up in the church, 24s.
Payd Jane Wright when Mr. Sayles and Mr. Watterhouse preacht, 9s.
Martha Wallis for a quart of sache sent for them 1s. 4d.
To Jane Wright when both Mr. Townes preacht, 5s.
Evidently Jane Wright and Martha Wallis were Bingley hotelkeepers. James Sales, a native of Pudsey, curate of Thornton, became minister under Vicar Todd at Leeds. He died at Pudsey in 1679. Jonas Waterhouse, vicar of Bradford, was ejected in 1662.

1653. Payd att an Excercize for Mr. Thompson and Mr. Coare, April 30, 2s. 2d. Exercize for both Mr. Townes 2s. 8d. Old Mr. Town preaching two sermons on Lord's day, 1s. 3d. Mr. Coare and Mr. Thompson at Excercize, Aug. 30, 2s. Mr. Town preacht Lord's day, 1s. Exercize both Mr. Townes, Nov. 7, 2s. 4d. Mr. Town, younger, preaching Sabbath day, 1s. Excercize when Mr. Summerton preacht, Nov. 29, 1s. 8d. Excercize when Mr. Coare and Mr. Thompson preacht, Feb. 17, 2s. 10d. Excercize when Mr. Town preacht, March 31, 3s. Mr. Howgill's dinner, Easter day, 6d. Why did not Mr. Howgill, the vicar, go home to his dinner?

1655. For the Protestants of the Duke of Savoy's affair, 4s. collection.

1654. Wyne April 8, (15 qts.), 9, 10, (5 qts.), 11, (3 pts.), 12, (2 qts.), 13, (7 qts. 1 pt.), 14, (9 qts. 1 pt.), 15, (27 qts.) Total, 67 quarts, 1 pint.

Oliver Heywood preached in Bingley Church at an exercise about 1654.

1659. Mr. Doughty for preaching, £4. Surely the vicar was ill at this time. Mr. Josiah Haldsworth for preaching 4 Saboths £1. Mr. Veach, the Scotchman, preached on New Year's day (end of March then), 4s. Mr. Kennion for his paines in preaching, £1. Mr. ffairebancke for 2 Saboth dayes, 15s., again 16s. (He would be at Luddenden at this time, and succeeded as vicar of Bingley in 1662.) Mr. Thornton and Mr. Walker preached. There was paid for wyne and ale when Mr. Hitch died 3s. 4d. Arvel or funeral feasts were then in full swing.

1661. Setting up the King's Armes, £1 16s. 0d. Charles II. had been restored in 1660.

Paid to preachers,—Mr. Jackson, six days, £1 9s. 6d. Mr. Kennion, June 19, £2; other four days £2 7s. 10d. Mr. Collier, of Bradford and Haworth, 6s. Mr. Barforth, Aug. 5, 1s. 6d. Mr. Marsden and his brother Mr. Marsden, 2s. 6d. Mr. Marsden two Saboth dayes 10s. Mr. Moore, 1s. 6d. Mr. Browne, 1s. 2d. He and Mr. Hetton, 10s. Mr. Broadley, 1s. 2d. Mr. Bullough three days administration of Sacrament, 16s. Mr. Smalewood, 28 Oct., &c., 21s. 6d. Cost of Mr. Thomas Smalewood and his man foure dayes, 4s. The Marsdens were two of the four sons of Ralph Marsden, Curate of Coley before Oliver Heywood, and all four were ejected ministers. Mr. Smallwood was ejected from Idle Chapel.

1662. Wyne and Suger when our vicar (Fairbank) first came.

These notes might have prepared us to believe that an early Nonconformist Church would have been established here, but such was not the case. The laity were partially prepared but it required the zeal of an outsider to requicken the old puritanism. This was done by the Rev. Oliver Heywood, of Coley, near Halifax, and the story best comes from his own diaries. [Heywood's Diaries and Register; 5 vols., edited by J. Horsfall Turner.]

1666. (Driven from home) returned secretly May 3, stayed there till May 16, "I spent two lords days at home with a considerable number of christians to my abundant comfort, oh they were refreshing days, and duties! I preacht to my neighbours several times in the week days and observed a solemne fast on May the 15, amongst almost 20 in my house, and god was wonderfully seen with us: the morning after, by sunrising I left mine owne house and went to Allerton to see my friends there, then visited Mr. Bentley at Bingley, whose condition is sadder than mine, for he is in the same house with some because of whom he cannot comfortably serve god, nor hath he the free exercise of his religion as he desires, and wisheth for any house of his own: thence I went to Menston and was all night with Colonel Charles ffairfax.

1667. Sep. 5, Thursday. I went to Bingley, visited some as I went and lodged at Marley Hall where I preached that night, the first meeting in private, I suppose, they have had in that parish; the

Lord graciously assisted and brought together a considerable number who were much affected. Who knows but some good may be done? The next day after, I visited my good friend Mr. Bentley who lives in that parish or rather is buried there, being much out of the world and out of public employment. I dined with him.

OLIVER HEYWOOD.

The Rev.* Eli Bentley, son of that esteemed minister, Richard Bentley, of Halifax parish, was born at Sowerby. He became Fellow of Trinity College, Cambridge. In August, 1652, he became assistant to Mr. Booth, the vicar of Halifax, and after Mr. Booth's death in 1657, Mr. Bentley held the Vicarage until the Restoration 1660, when he was ejected. The Five Mile Act drove him from Halifax, when he hid his usefulness at Bingley. In 1672 when the Indulgences were granted he returned to Halifax, and preached in his own house. He was a man of good abilities, a solid, serious preacher, of a very humble behaviour, very useful in his place, and much respected. He lived desired and died lamented, July 30, 1675, aged 4(9). He was buried in the south chapel of Halifax church,

---

* This title was seldom or never given to ministers at this time.

where the body of Oliver Heywood was afterwards placed, but unlike Mr. Bentley, without memorial stone. On a plain stone was recorded,—Eli Bentley, son of Richard Bentley of Sowerby, A.M., sometime Fellow of Trinity College, Cambridge, and late Minister of the Gospel at Halifax, departed this life July 30, 1675, in the 45th year of his age.

1667, Dec. The day after being Tuesday I went to Allerton, lodged at Widdow Hollins' house that night, on Wednesday (being that they call Christmas day) I went with my wife to Bingley, dined with Mr. farrand, lodged with my good friend Mr. Bentley, on thursday I preacht to a considerable number at Joshua Walkers in Marley Hall, went to Mr. Robert farrands home at night, there we lodged because of his wives weakness dined with his son Mr. Benjamin farrand at grange, thence after dinner we came home that evening, being Dec. 28, 1667, found all pretty wel at home, blessed be god.

1667-8, Jan. 8. Mr. Savil of Marley having sold his land and living a sharking wandering life, came to an alehouse near Ealand, called Nutters oth Coat, sate downe in a chaire, dyed immediately of an impostume as is thought.

1671-2, Jan. 1. Munday, upon call, I went to Bingley, preacht at Joshua Walker's house that night, the day after I went to Bramhup.

1671, Feb. 7, Wed. To Bramley, bapt. Sarah d. Elias Hinchball; same day to Cottingley, and bapt. John son John Hollins, preached there at night, home next day.

1672, Dec. 3. Tuesday, I went upon a call to Bingley, preacht at Mr. Farrands house, lodged there, had a considerable company, blessed be god.

1672, Augt. 13, I preacht at Micael Broadleys at Morton Banks.

1672, Aug. 13. I being in Bingley parish at severall times they were discoursing of the decay there is of persons of quality. Mr. Fairbank the minister there said to me there was a rot among the gentry, and I can say since I knew that place there is a decay of these houses and familys: Mr. Savile of Marley, Mr. Frank of Cottingley, Mr. Bins of Rushworth, Mr. Murgatrod of Greenhill, Mr. Currow of Nostrop, Mr. Johnson and others. Some are in debt, some imprisoned, some rooted out, title, name, some dead, posterity beggars, oh what unthriftines, wickednes, sloth, and gods curse for the same; this is a good lesson, Jno. 3, 33, Zech 5. 4.

1672. Declaration of Indulgence, Josiah Walker's house licensed as Presbyterian meeting house.

Thursday, Nov. 19, 1672, upon a call, I travelled to one Rich. Wilkinsons near Kighley, where I preacht and tho it be a barren place for religion yet there was a great number assembled and oh how was my heart wonderfully drawne out in prayer for the conversion of some soul! and many there were strangely affected, who knows wt good may be done in that ignorant prophane place! when I was preaching, one that heard me, all on a sudden cryed out A fi—— for him, what dost thou sit prating there! and opened the door and run away, and we saw him not again. I inquired after who he was, they told me it was one West of Keighley who was a great professor in the Antinomian way, then a quaker, marryed two wives at one time, but now is fallen off to drunkenness and horrible debauchery,—two great Antinomians heard me that day. At night, lodging at Joshua Walkers in Bingley, there came to me a man called John Wright, who hath not heard a minister preach scarce this ten years, we fell into discourse about ordinances, he said he was well satisfyed without, because he lives (as he sth) in the injoyment of god, and god hath promised that his people shall be all taught of god, and therefore need no teaching by man, &c.; the Lord did wonderfully help me in opening some scriptures speaking home to his case, answering his cavils, insomuch that he was silenced, and said as I said when I convinced him that if he was unconverted; ordinances were means of conversion, if converted ordinances were as necessary for edification, he confessed he was not without sin, yet I had much adoe to bring him off, having spent 4 or 5 houres in discourse, till I was weary, could not prevail with him for a promise but put-offs, I perceive he is an halfe witted man (!! after 5 hours.)

Dec. 4, 1672, being at Bingley, having preacht yesterday upon the subject of self-denyal at old Mr. Farrand's house, I found my spirit dull, tho' a little quickened towards the close of the day.

1672-3. Thursday, March 4th, I went upon a call to Bingley, preacht at Joshua Walker's house being licenced, there was a considerable company, god sweetly helped my heart both in praying and preaching on these words Act 16, 30 "wt. must I doe to be saved," wherein God helped me in many things extemporarily wch I knew were proper, the auditory being either prophane or Antinomians, or generally both: much of god was in that exercise, wt. the fruit will be god knows, whether conversion or hardening, however god hath helpt me to leave my testimony there in good sound earnest, and people were wonderfull attentive, some I saw much affected, god almighty grant a blessed effect. John Foster a choyce christian came to me after sermon and said Sr. you have brought strange things to our eares to day; I answered they are not strange to you, he replyed, no, but to that assembly they were, people are set on talking of them, tis thought some rich persons there were offended, I blesse god I am at a point with myself what people think of me so they may feel it wholesome good.

1673, Tu. April 22. I went to Bingley, preacht at Joshua Walkers with Mr. Whitehurst, we had a pretty assembly. Wednesday, I went to Pudsey, being desired by Mr. Farrand to talk with his daughter Mtris Milner about her marriage.

1673, June 10. I went to Bingley, preacht at Rushworth hall, Joshua Walker's house, had a large auditory, young Mr. Holdsworth preacht with me. I went to Bramhup that night.

1673, Thuesday, June 10. Mr. Holdsworth and I preacht in Rushworth Hall, for wch I procured a licence; providences are

J

strange in so disposing old Mr. Bins that owed it being a Justice of peace, and a great enemy to such men and meetings, a witty man, left his son in above £2000 debt, the son also prodigal apace increased it, was an implacable adversary to Joshua Walker, made him pay £8 for breaking up three-day work of land contrary to conditions writ tho' he had a verbal consent, yet Mr. Busfield, merchant of Leeds buys it, gave above £3000 for it, lets it to Joshua Walker, who hauing a licence makes use of it, and an exceeding convenient place it is, and we had a large assembly, blessed be god [his landlord hath now taken off that meeting. Postscript.]

1673. June 10, Thuesday, we had an excercize in Rushworth Hall near Bingley, God did wonderfully help my heart and many others, so that I saw many teares dropt down from many eyes, an ignorant prophane place. I was much carryed out in many expostulations for a work of conversion.

1673. Mr. Bins of Rushworth being Justice of Peace, dead some 8 or 9 yeares agoe left some three sons and 3 daughters, the eldest son hath been exceeding dissolute, spent excessively, the youngest children's portions being unpaid except one; Mr. Benson, Clark of the Assize, having lent him 700£ seeing all goe so fast feared his money, demanded it, put him upon selling his land, demanding also the other children's portions, and he hath sold it to Mr. Busfield of Leeds, who pays him £3000, excepting £100, whereof £700 goeth to Mr. Benson, £400 apiece to two sons, £300 apiece to two daughters, the rest to paying his other debts, and yet he is besotted, his brain crackt with drinking and in no capacity for any imployment, being unmarryed, &c.

Also, Mr. Thomas Murgatroyd hath lyen severall yeares prisoner in York Castle, making an escape, yrons were laid on him in the low jayle, where they have in processe of time almost eaten off his leg—that family is the most dreadful instance in the country, all that know tell strange passages of them.

1673. July 8, I went to Joshua Walkers at Rushworth Hall, near Bingley, to preach, Mr. Whitehurst preacht the former, his text was Lam. 3, 14, about saints experiences, but he had not one word in all his sermon reaching to the unconverted, my spirit was sore troubled, knowing the state of that people, being a numerous mixt assembly; I intended the subject of a token for good, but hearing his discourse changed my thoughts, treated of self-deceit from Sam. 1, 22, god did wonderfully assist, blessed be god; who knoweth what good may be done? many were affected. The morning after, riding over the moores to Bramhup (Mr. Dyneley's) though it was a terrible rain, yet my heart was much affected.

1673, July 8. God's mercy. As I was travelling to Bingley, over the heights, my horse had got a stone into his foot, I light to take it out, my horse having a sore neck with greasing for the scab, paused with me, came down upon me, yet blessed be god no worse.

1673, Sep. 5. At John Halls of Kipping, preaching with Mr. Whitehurst, I was much straitened and confounded in preaching, it may be because I was much straitened in time, or rather to confute my carnal confidence, for I must confesse I was self-conceited, having preached with him at Bingley, and conceiving myself much above him, now god set me far below him.

1673, Nov. 29. Micael Broadley of Bingley, being all night with me (at Northowram) told me that he had been a professor of religion many years, but I came to preach an excercise at Bingley church almost 20 years agoe upon that text 2 Cor. 4. 4, "if our gospel be hid its hid to them that are lost," his heart was so rivetted at that sermon that he thought the word was spoken to none but him, saw himself lost, yet kept councell, laments he opened not his case to me, I never knew of it til this night, blessed be god for this mercy to him, he is a gracious man.

1674. There is a man that rides up and down the country in white apparel, that talks at an high rate agt. ministers, ordinances, yea agt. scriptures as in Engl. and praiseth the hebrew bible only, which he pretends to have skill in, he is entertained by Mr. Cotes in Kildwick parish and John Drake of Pikeley, and others that pretend to perfection. Thomas Liedge (Leech) saw him yesterday in Bingley parish, being Dec. 28, '74, he rides upon a lusty black horse, hath a dog with him, pretends to be without money, hath eaten nothing but roots this 14 years, drinkes water, boastes that he baffled Mr. Rither and several other ministers, he goeth to severall houses, they send for neighbours, he talks much to them, makes people admire him. One man had crossed him in discourse, he took him by the hand, required him to kneel down with him, and let them pray that god would strike him that was in error; the man rusht from him and told him he thought he was a witch, wizzard or conjuror, would not meddle with him, some doubt whether he may not be a Jesuite, nobody can tell me his name, oh the danger of ignorant soules from such forlorn wanderers!

1674. Mr. Samuel Sunderland in Bingley parish, was robbed May 11, 1674, at night, there were nine thieves, they bound all persons in the house, bound him in his bed, went into his chests, took £2500 and went away with it; since I hear 8 of the thieves are taken; Lord, sanctify it to him. [Further notes will be found in the next chapter.]

1675, Dec. Preacht at Bingley, Morley, Sowerby, on three successive days.

1677. Nov. 27, Thuesday, preacht and lodged at Joshua Walker's at Rushworth Hall, god helpt.

28th, Mic. Broadley, my son and I rode into Craven thro' frost and snow.

30, frost broken and melted waters gave great danger to travelling, took our course by Gargrave, Skipton, travelled ou'r Rumbles moor, lodged and preacht that night at Mic. Broadley's to considerable company.

1677, Dec, 1. Saturday morning got out early, visited, prayed with and was much afflicted with Joseph Lister's case who buryed his son [David, brother of Accepted Lister] at Mr. frankland's [Academy] Munday last, a hopeful scholar.

1677, Dec. 31. Munday morning I went with Mic. Broadley, Tho. Leech, Sam Wilkinson to Morton Banks, by Rumbles moor, preacht there that afternoon, god graciously helpt, lodged at Henry Turners.

1677, Nov. 24. Micael Broadley & Dec. 30 Thos. Leech admitted members of Northowram Congregation.

1691. Abm. Broadley, Morton Banks, admitted.

1678, Mch. 26. Tu. forenoon, I rode to Bingley, baptized Ezekiel s. of Jonas Hainsworth, in my way, preacht at Josh. Walkers at Rushworth Hall about 3 aclock, god graciously helped. Wednesday morning with Tho. Leech, &c., into Craven.

1678, July 30. Tu. Morning, I rode to Tho. Leeches at Riddlesden Hall, there I preacht to a considerable number, and amongst them all bapt. his child David, god helped, there I lodged.

1678, Sept. 10. Tu. My wife & I went to Josh. Walkers, there I preacht in Rushworth Hall to a considerable assembly. At night John Hey and Mic. Broadley spent some time in prayer there, god helpt.

Wednesday morning, god sweetly drew out my heart in family prayer, oh wt. meltings. We called at John Hollins house.

1678, Oct. 15. I rode into Bingley parish, preacht at Thomas Leeches to a full company, god helpt on Joh. 6. 37, blessed be god, there I lodged.

Wednesday, I came home, called at Josh. Walkers, John Hollins.

1678, Dec. Munday morning I rode to Bingley, preacht at Joshua Walkers at Rushworth hall, found sweet assistance in praying, preaching on Luk. 14, 28, lodged there.

1679, June 18. 4th day morning, I rode towards Craven, called at Bingley, Rushworth, Kighley.

20th. 6th day, Heys came with me to Micael Broadleys at Morton Bank, where we had a solemne fast, god wonderfully melted my heart wn Jo(seph) Lister and myself were at prayer, oh, wt a day was it, blessed be god.

1679, July 17. 5 day morning, I with my son rode to Bingley, there I preacht at Joshua Walkers, god graciously assisted. Many friends out of Craven met me there, next day came home about noon.

1679, Oct. 21, took a journey towards Craven, visited J. Foster's family, and preached at Thomas Leache's to a considerable company. In the evening the Lord assisted Thomas Leach, Michael Broadley and myself in praying for the nation.

1680, Jan. 13. 3d day, I rode to Bingley, preacht at Joshua Walkers at Rushworth Hall, on Psal. 119, 158, "I beheld the transgressors and was grieved," had a ful assembly, god assisted; at night I set Josh. Walker, Mic. Broadley, Tho. Leech a-praying, I concluded, it was a good evening, blessed be god.

14th, after prayers I called of Mtris farrand at Bingley, discoursed and prayed with one Joseph Hainsworth's wife being in soul trouble at John Hollins at Cottingley, called of Joseph Lister, came home, tho' a stormy day.

Feb. 1680. Preached to a full assembly, at Mr. Leach's, Bingley, from this precious declaration of our Redeemer " Him that cometh unto me, I will in no wise cast out." It was a refreshing season to myself, and, I hope, to many others.

1680, March 23. I rode to Bingley, bapt. Jonas s. Jonas Hainworth, called on, prayed with Mtris. farrand who dyed next morning, preacht to a full assembly at Tho. Leeches on Job 14, 13, lodged at night. 24th, I got up early, called at Rushworth Hall, came home.

1682, May 25, I came to Riddlesden Hall where people were staying for me. Then God helped me in praying, preaching; lodged there; 26th, Friday we got up early, made ready, went to prayer, came altogether to Josh. Walker's to Rushworth Hall. There we stayed dinner. Then my sister and her son went back into Craven. We came forward, called at Jo. Hollins', Joseph Lister's, visited Mr. Smith at Kipping, (Thornton).

1683, June 19, Tuesday, rode to Bingley—dined with Josh. Walker, went forward to Bent Hall. 21st, Went to Riddlesden Hall, preached there. Came to Rushforth Hall. Lodged at Josh. Walker's. Friday, came to Stephen Wright's at Cottingley. Home.

1683, August 27, From Bradford travelled to Bingley, lodged at Josh. Walker's, Preacht. Tuesday 28th, we went towards Craven. 31 Friday, Came to Tho. Leeche's and so home.

1683, Oct. 25, From Keighley to Tho. Leeche's, preacht there that night. Lodged there. 26, went with John Walker to Baildon Hall, visited that gentlewoman, prayed, preached in her chamber, (Mrs. Baildon was probably ill; but persecution was specially rife in 1683-5.)

1683-4. Thomas Swain of Cottingley rose well of a good while, went to a thresher in the barn, told him of a cold he got at Andre(w)s fair, walkt into the fields, returning was taken suddenly, leaned on a gate, could get no further, they fetcht him on horseback, dyed at Jo. Hollins before they could get him home, this was Jan. 11, buryed at Bingley Jan. 13.

1686, June 1, Tuesday, rode to Bingley; up to Morton Banks, took Ab. Broadley with me, rode on to Bent Hall in Lothersdale, cousin W. Whitehead's. 3rd, By Skipton and Silsden. Dined at Tho. Leache's, called at Bingley; came to Joseph Lister's at Allerton.

There are several years' diaries that I have not yet discovered, so we may assume that there were many visits to Bingley that we have no record of.

1687. Thos. Leach built Riddlesden Hall in part of 1687, the new hall, April 1688.

1689, Dec. 27. John Dobson of Cottingley, son of Thomas Dobson of Bingley buried at Bingley, aged 31.

1689-90, Feb. 10. Anne wife to Joshua Walker, my dear friend, bur. at Bingley, aged 69.

1690. Gives Joshua Walker and others copies of his book.

1694-5, March 18, Monday called of Mr. Accepted Lister, did a weighty business with him about Bingley.

1695, July 30, Tuesday preacht in the meeting place at Bingley. Rode to Justice Farrand at Rushworth. Discoursed with Tho. Leech, returned; lodged at Robt. Walker's.

1695, August 10. Monday rode to Bingley. Tuesday writ the profession of Faith. Went after prayer to Joseph Lister's, read it to them. Consulted with Mr. Farrand, Mr. Whally, Tho. Leach, Mich. Broadley, &c., they thought well of it. I examined several communicants. Went to the chapel, prayed, preached. Then administered the Lord's supper to 13 or 14 after they had subscribed that profession. Had them all at dinner at Rob. Walker's, discoursed.

Here we have evidently the formation of the Congregational "Church" at Bingley, and very properly Mr. Heywood, after thirty years' casual labours at Bingley, was chosen to officiate as founder.

1698. Mr. Heywood distributed from Lady Mary Armine's fund, bequests to poor ministers; to Mr. Thomas Johnson, ejected minister £1, Mr. Matthew Smith, £1, Mr. Walker for Bingley £2, and a further grant of £10 to Bingley.

1701, Dec. 11, 5th day. Set myself to write a letter to Mr. Lister in answer to his, concerning that great dispute of his removing from Bingley. I was helped in it.

1701, 26 Dec. Abm. Broadley from Bingley dined with us.

1701-2, Feb. 15. Was carryed to my chapel. At night came Robert Walker, John Hanson, John Ramsden, talkt about Mr. Smiths remove to Bingley.

1701-2, Feb. 17. At dinner came Robt. Walker, about one o'clock came Mr. Dawson, Mr. Priestley, Mr. Bairstow to consult about Mr. Smith's staying at Warley or removing to Bingley, we framed a paper, subscribed our hands to it.

Mr. Heywood's Register* gives the following particulars of Bingley people, amongst hundreds of similar notices, mostly of Nonconformist families.

1671-2, Feb. Went to Cottingley to baptize a child.

Mr. Sam. Sunderland of Bingley Parish buried ffeb. 4, 1676-7, aged 74, a very rich man.

Emmat a poor woman in Bingley Parish buried April 2, Easter Tuesday, 1678, aged 100, some say 102, or 120; had cost the parish above £40 in poor leys. Another very old woman buryed at Bingley,

---

* Nonconformist Register, for Yorkshire and Lancashire, edited by J. Horsfall Turner.

West Riddlesden Hall.

Photo. by Geo. Hepworth.

April 21, 1678, her age not well known, grandmother to Thomas Leach wife.

1678, July 30, David s. Thomas Leach of Riddlesden hall christened.

Mrs. Crook, Riddlesden Hall, Thomas Leach's aunt died Aug. 22, 1679, aged 66.

John Waters of Morton Banks, buried Sep. 1679, aged 61.

Mrs. ffarrand of Bingley, second wife to Mr. Robert, Benjamin's father, died Mar. 24, 1679-80, aged about 80; rich widow, O.H.'s friend and hearer.

1684. John Hanson of Rhodes Hall (Wibsey) and Mary daughter of Joshua Walker, Bingley, married May 29.

1687, April 2, Mr. Fairbank, vicar of Bingley, died, aged 80, languisht long.

1687, June 9, Robert s. John Wright, Bingley, christened.

1688, July 26, Thomas Wade, Richard Wilkinson's father-in-law buryed at Bingley, aged 101.

1688, July 31, John Clayton his neighbour buried at Bingley, aged 83.

1689, Sep. 10, Sarah daughter of Robt. Walker, Bingley, bapt.

1694, April 8, Hannah daughter of Robt. Walker, Bingley, bapt.

1694, April 21, Mr. Thornton preacher at Horsford, usher at Bingley, went out well, found dead on Rundles More; lived at Morton Bank. Same day, James Kighley of Morton Bank found dead in his bed.

1695, Novr. Robert Leach . . . poor and wicked had been drinking on Lord's day, came home, fell into raging fits, died in two or three days.

1696, Aug. 13, Robert Hardcastle buried at Bingley, aged 72.

1697, April 13, Joshua Walker of Bingley, at meeting Lord's day twice, died Tuesday morning. Apr. 13, palsie, aged 71. April 15, my good friend buried there, aged 70.

1697, April 16, Joseph Lister's wife, Sarah, died, buried at Bingley on the 19th, aged 65.

1697, June 19, William Rushworth buried at Bingley, aged 74.

1697, July 3, Mr. Thomas fell buried at Bingley, aged 68.

1697-8, Feb. 19, Mr. John Walker married a daughter of William Rawson and William Lister of Bingley married a daughter of Dobson of Cottingley, Feb. 18, both of these young men stole their wives!!

1698, Dec. 22, Thomas Got of Bingley and Elizabeth Parkinson sister to Sarah Learoyd married at Bradford.

1699, Mr. Benjamin Farrand's wife was buried at Bingley, Nov. 24, aged 74, her son David came out of the south, fell sick, buried with her.

1699, Dec. Richard Wilkinson buried at Bingley, aged 63.

1700, Feb. 13, Mr. Benj. Farrand, Bingley, buried, aged 74.

1701, April 30. John Walker, Bingley, buried, aged 66.

1701, Oct. M(ichael) Maud of Cottingley, buried, aged 62.

1701-2, Jan. 7, Mr. Thomas Leach of Riddlesden Hall, my good friend, buried his wife at Bingley, aged 50.

1702, April 11, Matthew foster of Cottingley had not been well but breathed heavily, found by his wife, aged 74.

1702. Richard Walker of Bingley, long melancholy, then better, was found dead in his bed, buryed April 17, aged 64.

The venerable Heywood died soon afterwards.

The following particulars I extracted from the West Riding Sessions Rolls in 1873, but proceeded no further in my researches than the year 1700.

1672. Joshua Walker's house licensed; Indulgence Act.

1680. No papishes (papists) lived at either Morton or Bingley.

1689, July. At the Leeds Sessions, the houses of Thomas Leach of West Riddlesden, in Morton, and of Joshua Walker of Bingley, were recorded for religious worship under the Toleration Act. It was an abominable shame that the best men of the day should bow to either Indulgence or Toleration; the very words are galling.

1694, January. At Wakefield Sessions, the houses of John Walker, Bingley, Joseph Hammond, Bingley, Thomas Leach, junior, Morton Banks, and Martha Marshall, Bingley, recorded for religious services.

1695, July. Leeds Sessions, the house of Mr. Joseph Lister, in Bingley, was recorded.

1696, July. Leeds Sessions, the houses of Jonathan Widdop, Jeremie Heaton and Richard Shackleton, in Bingley parish, were recorded or registered, for Quakers or Friends.

1698, July. Skipton Sessions, the houses of Michael Broadley, Henry ffarrar, John Hollings, Benjamin Ferrand at Harden Grange, Richard Wilkinson and Thomas Whaley, all in Bingley parish were recorded.

I believe other applications were sent to the Archdeacons at their Visitations, but I have not examined the Archbishops' books of this period at York.

Mr. Dickenson, Heywood's successor at Northowram, continued the Register, and we must find space for a few more extracts by way of introducing certain more Bingley people, mostly Nonconformists.

1703, Sep. 30. Robert Walker of Bingley, died.

1706, Sep. 30. John, son of Mr. Thomas Wainman, minister at Bingley, born.

1708, Oct. 7. Samuel Starkey of Blakehill, and Margaret Gawthorpe of Bingley, married.

1711-12, Jan. 1. Robert Ferrand, Esq., J.P.. died.

1713-4, Feb. 2. Elizabeth, wife of Thomas Gott, buried.

1714, Oct. 21. William Clark of Hagstocks, Northowram, and —— Mitchell, near Bingley, married.

1716, Aug. 10. Isaac, son of John Hollings of Cottingley, buried; a hopeful young man designed for the ministry.

1717. Nov. 7. Mr. Thomas Leach, near Bingley, buried.

1719-20, Mch. 2. John Hollings, Cottingley, buried his wife at Bingley.
1721, Dec. 19. David Leach, near Bingley, and Mrs. Rachel ffenton of Hunslet, married.
1723, Nov. 15. Mary, dau. Widow Walker, Bingley, bur.
1724, April 25. John Hanson, Bingley, died of a few days' sickness; a young man unmarried.
1724, Sep. 8. Widow Susan Walker of Bingley, bur.
1726, Sep. 5. Isaac Wilkinson, of Westercroft, and Sarah Lister, of East Morton, married.
1728, July 29. John Hanson of Bingley, died in York Jail, buried.
1729, June 26. Mr. John Wainman, minister at Pudsey, and Mrs. Sarah Hollings of Bramley, married.
1729-30, March 31. Mr. Busfeild of Rishforth, near Bingley, a Justice of Peace, died suddenly.
1730. July 10. Mr. John Leache's wife, near Bingley, buried.
1730, Oct. 30. Mr. John Lambert Powell, and Abigail, Mr. Wainman's daughter, of Bingley, married.
1731, Dec. 18. Mr. Edward Farrand, of St. Ives, died.
1737. Joseph Hollings, of Cottingley, and Miss Marshall, near Rawdon, married.
1742. John Coates, gent., Morton Banks, married Elizabeth dau. Joshua Firth, gent., Kipping.
1742, Jan. 20. Mr. Wainman, minister at Bingley, buried his wife.
1743, Oct. 18. Mr. John Hollings, junr., died in Hunslet, buried from his father's at Cottingley.

It was not till May 1695, that the Nonconformists of Bingley had a resident minister settled amongst them, though the chapel, (which stood at the corner of Chapel Lane till recently, but transformed into cottages,) had been erected before the settlement. The meetings had migrated from Marley Hall, and Ryshworth Hall, and Riddlesden Hall, and other places, as shewn in these pages to a more central situation in Bingley.

We must introduce the father of the first resident minister because of his local influence, before treating more specially of the chapel history.

Joseph Lister, who was born at Bradford in June, 1627, became identified with Bingley. His mother's family were eminently puritan, two brothers being clergymen, one of whom (Edward Hill) was ejected in 1662, and the son of the other became a Nonconformist. Lister in his autobiography, printed in 1842, and reprinted by Abraham Holroyd in 1860, remarks that many good ministers and other puritans in 1639-1641, entertaining foreboding thoughts, concluding that popery was like to be set up, posted away to New England. Heywood and Lister had several friends amongst these emigrants. On one occasion when the Exercise was being held at Pudsey by rotation, where Mr. Elkanah Wales, the veteran preacher, was praying and preaching for six hours at a stretch, John Sugden came and stood in the chapel door, and said, in a lamentable voice : " Friends, we are all as good as dead men, for the Irish Rebels are coming." It turned out to be Protestant fugitives, and not Irish cut-throats. Profaneness came swelling upon them, and profane sports after the Book of Sports was issued. Lister being then fourteen was apprenticed to John Sharp (of Horton), Nonconformist; whose son (Thomas Sharp) was a noted ejected minister in 1662. The celebrated David Clarkson was kinsman to the Sharp's. Lister's narrative breaks off to record the sad condition of the district during the " Un "-Civil War. He mentions that when the enemies approached Bradford, horsemen were sent to Halifax, Bingley, and the small towns about, who presently took the alarm, and came with all speed, and such arms as they had, and stuck close to the inhabitants, and did very good service, Dec., 1642.*

On the Royalist side there was a Captain Bynnes, possibly the Bingley J.P., and the Saviles and Sunderlands were Royalists. July 2nd, 1643, Bradford was taken by the Royalists. " Oh ! what a day, what weeping and wringing of hands ! " Lister escaped after his master to Colne, by skulking in the hedges when troopers appeared, and by travelling in the dark. He returned to Bradford to find that his mother and Mrs. Sharp had escaped to Halifax, where he found them. Lister finished his apprenticeship at Sowerby, and mentions impressions he got at the Halifax Exercise Day, when Mr. Briscoe preached. In course of time he was advised to marry Sarah, daughter of John Denton, a gracious, holy man. He contrived to see what she was like, and then got his mother's leave, and applied to her father. The parents agreed to give each wedding portions, and as there was a law that justices should marry people, they, with four kinsfolk, went to Justice Farrar (at Halifax), and were married. Fourteen days afterwards his uncle, Mr. Edward Hill (Vicar of Crofton), agreed to give them a wedding sermon if they had not known each other since the justice married them, and marry them again, which he did ; as she had spent all the time at her own parents'. Lister speaks of his wife in the highest terms. They had two sons—*David*, who studied for the ministry under the Rev. Richard Frankland (an ejected minister), but died whilst a student, and was buried at Kendall, Nov., 1677 ; and *Accepted* (bapt. March, 1671), who became minister at Bingley.

Accepted Lister, as his Christian name alone would indicate, was born of Puritan parents, at Allerton, in March, 1671, and was educated under the Rev. Matthew Smith (of Mixenden), an author of some repute, and Nonconformist minister. Accepted was a sickly boy, afflicted with a great weakness in his joints, so that he could not go without crutches, yet when he grew up he was enabled to pray and preach two or three hours together upon them to the

---

* " Siege of Bradford."—Reprinted by J. Horsfall Turner, 2s.

awakening, warning, and comforting of many that came to hear him. Mrs. Lister's uncle (Samuel Bailey) having left them the tenancy of half his farm at Allerton, and other of her kinsfolk added to their wealth and comfort, so that they left Bradford and settled at Allerton, joining themselves to the religious community at Kipping-in-Thornton. During the persecution-years, " when preaching and praying were such crimes," private meetings were held at Sharp's, Horton, Lister's, and Berry's dwellings, and they were ministered to by the following ejected clergymen:—Messrs. Ryther, Root, father and son, Nesse, Marsden, Coates, and Whitehurst, and by a Mr. Bailey. They then got Mr. Matthew Smith from York, who left Kipping after ministering about eight years, to take the charge of the Mixenden congregation, on alternate Sabbaths along with Kipping. Accepted, being fit for University learning, was placed under Mr. Smith's tuition for about three years, and in the last year broke his thigh, in consequence of which it was feared he would not be able to stand to preach, so his father built a very convenient room for him to start a school, but a neighbouring schoolmaster reported him to the Spiritual Court at York, and he was refused a licence unless he would conform. Mr. Smith had held Kipping on alternate Sundays for some years, but left them entirely, in a hig. He, however, repented his rashness, and would have united the two places again, but the congregation refused; and they urged (for a considerable time) ACCEPTED LISTER to take the pastorate. He agreed for one quarter, and they renewed their invitation quarter after quarter. On October 17, 1693, he fell from his horse on returning from a preaching engagement at Leeds, and broke both his thighs. During the nine weeks he was bed-fast, he had a call to the congregation at Clifford near Tadcaster, but refused it, though dissatisfied with the dissensions at Kipping. It happened that some of the good men of Bingley came and desired him to go there every other Lord's Day and preach, and with the consent of Kipping people he promised for three months. The call was renewed and accepted. On Jan. 20, 1695, his horse's foot stuck fast in the ice, and he fell off and broke both his thighs again. The Bingley people rather than lose his services invited him to settle with them entirely, and urged that their chapel had a house adjoining it for the minister. He agreed, and the Bingley congregation " sent horses and carts and fetched us and almost all we had in one day." Thus writes the minister's father in his autobiography. This was in May, 1695, " And the Lord gave us favor in the eyes of all the inhabitants of the town (except two men) who behaved with great love and kindness towards us; and yet but few of the town's people came to hear my son preach—but the congregation chiefly consisted of persons that came from other places. Having been here about two years, my dear wife died, and she lieth asleep in this place. . . . . About three years after my wife's death, I was attacked by a most violent fever, which was then very fatal in the neighbourhood. Under this distemper, I was afflicted with very great sweating, and extreme coughing for two or three hours together, with but very little intermission ; and also with the most afflicting thirst I ever experienced, and for a week or ten days I was regarded as a gone man, yet I was raised up. During our stay at Bingley, my son had many calls from the church at Kipping to return to them again, and all the good people at Bingley were often desiring him to accept of the office of a settled pastor amongst them. He was much embarrassed, and sought the advice of neighbouring ministers, who had a conference together, but came to no conclusion, fearing to offend either Kipping or Bingley; but Mr. Whitaker, of Leeds, and Mr. Noble, of Morley, declared in favour of Kipping. After long deliberation he acquiesced, and thirty men with as many horses and carts as could carry all we had away fetched us to Kipping, July 22, 1702." Joseph Lister resumed his duties as a deacon, and the son became the faithful pastor until Feb. 25, 1709, when he died. In a fortnight the father died, and was buried March 14, 1709.

Mr. Whitaker's *Sermons*, 8vo., 1712, contains "A Sermon on the Death of Mr. Joseph Lister, of Kipping."

Accepted Lister was ordained by three ejected ministers, who will ever shine amongst the noblest men Yorkshire ever had. These were Frankland, Heywood, and Thorpe (of Hopton); and other ministers were present. The ceremony took place at Horton, near Bradford, June 6, 1691. His thesis was—*An vere fideles de sua salute certi esse possunt?* He took the affirmative. He was then examined in Hebrew, Greek, and other parts of learning, delivered his confession of faith, and answered to various interrogatories respecting his objects in entering the ministry, &c. After this Mr. Thorpe prayed over him, and in the midst of this prayer the ordaining ministers laid their hands upon him. A Bible was then presented, and they gave him the right hand of fellowship. Then followed an exhortation to him and two others then ordained, and to the people. The service lasted six or seven hours, after which they dined at Mr. Sharp's. Mr. A. Lister published a sermon preached in Call Lane Chapel, Leeds, entitled, "Christ's Coming, the Believer's Comfort," on the death of Benjamin, son of Joshua Dawson, of Leeds. On Sunday, Feb. 21, 1708-9, he preached twice in his chapel, and died on the 25th, of apoplexy.

Oliver Heywood's concern for him at Bingley will be found in his diaries under dates, March 1694-5, and Dec. 11, 1701.

Heywood's successor, (Rev. Thos. Dickinson) in the Northowram Register says, "A. L. was an excellent preacher; a little helpless body; but a great and sound soul." The eccentric John Dunton of London, in his *Panegyricks* (1818,) says "A L. is a little man, but one that has a great soul, rich in grace and gifts, of a strong memory, good elocution, ACCEPTED with God and all good men, and one that serves God faithfully in the Gospel of his Son; naturally caring for the good of souls, and longing after them in the bowels of the Lord Jesus."

Accepted Lister married Mary Whitehead on April 11th, 1705. In 1718 she married Robert Richmond, minister at Cleckheaton, and surviving him she had as a third husband, John Willis of Wakefield. On the gravestone at Thornton Church, near where the south wall stood, is a stone with this inscription:—

HERE LYETH THE BODY OF MR. ACCEPTED LISTER, MINISTER OF THE GOSPEL, WHO CHANGED THIS FRAIL LIFE FOR A BETTER, FEBRVARY THE 25TH. 1708-9 ANNO ÆTATIS 38, AFTER HE HAD BY HIS ABVNDANT LABOVRS VERIFIED HIS OWN MOTTO—IMPENDAM ET EXPENDAR.

In my *Yorkshire Notes and Queries*, Vol. I., p. 177, &c., will be found twelve pages of notes taken at Kipping by a hearer, and chief supporter of that congregation, with interesting notices of the deaths of Mr. Lister and his father.

On Mr. 'Ceppy Lister's removal, the Rev. Matthew Smith served the congregation frequently, and he was invited to settle here, but declined. He was a very learned man, an M.A. of Edinburgh University, and author of a pamphlet entitled, "The True Notion of Imported Righteousness and our Justification thereby." This he supplemented by a "Defence," and his son published some of his sermons in a small volume. Mr. Heywood and others were apprehensive of Mr. Smith's want of orthodoxy, but unjustly so, and he does not seem to have favoured his removal to Bingley. (Feb. 15, 1702, *Diaries*.) He was succeeded at Mixenden by his son, Rev. John Smith.

Mr. Thomas Ferrand, of Bradford, in a letter to Mr. Thoresby, of Leeds, March 15, 1703-4, gives us a glimpse of local history at Bingley. Mrs. Walker had evidently applied for a grant of money towards Mr. Wainman's support as minister at Bingley from the Stretton Fund, London:—

"Sir, Mr. Lister is some time ago removed from Bingley, and they have there now a very hopeful young man — one Mr. THOMAS WAINMAN—whose ministry is so acceptable to the people that the congregation is increased since he came there. I have sent your letter forward to Bingley, and I hope, good sir, you will pardon what the widow (Mrs. Robert Walker) writ to you, for it's from a hearty zeal she hath to propagate the Gospel in that place. Sir, her husband built a chapel and lofted the same at his own charge, say for about £15, as I remember he had from his father and an uncle. The salary as I am told is very small, not above £16 a year, to the minister."

Mr. Wainman had previously held the pastorate of Eastwood, near Hebden Bridge. He had been educated, like most of the Northern Nonconformist Ministers, under the Rev. Richard Frankland, at

Rathmell, near Settle; and at other places to which Mr. Frankland had been compelled by persecution to remove. In 1715 he had a congregation of about 250 persons, of whom 17 were freeholders and Parliamentary voters. At that time Idle Nonconformists had just withdrawn from Bingley, and re-united as a congregation and built themselves a chapel, but the Keighley members are included in these figures, for they did not withdraw till 1730. Mr. Wainman was also assisted from Lady Hewley's Fund for Poor Ministers. He has always had the reputation of having been a pious and zealous man. He was buried in the Parish Churchyard at Bingley, and his gravestone still bears the inscription—" In Memory of the Rev. Thomas Wainman of this town, who died Jan. 8, 1746, in the 68th year of his age. His delight was in the law of the Lord, and in that law he meditated day and night."

From 1746 to 1752, his son, the Rev. John Wainman, of Pudsey, frequently supplied the pulpit in exchange with Mr. Fenton, who was the nominal minister at Bingley.

In 1753, the REV. THOMAS LILLIE, a Presbyterian, "A Calvinist, and somewhat Latitudinarian," who wrote under the signature of "Cornelius" in Priestley's *Theological Repository*, succeeded to the Bingley ministry. He had been educated in Scotland. He received grants from the Hewley Fund. He published a sermon on the "Death of Mrs. Phillips" (wife of the Minister at Keighley) preached there July 11, 1784. Printed by J. Nicholson & Son, Bradford; 8 vo., 52 pp., which is supposed to be the first Bradford printed book. "This sermon was a well-composed discourse, but wanting in an exhibition of the doctrine of atonement, though the text (Ps. xxiii. 4) might have naturally led in that direction." Mr. Lillie died May 3, 1797, aged 77, after a pastorate of 44 years, and was buried in the Old Independent Chapel. His remains were removed to the new chapel in 1819, and a tablet to his memory is preserved:—" In memory of the Rev. Thomas Lillie, who departed this life May 3, 1797, aged 77 years. His mortal remains were interred in the Old Chapel, Bingley, where he had been the diligent, peaceful, useful, and much-respected pastor forty-four years. His remains were removed to this place, Oct., 1819. The memory of the just is blessed." A notice of him appeared in the *Protestant Magazine*, May, 1832. The Rev. John Calvert preached his funeral sermon. The present chapel register begins with Mr. Lillie's ministry. The books giving the births and baptisms 1754-1837, and the burials, 1818-1837, are at Somerset House, London. The congregation consisted of persons from Eldwick, Morton, Cottingley, Harden, Wilsden and Allerton, besides Bingley. Mr. Lillie's last entry in the register was April 12th, 1797, the baptisms of Joseph and Barnard, sons of William and Mary Hartley, of Harden. There seems to have been only one burial in the chapel before his own, and there was then no grave-yard. In Oct. 1794, the tax on births and burials was taken off.

The REV. WILLIAM STEPHENS was chosen by the congregation to succeed Mr. Lillie. He had been upon the stage, but had abandoned the theatrical profession, and the novelty of his appearance in the pulpit excited curiosity and rendered him popular. Failing to prevail on the people to erect a new chapel, he resigned. He removed to Aberdeen, and changed to another denomination, in which he laboured many years. Mr. Stephens was at Bingley about two years.

In 1800 the REV. ABRAHAM HUDSWELL accepted the call of the church, and on the 16th of June, 1801, was ordained, the officiating ministers being the Revs. Sugden, Calvert, Holgate, Jonathan Toothill and Williams. He was a most pious and gifted, a zealous and able preacher, a well-read theologian, orthodox in his teaching, eloquent and impressive in his address, and held highly in regard and love by his people. His son, the Rev. William Hudswell was born at Bingley. In December, 1816, he left Bingley for Morley, and whilst there was deprived of the Lady Hewley grant of £16 owing to the Hewley chancery suit. He died at Morley, Feb. 27, 1838, after a long illness. On the next page will be found a facsimile of Mr. Abraham Hudswell's writing.

The REV. ABRAHAM CLARKSON, of Mixenden, succeeded at Bingley in August, 1817. He was born at Earlsheaton in 1783, his parents being conformists. He heard the Rev. Thomas Taylor, of Ossett, preach in a house at Earlsheaton, and determined to become a minister. In 1811 he became a student under the Rev. W. Vint of Idle, and served his first office for two years at Mixenden. Soon after his settlement at Bingley, measures were adopted to erect a new chapel, as the old one was incommodious and inadequate for the increased congregation. The new chapel was opened April 29, 1818, to hold 500 people, and the cost was about £1200. It has been enlarged since. The ordination of Mr. Clarkson seems to have been postponed till June 10, 1818, when the Revs. Vint, Scott, Pool, and Jonathan Toothill officiated. Mr. Clarkson's pastorate was very successful, and he conducted monthly services at Cottingley, Eldwick, Harden and Morton. Owing to failing health, he resigned in 1837, and retired to Batley. He died on May 4th, 1850, and the Rev. Jonathan Sutcliffe of Ashton-under-Lyne, aptly said that Mr. Clarkson's religion was not a new dress but a new nature, not a holiday but an every-day garb, worn with the ease of natural habit, not with the stiffness of an assumed attire.

The REV. JOHN PROTHEROE (from Neport-Pagnel Academy) was the next minister, and held office just two years—April 1, 1838, to April 1, 1840. His last two sermons were a discourse on the death of an old deacon (John Illingworth), and a farewell address, Acts xx., 32. He was an amiable and cheerful minister, and much esteemed. In 1838 the branch chapel at Harden was erected, to seat 250 people, but the people were not formed into a church until three years afterwards. Mr. Protheroe removed to Bulford, Wiltshire.

1 Pet. 1.3 [shorthand symbols]

As we are by nature sinners, born in sin & concieved in iniquity; our natures are consequently depraved, defiled & poluted, from the crown of the head to the sole of the foot, we are all wounds & bruises & putrifying sores, sin is so ingrafted in our nature that we cannot love, or take delight in any thing else, we live and indulge in it because we love it, the bias of our minds is on the side of sin. What was it that expeled the angels out of heaven, & made Devils in the regions of hell? It was sin. What was it that drove our first parents out of Paradice, where they enjoyed the presence of God their maker? It was sin. What was it that introduces misery into our world but sin? Why was it that God destroyed the inhabitents of the old world with water &c. but sin. Why was it that God destroyed the Egytians in the red Sea & slew the children in the wilderness, and permitted none who came up out of Egypt save Caleb & Joshua, to enter into the promised land? It was for sin. Why was it that God permitted his own people to be overcome by the Chaldeans, & carried captive into babalon, to be subdued under the government of the Roman Emperors, and controled by their petty Kings, but for their sin? What was it introduced misery with its long catalogue of woes into our world once the seat of heavenly bliss? It was sin. How is it that death in all the dreadfulness of its form, & awfulness of its consequences sweeps away one generation after another, and will soon sweep us? It is sin. — For sin when it is finished bringeth forth Death. — & all being by nature such great sinners, there must be a change, before we can be prepared for heaven; and if we have but experienced this great change, we shall exclaim with the apostle in the words Blessed —

MR. HUDSWELL'S WRITING.

The Rev. William Atherton, from Middleton in Lancashire, succeeded at Bingley, Jan. 3, 1841. Though he had not enjoyed the advantages of a college training, yet by energy, strength of mind, and fluency of utterance, his powerful, dramatic, and impressive preaching drew large audiences to hear him; necessitating internal alterations at the chapel to afford accommodation. The church membership was largely augmented. The Sunday School was crowded, and the chapel had to be enlarged in 1845. In the same year Morton Chapel was erected to seat 340 people, though services had been held there for many years. With great reluctance the people at Bingley submitted to Mr. Atherton's removal to Idle, and he left with great regret, though feeling it to be his duty. They presented to him a valuable service of plate. Mr. Atherton entered on his labours at Idle on Oct. 1, 1848, where a new school was completed in the Spring of 1849; and a new chapel was opened on Good Friday, 1850. He was suddenly cut off, dying at Wigan, July 16, 1850, in his 34th year. A portrait of him will be found in "Nonconformity in Idle," and a fine eulogium in the Congregational Year Book, 1863.

The Rev. William Orgar (untrained), from Stubbin, Elscar, followed Mr. Atherton at Bingley after two years' interval. He held the pastorate for eleven years, and removed to Morley in 1861. To him also, as a token of their esteem, the people at Bingley presented a handsome service of plate. In 1855 there were about 200 scholars in the Sunday School. A memoir of Mr. Orgar appears in the Yorkshire Congregational Year Book, 1874, two pages.

The Rev. Ebenezer Sloane Heron (untrained), who had laboured in Bradford and Denholme, but had more recently ministered at Ilkeston, in Derbyshire, for six years, accepted a unanimous invitation from both church and congregation to settle at Bingley in Nov., 1861. The congregation was in an apathetic state at this time, but a new life became manifest early in 1862. On July 20, 1862, to supply a need and in commemoration of the Ejectments of August 24, 1662, the corner-stone of a Memorial Bi-centenary Sunday School was laid by Alderman Brown, of Bradford. The School, which cost £690, was opened with great demonstration, Nov. 19, 1862; when Mr. W. Murgatroyd, J.P., Rev. Dr. Campbell, Rev. J. P. Chown, and others took part.

A very brief "History of Independency in Bingley" by Joseph Stephenson, was reprinted in a 12-page pamphlet in 1863 by Edward Baines & Sons, Leeds; from the "Congregational Register," W.R. Yorks., of that year.

In 1864 the people of Cottingley built a Town Hall there, and the inhabitants who had mostly attended Bingley Chapel and the preaching station at Cottingley, commenced Congregational services in their new hall. A most disastrous dispute arose between Mr. Heron and the bulk of his congregation, which resulted in a temporary secession, the seceders worshipping for a time in the

Oddfellows' Hall; and as reconciliation seemed impossible a law-suit was instituted, and Mr. Heron was ejected. Mr. Heron on leaving Bingley, bought a farm in Tennessee with subscription given to him here. From Nov., 1865, to 1867, at least three pamphlets and six fly-sheets were printed, containing the bitterest remarks that could be penned by both sides. "Bingley Chapel Case: Evidence of the

Rev. E. S. Heron.

Rev. Daniel Fraser, D.D., and the Rev. Ebenezer Sloane Heron," 16 pages, no date or printer's name. "A Tale of Christmas Eve; or a New Version of Paradise Lost, which did *not* appear in the 'Yorks. Post,' Dec. 26th, 1866; corrected by Toney Eavesdropper, Bingley." 16 pages, Harrison & Son, Bingley. Mr. Thomas Rushforth is stated to have been author of this rhyme. "An Apology for the

Minister and Friends of the Independent Chapel, Bingley, 1867." 31 pages, Wm. Green, Myrtle Place, printer.

Dr. J. M. Heron, a Medical Missionary at the Royal Palace in Corea, 1889, is son of the Rev. E. S. Heron, of Bingley.

The REV. J. H. J. TAYLOR, of Colne (trained at Bristol), followed Mr. Heron at Bingley, but resigned the pastorate after four years, and withdrew from the ministry.

The REV. JOSEPH MARTIN followed, Oct. 1, 1876, and still presides over a large and happy community. In Jan. 1883, a Chapel Manual, 16 pages, was first issued, printed by Edward Foulds, Ireland Bridge. In 1889 extensive alterations were made in the chapel interior at a cost of £850.

In 1855 Harden and Morton Pastorates were both vacant. In 1861, Mr. M. A. Wilkinson, previously a Wesleyan Methodist, from Bradford, was settled at Harden, where were 170 scholars. Morton had 150 scholars, but no resident minister. Mr. Wilkinson removed to Pickering in 1885. The Rev. John Milnes, M.A., from Airedale College, was ordained at Morton in May, 1864, but both were vacant before 1870. The Rev. J. Paul Ritchie (trained at Airedale) settled at Harden in 1871, but left in 1875 for Bradford. Rev. Edwin Morton was at Harden a short time.

The Rev. Joseph Harrison, a native of Craven, had held pastorates in Essex and Cambridgeshire; became minister to the Baptist congregation at Bingley, but a Baptist minister officiated at the bi-monthly communion service. He was a plain-spoken, earnest man, inclined to Baxterianism. He then kept a school, and formed an Independent congregation at Wilsden before 1793, during which year he resided at Harden Beck. In 1795 Wilsden Chapel was built for him, and a parsonage erected soon after. He removed to Bury soon after 1801, but came to Allerton afterwards, where a chapel was built for him in 1814. The second minister at Wilsden was the Rev. Samuel Baines, a native of Ossett, born 1773, a student under the Rev. W. Vint, and pastor at Wilsden from June, 1806, till 1834. He married Mr. George Tweedy's daughter, and their son may be well regarded as the Cottingley benefactor. The Rev. S. Baines died May 27, 1835.

---o---

THE SOCIETY OF FRIENDS OR QUAKERS.

We must briefly refer to one of the strictest of the Puritan off-springs—the followers of George Fox—of whom local items will be found in Fox's *Journals* and Besse's *Sufferings of the Quakers*. In addition to these, the following are taken from the Keighley Quaker Register as printed in my " Yorkshire County Magazine " :—

		Old Style.
Mary Brigg d. Thos. of Harding	Born	25.1.1676
Jereh. s. Ric. Shackleton	...	30.8.1683
John ,, ,,	...	17.3.1686
Ric. s. Ric. Shackleton of Harding	...	31.9.1688

164   ANCIENT BINGLEY.

Hanh. d. John Taylor, Harding	20.1.1690
Ruth d. Timothy & Esther Maud, Castlefield	2.9.1690
Roger s. Rich Shackleton, Hardein... ...	8.5.(July)1691
Martha d. Tim. Mawde	28.10.1692
Moses s. Tim. Esther Maude, Castlefd ...	5.11.1693
Mary d. Ric. Shackleton, Harden	15.1.1694
Mercy d. Tim. & Esther Maud, Castlefd. ...	6.12.1695
Abm s. Ric. Sarah Shackleton, Harden ...	27.8.1696
Debora, Tim & Esther Mawd, Castld. ...	10.9.1697
Hanh. ... ,, ,, ...	22.3.1699
Tim. ... ,, ,, ...	27.8.1700
Mary ... ,, ,, ...	17.9.1701
Tim ... ,, ,, Crossflat ...	14.10.1703
Jonathan } Jonathn & Lidia Taylor, Ravenroid Rebeckah }	19.9.1705
Elijah s. John & Sarah Lee, Ravenroid ...	7.11.1723
Hanh. Thos. & Hanh. Lister, Gilstead ...	20.5.1726
Esther d. Tim. Maud junr., & Ann, wife of, Gauthorp Hall	3.2.1727
Tim. s. Tim. Maud junr., & Ann, Ravenroid...	3.1.1729
Wm. s. Timothy ,, ,, ,, ...	12.6.1732
Joshua s. John & Debora (née Maude) Stansfield, Morton	6.12.1735
Esther s. John Stansfield. Morton	16.1.1737
Ann d. John & Ann Stansfield.	6.5.1738
Cornelia d. Wm. & Cornelia Horsfall, Haworth	21.10.1765

Richd. Shackleton, of Harding, bachelor, Sarah d. Thos. Brigg, Calversike hill, spins., mar. at Calversike 30.9.1682.

Mar. of Jeremy Brigg of Calversike to Eliz'th. Davis of Kildwick, at Shackleton's House, Harden, 1690.

Mar. of Zach. s. Zach. Yewdall of Idle and Martha Pearson of Thornton, at Timothy Maud's Castlefield, Bingley, in Keighley Meeting, 1694.

Wm. Wade of Steeton and Eliz'th Atkinson of Colne mar. at R. Shackleton's, Harden in 1695.

James Hustler, Bingley, yeoman, and Elizth Rawson, Stubbin House, Bingley, widow, mar. at Rawdon, 13.5.1698. The intention was pub. at Braithwaite.

Jas. Wilcock, Calverley parish, son of John W., Maningham, broad clothiers, married Phebe d. Jerem. Heaton, Ravenroid, Kersey maker, at Kighley Meeting Place 4.4.1712.

Robt. Walker, Healey in Batley, & Ruth d. Tim. Maud Crossflatts, mar. at Tim. Maud's house 2.12.1714.

Tim. Maud, junr., & Ann Walker, intention published 26.3.1725.

Thos. s. Christr. Foster, Rilstone, and Mary d. Wm. Lister, Bingley, 1729.

John s. Joshua Stansfield of Sandbeds, Bingley, and Deborah d. Tim. and Esther Maud of Gauthorpe Hall, at the Public Meeting House at Springhead nr. Bingley 28.8.1733.

Some are buried at the Friends' Burial Ground at Crossflatts, Bingley. Burials.
1675.5.6. John s. Joshua Dawson of Jackfield in Bingley, bur. at Coversett hill, 7th
1682.21 Nov. George s. John Millner of Harding, bur. at Calversick hill, Keighley, 23rd.
1689.2.9. Anthony Browen of Harding at Calversike, 5th.
Joshua & Mary Dawson, late of Addingham, were bur. in 1690 and 1692 respectively.
1695.6.3. Moses s. Tim. Maud, Castlefields.
1696.25.6. Hannah   ,,   ,, ...   27th.
1700.8.2. Elizth Shackleton, Harden, widdow, aged; bur. 12th.
1700.23.10. Timoth s. Tim. Mawd, Castlefd., bur. at Calversike on 27th, aged 2 months.
1701.18.5. Mary child of Timothy and Esther Mawd aged 11 days; first that was buried at Crossflatts.
1703.28.2. Sarah wife Richard Shackleton, Harden, aged 45 years, 5 months.
1703.2.4. John s. John Taylor, Hill-end, Harden, about 28 yrs., bur. in Tim. Mawd's ground at Crossflatts on 6th.
1704.24.10. Ric. s. Ric. Shackleton, Harden, 16 yrs., bur. at Crossflatts on 28th.
1705.29.1. Richard Shackleton, Harden, above middle age, bur. at Crossflatts, 1st, 2nd mo.
1706.29.2. Jonth. s. Jonth. & Lidya Taylor, Ravenroid, abt. 32, bur. at Crossflatts.
1707.24.3. Jonth. Taylor, Ravenroid, about 32 (see last entry), bur. at Crossflatts.
1709.25.7. James Hustler, Bingley, aged.
1711.16.2. Thos. England, Lees in Bingley, bur. at Kighley Meeting house, aged.
1712.19.2. Frances Myers, widdow, of Crossflatts, bur. there, aged.
1713.24.7. Saml. s. Wm. Lister, Bingley, 9 months, bur. at K.
1716.20.4. Sarah d. Jonth. Bottomley, Hainworth in Bingley, bur. at Calversike.
1726.12.9. Elleanor wife Wm. Lister, Bingley, bur. at Friends place, Whitby.
1728.21.12. Sarah Roads, Lees in Bingley, above 80, bur. at Kighley.
1732.1.10. Robt. Walker of Bingley, bur. in his orchard at Bingley, abt. 40 yrs. of age.
1732. Jerry Frankland, Elwick, a leading Quaker.
1733.—.1. Judith d. Joshua Stansfield, by first wife, of Sandbeds; aged 16, bur. at Keighley.

1733.—.2. Jeremiah Heaton, Ravenroid, about 80, bur. at Crossflatts, on 29th.
1734.13.3. Timothy Maud, Gauthorp Hall, 73rd year, buried at Crossflatts on 16th.
1734.21.8. Sarah wid. Jereh. Heaton, Ravenroid, aged 88, bur. in Friends' burying place at Crossflatts.
1763.22.7. James Hustler, died at Dub, near Bingley, aged about 85, bur. at Crossflatts.
1765.25.10. Cornelia wife Wm. Horsfall, Haworth, dau. Joshua Brigg of Calversike hill, aged 28, bur. 1765 ; her dau. Cornelia bur. in 1766.
1767. Jeremy Marshall of East Morton, yeoman, a leading Quaker at this time.

Amongst those who left this country during the persecutions of 1683-4—the very climax of intolerance, when every prison in the land was full of dissenters—was John Parker, of Ravenroid (a Quaker), who settled in Pennsylvania, where his descendants still reside.

THE BAPTIST CAUSE.

Amongst the pupils of Mr. W. Hustler at Bingley, about the year 1675, was John Moore, a native of "Okeworth Hall, near Kighley," born 1662. He had been under the tuition of Mr. John Moore, of Pendle, before he became a scholar at Bingley. He became a Baptist under the ministrations of the celebrated itinerant William Mitchell of Rawdon and Heaton, and several local dwellings were licensed for preaching in their names, but few causes were permanently established in this neighbourhood by them. Mr. Moore became an ordained minister and settled at Northampton, where he published a volume of sermons preached in Heaton, &c., in 1703, 1711 and 1719. The book was printed in 1722, and reprinted in 1854. The isolated families of the Baptist persuasion who resided here from that time to 1760, journeyed to the chapels at Haworth, Sutton, &c. The Rev. John Beatson, who is said to have been a native of Cottingley, became the minister at Sutton in Craven in or before 1768, but removed to Hull in 1770. His wife died in 1774, and the Rev. James Hartley, of Haworth, preached her funeral sermon which was printed. Mr. Beatson also was an author. The estimable John Fawcett of Bradford, (afterwards the Rev. Dr. Fawcett of Hebden Bridge), born in Jan. 1740, married Susannah, the eldest daughter of John Skirrow of Bingley, who was about six years older than her husband. They were married about 1759. She died March 30th, 1810, and the learned Doctor in July, 1817. Mr. Skirrow had been one of the leading Methodists up to the time of his daughter's marriage, and there can be little doubt that his son-in-law had much to do with his change of theological tenets, and thus to the formation of the Baptist Chapel at Bingley. Mr. Skirrow, previously an energetic local preacher and class-leader amongst the Wesleyans at Bingley, was charged with preaching Calvinistic doctrines. The Superintendent of the District severely censured him, and publicly excluded him and nearly the whole of his class, expelling him from the pulpit and the chapel which he had been a principal means of erecting. Mr. Fawcett, then a member of the Baptist Church at Bradford, preached a sermon at Bingley, and baptized Mr. Skirrow and nine other persons in the river Aire. This led to the formation of the Baptist Church in Bingley. At first the congregation met in a room, and were ministered to by Mr. Fawcett and neighbouring ministers and local preachers. In 1764 a chapel was erected in the Main Street, where the new Co-operative Stores now stand; in which undertaking the Rev. James Hartley, of Haworth, rendered considerable assistance. In 1765, Mr. Butterworth, a member of the Baptist Church at Goodshaw, came to labour as minister, but he only remained a short time.

In 1768, Mr. John Dracup, a native of Idle, was ordained, and his stay at Bingley was short. He removed to Rochdale, then to Steep Lane near Hebden Bridge, for 17 years, then to Rodhill end, and again for 11 years to Steep Lane, where he died March 28th, 1795. The Bingley pulpit was supported by local ministers and laymen till 1779 when Mr. William Hartley came, and was ordained by the Revs. W. Crabtree of Bradford, and John Fawcett, Wainsgate, near Hebden Bridge. He retired at the close of 1790 owing to disputes in the Bingley church, removing first to Newcastle and thence to Stockton, where he died at the age of 82. I find him recorded as minister at Halifax from Dec. 1792 to Sept. 1795, when he settled at Lockwood until Nov. 1804. He was a member of Wainsgate and minister at Halifax from 1772-6, before he came to Bingley.

The Rev. Joseph Harrison, who had been Independent Minister at Skipton, settled over the Baptist cause here, and occupied the pulpit with great acceptance for about three years, during which time galleries were erected in the chapel. He was, however, never ordained pastor of the church, nor did he administer the Lord's Supper. Troubles began, and his ministry ended abruptly about 1800. Mr. Abraham Greenwood became pastor. In 1806, Mr. John Greenwood succeeded his name-sake, and held the office till 1811.

During the years 1811 to 1820, the pulpit was supplied by locals again, and by students from Horton Academy. Amongst the most popular supply was William Garnett, a member of the Baptist church at Idle, who rendered considerable assistance to the destitute church. He sometimes reminded his hearers that his tongue was not tipped with silver, and that he had never rubbed his back against the walls of an academy. Long neglect greatly reduced the number of the congregation, so an effort was made to secure a resident minister.

Mr. Bottomley, a student at Horton, accepted the unanimous call to the pastorate, and he was ordained in May 1820. He resigned in 1825, having laboured with considerable success.

Mr. McKeog was then invited to occupy the pulpit. In consequence of the chapel roof being deemed insecure, it was removed about this time, and an enlargement took place at considerable cost. This was followed by expensive legal proceedings, and events of a very painful nature, in which the minister according to the people's statement took a wicked part. The church was broken up, and the chapel doors were closed for eight months.

In Nov. 1831, the place was re-opened for divine worship by Mr. Wm. Fawcett, of Ewood Hall, late of Sutton. He was from Hebden Bridge church, and had been minister at Barnoldswick. In 1832 the church was re-formed, and Mr. D. Taylor, a Horton student, was ordained pastor. In 1837 he removed to Hedon.

In 1841, Mr. W. C. Bottomley was invited to return, and he accepted the call. There were then 33 members, an increase of seven during the year. They had four preaching stations, and a Sunday School with 36 teachers and a hundred scholars.

The Rev. Miles Oddy, formerly Baptist minister at Haworth retired to Bingley after 45 years service there, in 1830, and died at Bingley in March, 1841, aged 85 years.

After Mr. Bottomley, the ministers have been Messrs. Rodway, Burton, Dawson, Forth, Hanson, Cossey, and Lewis successively.

Copy of Tablet removed from the old Baptist Chapel to Bingley Cemetery—

"In Memory of Edward, son of John Skirrow, of Dubb, he died March 1st, 1785, aged 41 years.

Also of the above John Skirrow, he died Nov. 22nd, 1785, aged 75 years.

Also of Jane, wife of the above John Skirrow, she died May 31st, 1797, aged 86 years.

And also of John and Elizabeth, son and daughter of Timothy Skirrow, of Low Laithe, and grandchildren of the above John, who died in their infancy.

BAPTIST CHURCH, 1897.

"Why should we weep for those who die in Jesus and are blest;
Their happy spirits upward fly to their eternal rest."

Also Elizabeth, daughter of the said John Skirrow, who died May 6th, 1816, aged 62 years.

Also of the above-named Timothy Skirrow, who died Nov. 30th, 1824, aged 76 years.

The remains of the above with others, were removed from the old Baptist Chapel, and re-interred here Nov. 24th, 1877."

CULLINGWORTH BAPTISTS.—In the summer of 1835, two ministers in the neighbourhood, encouraged by a liberal promise of assistance from a tradesman in Cullingworth, consulted together for the establishment of a Baptist interest in the place. Having obtained a room called the Lodge, it was opened in Feb. 1836 for divine worship, and the attendance and good spirit were encouraging. In March, a Sunday School was established with great promises of success. In May, Mr. Harvey, a student at Horton College, consented to occupy the pulpit during the holidays, and his services were very acceptable. On the 15th of June, 1836, seven persons were baptized in the stream at the bridge, and a church was formed consisting of twenty-two persons. Messrs. Godwin, Saunders, Foster and Jordan took part in the ceremony. In Oct., 1837, the chapel was opened for worship, and in January 1837, Mr. Harvey consented to become minister, but in March 1838 he resigned, much to the regret of the people. By depression of trade they had many difficulties to encounter. After his removal the cause became greatly enfeebled, the numbers declined: an attempt was made to unite the churches of Cullingworth and Bingley, but that was found impracticable. Students and locals supplied the pulpit till March 1842, when Mr. J. Green, of Soham, accepted the pastorate. There were then 50 members, and a school with 45 teachers and 110 scholars.

PRIMITIVE METHODISM IN BINGLEY PARISH.

Keighley and Bingley were missioned in this cause by the Rev. Thomas Batty in the summer of 1821. He laboured most successfully in the streets and a settled congregation was gathered. On Sunday, Sept. 16, 1821, he conducted the first Primitive Methodist Love-feast in a large wool-warehouse in Keighley, and just after the service had concluded the floor gave way with a tremendous crash. The building was three storeys high, and the meeting was held in one of the upper rooms. The people fell down into the lower room, and sixty persons were injured, and a woman died through her injuries. It was feared the cause would receive its death-blow with this accident, but increased earnestness added new converts. The Keighley ministers established a branch in Bingley, holding services in the streets and in cottages, until chapels were built. East Morton chapel was opened Feb. 17, 1828; Wilsden in 1843, Harecroft in 1852, Denholme in 1884. The first Bingley Primitive Methodist Chapel was in York Place, and was bought by Mr. Harrison who pulled it down and erected a larger edifice for his printing works, but it is now used by the Liberal Club. The New Chapel was erected in St. John Street, Hill Street, and branches have been established at Denholme Clough, Ryecroft and Crossflatts.

LIBERAL CLUB, BINGLEY.

The following is a list of the travelling preachers:—

1821, Rev. T. Batty
1822, Rev. J. Hewson
1823-4, Rev. J. Clewer
1825-6, Rev. J. Ambler
1826-7, Rev. J. Bowes
1827-8, Rev. J. Spencer
1828-9, Revs. J. Browning and J. Graham
1829-31, Revs. F. N. Jersey and T. Page
1831-33, Rev. J. Clewer
1833-5, Revs. R. Kay and M. Mose
1836-7, Revs. S. Tillotson and J. Crampton
1837-8, Revs. R. Hill and R. Keely
1838-9, Revs. R. Hill and A. Gee
1839-40, Revs. R. Hill and T. Hatfield
1840-2, Revs. M. Lee and A. Kirkland
1842, Rev. R. Davies
1843, Rev. D. Tuton
1844, Rev. J. McPherson
1845, Revs. G. W. Armitage and T. Swindell
1846-7, Revs. G. W. Armitage and J. Clarke
1848-9, Revs. C. Smith and G. Normandale
1849-50, Revs. J. Headley and J. A. Bastow
1850-52, Revs. A. McKechnie and J. Parrot
1852-4, Revs. J. Simpson and R. Tanfield
1854-5, Revs. J. Simpson and H. Crabtree
1855-6, Revs. J. Dodsworth and H. Crabtree
1856-7, Revs. J. Dodsworth and G. Hutchinson

PRIMITIVE METHODIST CHAPEL, BINGLEY.

Bingley was now made a branch of Keighley Circuit, 1857, and the Rev. Richard Brook was the first preacher that lived in Bingley.

1858, Rev. Richard Brook
1859-61, Rev. A. McKechnie
1862, Rev. John Snowden
1863, Rev. Jeremiah Dodsworth, senr.
1864-6, Rev. John Rumfit
1867-9, Rev. Henry Hatherley
1870-1, Rev. William Bennett
1872-4, Rev. Jeremiah Dodsworth, junr.

1875-7, Rev. Thomas Mitchell and
    Richard Stead Blackburn
1878-9, Revs. Thomas Mitchell and
    Benjamin Robinson
1880, Revs. Michael Sullivan and
    Benjamin Robinson
1881, Revs. Michael Sullivan and
    Thomas Shaw
1882-3, Revs. John Swales and
    John Phillips
1884-5, Revs. A. McKechnie and
    John P. Osborne
1886-8, Revs. A. McKechnie and
    John Maylard, supernu.
1889-92, Revs. Mark Knowlson
    and John Maylard
1893-5, Revs. Joseph Hucknall
    and John Maylard
1896, Revs. Wm. Thoseby and
    John Maylard

REV. A. McKECHNIE.

The Rev. John Maylard died Aug. 11, 1896, aged 79.

Bingley became an Independent Circuit in 1864. The Rev. John Simpson published several small works, but he did not reside in Bingley. Rev. J. Dodsworth was author of "The Better Land," and the Rev. A. McKechnie has issued several lectures:—"Right Sort of Stuff to make a Man." "Right Sort of Stuff to make a Woman." "Sugar Plums for Big Babies." "Sugar Candy for Spoiled Husbands."

MORTON BANKS PRIMITIVE METHODIST CHAPEL.

Morton Banks or Riddlesden Primitive Methodist Chapel is in Keighley Circuit. Before the erection of this chapel, services were held in an out-building at Brow Top, Morton Banks. The foundation stone was laid in August, 1843, and the chapel opened Jan. 7, 1844; the trustees being Messrs. Geo. Ickringill, John Ickringill, junr., John Watson, Saml. Thomas and Jas. Emmott, Samuel and Thomas Johnson, William and Frank Weatherall, David Fortune and Thomas Walmsley. In 1896 two vestries were added, and the chapel enlarged. It now will seat 120, and there are 65 scholars and 16 officers and teachers.

MICKLETHWAITE METHODIST FREE CHURCH OR WESLEYAN REFORMERS. This cause began in 1853 in a cottage-house in Micklethwaite, and removed in 1854 to a large room in a farm yard near, till the present chapel was built in 1875. The corner stone was laid April 3, 1875, by J. W. Wright, Esq., who had given the ground, and the chapel was opened Dec. 4, 1875. Although called a United Methodist Free Church it joins with the Wesleyan Reform Union.

At Harden is a Wesleyan Reformers Chapel, and in Bingley the Christian Brethren or Independent Methodists and Salvation Army have places of worship. The Spiritualists formerly held meetings in Bingley, but the society is now defunct.

CHRISTIAN BRETHREN CHAPEL.

WESLEYAN METHODISM.—The "Old Body" have a chapel in Mornington Road, and a Mission held in the Hill Street Day Schools, Bingley, one each also at Gilstead, Eldwick, Morton, Micklethwaite, Riddlesden or West Morton, Harden and Cullingworth. The chapel

WESLEYAN CHAPEL, CASTLEFIELDS.

at Castlefields cost about £1,100. The foundation stone was laid April 22nd, 1871, by Mr. Miller Marshall, of Shipley, and was opened in September. The Sunday School (now numbering 150 scholars) was built later. Services were previously held in a cottage in Well Street. The Wesleyan Chapel at Morton Banks was built in 1883, before which date services were held in a room over two cottages at Barley Cote, and known as Barley Cote Chapel. There are now about 80 scholars in the Sunday School. As the full records of the Methodists here have been gathered by the Rev. J. Ward into a small volume, and by my esteemed but departed friend Hartley Hartley in a lecture and in an article in the *Methodist Recorder*, Dec. 1893, I refer the reader to those sources at present.

A Chronological Chapter.

BINGLEY has taken its due share in all the events of the past four hundred years, and I need only record the main local items which link its history with that of the nation. It would be easy to elaborate this chapter to any extent but space demands that it must be condensed. Of the struggles of the Wars of the Roses I have nothing of local interest to record, the common people were becoming emancipated from feudal serfdom, the yeomanry were combining manufacturing and farming, religious freedom was gaining ground, the power of Kings was challenged by a new aristocracy, and the general prosperity of the country began with the three-fold Reformation against Romanism, King-craft and Ignorance.

A School existed in Bingley in Roman Catholic times, and as will be found in the chapter on Charities, so early as 1529 certain lands were appropriated for the maintenance of a schoolmaster.

I have not met with the names of the Bingley men who fought at the sore battle of Flodden Field in September 1513; but besides Henry Currer, of Farnhill, at least eleven Morton men followed the "Shepherd" Lord Clifford to this conflict;—John Rogerson with a bow, able horse and requirements, Richard Holymake, William Butterfield, William Rogerson, and William Sharppe with bows, and John Fuller, William Leche, John Leche, William Adamson, Edmund Dobson and Adam Wodde, bill-men. As about fifty Keighley men joined, it is probable that an equal number at least went from Bingley.

In 1524 (15 Henry VIII.), parliament made a grant to the King to assist him to fight the French, and from the Skyrack Wapontake return, we learn the names of the chief inhabitants and their relative wealth by the sums they were required to pay.

VILLA DE BYNGLAY.—Thomas Megelay for goods, 20s. John Bene for goods, 5s. Antony Eltofts, gent., for lands, 10s. Thomas Eltofts for labour, 4d. Crystofer Rauson for lands, 12d. Thomas Morgatroyt for lands, 12d. Roger Thornton for goods, 12d. Richard Wilkynson for goods, 12d. Edward Fether for labour, 4d. John Elyngpage for labour, 4d. William Bryster for labour, 4d. Robert Kyghelay for labour, 4d. John Mawblay for labour, 4d. John Ferrand for labour, 4d. Henry Megelay for labour, 4d. Antony Forster for labour, 4d. William Long for labour, 4d. John Morgatrowyd for labour, 4d. Hugh Glover for labour, 4d. Total 19. Sum—£2-3-0.

VILLA DE MORTON.—Walter Paslow for lands, 13s. 4d. Costene Mawyd for lands, 4s. William Rogerson for lands, 12d. Arthur Mawde for lands, 12d. John Rogerson for goods, 12d. Richard Buttler for goods, 12d. John Beanlands for labour, 4d. Edmond Dobson for goods, 12d. Thomas Buttler for goods, 12d. William Wod for goods, 12d. Total 10. Sum—£1-4-8.

The villa of Bayldon has only seven names; Ylklay, six; Haworth, eight, sum 12s. 2d. Schyplay, William Pykkard, only, for 40s. guds, 12d. Bradford had twenty-three, sum £4-2-10. For this purpose lands were assessed at 12d. in the pound; goods at 6d.; wages or labour at 6d. in the pound.

From time to time the county has had to rearrange the township rates. On the 44th Elizabeth the proportions in this district were: Baildon 5d., Ilkley 6d., Morton 6d., Bingley 9d., Otley 10d. In 1584 the proportions were Bayldon 3s., Ylkeley 3s., Morton 2s., Byngley 10s., Otley 18s. (From original MS. in my possession.)

In September, 1574, as at the rebellion of 1537, the Pilgrimage of Grace, the Catholics of Craven were agitating for the restoration of the ancient faith, and amongst the adherents to the old creed who were supposed to favour Mary, Queen of Scots, were Mr. Paslew of Riddlesden, and Sir John Neville of Liversedge. Paslew, the abbot of Whalley, who was hanged for taking part in the Pilgrimage, was a member of the Riddlesden family. Neville's rent-book for Liversedge includes some outside rents at Bingley, and in the record we meet with the usual stipulations, which were never enforced, of requiring the tenant to pay, *if demanded*, a rose, a peppercorn, a hen, &c.

BINGLEY.—John Beanland, of Morton, hath a messuage and croft, and certain acres of land for the which he payeth Carye yearly iis. iid. And unto Mr. Paslewe, who they say is their Chief Lord and under age, and in custodie of Mr. Lee, xiiis. iiijd.—And the Earl of Cumberland a hen yearly, which they call a castle hen.

MORTON.—John Turner and Henry Turner, for the like messuage in Morton to Mr. Carye iiis. xd. He payeth to Mr. Paslewe yearly viiis. viid., and to Skipton Castle a hen likewise.

PRESTETHORP.—Thos. Green, of Prestethorpe, hath a cottage and a gardensteede, for the which he payeth yearly to Mr. Carye xiid.

BINGLEYE.—William Farrande, a cottage in Bingleye with a gardensteede in Bingleye iiid."

The Parish Registers, it will be seen, date from 1577.

It is about 320 years since our Yorkshire worthy, Christopher Saxton,* brought out his remarkable maps, and I was amused to find the same names on a sign board at Morton this year, the family coming from Leeds and Dewsbury, the old homes of the Saxtons. On page 47 will be found a copy of the Bingley part of Speed's Map, 1610. John Speed copied, as did Morden and Bowen (page 48), from Saxton's careful survey. From that date to this, we have short accounts of the district as recorded by casual visitors, two of which, besides Dodsworth's as given in a previous chapter, we reprint.

Harrison, the old topographer, carefully describes the courses of the Yorkshire rivers. He says that "the Air, after receiving a water from Sutton and two rylls from the north, runneth by Reddlesden, and over against this towne the Laycock and the Worthe doe meet

---

* Died at Leeds in 1587.

withall in one channel as the Morton water doth on the north, somewhat lower; thence it goeth to Risheforthe Hall, and so to Bingley."

Dr. Whitaker says, "Bingley affords a rich, woody scene, commanding two valleys almost equally beautiful. In the smaller of these valleys is Old St. Ives, which commands a well-wooded vale, in

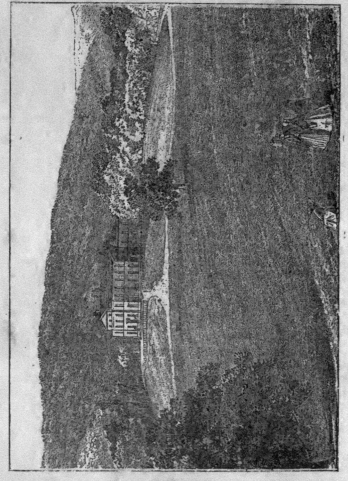

Old St. Ives, taken down in 1859 by Wm. Ferrand, Esq., and Harden Grange built there.

which are many beautiful knolls clothed with timber. From these woods the late proprietor, by means of judicious thinnings, derived for many years a considerable income, without injuring their picturesque effect. On the whole, in extent of view, richness of scenery, and wild and rocky distances, every situation in Airedale to the northward must yield to St. Ives."

In the reign of Queen Elizabeth there was a general stir in purchasing and selling land in the West Riding. The profits from the woollen manufacture enabled the smaller farmers to command ready-money wherewith to secure small estates from the older yeomanry, who had lands but no great amount of capital. Many of the families had sons in London and Hull who became immensely wealthy; and we only give a few examples of transfers (out of the many that might be recorded) to indicate these families.

1581. Christopher Mawde alias Mohaute, brother of Arthur Mawde, owed Anthony Fell of Morton Banks, yeoman, £160.

1587, June 1. To all christian people, Anthony ffell of Morton Banck, in the parishinge of Binglaie, yeoman, sendeth greeting in our lord god everlastinge, granted his messuage in the occupation of Robert and Edmund Turner at the yearly rent of vs., a messuage in the occupation of Christopher Broadley of East Morton, a messuage in the occupation of John Hargreaves, ditto John Butler, ditto Jenit Stephenson, ditto Brian Lister, ditto Christopher Beanlands; to John Asden of Scofeld in Cowline, and Wm. Sharpe of Harrodhill, Keighley, for the proper use of James Asden of Scofeld, yeoman, Ann, Margaret and Isabell, daughters of said Anthony fell for eight years, and after that time to the use of Thomas Fell, eldest son of said Anthony.

1587, 30 Jan. A Latin deed in the writing of the great local conveyancer of that time, Lawyer Midgley, records, To all the faithful in Christ, George Rodes of East Morton, clothier, conveyed a close called Over Intacke, (land *taken in* from the moor), a close called the High Croft end, and the Middle high croft and his messuage in East Morton, bought from Francis Paslew of Methley, gent., 33 Eliz., to Thomas ffell of East Morton, yeoman.

1595, 24 Jan. Indenture between George Rodes and Jennett his wife, and the said Thomas ffell, son of Anthony ffell, deceased, whereby Rodes sold to Thomas ffell a close called Brode Yng in East Morton, abutting on the lands of Sir Thomas ffayrffax knight, late in the occupation of Wm. Whittingham, purchased from ffrauncis Paslewe of Riddlesden, gent.

1597, 30 Jan. Indenture between George Rodes, clothier, and Bryan Lister, youngest son of Thomas Lister, yeoman, Morton, for £37, G. R. sold the messuage where he dwelleth with barn, orchard, garden, fold, &c., except the orchard in the middle high close, with common rights, turf and stone digging, owing suite to the Courte of the Mannor of Riddlesden, and suite to the Milne there.

1617, May. Nicholas Walker of Gawthorpe, gent., conveyed lands at Gilstead to William Currer of Staple Inn, London, gent.

1636. John Bynnes of Rishworth, Esquire, and Elizabeth his wife, conveyed lands to Edmond Farrand, of Bingley, tanner, as did

L

their son Abraham Binns, Esquire, who sold Ryshworth estate to William Busfeild, Esquire, in 1672.

In 1621, Dodsworth visited Bingley, and records (Harl. MSS., 1997), the arms he noticed in Bingley Church. These arms were restored in the East Window in 1848, by Johnson Atkinson Busfeild, Esq.

The following lists serve as a census of the population of the parish in 1621 and 1627.

1621. Subsidy Roll: Wm. Busfeild of Leeds, gentleman, principal collector for the Wapentake of Skyrack, under the seal of Henry Savile, Knt. & Bart., and Henry Goodrick, Knt; 1s. 4d. in the pound for land and 1s. for goods.

BINGLEY:	£	s.	d.		£	s.	d.
Anthony Walker	4,	Tax 5	4	William Smith	1,	Tax 1	4
Abraham Bynnes	3,	,, 4	0	John Dobson	1,	,, 1	4
William Currer	2,	,, 2	8	Robert Blakey	1,	,, 1	4
Edwd. Brooksbank	2,	,, 2	8	John Bynnes	1,	,, 1	4
John Oldfield	2,	,, 2	0	Robt. Buttler	1,	,, 1	4
Willm. Franke	1,	,, 1	4	John Rawsonn	1,	,, 1	4
John Rawsonn	1,	,, 1	4	Michael Dobsonn	1,	,, 1	4
Thomas Elison	1,	,, 1	4	Samuel Longbothome	1,	,, 1	4
William Whitakars	1,	,, 1	4	William Walters	1,	,, 1	4
John Murgatroyd	1,	,, 1	4	Thomas Oldfield	1,	,, 1	4
Arthur Rawson	1,	,, 1	4	Alice Hudson	1,	,, 1	4

The above were taxed for land; the following were large tradespeople or merchants, and taxed for goods:

Robert Mydgley	3,	,, 3	0	John Mylner	3,	,, 3	0
Thomas Blakey	3,	,, 3	0	Thomas Leach	3,	,, 3	0
William Waddington	3,	,, 3	0	Elizabeth Long	3,	,, 3	0

Baildon had only three taxed for lands and five for goods: total 24s. 4d. Esholt was then held by two gentlewomen in equal portions, Dorothy Thompson and Elizabeth Sherburne. Leeds raised £10 5s. 6d. Otley £1 7s. 4d.

MORTON:		£	s.	d.	
	John Rishworthe	6 land,	tax 8	0	
	Thomas Mawde	3 ,,	,, 4	0	
	Thomas Brooke	1½ ,,	,, 2	0	
	Alex. Wood	1 ,,	,, 1	4	
	William Leighe	1 ,,	,, 1	4	
	Thomas ffell	5 goods	,, 5	0	
	Arthur Currer	4 ,,	,, 4	0	
	Willm. Hanworthe	3 ,,	,, 3	0	
	Thomas Byrrey	3 ,,	,, 3	0	Sum £1-11-8

In 1627, another Subsidy Roll signed by John, Lord Savile, Henry Savile, Bart., Thos. Bland, Knt., was 4s. in the pound, and realized as follows:—

Byngley:	£	s.		£	s.
John Savile, gent.,	3 land;	12.	Thomas Keighley,	1 land;	4
Anthony Walker	4 ,,	16.	John Rawson	1 ,,	4
John Bynnes	3 ,,	12.	Michael Dobson	1 ,,	4
John Dobson	1 ,,	4.	Henry Johnson	1 ,,	4
Henry Rawson	1 ,,	4.	William Waters	1 ,,	4
John Murgatroyd	1 ,,	4.	Thomas Owldfeild	1 ,,	4
William Whittacres	1 ,,	4.	George ffarrand	1 ,,	4
Robert Blake	1 ,,	4.	Henry Butler	1 ,,	4
Thomas Elleson	1 ,,	4.	Robert Walker	1 ,,	4
William Franke	1 ,,	4.	William Waddington,	3 goods;	8
William Midgley	1. ,,	4.	William Kigheley	3 ,,	8
Joshua Bailie	1 ,,	4.	William Smithe	3 ,,	8
Robert Butler	1 ,,	4.	Richard Hardie	3 ,,	8
				Sum £7 10s.	
Morton:	£	s.		£	s.
John Risheworth, gent.	4 land;	16.	Francis Lister	1 land;	4
Thomas Mawde	3 ,,	12.	Christopher Clapham	1 ,,	4
Thomas ffell	1½ ,,	6.	William Hayneworthe	1 ,,	4
Thomas Waters	1 ,,	4.	William Leache	1 ,,	4
Edward Turner	1 ,,	4.		Sum 58s.	

Ilkley raised 42s., Baildon 52s., Leeds £23 10s,, Otley £3 4s.

An assessment made April 28, 1634, by Anthony Fell, Walter Milnes, Isaac Hollings, and John Faireburne, churchwardens;. and George Beaulande, Simeon Collier, Thomas Ellison and John Whitley, overseers, for releivinge of the pore impotent in the parishe was raised as followethe.

Morton 11s. 2d., Micklethwaite with Elwick and Priesthorpe 13s., Harden and Marley, Lees and Hainworth 13s. 2d., Bingley and Cottingley 6s. 2d. Total £2 3s. 6d. Confirmed by T. Fairfax and Richard Sunderland, Justices of the Peace. The amount was raised from 167 ratepayers.

An idea of the management of poor affairs in 1639 may be gathered from the following extract from the Sessions Rolls, which I copied from the originals in 1873.

At Wakefield Sessions, 12 July, 14 Charles I.

Forasmuch as this Court is informed upon the behalfe of diverse poore people inhabitants within the parishe of Bingley, viz:—George Turner, Jane Illingworth and Anne Longbothome, that they, being placed in diverse several cottages within the saide parishe, are fearfull that they are subject to the dangers of the Lawe; and further that there are diverse other poor people, viz:—William Hudson and William Smith, now destitute of houses, and are hereafter likely to be in danger of the Lawe if they should have cottages built or assigned them for their habitations, This Court ordereth that the said parties who have houses already assigned them shall continue without danger of the Lawe, and that the other said parties shall continue and remain in such houses as shall be hereafter assigned unto them by the church-wardens and overseers of the poore there, without danger unto themselves or anie other of the parishioners.

The law referred to was the statute of 31 Eliz. against erecting and maintaining cottages, or converting buildings into cottages, unless four acres of ground at the least of his or her freehold, lying near to such cottage were attached and cultivated, under penalty of £10 for the offence, and £2 a month for occupancy. Market towns were exempted. There was to be no more than one family in any cottage under penalty of 10s. per month. By the Act, 43 Eliz., church-wardens and overseers were allowed to agree with the lord of the manor to build cottages on the waste, or otherwise as ordered by justices, for the impotent poor, also to place an inmate or lodger, or more families than one in one house, hence this application from Bingley.

The great trouble of modern times happened to the nation when the stupidity of the Stuarts hurried on the Civil War. Bingley had its share as is shewn in Joseph Lister's autobiography, and it has always been a tradition that a skirmish took place on Harden Moor, where the soldiers' graves are still shewn. At St. Ives, anciently Harden Grange, may be seen the table on which Fairfax wrote despatches.

Behind St. Ives, on the summit of the moor, with plantations on each side, is an open space where tradition says that about 200 soldiers were interred in the time of Sir Thomas Fairfax. I strongly believe this to be a great exaggeration, for no civil-war tract or local record corroborates it. Various ill-defined mounds covering about a hundred yards in length, may be noticed. The nearest approach we can get to the date of the Harden encampment is in June and July, 1644, before and after the great conflict at Marston Moor, near York. A few war implements, swords and spears, have been found in the parish, bearing further evidence of a skirmish. The Parliamentarians would be quite as likely to bury the slain of either party on the site of the battle as in consecrated ground, and such was the unsettled condition of the vicars and people that the silence of the burial registers of 1642-8 does not disprove that there was no battle. Even the burials of ordinary inhabitants are often left unrecorded. That detachments lingered about here for some years is well known.

In Keighley Church Register we find:—

1643, Dec. 7. A souldier yt was found slaine on the moor, buried.
„ Jan. 16. Two souldiers.
1644, June 18. A souldier of Coll. Crumwalls.
„ June 28. Two souldiers slayne at New Brigge.
„ Feb. 14. Fower souldiers buried.
164⅞, Mch. 25. Humphry Bland, a souldier.

In Bingley Register:

1647, Sep. 24. A Scottisheman, a souldier.
„ Oct. 1. A Scot, a souldier.

St. Ives (formerly Harden Grange), Fairfax Table, &c. *Photo. by H. England, Esq.*

As in the days of the Romans, so at this period the armies must have occasionally crossed Harden Moor on their journeys between York and Manchester, and so late as the 1745 rebellion, bands of Scotch rebels traversed the same road. A Morton man, Oliver Mitchell, found near the Druids Altar, a few years ago, a small box containing Scotch coin.

Under date April, 1655, we meet with an interesting document written by John Bynnes, of Bingley, to his neighbours first, and then to the Justices of Peace, who ordered these "Proposals for the Relief of the Poor" to be put into execution in the West Riding four years after. He complained of defective distribution of alms in the time of dearth and sickness, whereby the old, lame, sick and indigent poor were almost perished, whilst the sturdy, lustful, wasteful and debauched poor were grown more idle and dissolute, spending their week-day earnings in drunkenness on the Lord's Day, no notice being taken thereof by the officers, and begging meat when not working. The law of God and the land say there shall not be a beggar in Christ's Commonwealth. Even the Turks take better course in government. The Churchwardens and Overseers are God's allmoners and responsible to keep the poor from want. It is their duty to lycence any poor to beg. The number of poor has increased, and the monthly assessment groweth colder. Half the charge will do if properly distributed and gospel-like conversation be restored. It is proposed (1) that the officers and discreetest inhabitants take consideration of every poor family, and monthly supplies be given in money. (2). Lycenses to beg be given to such as cannot work, but none others allowed. (3). The Lycensed have districts or begging quarters assigned in the parish for set days, and none out of the parish. (4). To punish the poor who beg without licence, by withholding their other allowances. (5). Work must be provided for them by the town, and their wages assessed. (6). Everyone liable to have poor apprentices, even poor people, have one assigned. (7). One of the lycenced beggars shall keep ward by day for vagrant rogues, to apprehend such, and the wardman to be kept by the village. (8). Money spent wastefully or riotously at funerals should be given to the poor fund.

The Hearth Tax was an imposition of 2s. on every hearth or stove, in all dwellinghouses. It was first demanded in 1662. From the 1672 Tax we get a true estimate of the houses (except smallest cottages) in Bingley. The figure after the name shews where there were more than one fire-place to the house:

Thomas Smith	Mr. Bentley, 3	Edward Skirro, 2
Mary Smith	Michael Slater	Abraham Sharpe
Thomas Keighley, 2	Thos. Scarrow	Jerome Green
William Scott, 3	Thos. Murgatroyde, 6	Arthur Pickles
Robert Leach, 3	Robt. Hardcastle } 3	James Keighley
James Keighley, 2	(p Thos. Rushworth)	Stephen Hogg

ANCIENT BINGLEY.

Jonath. Longbotham	John Rhoades	Robert Illingworth, senr.
Stephen Hudson	Henry Shaw	Robert Illingworth, junr.
Mr Michl Longbotham, 4	Henry Shaw	William Tayler
John Turner	Henry Midgley	Richd. Thackwray
William Hartley	William Midgley	Nichos. Stead, 3
Robt. Emmitt	Robert Midgley	Walter Midgley
Widow Longbothom	Richd. Midgley	Thos. Milner
William Crowther	James Holmes	John Mitchell, 3
Martin Lister, 4	Mr. Ben. ffarrand, 8	Thos. Booth, 5
Rich. Tompson, 2	S. Sunderland, Esq., 8	Widow Heaton, 4
Ed. Lupton, sen., 2	John Wright, 2	James Illingworth, 2
Widow Lupton	John Longley	Stephen Waide
William Lupton	Mr. Benj. ffarrand, 4	George Oldroyde, 4
William Whittacres	Willm. Dobson, 5	Abra. Robinson
Nathan Binns	Abra. Parker, 5	John Clayton, 3
Richd. Garnitt	Thos. Blakey, 4	John Widdop
Jonas Mann	William Morley	Joseph Dawson, 3
Edward Ambler	Thos. Blakey, jun., 2	Richard Francke, 4
Jerom. Tompson, 2	Will. Hall	Isaac Leech, 2
Thos. Dodson	Robt. Hall	Grace Dickinson
James Booth	Ric. Wilkinson, 2	Widow Farrer
Thos. Beane	James Whitakers	Widow Hudson
Samuel Wood	Charles Rogers	James Robinson
Robert Tennant, 2	John Smith	Richard Walker
Thos. Tennant, 2	William Bothomley	Thos. Whitley, 2
Robt. Denby, 3	Charles Waddington	John Rawson, 3
Widow Rawson, 2	Jacob Scott, 2	Thos. Lister, 4
Christopher Garnett	John Smith	Michaell Wade, 2
(torn)	John Pickles	Robert Lupton, 2
John Briggs	Widow Wilkinson	William Marvill, 4
Thos. Haley	Richd. Hargreaves	James Woodhead, 2
William Booth	Richd. Sugden	Robert Blakey, 2
John Ellison, 2	William Longfield	Jonas Appleyard, 4
Jonas Whitacres	Robert Oldfeild	Thos. Rushworth
William Waddington	Walter Waddington	Geo. Hudson
Widow Wilkinson	Widow Smith	John Holdroyd
John Ellison	Constance Waddington	John Hodgson
John Hollingrave	William Waddington	Widow Holmes, 3
John Leach	John Roades	Brian Lister, 2
Geo. Butler	Robert Wright	John Earthburne
John Moore	George Sugden, 2	Thos. Swaine, 2
Richd. Wright	James Holmes	John Lister
Richd. Driver	Roger Shackleton, 4	Total—434(?).
Edward Mercer, 2	Joseph Waide	

These p'sons ffollowing are discharged by certificate:
Nicholas Gleadall, 1   John Hartley, 1   Benj. Clarkhouse, 1
William Clarke, 1   John Kitchin, 1   Omitted by reason of
George Wainman, Collector, Stephen ffarran, Constable. [poverty, 9

ANCIENT BINGLEY.

Baildon had 109 taxed, Barwick-in-Elmet 278, Ilkley 114, Leeds 2479, Otley 278.

Morton:

Mr. Edmond Starkie, 16
Mrs. Crooke, 4
Thos. Mawson
Willm. Mitchell, 3
Christr. Beanland
Mercy Berry, 2
Abra. Leech
Thos. ffell
John Lister
Thos. Lister, 3
John Walters, 2
John Smith
Widow Hainsworth
Thos. Lister, senr., 2
Michael Bradley
Michael Wood, 3
George Turner
John Wood, senr.
Abra. Longbotham
Henry Turner, 2

Will. Rusforth
Anthony Inkeringall
Jer. Phillips, 2
Christr. Berry
Christr. Smith, 3
Thomas Leach, 2
Stephen Wilkinson
John Leach, 2
George Beanland, 2
Willm. Emmott
Will. Blakey
James Atkinson
Thos. Hainworth, junr.
ffran. Smith
Willm. Spence
John Rogers
John Clapham
John Coates
Thos. Sharpe, 2
Thos. Wilkinson, 3

Thos. Smith
Robt. Sugden
Samuell Coates
Thos. Rogers, 3
Richard Hudson
Jona. Shackleton, 4
Thos. Butterfeild
Christr. Calverley
John Hall
Thos. Butterfeild
Robert Wright, 2
John Atkinson
John Maskew
James Widdop, 2
Margaret Wilkinson
Mr. Thos. ffell, 9
John Catley
Total—109.
Omitted by reason of poverty, 2

Roger Hardcastle, Collector; Chrofer. Calverley, Constable.

An exemption was allowed to those who were too poor to pay poor rate and church rate, or who produced a certificate, signed by the Minister and a Churchwarden or Overseer, testifying that the annual value of the house was not more than 20s., and that no one residing in the house occupied lands or had goods and chattels to the value of £10.

I calculate that these lists give about 300 houses, and a population therefore for the whole parish of a little over 1500.

We have previously given Mr. Oliver Heywood's account of the great robbery of Samuel Sunderland, Esquire, of Hill End, Harden, May 11, 1674. An old account gives the story as follows: "The Sunderlands were distinguished both for eminence and opulence.

REV. E. R. LEWIS, (Baptist), *see p.* 168.

One of them resided at Arthing Hall (error for Hill End, near Harden Hall), near Bingley,—a man whose master passion was the amassing of wealth, and whose circumstances gave him every possible opportunity of gratifying his ruling propensity. The system of hoarding prevailed to an almost incredible extent, and he was deemed to be the wealthiest man who had the most coin in his coffers. [The writer had poor authority for such sweeping assertion.] The gentleman in question was so rich that in a private apartment in his house he had two small shelves upon which his bags of money were arranged, and upon which too, there is little doubt, that he often gazed with fond, with foolish, and with dangerous delight. [The writer has again drawn on his imagination, probably, in both these statements. The tradition has been handed down that the gold was stored in an iron box, and though the present Mr. Ferrand had not heard that he owned this box, the Steward was aware of it. Mr. Ferrand took me into an outbuilding to see this box—nearly three feet long and two feet deep—which had been opened lately, and the elaborate lock had snapt with decay. The old family of Rishworth bought an elaborate inlaid oak chest at the Parker Sale, which had descended to them from Samuel Sunderland, Esq., and tradition has handed down for certainly a century that the bags and iron box were deposited in it. It is still a beautiful piece of wood work, with a key the size of an ordinary cottage door key.] Hoarding, in all ages, has acted as a premium upon robbery, and as an incentive to murder. Two men who resided at *Collingham*, reckless, dissipated, and in all probability ruined in their circumstances, determined to repair the effects of their own profligacy by seizing the gold treasured up at Arthing Hall. In order to bewilder their pursuers in the event of alarm, they obtained the agency of a blacksmith in their village to shoe their horses backwards way, meaning no doubt to change their route on return, and thus completely to baffle the human bloodhounds who might be set upon their track. In the dead of the night they broke into Mr. Sunderland's house, they took away nearly the whole of the bags which occupied the first of the shelves, and they succeeded in accomplishing their retreat, notwithstanding that their operations were distinctly heard by Mr. Sunderland's family; and every individual upon the premises was prepared to raise an instant hue and cry as soon as they had gone. So large was the quantity of money with which these men had loaded themselves, that their

THE CHEST.

horses became jaded by the unwonted burden, and they were compelled to throw part of their booty away as they rode over Blackmoor. This money was found soon afterwards by some inhabitants of Leeds. The robbers safely arrived at Collingham, exulting in the successful accomplishment of their enterprize, and they proceeded immediately to make a division of the spoil. Detection however, followed close upon the heels of crime. In the meantime all was consternation at Arthing Hall, the inhabitants of the solitary mansion were involved in dismay, and it was not until some time after the sound of the horses' hoofs had died away, that they ventured to ascertain the extent of their loss. When they opened the door where the treasure had been deposited they found a dog, which the robbers had brought with them, and which in the hurry and confusion of departure had been left without any means of egress from the house. It was instantly perceived that this animal would be the means of effecting the discovery of the culprits. A party well-mounted and armed was soon collected. One of the dog's legs was broken to prevent its running too fast for the horses; it was no sooner liberated than it took the direct road to Collingham, it led the pursuers to the very house of its masters (?), the door was burst open, and the robbers were seized in the very act of counting over the money. The amount said to have been taken was £2500 in gold and silver. One account states that they resorted to a public-house at Collingham, and whilst they were dividing the booty, the landlord hearing a dispute and the sound of coin, went softly into the room above, and peeping through chinks in the floor, saw the money and heard sufficient to satisfy him that a robbery had been committed; upon which he joined the robbers, and declared that unless they would let him share he would inform against them. Thereupon he received his portion and became a partner in the crime. They were all taken to York Castle, tried, and found guilty, and condemned to

REV. J. MARTIN, (Congregational) see p. 166.

die. When the Judge was passing sentence of death, one of the culprits laughed, and on being rebuked by the Judge, he said, "I was only thinking, my lord, that the publican has come in for his share." From this arose the common saying, "Like the landlord of Collingham, you'll come in for your share." When the day of execution arrived, the hangman was not to be found, and it is said that "a young appentice of one of the thieves was compelled to execute the prisoners. In horror, though but slightly guilty as an accessor, he criminated himself, was condemned, and suffered death with the rest." I must say that I have not met with the actual proof of these details, and believe there is some exaggeration, for the writer betrays a special bias against the worthy squire, who was one of the greatest benefactors to the churches and grammar schools of the parishes of Halifax, Bradford, Calverley, Bingley, &c. It is further recorded that when upon his death-bed he caused his money-chest to be opened and took a solemn farewell of it. "Mrs. Mary Midgley, of Moortown, Leeds, his niece, was accustomed in her old age to tell how the day after the robbery he took her to see the empty shelf." Notices of Mr. Sunderland and Captain Langdale Sunderland will be found in the chapter on the families of this parish.

BRIDGES OF THE PARISH.—The following notes on the Bridges of this Parish—1650-1700—I extracted from the original Sessions Rolls at Wakefield in 1873.

COTTINGLEY BRIDGE, over Ayre, parish of Bingley,—In Book of Bridges, *v* li allowed at Barnsley Sessions, the 19th Oct. 22 Car. and estreat not made, now to be estreated. Order Book, Pontefract, Ap. 23 Car., C. 6.

Presentment. Indictment Book, Wakefield, 17 Jan. 1649, C 11.
Presentment. Indictment Book, Wakefield, Oct. 1664, G.
A great floode hath taken away the foundations so that the whole Bridge is shrunke; on view and certificate £300 estreated for rebuilding. Order Book, Wakefield, Oct. 1664, F. 187.

£200 having been already estreated, £100 the balance now estreated, Pontefract, Ap. 1665, G 2. Estreat for this and other Bridges. Rolls, Pontefract, 1675.

Presentment. Indictment Book, Leeds, July 1677, M 127.
Mr. Calverley and Mr. ffairfax to view it. Indictment, Leeds, July 1677.

New Order, proceedings to be certified. Order Book, Leeds, July 1677, I 66.

Particulars of estreat. Rolls, Leeds, July 1677.
Presentment. Indictment Book, Pont. Ap. 1682, O 52.
Presented, charged on Riding, to be viewed, &c., and certified. Order Book, Pont. Ap. 1682, K 40.

£10 on the Riding. Rolls, Pontefract, Ap. 1682.
£20 certified as needed and estreated. Order Book, Leeds, July 1682, K. 52.

Rustic Bridge, The Grange.

Photo. by H. England, Esq.

COTTINGLEY BRIDGE.

Schedule, Repairs. £36 estreated. Rolls, Wakefield, Jan. 1682.
Surveyors discharged. Order Book, Pont. Ap. 1683, K 87.
Report of Viewers on completion. Rolls, Pont. Ap. 1683.
£2 estreated for this. Order Book, Pont. Ap. 1690, L 121.
£50 estreated for this. Order Book, Pont. Ap. 1698, M 176.

BINGLEY OR IRELAND BRIDGE.—For many years past repaired by the parish and the money raised by Constable Assessment; but they say it was formerly a Riding Bridge, and that with other Riding Bridges it is in a direct line to Bradford. It is a wood-bridge, and only " passable by horse or foote, not by carte, and goes upp a hill to the moores, an obscure way not vsed by any strangers as we are informed. It would require £80 to repair it if wood, such wood being scarce, but if built of stone would cost £450; but there is no necessity of makeinge it passable for carts for there is noe cart way to nor from it, and Cottingley Bridge being as gain as it is. John Bynnes, Esq., J.P., did agree that if the Riding built a stone bridge at Cottingley the parish would maintain Bingley bridge."

Such was the report of H. Wood and W. Briggs, appointed by the Justices, May 1683. Rolls, Leeds, July 1683.

Presentment not charged.

Indictment at Wakefield, Jan. 1685. Rolls. P. 125, Indictment Book.

On Traverse this day, court is satisfied in reading several antient records of this Court, &c. The Jury found it an antient Riding Bridge. To be viewed & cost of rebuilding ascertained and certified & 200£ estr. 270£ estreated. Charged as a Riding Bridge. Pontefract, Ap. 1686. L 2, Order book.

30 li estreated for making a causey West end of Bridge. Rolls and Order Book, Pontefract, April 1687. L 38.

MARLEY, ALIAS MARLOE BRIDGE, over Ayre, Bingley Parish.—I have no memorandum shewing when this bridge was last destroyed.

Presented, not charged. Pontefract, Ap. 1656, D.

In decay being builded by the Wap. of Skyrack the last time, and the ford thro the water where carts and carriages pass with wyne, oil, and iron from the City of York to the Market towne of Keighley is worn with pitts so as it is very dangerous to passengers. Dan. Mawde. Wakefield, Oct. 1661, F 97.

Bingley Inhab. Presentment. Leeds, July 1670, H 124.

Complaint by inhabitants that Morton will not contribute, referred to Justices. Wakefield, Oct. 1680, I 188.

Same, Petition of Bingley Inhabits. Skipton, July 1680.

Same, Petition of Bingley Inhabits. Wetherby, Jan. 1680.

Skyrack. Presentment. Indictment Book, Leeds, July 1687, Q 20.

Skyrack. Presented, charged on Wapentake to be viewed. Order Book, Leeds, July 1687, L 45.

Skyrack. Indictment, Leeds, July 1687.

Skyrack. £150 certified and estreated on Skyrack. Order Book, Wakefield, January 1687, L 56.

Wood bridge will cost £80. Stone £150. Report of Viewers. Rolls, Wakefield, Jan. 1687.

Traverse to be tried at Rotherham, not at Leeds. Order Book, Pontefract, Ap. 1688, L 65.

Sum to estreat on traverse. Order Book, Leeds, July 1688, L 67.

GILBECK BRIDGE, over Gilbrooke, between Otley and Bradford.

Bingley. Award process. Wakefield, Jan. 1658, Indictment Book, E 158.

STOCK BRIDGE, over Ayre, in Kighley and Morton, between Keighley and Otley, dividing Skirack and Staincliffe.

Presentment. Indictment Book, Skipton, July 1664, G.

Presented to be viewed by two Justices in each Wap. who are to examine how or by whom it hath formerly been repaired, and whether the same be of so great and general use for the country as is alledged, and whether they conceive it to be fitting that the same be inserted in the Book of Bridges, and certify to next Sessions at Pontefract. Order Book, Wakefield, July 1664, F 173.

On petition on behalf of the Country adjacent to Kighley, view ordered, &c., proceedings to be certified to next Sessions. Order Book, Pontefract, May 1671, H 28.

Order reciting prior proceedings and certificates, and that the Bridges next above and below over Ayre are Riding Bridges, and this is as considerable as either of them, and fit to be inserted in the Book of Bridges to be repaired at the general charge; and if not repaired the country will be stopt, and trading between Lancashire and Eastern parts of Yorkshire quite laid aside; also the said bridge must be new built, and cannot consist of less than two arches, in regard the river is 28 yards broad and in regard materials are so far remote, not less than £400 will rebuild the said Bridge with stone sufficient and suitable to other Bridges upon the said River, as namely, Apperley Bridge, which they think fit and desire may be a pattern. £350 estreated on Riding and Surveyor appointed. Order Book, Skipton, July 1671, H 41.

The same as above. Copy of Estreat. Skipton, 1671, Rolls.

Kighley and Morton. Charged on those places, ordered discharged. Indictment Book, Pontefract, April 1672, K 55.

Not to be inserted in the Book of Bridges, for the future to be repaired by the Riding, being found at these Sessions to be repaired at the sole charge of Kighley and Morton. £50 already paid to be paid back. Order Book, Pontefract, April 1672, H 68.

Several Chief Constables in arrears ordered to pay, and that accounts be taken. Order Book, Pontefract, April 1673, H 105.

Surveyor's Accounts to be taken. Order Book, Knaresbro', Oct. 1673, H 126.

Riding. £200 estreated on Riding. Order Book, Pontefract, April 1674, H 138.

BECKFOOT BRIDGE, BINGLEY.

STOCK BRIDGE continued. Accounts to be taken. Order Book, Wetherby, Jan. 1677, I 83.

Stainc. and Ewcross. Presentment. Indictment Book, Pontefract, April 1682, O 51.

Stainc. and Ewcross. Presented, charged on Wap. to be viewed and certified. Order Book, Pontefract, April 1682, K 39.

Inhabs. of Kighley, West and East Morton. Presentment. Indictment Book, Leeds, July 1682, O 75.

Its position on highway. Rolls, Leeds, July 1683.

Kighley and Morton Bank. Presentment (not guilty). Indictment Book, Wakefield, Oct. 1687, Q 37.

Kighley and Morton Bank. Indictment. Rolls, Wakefield, Oct. 1687.

Kighley and Morton Bank. £50 estreated on Morton Bank and Kighley for repair. Order Book, Wakefield, Jan. 1637, L 56.

Record on traverse, Kighley and Morton Bank ought not to repair. Indictment Book, Pontefract, Ap. 1688, Q 79.

Presentment. Indictment Book, Leeds, July 1688, Q 86.

Riding. Indictment. Rolls, Leeds, July 1688.

Report of Viewers, £38 required, referred to Weth., estimated at cost. Rolls, Knaresbro', Oct. 1688.

To be viewed and certified. Order Book, Skipton, July 1689, L 77.

To be viewed and certified. Order Book, Wakefield, Jan. 1689, L 110.

£5 estreated for repair. Order Book, Pontefract, April 1690, L 121.

Riding. £6 estreated on Riding for repair. Order Book, Skipton, July 1697, M 151.

In 1692 the land tax on real estate produced, at 4s. in the pound, in Bingley, £150 6s. 0d. ; in Morton, £79 (with £3 15s. 0d. personall); in Baildon, £59 ; Ilkley, £56 ; Otley, £85.

In 1705, at 4d. in the pound, the Constable lay or assessment realized £60 5s. 8d. for Harden in 74 items ; £61 19s. 0d. for Micklethwaite in 70 items ; and £29 0s. 4d. for Bingley in 40 items, including lime delves ; total, £151 16s. 4d.

The proportions as recorded at Pontefract Sessions in 1711 were : Bingley, £30 2s. 2d.; Harden, £57 19s. 4d.; Micklethwaite, £62 9s. 6d.; total, £150 11s.

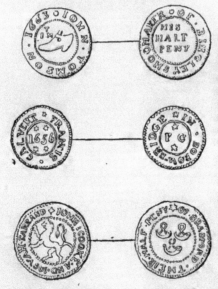

BINGLEY TOKEN.—After the Civil Wars, tradesmen were allowed to issue tokens in place of the ordinary coinage, and the tradesmen were responsible for cashing them, as bank-notes of to-day carry the impressed value against the issuing bank. I only know of one Bingley tradesman who issued them, but possibly many more issued them, as they were mostly called in and destroyed. On the obverse—

IOHN TOMSON. 1663 $^{T}_{IM}$, figure of a shoe.

On the reverse—OF BINGLEY, SHOOMAKER. HIS HALF PENY.

TOKENS—TOMSON OF BINGLEY, FARRAND, &C., OF BRADFORD.

VOTERS AT THE ELECTION OF MEMBER OF PARLIAMENT FOR YORKSHIRE IN 1741-2 (JAN. 13, &c., O.S.),

FOR GEORGE FOX, ESQ.

Bingley.—William Ambler, Benj. Birks, Jerem. Booth, Joseph Booth, John Bottomley, John Butterfield, Thomas Dobson (gent.), Thomas Dobson, Timothy Dobson, John Ellison, Joseph Hartley, Peter Heaton, Chistopher Hickeringale, John Hodgson, John Holdsworth, John Hudson, James Knipe, Richard Leach (clerk for Wilsden land), Robert Leach, Thomas Lister, James Maud, John Maud, Thomas Morvill, James Murgatroyd, Roger Shackleton, James Smith, John Smith, Joshua Smith, Thomas Spencer, John Walker, Robert Watson, John Whitley, George Barrowclift, Thomas Booth, Wm. Butterfield, Thos. Ellinthorpe, John Garnett, Samuel Hird, Jos. Maud, John Middlebrook, David Midgley, John Murgatroyd, John Rhodes, Christopher Smith, Thomas Smith.

Cottingley.—W. Lamplugh (clerk), John Lister, Oldroyd Skirrow, John Booth, Timothy Maud, of Gauthorpe.

Harding.—John Jewitt, Wm. Leach, John Lancaster, Richard Midgley, Richardson Ferrand, Esq.

Micklethwaite.—Thos. Wilkinson, Wm. Wilkinson.

Morton.—John Berry, Wm. Beanland, John Dalton, Jacob Elstone, John Greenwood, Joshua Hainsworth (of Morton Bank), Joseph Horner, Bryan Lister, Wm. Skelton for North Cave, John Wilkinson, James Parker (of Morton Bank), John Thornton.

Rushworth.—W. Busfeild, Esq.

St. Ives.—Samuel Whaley, for land at Keighley.

Thwaites.—Thomas Rushworth for Bingley lands, Wm. Clapham.

Woodhouse-in-Bingley.—Wm. Bottomley for Calderside hill.

FOR CHOLMLEY TURNER, ESQ.

Bingley.—Richard Hartley (clerk), Samuel Holmes, Thomas Laycock, Wm. Lister, Thos. Lister, Richard Wallis.

Cottingley.—Bryan Lister, Joseph Hollings.

In 1744 a Bill to make the Aire navigable from Cottingley to Inghey Bridge in Craven was dropped in Parliament.

In 1747, from a list printed at York after the Scotch Rebellion, there had been collected for the defence of the County, from Bingley £71, Keighley £104, Bradford £256, Huddersfield £35. The local woollen and worsted trade was rapidly increasing at this time, and the introduction of shalloons and calimancoes in 1750 promoted further prosperity. In 1753 the old Market Place and Butter Cross were restored at Bingley, and Tuesday adopted as the Market day. It may have been held on Tuesdays before this date, but its original day was Sunday. In this year, June 1753, the great Rebecca Riots for demolishing turnpike gates took place, and mobs gathered from Otley, Yeadon, and most of the villages of Airedale and Wharfedale, and proceeded to pull down the structures at Apperley Bridge, Kirkstall, Bingley, Bradford, Bellybridge (Bailiffe-bridge), Bridge

House (Brighouse), Cleggheaton (Cleckheaton), &c. Again in August, they burnt the gates at Apperley Bridge, Bellybridge, and Bridge House.

On Friday, August 17th, 1764, Lydia Longbottom, of Bingley, was publicly whipt through the Market at Wakefield, for reeling false and short yarn, the town bailiff carrying a reel before her.

In 1774, a great impetus was given to the prosperity of Bingley by the completion of the Canal, of which more anon.

MARKET, STOCKS, AND FIRST WESLEYAN CHAPEL.

As Bingley is an antient Market town both by charter and custom, as it is provided with a good Market House and Cross lately repaired at a considerable expense, and also furnished with standard weights and measures, as the situation is in every respect an eligible one, and it seems to be the prevailing opinion that the Market which has for sometime been lost may without much difficulty be revived, to the very great improvement of the town and neighbourhood, We, to bring this about, have at a meeting this 11 Nov. 1775, mutually agreed with each other that we will faithfully observe and keep the following resolutions:—

(1.) The Market shall be held on Tuesday, 19 Dec., and forwards weekly, unless on trial some other day be found better. That we will not by ourselves or agents for one year to commence on said day buy or sell any wheat, rye, barley, oats, beans, or any other kind of grain (malt excepted) in any other place than the open market, and that not by sample nor any quantity less than a sack containing Winchester bushels.) That we will not buy or sell any butter, eggs, fowls, ducks, geese, turkeys, pidgeons, potatoes, apples, onions, or other vegetables (pease only excepted) any otherwise than in the Public Market.

(2.) That we will not buy any shambles meat off any butcher in the town who shall refuse to erect a stall in the neighbourhood of the Market Cross for the convenience of people who come to the Market. Neither will we buy any beef or bacon for salting which has not previously been exposed to sale in the Open Market.

That we will give all the energy that is in our power to all dealers in hardware, tins, braziery, goods, hats, &c., residing in the neighbouring towns and villages to bring their commodities to this Market.

(3.) That we will endeavour to prevail on dealers in sea fish who come this road to bring the same regularly to Market.

St. Ives (formerly Harden Grange). *Photo. by H. England, Esq.*

That the following gentlemen be Committee to work out these resolutions :—

Messrs. B. Ferrand, H. Wickham, J. A. Busfeild, J. Lobley J. Peile, J. Leach, John Harrock, Jas. Murgatroyd, John Booth, J. Heaton, Thos. Dobson, Jas. Hulbert, — Oliver, and Francis Lister.

(Signed) Jonas Horsfall, Timothy Horsfall, Josh. Longbottom, W. Horsfall, (about 108 names).

Ancient Entrance to HARDEN GRANGE (now called St. Ives). with Arms of Ferrand, &c., 1636.

Bingley Families.

ROBERT BENSON, (Baron Bingley).

Benson Arms—Argent three trefoils in bend sable, cotissed gules.

Robert Benson, of Wrenthorpe, Wakefield, Clerk of Assize, M.P. for Aldborough in 1673.
=Dorothy dau. Col. Toby Jenkins, of Grimston.
Robert, Lord Mayor of York in 1707, Chancellor of the Exchequer, Baron Bingley in 1713, built Bramham Hall; died 1730, portrait in York Guildhall, from which the illustration is taken.
=Elizabeth, dau. Heneage Finch, first Earl of Ailesford.

Harriet, only daughter, married in 1731.
=George Lane Fox, Esq., created Lord Bingley, Baron of Bingley, May 4, 1762; Lord Mayor of York in 1757, M.P. for Yorkshire 1758; died in 1772.
Robert Lane Fox, only son, died without issue in 1768; title again became extinct.
George, (son of Henry Fox and Frances née Lane) had a brother Sackville Lane Fox, whose son James, M.P. for Horsham was heir to his uncle (Baron Bingley). He died in 1821 leaving a son, Sackville Walter Lane Fox, Esq., who married the only daughter of the Duke of Leeds. Their son was Sackville George, Baron Conyers. (Fuller pedigree in *Yorkshire County Magazine*, Vol. III., pp. 36-7.)

FERRAND OF SKIPTON AND ST. IVES.

Arms.—Argent on a chief gules two crosses flory vair, a cinquefoil azure for difference.

Crest.—A cubit arm erect, vair, charged with a cinquefoil gules, in the hand a battle axe proper.

Motto.—Justus propositi tenax.

The Arms are arms of patronage compounded of the arms of the Earls of Albemarle of Skipton Castle, of which the Ferrands were wardours. Fuller details of the pedigree will be found in the 3rd edition of Whitaker's *Craven*, and in a privately printed history of the family by J. A. Busfeild, Esq.

Roger Ferrand, of Skipton, married Isabel, dau. and sole heiress of William de Altaripa (Dawtrey), of Carlton; and their son, Robert,

LAKE AND BOAT-HOUSE, ST. IVES.

Photo. by H. England, Esq.

was father of William (A), Richard and Thomas. Richard, London citizen, died in 1560, and was buried in Beverley Minster, where an elaborate brass still exists to his memory. In his will he mentions brothers Roger and Harry Ferrand and a sister Maude. Thomas was also a London citizen, and died in 1536, leaving issue. In his will he mentions Skipton Church.

(A.) William, the eldest son, of Skipton, married a Tempest, and their son, Christopher, was father of William, of Skipton, and Carlton, and received the Grant of Arms in 1586. This grant is printed in the family history. He had two sons—Thomas, of Skipton, and William, of Westhall in Ilkley. The elder was father of Edmund, of Carlton, Bryan of Flasby, and Eleanor, who married Thomas Heber, of Marton. Edmund married a Wentworth, and their elder son Thomas was killed on the Royalist side at Preston, whilst the second son, Edmund, who had married a daughter of Francis Malham of Elslack, Esq., sold Carlton in 1651.

Christopher and Alice Ferrand, of Bingley, were parents of Richard Ferrand, of Bingley, and of Robert, who was buried at Bingley in Nov. 1593. This Robert made his Will in 1591, wherein he mentions his mother, his wife Margaret, and his brother Richard's children. The Robert Ferrand, who held lands in Priesthorpe in 1558 was probably his uncle. The wives of the two brothers were named Margaret. Richard held lands in Bingley and Castlefields in 1597; he died in 1641; his children being:—

(1) George, (2) Edmund (bapt. Aug. 1592, married in Aug. 1620, Isabel Wood, buried Nov. 1663), (3) Robert, (4) Stephen of Harden (bapt. June 1600, married in Dec. 1624, Mary Walters, buried Feb. 1684), (5) Agnes, bapt. 1579, married John Bean, of Gilstead, (6) Mary, bapt. 1581, married Samuel Holeride, of Bingley, (7) Alice, bapt. 1586, married Wm. Wiley, of London, (8) Anne, bapt. 1594, married William Crawshaw, of Wilsden.

George, the eldest, bapt. at Bingley Jan. 5, 1577, had a son, Thomas, born March 1615, Will dated 1662. Thomas's wife was named Elizabeth, and they had two sons—Joshua the younger, and Stephen, who married in 1672, Mary Hollings, of Allerton. He died in 1684, and his widow married Abraham Binns, of Ryshworth. Stephen's only son was Thomas Ferrand, M.A., Trin. Coll., Camb., Vicar of Bingley, who was bapt. here 9 June 1680; married in June 1705, Martha, dau. of John Dobson, gent., of the Vicarage. The Vicar was buried here 15 Dec. 1740, and his widow in March 1762, aged 84. Their seven children were:—

(A) John, bapt. Nov. 5, 1706, M.A., Trin. Coll. Camb., Vicar of Messingham, who died in 1759, and his only issue, Gerrard, d. in 1779, aged 27, unmarried; (B) Thomas, bapt. 21 Dec. 1709, Fellow of Trin. Coll. Camb., died 1741 unmarried; (C) Benjamin, Lieut. R.N., bapt. Nov. 1713, killed at Porto Cavello, unmarried; (D) Stephen, of Blythe, bap. Mch. 1717, died unmarried March, 1788; (E) Mary died young, (F) Sarah bapt. Aug. 1720, married John Siddall, gent., of Bingley;

she died in 1772; (G) Anne, married in 1740 to Rev. Joshua Waddington of Harworth and Walkingham. Their eldest son Thomas Waddington-Ferrand is the ancestor of G. T. W. Ferrand, Esq., of Aldeburgh, Suffolk.

Resuming the line of Robert, third son of Richard and Margaret Ferrand, both of whom died in 1641, he was baptized at Bingley, 6 Nov. 1597, and entered his pedigree at the 1665 visitation. He resided at Harden Grange, and was buried Aug. 7, 1674. He married in 1624, Anne dau. of Thomas Newton, Esq., of Daventry; she died 6 Jan. 1667. Their issue was *Dorothy*, wife of Ambrose Metcalf, of Hull; *Anne* who married first Robert Milner, Esq., of Pudsey, and secondly Samuel Jenkinson, Esq., of Horbury; and *Benjamin*, only son, of Harden Beck, aged 41 in 1665, buried at Bingley 14 Feb. 1699. Sir Walter Calverley, of New Calverley, now called Esholt Hall, says in his Note Book—"I was at the burial of old Mr. Ferrand who was interred at Bingley. We had only gloves, 15 Feb. 1699, O.S." He married at Bingley in Dec. 1645, Martha dau. Edward Brooksbank, Esq., of Wilsden; she died Nov. 1699. They had eight children :

(1) Robert, (2) Edward, (3) David, major in the army, died *s.p.*, bur. at Bingley 24 Nov. 1699, (4) Samuel, (5) Anne bapt. June 1650, married in May, 1671, Thomas Fluid, Esq., Leicestershire, (6) Lydia bapt. 8 March, 1652, married Thomas Whalley, gent., of Winterburn, (7) Mary bapt. 25 Jan. 1658, married Richard Pindar, Esq., Kendall, and (8) Martha bapt. June 1668, married Stephen Fyshe of Settle.

We must follow three of these lines, the descendants of Robert, Edward and Samuel.

(I) Robert Ferrand, of Harden Grange. bapt. 9 Dec. 1647, J.P. and D.L. for Yorkshire, buried 5 Jan., 1711.
=(1) Barbara Bradgate of Ullesthorp, Leicester : bur. 1685.
  =(2) Anne dau. Hugh Currer of Kildwick, Esq., widow of Wm. Busfeild, Esq., of Leeds; she died in 1712.
Robert, Harden Grange, bapt. Dec. 1687, bur. Sep. 1742, unmarried.

Benjamin, of St. Ives, Capt. W. R. Militia, born Sept. 1676, married first Anne dau. Henry Currer, Esq., Kildwick, in Dec. 1707, she died *s.p.* July 1727. He married secondly

Bradgate, M.A., Trin. Coll., Camb., Vicar of Bradford, *portrait herewith*, bapt. May 1682, bur. in Bradford Church, May 1709, unmarried.
  Mary bapt. Jan. 1677, married Thomas Roebuck, Esq., of Heath.
  Anne, bapt. Aug. 1679, married John Cockcroft, Esq., of Bradford.

=Sarah dau. & coh. Thomas Dobson, Esq., of the Vicarage. She married secondly in 1737 Gregory Rhodes of Ripon, and was buried at Bingley in 1785.
Benjamin, of St. Ives, lord of the manors of Cottingley, Oakworth, &c., major of W. R. Militia, J.P. and D.L., bapt. May 1730, died unmarried Oct. 1803, aged 73.

REV. BRADGATE FERRAND.

(II) Edward Ferrand of Harden Beck, bapt. May 1656, buried Dec. 1742. He married Jane dau. of William Richardson, Esq., of Bierley. She was buried at Bingley, 3 April, 1716. Issue:—

Richardson, of Harden, J.P., bap. 21 April, 1692, died 31 Aug. 1745, married 24 May, 1728.
=Mary, dau. Wm. Busfeild, Esq., J.P., of Ryshworth; She died 8 Feb. 1754.

Jane, coh.=Robert Stansfield, Esq., of Esholt.
Mary, coh.=Henry Currer, Esq., and 2ndly Peter Bell; died s.p.

John, of Stockton, bapt. April 1697, bur. at Bingley, Aug. 1729.
=Maria Hewdick of Rotterdam. She died July, 1744.
Richardson, of Stockton, bapt. there 1723, married Feb. 1745; died 1769.
=Anne dau. Rev. Geo. Walker. She died in 1771.

Jane died unmarried.

John, b. 1747, d. at Sedgfield, in 1790, married in 1772.	George, b. 1750, d. s.p.	Richardson, b. 1759, Mayor of Stockton.	Esther, =Benj. Lumley, Stockton.	Anna Maria, =Wray, Stockton.

=Sarah, dau. Edwd. Dale, Esq., Stockton; she died at Bath in 1825.

Edward	Walker	Jane	Sarah=Currer Fothergill	Anne Catherine
A	B	C	D Busfeild, B.A.	E

A. Edward Ferrand, Esq., J.P., D.L., of St. Ives, born 14 Dec. 1777, at Barnard Castle, died 21 March, 1837, having married 31 Jan. 1809, Frances, dau. & coh. of W. Holden, Esq., Baildon. She died 9 Jan. 1861, aged 71, leaving an only daughter, Frances, who married in Dec. 1840, R. P. Amphlett, Esq., M.A., Q.C., M.P., who in 1874 was made a Baron of the Exchequer, and received Knighthood, and in 1876 was made Lord Justice of Appeal and Privy Councellor; their only child William Ferrand Amphlett died an infant in Feb. 1846.

B. Walker Ferrand, of Harden Grange, Esq., J.P., D.L., M.P. for Tralee, Captain in the army, Major and Lieut. Col. of Bradford Local Militia, *portrait herewith*, born June 5, 1780, married 1st his cousin Katherine Maria, only child and heir of Gen. Wm. Twiss, R.E.; she died Feb. 1827, aged 50; W. F. married 2ndly in Jan. 1829, Margaret, dau. John Moss, Esq. She died 5 April, 1845, aged 38, and he died *s.p.* 20 Sept. 1835.

C. Jane Ferrand, born Sept. 1775, married in April, 1794, to the Rev. C. B. Charlewood, Staff., and died in 1798, leaving issue a son and daughter, but the son died unmarried in 1817 aged 21, and his sister, Sarah, married in 1829 Charles Wm. Martin, grandson of John, 3rd Duke of Athole, and had issue.

WALKER FERRAND, ESQ., b. 1780, d. 1835.

E. Anne Catherine Ferrand, born May, 1787, married 1st Edward Surtees, Esq., in 1809, and had an only son W. E. Surtees, D.C.L., J.P., D.L., High Sheriff for Durham, 1866, &c., and 2ndly G. T. Monkland, Esq., Captain.

D. Sarah Ferrand, born July 25, 1783, married Feb. 1805, died 30 May, 1854. In 1837 in compliance with the will of Benjamin Ferrand, Esq., she by sign manual resumed the surname Ferrand.

=Currer Fothergill Busfeild, B.A., of Cottingley Bridge, born 23 Jan. 1777, died June 30, 1832.

1	2	3	4	5	6	7
William *portrait below*	Walker	Currer	Johnson Atkinson	Benj. Ferrand	Jane Ferrand	Sarah Dale

8	9	10	11	12	13
Katherine Maria	Elizabeth Octavia	Mary Anne	Anne Isabella	Caroline	Emily Lucinda

W. Busfeild-Ferrand, Esq., b. 1809, d. 1889.

1. William Busfeild-Ferrand, of Harden Grange and St. Ives, *portrait herewith*, M.P. for Knaresborough 1841-7, and for Devonport, 1863-5, J.P. and D.L., born 26 April, 1809, married first in 1831: assumed in 1839 the name Ferrand.

=Sarah, dau. Capt. John Priestley; she died 3 Dec. 1832.
 =2ndly, in Aug. 1847, Fanny Mary Stuart, dau. of Lord Blantyre.

| William Ferrand, J.P., D.L., b. 1831, d. unmarried 1 Sept. 1865. | Sarah Harriette Ferrand, =Edward Hailstone, Esq., F.S.A., Horton and Walton Hall, in June 1855. | Hugo Ferrand, b. 10 Oct. 1848, d. 14 June, 1877 unmarried. |

Etheldreda Lilla, b. Oct. 1858.   Wilfrid Edward, b. Aug. 1864.

A granite obelisk within the park, at St. Ives, near the moor and lake, was erected by his widow, to the memory of Mr. Busfeild Ferrand, recording that he was M.P. as before stated, and also a Magistrate for nearly 50 years, during a great portion of which time he presided as Chairman of the Keighley Petty Sessional Division in perfect harmony with his fellow magistrates, and that in early life he took an active part in support of the Ten hours Factory Bill, and after 17 years of ceaseless effort he assisted as M.P. for Knaresborough in carrying it through the House of Commons. He brought under notice the iniquities of the Truck system, and a stringent law was passed to compel payment of wages in current coin of the realm. He vigorously exposed the harsh clauses of the New Poor Law until they were removed from the Statute Book, and he was the firm denouncer of all corruption amongst public men. He planted about 400 acres of wood for the benefit of the property and to beautify his native place. He died March 31, 1889, aged 79. Close by the monument is an arbour that was the favourite resort of Lady Blantyre, mother of the Hon. Mrs. Ferrand. The latter lady died in 1896 at Cannes, aged 80.

2. Walker Busfeild, of Cottingley Bridge, born 10 Sep. 1811, died 16 Sep. 1855, married 19 Oct. 1841, Emma dau. Edmund Broderip, Esq., J.P., and had three children, *Walker*, [born 1843, married Marianne dau. W. B. Naish, Esq., J.P., (his mother's step-daughter), and had a daughter Marian May B.]. *Emma* married Edmund, son of Edm. G. Broderip, Esq.; and *Gertrude Augusta*.

3. Currer Busfeild, born 3 Nov. 1812, died 13 Sep. 1848, married 23 Nov. 1839, Sarah dau. P. Tuer, Esq., and had a son Currer Fothergill Busfeild, Lieut., born 15 Sep. 1840.

4. Johnson Atkinson Busfeild, *portrait herewith*, of Upwood, J.P., born 7 Jan. 1814, died 19 Sep. 1882, married 10 Nov. 1832, Mary Elizabeth dau. John Priestley, Esq., Captain 32nd Regt., and had issue—

(*a*) Johnson Atkinson, born 16 Sep. 1833, d. 18 Nov. 1838.
(*b*) Currer Fothergill, born 6 Oct. 1834, d. 10 May, 1839.
(*c*) William Busfeild, now Ferrand, *see postea*.
(*d*) Johnson Atkinson, born 4 Oct. 1853, died 1 Dec. 1859.
(*e*) Mary Skelton Busfeild married 13 July, 1864, R. Townley Woodman, Esq., J.P., and D.L., of Maescelyn, co. Brecon.
(*f*) Sarah Ferrand Busfeild, died 26 Dec. 1854, aged 13.
(*g*) Caroline Christiana married 23 March, 1871, her second cousin Lieut. John Busfeild.

J. A. BUSFEILD, ESQ., 1874.

(*h*) Louisa Emily married 21 April, 1874, her second cousin, Capt. Wm. Busfeild.

(*c*) William Busfeild, of The Hills, Bingley, afterwards of Morland Hall, Westmorland, born 15 Jan. 1838, married 19 April, 1865, Emily, youngest daughter of Alfred Harris, Esq., J.P., D.L., of Oxton Hall, Tadcaster, and had issue—

(1) William Harris Busfeild, now Ferrand, born 9 March, 1873, late Lieut. Yorks. Artil., J.P. for West Riding, married 1 June,

1897, Constance, second daughter of Colonel The Hon. Augustus M. Cathcart.
  (2) Emily Mary married in 1887 Edward Pelly Woodman, Esq.
  (3) Guy Ferrand Busfeild, born 14 July, 1881.
  Mrs. Busfeild died 16 July, 1881, and Mr. Busfeild married, secondly, 26 Sep., 1883, Florence Annie Letitia eld. dau. of the Hon. Amias Charles Orde Powlett of Thorney Hall, Yks., and has issue—
  (4) Amias William Powlett, born 7 Apr. 1887.
  (5) Stafford Hubert, born 1 March, 1888.
  (6) Florence Marjorie.
  (7) Hermione Monica.
  Mr. Busfeild on becoming the devisee under the will of his paternal uncle, Wm. Ferrand, Esq., of St. Ives and Harden Grange, who died 31 March, 1889, assumed by Royal Licence 18 March, 1890, the surname and arms of Ferrand in lieu of Busfeild. He is a D.L. and J.P. for the West Riding and a J.P. for Westmorland. He resides at St. Ives, the ancient name of which was Halton Grange, afterwards Harden Grange, which mansion he has greatly enlarged and beautified. An interesting series of family arms adorn the windows. Our accompanying illustrations give views of the Mansion from the West, of Fairfax table, and of the ancient doorway. For the privilege of reproducing these views and several photographs I am indebted to Mr. Ferrand, as also for the kind manner in which he has made me welcome in my researches at St. Ives. His father printed privately a history of the Family and compiled several unique and handsome volumes, copiously illustrated, containing materials for the history of Bingley, and these invaluable manuscripts have been generously placed at my disposal, and my greatest difficulty has been to condense into a small volume the interesting notes gathered by the late Mr. Busfeild of Upwood, with true antiquarian instincts.
  The family memorials in Bingley Church include—
  Hic jacet (Here lyeth) the body of Mr. Edward, son of Neall Hewit, Esq., of Dunton Basset in Leicestershire, who departed this life Oct. 1, 1698, in the 27th year of his age, being a boarder with Mr. Edward Ferrand of Harden.
  Arms. Argent on a chief gules two crosses flory vair a cinquefoil for difference. On an escutcheon of pretence gules on a mount vert a swan argent membered collared and chained or. In the Abbey Church of Bath lieth the remains of Sarah Ferrand of Cottingley House, relict of John Ferrand, Esq., of Barnard Castle, who died 17 Feb. 1790, aged 44, and is buried at Sedgfield, Durham. She died 3 May, 1825, aged 74.
  On a slab in the nave floor—
  Benjamin Ferrand, Esq., of St. Ives, d. 20 Oct. 1803, aged 73.
  Edward Ferrand, Esq., of St. Ives, d. 21 Mch. 1837, aged 59.
  Frances, widow of said Edward, d. Jan. 9, 1861, aged 71.
  Mr. John Sedgwick, formerly of Leeds, late of this place, died Aug. 13, 1791, aged 75 years, and Sarah his wife died May——.

In the North aisle—

On the 29 July, 1747, was buried the body of Thomas Dobson, Esq., of the Vicarage, who married Ann, dau. of Wm. Beaumont, Esq., of Darton, by whom he had three children, John, Sarah and Martha. John died a student of Lincoln's Inn, and was buried there 4 March, 1732; Martha was married to Miles Staveley, Esq., and was interred at Ripon in May, 1738; Sarah was married to Benjamin Ferrand, Esq., of St. Ives, to her first husband, and to Gregory Rhodes, Esq., of Ripon, to her second husband. She was here interred 11 April, 1785, and directed this monument to be erected in testimony of respect for her family.

WM. BUSFEILD, ESQ., of Ryshworth, b. 1674, ob. 21 March, 1729.
(*From Kneller's painting*).

Arms: On a lozenge, per fess, first coat in chief, argent on a chief gules two crosses flory vair for *Ferrand;* second coat, in base, argent on a cross engr. between four lions rampant gules as many bezants for *Rhodes;* and on an escu. of pretence argent a fess nebuly between six fleurs-de-lis gules for *Dobson.*

Benjamin, only son of Benj. Ferrand, Esq., of St. Ives, and Sarah his wife, dau. of Thos. Dobson, Esq , of Vicarage. He died at Buxton unmarried 20 Oct. 1803, aged 75. *Arms,* as before, with crest, an armed arm embowed holding a battle-axe.

Arms: Baron and femme; quarterly 1 and 4, Busfeild, 2 and 3 Atkinson; impaling quarterly 1 and 4 Ferrand, 2 and 3 Dale;

ELIZABETH FOTHERGILL, Wife of William Busfeild, Esq., of Ryshworth, b. 1671, ob. 24 April, 1726.

(From Kneller's painting)

motto: In medio tutissimus ibis. Currer Fothergill Busfeild of Cottingley Bridge, youngest son of Johnson A. Busfeild, Esq., and of Elizabeth Busfeild of Ryshworth, his wife, lived 55 years, died 30 June, 1832.

Mary Anne Busfeild died 24 Oct. 1817, aged 1; Annie Isabella d. 22 Jan. 1824, aged 4; Jane Ferrand d. 17 Mch. 1824, aged 17; Sarah Dale died 9 July, 1825, aged 17. Sarah Ferrand erected this monument. She died 30 May, 1854, aged 70.

On the front of the Ferrand pew, over the vestry, in oak, is the shield—

Per pale *Ferrand*, with escutcheon of pretence, viz., two chevrons appointè, that in chief reversed and in chief and base a cross crosslet for *Twiss*, impaling, ermine a cross patty sable for *Moss;* motto. Justus propositi tenax. Walker Ferrand, Esq., of Harden Grange, married first, Catherine dau. & heiress of General Twiss, and secondly, Margaret dau. of John Moss. Mr. Ferrand died 20 Sep. 1835.

Caroline wife of Wm. Busfeild, Esq., M.P., of Upwood, eldest daughter of Capt. Charles Wood, R.N., sister of Sir Francis Lindley Wood, Bart., died 8 April, 1839. Mr. Busfeild was three times M.P. for Bradford. He died 11 Sept. 1851, aged 78.

Arms: Sable a chevron between three fleurs-de-lis or, *Busfeild*, quartering vert a buck's head couped within a bordure engrailed or, *Fothergill*. Ann dau. of Hugh Currer of Kildwick, Esq., widow and relict of William Busfeild, Esq. of Leeds, merchant, and widow of Robert Ferrand, Esq., and mother of William Busfeild, Esq., of Ryshworth, died 9 Nov. 1712, aged 63. Also Elizabeth dau. of Abraham Fothergill of London, wife of William Busfeild of Ryshworth, died 24 April, 1726, aged 55. William Busfeild died 21 March, 1729, aged 56. Also William Busfeild of Ryshworth Hall, their eldest son, died 31 Oct. 1748, aged 50.

Johnson Atkinson Busfeild, D.D., rector of St. Michael's, Wood Street, London, and 22 years curate of Carlton in Craven, where he was interred: born July 4, 1775, died Jan. 12, 1849. Johnson, his youngest son, born 19 Aug. 1825, died 22 Jan. 1830.

On a slab in the nave floor—

Walker Ferrand, Esq., of Harden Grange, died Sept. 20, 1835, aged 55. Catherine Maria, his wife, only daughter of General Twiss, R.E., who died 15 Feb. 1827, aged 50. General Twiss, R.E., died at Harden Grange, 14 March, 1827, aged 82; Elizabeth his relict, died 7 July, 1835, aged 94. Margaret relict of Walker Ferrand, eld. dau. of John Moss, Esq., died 5 April, 1846, aged 38.

Elizabeth Busfeild, sole heiress of William Busfeild, Esq., of Ryshworth Hall, and wife of Johnson Atkinson Busfeild, of Myrtle Grove. She died 5 Nov. 1798, aged 50, leaving three sons and one daughter. Also the above Johnson Atkinson Busfeild, (eldest son of the Rev. Christopher Atkinson, B.A., vicar of Thorp Arch,) who died 26 March, 1817, aged 78, J.P. and D.L. for the West Riding for 36 years. Susanna, second wife of Johnson Atkinson Busfeild (and relict of

Rev. Johnson Atkinson Busfeild, D.D., b. July 4, 1775,
d. 12 Jan. 1849.

John Dearden, Esq., of The Hollins,) died 26 Dec. 1812. Jane, daughter of Johnson Atkinson and Elizabeth Busfeild, married Major Chas. Jones, and died 20 March, 1818, aged 37. Mary Susanna, wife of Rev. Johnson Atkinson Busfeild, D.D., and dau. of Joseph Priestley, Esq., of Whitewindows, Halifax, buried in St. Marylebone.

A brass plate let into a pier in the north chancel aisle records—
Inscriptions on tombstones existing in this chapel at the time of its restoration, A.D. 1870.

Hic requiescit in pace Anna Hugonis Currer de Kildwick filia Will. Busfeild de Leeds gen. et Robert. Ferrand de Harden Grange armiger. relicta et Wm. Busfeild de Ryshworth armig. mater amantissima ob. 9 Nov. an. æt. 63, sa. 1712. Hic requiescit in pace Willielmus Roberti Stansfield de Bradford gen. filius et Will. Busfeild de Ryshworth arm.

ELIZABETH, sole heiress of Wm. Busfeild, Esq., of Ryshworth, b. 1748, married, 1765, to Johnson Atkinson, M.D., ob. Nov. 5, 1798.

ex filia nepos. ob. 1 Dec. æt. 2 do, s. 1727. Hic requiescit in pace Elizabetha Abrahami Fothergill de Londino, genr. obsequens filia et Will. Busfeild de Ryshworth armig. charissima conjux, ob. 24 April æt. 55 sa. 1726; et ipse Gulielmus Busfeild qui obiit 21 Martii, anno æt. 56, salv. 1729.

On a brass— | W. B. 1748. |

On a tombstone in the south aisle there was formerly to be seen the inscription—George Ferrand of Priesthorpe, died June ye 8, anno 1738, ætat 31. Also Elizabeth his wife who dep. this life 29 Jan. 1752, aged 45.

ATKINSON-BUSFEILD.—A pedigree of the Atkinson family running back to their home in Westmorland two centuries ago will be found in my *Yorkshire Notes and Queries*. Our present connection starts

RYSHWORTH HALL, BINGLEY.

with the Rev. Christopher Atkinson, vicar of Thorp Arch, of Queen's Coll., Oxford, born 1713, died July 11, 1774. His widow, Jane, dau. Wm. Johnson, Esq., of Old Hall, Kendall, died at Thorp Arch in 1791. At the father's death in 1774, there were twelve children living, the oldest of whom, Johnson Atkinson, born in 1739, 8th wrangler, Queen's College, Cambridge, married in 1765, Elizabeth, dau. and heiress of William Busfeild, Esq., of Ryshworth, and afterwards he assumed the surname Busfeild. His brother was Miles Atkinson, B.A., born at Ledsham in 1741, vicar of Kippax and of St. Paul's, Leeds, author of "Practical Sermons," 2 vols., portrait, 1812. His family numbered seven sons and four daughters. Johnson Atkinson Busfeild's second brother was Christopher Atkinson, M.A., born 1755, Trinity College, Cambridge, 5th wrangler, of Wethersfield, died 1795, who married the sister of Lord de Tabley. The fourth son of this remarkable family was the Rev. Wm. Atkinson, M.A., born April 1758, a man who figured prominently in Bradford as a controversialist and died in 1846, aged 88. He was grandfather of the late Sir Matthew W. Thompson, Bart., of Guiseley. The eight daughters of the Rev. Christr. Atkinson, of Thorp Arch, were—Jane, Agnes, Margaret, Ann, Isabel, Dorothy, Elizabeth and Mary, four of whom married.

JOHNSON ATKINSON BUSFEILD, ESQ.,
of Myrtle Grove, b. 1739, ob. 26 March, 1817.
(Col. of Bradford Volunteers).

In Guiseley Church are three monuments to the Stansfield family, of Esholt, who are still landowners in this parish, and represented by the daughters and co-heiresses of General Crompton-Stansfield.

In the south transept, south side, marble monument :—

S. M. of Ann Rookes, wife of William Rookes, Esq., and heir at law of Robert Stansfield of Esholt Hall, Esq., died Feb. 12, 1798, aged 68. She was daughter of Robert Stansfield, and grand-daughter of Wm. Busfeild, Esq., of Ryshworth.

Another monument,—

Arms: Crompton, Vert on a bend argent double cotised ermine, a lion passant gules between two covered cups or, on a chief azure three pheons or. On escutcheon, Rookes and Stansfield quarterly.

Maria, wife of Joshua Crompton, Esq., married 1786, died 1819, aged 56; eldest daughter and co-heir of William and Ann Rookes.

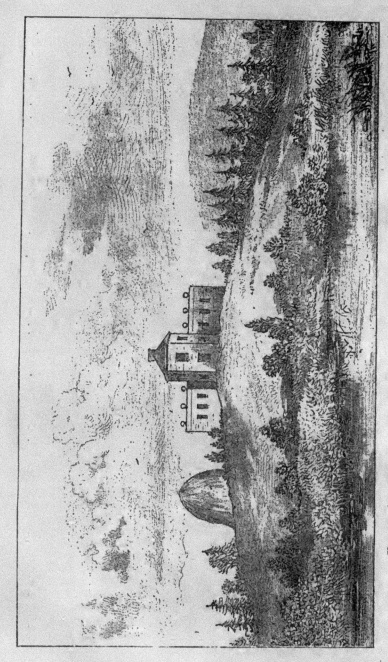

Upwood, about 1790, when a Shooting Box, from a sketch by W. Busfeild, Esq., M.P., Upwood.

Urwood in 1874

On the west side of south transept, Guiseley, on a marble monument:

Arms: Vert, three goats trippant argent (Stansfield), surmounted by an escutcheon of pretence argent, on a chief gules two crosses flory vair (Ferrand). Crest, a lion's head erased or.

S. M. of Robert Stansfield of Esholt, Esq. He married Jane eldest daughter and co-heir of Richardson Ferrand of Harden, Esq., and by her had two daughters who died in their infancy. He departed this life Sept. 14th, 1772, aged 44 years. [Eulogy on this worthy gentleman]. He was the son of Robert Stansfield, Esq., of Bradford, by Anna his second wife, the eldest daughter of William Busfeild, Esq., of Ryshworth.

THOMAS BUSFEILD, ESQ., Ryshworth Hall, b. July 27, 1699, died Sep. 4, 1772.

Painting at Esholt Hall.

"Jane Stansfield, relict, died June 18, 1796, aged 65. Her conduct as a wife was irreproachable, and her widowhood of 24 years was spent in unaffected piety and universal benevolence to all around her, particularly to the afflicted and distressed."

In 1837 a remarkable Parliamentary contest took place at Bradford when Mr. Hardy and Mr. Lister, the retiring M.Ps., were joined by two other candidates, Wm. Busfeild, Esq., of Upwood, a whig, and his nephew, Wm. Busfeild, Esq., of Milner Field. Messrs. Lister and Busfeild (Upwood) opposed Messrs. Hardy and Busfeild junior, and the first two won the seats.

In the same year, 1837, a grant was made by Garter King of Arms to Sarah, widow and relict of Currer Fothergill Busfeild, Esq., of Cottingley Bridge, second daughter of John Ferrand, Esq., of Barnard Castle, to take the arms and surname of Ferrand upon succeeding to the St. Ives Estate on the death of her brother Edward Ferrand, Esq., without male issue.

Sketch Pedigree of Busfeild—*Arms* as entered at The Heralds' College.—Arg. a chevron invected gu. gutte d'eau between three fleurs-de-lis vert in the centre chief point a saltire couped of the second. Crest, on a wreath of the colors a cubit arm in armour ppr. charged with a saltire as in the arms, holding in the hand ppr. a fleur-de-lis within an annulet or.

William Busfeild, Esq., Mayor of Leeds in 1673, died 1675, purchased Ryshworth Hall; son of William son of James B., Leeds, who died in 1613.
=Ann, dau. Hugh Currer, Esq., Kild^k She marr. 2ndly, Robt. Ferrand, Esq.

William Busfeild, Esq., J.P., Ryshworth, died 1730.
=Elizabeth, dau. Abraham Fothergill, Esq., d. 1726.

| William, d. 5 Nov. 1748. | Thomas, b. 1699, d. s.p. 1772. | Fothergill of Manchester, d. s.p. 1761. | Charles, Lisbon Merchant, d. s.p. 1735. | Ann(c) (*next page*.) |

=Mary Wilkinson, d. March 1796, having married 2ndly, Edward Kenion and had issue Edward Kenion, Mary Kenion (married Rev. Miles Atkinson, Leeds,) and Phœbe Kenion (married James Murgatroyd, gent., Bingley).

Elizabeth, b. 1747, d. and heiress, *portrait, page 207*, d. 1798, mar. 1765,
=Johnson Atkinson, M.D., J.P., D.L., Ryshworth and Myrtle Grove; took the name Busfeild on the death of his wife's uncle, Thomas.

| William, b. 1767, d. 1770. | William, of Upwood, b. 1773, J.P. D.L. and M.P. for Bradford, from 1837 to 1851. | Johnson Atkinson B., D.D., b. 1775, marr. in 1798 Mary S. Priestley. | Currer Fothergill b. 1777, mar. in 1805 Sarah |

(*a*)   (*b*)

(a) =in 1800, Caroline dau. Capt. C. Wood.

(b) Ferrand.

Jane B. mar. C. Jones, Esq. Major 18th Hussars.

(c) Ann Busfeild married in 1723, d. 1757.
=Robert Stansfield, Esq., Esholt. = 1st wife Elizabeth dau. heir Thomas Sharp, Esq., Horton.

Robert, d. s.p. 1772.   Wm. d. sp.   Thos. d. s.p.   Ann, d. 1798. =Wm. Rookes, Esq., Esholt, d. Nov. 1789.   Faith=R. G. Sawrey, Esq. a quo Sir F. Sharp Powell.

Anna Maria=Joshua Crompton, Esq.

a quo Misses Crompton-Stansfield, of Esholt Hall.

The following brief account of General Twiss has been supplied by Mr. Ferrand.

LIEUTENANT GENERAL WILLIAM TWISS.
Colonel Commandant in the Royal Engineers.

This Officer entered the Military department of the Ordnance in July, 1760, he obtained a commission in the Corps of Engineers in Nov., 1763; and was promoted to lieutenancy in April, 1771. From 1762 to 1771 he did duty as an Engineer in the garrison at Gibraltar, and from 1772 to the end of 1775 was employed on the new fortifications constructing for the defence of the dockyard at Portsmouth.

Early in 1776 he embarked with General Burgoyne and the army he commanded for Canada, and landed at Quebec in June, when he was nominated Aide-de-camp to Major General Phillips. He was with the army in pursuing the Americans up the river St. Lawrence and was in the affair at the Three Rivers on the 8th June, and proceeded with the army until the Americans were driven out of Canada, and embarked in their fleet and boats on Lake Champlain in July. He was then appointed by Sir Guy Carleton, the Commander in Chief, to be comptroller of works, and to superintend the construction of a fleet for Lake Champlain, with gun-boats and batteaux, for conveying the army over the Lake, and with the able assistance of the naval department, over which the late Admiral Schank was made Commissioner, they began in the middle of July the necessary preparations for so arduous an undertaking, and at a time that Government had neither vessel nor boat on Lake Champlain, nor the smallest building for barracks, storehouses, or workshops. Notwithstanding all which, a numerous fleet was constructed, which fought and defeated the enemy at Valcour Island on the 11th and 12th of October, and obtained the naval superiority during the whole war. He then proceeded with the army to Crown Point, and with it returned and wintered in Canada.

GENERAL TWISS.

In the spring of 1777 he was appointed Commanding Engineer under General Burgoyne; and in July was with the army at the investment of Ticonderoga, where the Americans had employed many thousand men, during eight months, in fortifying Mount Independence; but from the position which the army took, these works were immediately abandoned. He served with the army the whole of the campaign, and was present at all the general actions, and was included in the convention of Saratoga, but was, with other officers, exchanged a few days afterwards and returned to Ticonderoga, when he assisted in the evacuation of that port, in November, 1777.

In 1778 he was sent by General Sir F. Haldimand to Lake Ontario to form a naval establishment on the east side of that lake; and was afterwards employed in different parts of Canada as Commanding Engineer, until the peace in 1783, when he obtained leave to return to England. In 1785, he was employed as Secretary to the Board of Land and Sea Officers, appointed under the King's Sign Manual, to report upon the defences of the dockyards of Portsmouth and Plymouth. From 1785 to 1792 he was employed as an Engineer at Portsmouth, where many new works were constructing, particularly

Myrtle Grove, built by Johnson Atkinson Busfeild, Esq., 1770.

Cumberland Fort, at the entrance of Langston Harbour. In 1794 he was appointed Lieutenant Governor of the Royal Academy at Woolwich, which station he held until he succeeded to be Colonel Commandant of Royal Engineers in 1810, when by the rules of the service, he was removed; however, during this period, he was employed on the following services:—

Between 1792 and 1799, in augmenting the defences on the coasts of Kent and Sussex, particularly at Dover Castle. In 1799, upon Colonel Hay of the Engineers being killed in Holland, he was sent as Commanding Royal Engineer under the Duke of York; and remained there until the evacuation of that country was completed.

In 1800, he was sent to visit the Islands of Guernsey and Jersey. In 1802, he was ordered to make the tour of Ireland, and report respecting its defences. In 1803, he was again sent to the coasts of Kent and Sussex; and in 1805 was directed to carry into execution the system of detached redoubts and towers which Government had adopted for the defence of that sea-coast, and was finished about the year 1809: he was also one of the Engineers sent to report how far the same system was applicable to the Eastern Coast. In 1810, after an active service of 50 years, he obtained leave to remain unemployed and retired into the country.

He purchased at this time Myrtle Grove, near Bingley, where he resided for nearly twenty years. He married in 1775, Elizabeth, daughter of Richard Wood, Esq., of Hanger Hill, near Ealing, Middlesex. The only issue of the marriage, a daughter, Catherine Maria, married in 1805 Walker Ferrand, Esq., of Harden Grange, Bingley.

The General died at Harden Grange, the residence of his son-in-law, the 14th March, 1827, aged 82, and was interred in Bingley Church.

SUNDERLAND.—The Sunderlands derive their surname from the place Sunderland in Halifax parish, where for more than six centuries they have been amongst the chief gentry. I must refer to my books on Brighouse and Coley Hall, and to Watson's "Halifax" for further particulars. In the Bingley Church tower is a fine slab to the memory of the gentleman who was robbed at Harden. The stone is 6 feet 2 inches wide, with a bordure of ornament formed of SS, but has recently been covered by boarding for choir surplices. The inscription reads— " D. O. M. HIC REQUIESCIT IN PACE SAM. SUNDERLAND ARMIGR. QUI ECCLESIIS SCHOLIS ET PAUPERIBUS CENTUM LIBRAS PER ANNUM LEGAVIT; NATURÆ DEBITUM SOLVIT 4to DIE FEBRUARII ANNO SALUTIS 1676. VIVIT POST FUNERA VIRTUS."

Arms.—Three lions passant in pale. Crest, a goat's head erased; but the fuller rendering is:—party per pale or and azure, three lioncells passant counterchanged. Crest, on a helmet a goat's head erased.

Richard Sunderland, of High Sunderland, Halifax.

Richard, s. of High Sunderland; will 1573.
= Agnes Rishworth, of Coley, ?Ann Rishworth, of Riddlesden.

Richard, Esq., J.P., d. 1634. = Susan, dau. SirRich.Saltonstall.

Abraham, of High Sunderland, bequeaths legacies to Rishworths of Bingley.

Grace, Mary, both sisters, in their Wills 1574, gifts to Rishworths, of Haworth.

Abraham. =

Samuel, b. 1600, of Harden. (Thoresby, p.583), London merchant with Peter.

Peter, b. 1617, d. 1677. = Mary, d. Rich. Buck, Idel. She married for third husband, RichardShuttleworth.

Robert.

Mary, = in 1629, Edward Parker, of Browsholme.

Langdale, Captain in Royalist Army, had lands at Baildon, Morton, &c., p. 244-6, *Bradf. Antiq.*

The descendants of Capt. Langdale Sunderland, of Ackton, near Pontefract, sold their Bingley possessions, and their pedigree down to the present date will be found in my *Yorkshire Genealogist*, p. 209. Samuel Sunderland, of Harden Hill End, was a benefactor to a large number of the Churches and Grammar Schools of Halifax, Bradford, Bingley, Idle, Leeds, Thornton, &c. He is said to have left £17000 in cash, and £1200 a year from land. The robbery before mentioned is estimated at £2000 in silver and £500 in gold.

Peter Sunderland, Esq., of Fairweather Green, Bradford, like his brother Samuel, was benefactor to many local schools and churches; and founder of the Lectureship at Bradford Church. He refers in his will, 1677, to Henry, son of Francis Atkinson, gent., his kinsman; gave lands to Walter Laycock, of Oxmanthorpe, near York; to Peter Bielby, his nephew, in trust for Thomas son of Edward Parker, Esquire, deceased, of Marley Hall, "my late nephew," lands in Allerton. To Langdale Sunderland, nephew, £300. To Bryan, son of the said Langdale, "a cabinet which was my brother Robert's, and a gold ring which was my cousin Sowden's." He was a puritan as shewn by the conditions of his Bradford Lectureship. There is a monument to his memory in Bradford church, where he was interred. "Bradford Antiquary," pp. 11-12, James' "Bradford."

RISHWORTH. Arms, argent a bend sable between an eaglet displayed vert and a cross crosslet sable (a ring on the bend.)

Robert Rishworth, gent., of Coley.
= Cecily, dau. Thomas Methley, of Thornhill.
John of Coley.
= Joyce, dau. Robert Nevile, of Liversedge, gent.
Robert of Coley.
= Grace, dau. John Blythe.

Christopher.
```
   ┬
John of Coley.
   ┬ dau. of Walter Paslew, of Riddlesden, co-heiress of Francis,
   │   her brother,
   ├──────────────────────┬──────────────────┬─────────────
John of Riddlesden.*     Phœbe.             Agnes.
   ┬ Ann, dau. Edmund    = William Savile   ┬ Richard
   │   Townley, of Royle.   of Hollinedge,  │   Sunderland.
   │                        Elland.         ↓
Richard, living 1630, who with │ his father sold Riddlesden to Mr.
   Murgatroyd.                   Robert.
 = dau. ──── Butler,
```
Henry de Rishworth inherited Coley near Halifax, from Henry de Coley about 1320, see "Memoirs of Capt. Hodgson of Coley," and the Rishworths held Coley until near 1600, when the Sunderlands purchased it. No satisfactory pedigree of the Rishworths has yet been compiled, though the Rishworths of Haworth, Bingley, &c., have given many connecting links in their Wills. At some time the following notes may be serviceable—John Rishworth, Esq., of Coley, and his son Alexander (whose wife was named Beatrix) disposed of Coley to the Sunderlands.

Umfri Rishworth of Haworth, gent., mentions in his Will dated 1539, his wife Isabel and daughter Elizabeth.

John Rishworth of Haworth, Will dated 1557, mentions his wife Margaret and their children, John, Umphry, Thomas, William and Isabel. William had a daughter Margaret at that time, and John, who made his Will in 1569, had married Isabel, probably a Sunderland, for she refers to that family in her Will dated 1577. Their children were John (the father of Robert), Henry (whose Will dated 1584 mentions his children, Abraham, William and Isabel), Christopher (whose wife was named Alice), Anne, and Janet who had married Richard Byns, according to the father's Will dated 1569.

Richard Rishworth, gent., Haworth, and Alice his wife (1580) were parents of Christopher, Richard, Mary and Dorothy; and I believe the Rishworths of Bolling Hall and *Rushworth* the Historian, kinsman to the Tempests and Lord Fairfax, were of their family. It is to be hoped that T. H. Rishforth, Esq., of Coley Lodge, Ealing, may be able to complete the family record. The family is represented in Bingley still by the gentleman who owns an elaborate inlaid oak chest purchased by his ancestor from the Sunderland-Parker family, believed to be the chest from which the treasure was stolen. Thomas Rishworth of Thwaites House, died 29 Sep. 1809, aged 70. Amy his wife, died 14 March, 1818, aged 69. Amelia, their daughter, wife of Thomas Whitley, of Birgley, died April 20, 1841, aged 58. Elizabeth wife of John Craven of Walk Mill (that is fulling mill), Keighley, died 25 June, 1859, aged 74. These dates are taken from the monument in Bingley church.

* In 1634, he and his two sons Richard and Robert, conveyed East Riddlesden to Robert Townley, of Newhall.

Alexander Ryshworth, of Heath, Esquire, and Beatrix his wife, with Richard their son, conveyed the Manor of Haworth to Martin Birkhead, Esq., of Wakefield, for £600. Alexander had a brother Thomas, gent., of Stanroyde in Lancashire. Nathaniel Birkhead, Esq., son of Martin, sold in 1636, Harden or Halton Grange, with a fulling mill, to Robert Ferrand, Esq. (*Haworth Past and Present.*)

BIRKHEAD.—Richard Birkhead of Halifax parish, Will in Calvinistic form, dated 1544, mentions his wife Elizabeth, and from it we learn that he held lands in Halifax, Wakefield, Crofton, &c. Their children were Richard, Martyn, Thomas, John, Robert, Anne, Sibell, Elizabeth, Isabel and Margaret.

Martyn, the second son, of Wakefield, was the gentleman who bought Haworth Manor, (see *Haworth Past and Present*), and he had possessions in Bradford, Southowram, &c. He made his Will in 1590, and mentions his wife Mary and two sons Nathaniel and Daniel, both of whom held properties in Harden and Haworth. Haworth, with lands in Harden, passed to Nicholas Bladen, Esq., of the Inner Temple, and by him they were conveyed to William Midgley, gent., of Haworth, and from the Midgleys in 1811, Haworth Manor passed by purchase to the Trustees of Benjamin Ferrand, Esq.

ELTOFT.—Arms: three chess rokes sable. The Eltofts held Ryshworth and Elwyck lands under Richard Astley for £10, in 10 Henry VIII, when Christopher Eltoft died. His son, Anthony Eltoft, made his Will in 1537. It is dated from Rishworth Hall, and he directed that his body should be buried at Bingley (probably in the Eltoft or Rishworth chapel, at the parish church). He left lands at Farnhill to his son Thomas, and gave £40 each to his children Anthony, William, John, Jane, Margaret and Dorothy. Edmund, the eldest son, inherited Farnhill Hall. Anthony Eltoft died July, 29 Henry VIII, leaving his wife Maud executrix.

Sir Robert Bindloss of Berwyk, married Mary Eltoft, a descendant, and Farnhill thus became the property of her son Sir Francis, the father of Sir Robert, (1647).

Eltoft, quartered the arms of Copley, argent a cross moline, from Adam de Copley, alias Adam de Oxenhope. They also quarter Marley, Stapleton of Quarmby, St. Philbert, Aldburgh, Godard and Remston.

William Eltoft, of Darnton, Durham.
|
|———————|
William Eltoft, from Darlington, (Harl. MS. 1487), had four
    bovates of land in Oxenhope, 1409.
= Agnes, dau. and h. Robert de Farnhill.
Henry.
=
    Christopher, held lands in Oxenhope, temp. Hen. VII.
      Died 10 Hy. VIII., his son Anthony aged 19.
    = sister of Sir Richard Tempest, of Bolling.

Anthony of Rishworth.   William, held lands in Oxenhope.
= Mawde, d. and h. Thomas Stapleton, of Quarmby.
    ? Matilda, d. Sir John Nevile, Liversedge.

Jane, Thos. Anthony, Wm., John, Margaret, Dorothy, Edmond,
= Arthur Mawde, of Riddlesden.   *
*Edmond, (eldest), of Farnhill, captain.
    =Agnes, dau. Sir W. Fairfax, of Steeton.
        = Agnes, Lady Everingham.

Mary,   Anne,   Edmund, J.P., lands in Oxenhope, 1577,
 = Wm.   = Stephen   = Jane, d. Sir Francis Hastings.
 Middleton, Tempest.   Thomas, aged 16 in 1585. *(Glover's*
 of Stockeld | *Visitation.)*
 and Ilkley.   Edmund.

OLDFIELD.—Indenture, 1562, whereby Edmond Eltoft of Farnhill sold to John Oldfield of Bingley, a messuage bounded by Bothomlands, Bouldoles, Brerehy lands, Castle, Milnwro, Eyre river, &c.

The Oldfields were an old Gilstead family and owned Milner Field and other messuages in Gilstead.

Thomas Oldfield, of Gilstead.
= Sarah, widow in 1633 or before.
John Oldfield, of Rotherham, died 1635, O.S. March 20.
= Isabel, dau. of Wm. Emery, died in 1642.

John of Manchester,   Emery of Manchester.   Alice.   Marie.
 woollen draper, &c.,   ⅄
 d. June 1662.
= Mary Booth, married May 30, 1654, at Stockport.

John, bap.   Humphrey, founder of Salford Library, bap.   Thomas,
at Salford, Dec. 27, 1657, unmarried; his two Wills are   bap.April
Feb.1654-5. printed in *Manchester Notes and Queries*, Oct. 28, 1661,
   ⅄   Jan. 1887-8. He died Nov. 25, 1690. *Arms,*   un-
             3 garbs, 2 and 1, crest on a garb, a bird   married.
             statant to sinister.

John Oldfield of Rotherham, yeoman, and John Rawson of Greenhill, in Bingley, make an agreement respecting two closes of Oldfield's named Ealand and Walkerclose in Gilstead, in the tenure of Henry Johnson, agent, and Giles Beane, yeoman, 1633, whereby Rawson enters bond to pay ffiftie poundes unto Sara Oldfield, widowe, late wife of Thomas Oldfield, father of said John, for payment of £5 10s. yearly to her as dower, reserving a "redd rose in tyme of roses if the same be demaunded." John Oldfield signs in a good bold hand. Inquisition post-mortem was taken at Bradford in Sep. 1636, when it was found that he died seized of messuage and twenty acres in

Gilstead, subject to a mortgage of £120 to John Rawson, and lands in Rotherham, and his son John was then 9½ years old. The inventory of his personal effects amounted to £266, a goodly sum in those days. John the son, who married Mary, daughter of Humphrey Booth, of Salford, paid off the Gilstead mortgage in April 1654, the messuage late in the tenure of John Slater and then Thomas Oldfield and now of George Beeston, and the closes called Narr and Far Royds, Smithie Croft, Overshaw, Nethershaw, (now Ynge and Ould Roydshill), Walker close, Ealands, Dowley, By-the-burnt-Cake and Lightfoot close, which with lands in Rotherham, Kimberworth and Marshborough (? Masbro') formed the real estate. Marriage settlement, May 8, 1654. Mary Booth's portion was £200, signed by her cousin, Robert Booth, afterwards Sir Robert, Chief Justice of Ireland.

RAWSON, of Shipley. Arms, fess sable and azure, Castle with four towers argent: possessions in Bingley parish.

—— Rawson ⊤ —— dau. of Gascoigne.

William R., Shipley, died s.p.   Lawrence,
= Barbara Hawksworth.   ⊤ —— Hawksworth,

William,   John,   other children.
⊤ Martha, dau.   = Sarah, dau. W. Farrer, Idel.
Ric. Pollard.
William
= Mary, dau. Thos, Lister, Manningham.

KIGHLEY, of Kighley and Riddlesden.
Richard K.

Sir Henry, 21 Edw. I., married Ellen, dau. Sir. Hugh Venables.

Henry, 4 Ed. II.

Gilbert, knight, gravestone at Keighley.
⊤ Margery Hornby, wid. of Sir Robt. Urswick.
Richard, 20 Edw. III.

William, 36 Edw. III.

Henry ⊤ Margaret, dau. Sir Robt. Hesketh.
   Henry ⊤ Cecilye, dau. Sir Thos. Butler
     George. 1 Hy. VIII.⊤Anne, dau. Laurence Warren, Esq.
       Henry ⊤

Ann = Sir Wm. Cavendish.   Thomas Worsley, Esq. = Kathrine.
Laurence Kighley, of Newhall ⊤ Isabel, wid. Sir. Robt. Plompton.
       Richard ⊤ dau. of Wm. Calverley, Esq.

Edward ⊤ Anne, dau. & h. W. Goldesburgh.   Margaret = W. Gascoigne
   Leonard, of Newhall, 32 Eliz.   Esq.

ANCIENT BINGLEY. 223

BRIGGS. Abridged from *Ilkley Ancient and Modern*.

Francis Brigg, joiner, Otley, Ilkley and Bingley successively; restored Bingley Market Hall.
= (1), Sarah, dau. Henry Jennings, of Ilkley, bap. 1727, married at Ilkley, April 21, 1748.
= (2), — a quo Briggs of Bingley.

James, merchant, of Leeds. JamesBriggs, M.D., Brighton and London, d. s.p. = FrancesVincent, niece of Dean V. of Westminster.

Mary, bap. at Ilkley, Mch. 26, 1749, =James Horsfall, Rastrick. a quo the Horsfalls of Brighouse.

two other daughters

BRIGGS ARMS.

In Bingley churchyard is a tombstone to the memory of another of the numerous Brigg or Briggs family, and a rude oil portrait of the veteran sexton is in existence. "To the memory of Hezekiah Briggs, who died August 5th, 1844, in the 80th year of his age. He was sexton of this church 43 years, and interred upwards of 7000 corpses.

Here lies an old ringer beneath this cold clay,
Who has rung many peals both for serious and gay;
Through grandsire and trebles with ease he could range,
Till death called a bob which brought round the last change."

HARTLEY AND HUDSON. From monuments in Bingley Church, we gather that the Rev. Richard Hartley, A.B., 48 years vicar of this parish, died April 20, 1789, aged 75. [He is stated to have been born at Eldwick Hall, Sep. 5, 1714.] He was twice married, first to Ann, daughter of John Perkins, M.D., of Netherton near Wakefield, by Elizabeth, relict of Sir Wm. Thornton, Knt., of Thornville, near York, by whom he had two children, Thomas and Ann. She (the wife) died August 10th, 1745, aged 24 years, and was buried here. Thomas was buried at Harrogate, Sept. 29, 1772, aged 31 years, and Ann died unmarried 2 Aug. 1815, aged 71 years. His second wife was Martha dau. Rev. Thomas Hudson, A.B., Master of the Grammar School at Bingley, by whom he had issue Martha and Richard, the former marrying Mr. Peter Tolson of Leeds, and the latter becoming Vicar of Bingley. Their mother died Sep. 1, 1764, aged 40, and was buried at Bingley.

The Rev. Richard Hartley, D.D., the son, born at Bingley, was 45 years Master of the Grammar School at Bingley and Vicar 39 years. He died Oct. 26, 1836, aged 72. His first wife, named Charlotte, died April 11, 1820, and his second wife, Mary, eldest daughter of the Rev. Richard Hudson

REV. R. HUDSON.   HARTLEY HARTLEY.

of Hipperholme, survived him and was buried at Spofforth, 28 March, 1844, aged 63.

There have been Hartleys in Helwick (Eldwick) for a long period, one of whom, William was father of William Hartley of Helwicke Hall, whose son Joseph Hartley, a farmer and butcher, born in Bingley, lived at Helwick Hall. He was lost in the snow coming from Halifax market, Nov. 16, 1791, and was buried in Bingley churchyard. His son John Hartley was born at Helwick Hall, May 29, 1780, and Col. Joseph Hartley of London, is his son.

From another of the local branches sprang my late friend Hartley Hartley, whom I induced to work up the local history by gathering the traditions of the district. The Methodist section he had fairly done, and he copied at my suggestion the old Churchwardens' book which we read together for correction. We then copied the Parish Registers, mostly together, one reading whilst the other wrote, but when he had got well acquainted with the caligraphy sickness overtook him, and he was suddenly cut off to the great regret of a numerous acquaintance, and he was buried in the Wesleyan chapel-yard at East Morton. His motto was very apt, HEARTILY, HEARTILY, AS TO THE LORD.

ANCIENT BINGLEY.

Rev. Thomas Hudson, A.B., Curate of Idle, Master of Bingley Grammar School, died 13 May, 1756.
= Martha Rocket, married at Bradford 21 Dec. 1723, died 28 Nov. 1775, aged 75.

Thomas,	Richard,	Martha,	Mary,	Elizabeth,
B.A., Fell.	B.A., Fell.	married Rev.	d. 8 Nov.	d. 27 May,
Christ Coll.,	Queen's Coll.,	Richd. Hartley,	1763,	1781,
Camb.,	Camb. 53 years	as above stated,	aged 29.	aged 55.
Master of	Master of	she was bapt.		
Bingley	Hipperholme	at Bradford, 3 Dec.		
Gram. School,	Gram. School,	1724, her father		
d. July 1785,	*portrait herewith*,	being then		
aged 51.	65 years	Curate of Idle.		

Lecturer at
Halifax Parish Church,
Incumbent of Bolsterstone, near Sheffield,
Vicar of Cockerham, died 28 March, 1835,
aged 89, buried at Coley.

GREENWOOD. *Arms*—Sa; a chevron ermine between three saltiers couped argent. Party per fesse, sable and argent, a chevron ermine between three cross saltiers, countercharged argent. Crest, a tiger sejant, or.

James Greenwood, of Keighley.
|
John, born July 6, 1730, died Mch. 10, 1807.
=Ann Barwick, d. June 1810, aged 70.
John, born Sep. 8, 1763; died Oct. 11, 1846.
= (2) Sarah, eld. dau. Wm. Sugden, Esq., Keighley; died 1803, aged 26; buried at Keighley.

Frederick, born Jan. 15, 1797, of Ryshworth Hall, 1828-48; of Norton Conyers. =Sarah, dau. Saml. Stainforth, Esq.	Edwin, b. 1798, d. unmarried 1852.	Ann, b. 1795, = Rev. Theodore Dury, of Keighley.	Matilda, b. 1799, =Rawdon Briggs, Esq., M.P., Halifax.	Sarah Hannah, b. 1805, =John Benson Sedgwick, Esq., of StoneGappe.
John, b. at Ryshworth Hall in 1829; M.A. of Oxford, M.P. for Ripon. =Louisa Elizabeth, dau. N. C. Barnardiston, Esq.	Mary Littledale. = Major Hawkins.	7 children.		

Frederick B.	Charles S.	Edwin Wilfrid.	Clara Louisa.

o

STARKIE. Nicholas Starkie, Esq., of Huntroyd, Lancashire.

Nicholas S., Esq., of Riddlesden.   William, of Manchester.

Nicholas Le Gandre Starkie.   Thomas, of Frenchwood.
=Frances, dau. Walter Hawksworth.

Nicholas, of Frenchwood and Riddlesden.

Elizabeth Susannah, died 1862.   Katherine   [d. 1860.
=Col. H. Bence, d. 1861, aged 73.   =Capt. E. C. K. Bacon, R.N.,

Henry Alex. Starkie Bence, inherited half of Riddlesden.
Edw. Starkie Bence, of Kentwell, High Sheriff of Suffolk.

Two coheiresses, whose husbands Commander W.F. Jackson, R.N., and John Thomas, Esq., each acquired a 4th part of Riddlesden.

PEILE of Gilstead. Arms,—Argent, a bend sable between two mullets pierced sable.
Jonathan Peile, Esq., from Otley, b. 1708, d. Sep. 1782.
= Ann Booth, died 1785, aged 70. Monument in Bingley Church.

Jonathan, d. s.p.
John, d. s.p.
Benj., d. s.p.
Thomas, of London, d. s.p.

Christopher, of Civil Service, Bombay; of Bath, d. 1873.
=Jane Taylor.

Solomon, of London.

Booth, d. s.p.
Sarah.

John Henry, Civil Service, Madras; Brighton, sold Bingley estates in 1843.

= Jane, d. Lt.Col. Henry Powlett, of Carisbrook.

Christopher Fountaine, Captain, Madras. d. 1824.

FELL.—A monument in Bingley Church tower bears the inscription INFRA REPONUNTUR EXUVIÆ THOMÆ FELL DE MORTON GENS. QUI OBIIT primo Julii anno ætatis suæ lxviii, salutis nostræ mdcxcvii Joshua & Martha pignora Elhara sui ut fine sic situ parum distant quibus nil fellis prætor nomen erat quos genio pares, amis non longe dispares ævo immaturos pietate maturos Mors paiter rapuit immatura Hac obiit 6º Julii anno ætatis xv, Dom mdcxcvii Ille obiit 19º Junii Anno ætat xiii Dom mdcxcix.

The Fells are mentioned in both Bingley and Keighley Registers from the earliest pages. Thomas Fell died in 1745, leaving his property to his wife for life, with remainder to his cousin Solomon Fell, from whom it passed to his only daughter Pleasaunce, who married the Rev. Wm. Penny.

FERRAND.—The following paragraph, referred to on page 196, was overlooked at its proper place. Samuel Ferrand, bapt. at Bingley 24 Feb., 1664, rector of Todwick, vicar of Rotherham, married (1) in 1687, Ann Marsh, and had issue, Benjamin, a clergyman, Edward, Fytch William, and others.

LEACH. On a fine marble tablet in the Church are the arms of Leach,—Ermine on a chief dancetty gules, three ducal coronets or. Crest a naked arm, hand grasping a snake. Under a stone in the Porch marked D.L. lieth

DAVID LEACH of West Riddlesden Hall, gentleman. He died 8th August, 1752, aged 56, leaving an example to posterity how great works are to be accomplished by Faith and Perseverance, to the attainment of felicity and for the public utility to succeeding ages. Ann his daughter, died April the 16th, 1744.

On another tablet are the arms, colouring nearly obliterated, Baron and femme, *Leach* quarterly,

LEACH ARMS.

impaling ermine on a chief indented azure two estoiles or. *Rayner* quartering a chevron, &c.

THOMAS LEACH of the Honourable Societies of Gray's Inn and Staple Inn, Middlesex, Principal of the latter place, was buried here 16 June, 1763, aged 63. He was eldest son of Abraham Leach of this parish, by Hannah, third daughter of John and Elizabeth Rayner of Liversedge and Holme Shayes in this county. To whose memory and to his only brother John who died in Jamaica, April ye 3rd, 1725, this stone was erected by his executors.

Thomas Leach of West Riddlesden Hall, gent., died 4 May, 1796; his wife Hannah, 7 April, 1788, aged 60, his wife Elizabeth, 11 July, 1807, aged 58. Also Jane, wife of William Leach, died 20 Nov., 1822, aged 58. Also Thomas, son of said Thomas and Hannah, died June 10, 1841, aged 79. *Arms*, 1 and 4 Leach, 2 and 3, argent a lion rampant, gules.

The Leaches obtained Riddlesden in 1634, by the marriage of John Leach and the heiress of Mawde, and when this line became extinct in 1854 the Greenwoods purchased the estate. The three crowns on the arms are said to have been granted because one of the progenitors entertained the kings of England, France and Scotland at his house near Windsor! From a pedigree filling 13 pages of parchment, beginning with John Leche of Shelf, near Halifax, 1430, I have printed the well attested descent in my *Yorkshire Genealogist*, Vol. I., 143-150, and therefore need not repeat the whole again.

On gravestones near the south porch are inscriptions to the memory of the Rev. Richard Leach, schoolmaster, who died in 1742, aged 40; one in Latin to the memory of John son of Robert Leach, 1708; a third to David Leach, died 1752, aged 56, Rachel, his wife, of West Riddlesden Hall, 1779, aged 89, William and Ann their children, Lydia Sunderland of Blackburn, niece of Rachel Leach, died 1795, aged 80, and Rachel, daughter of David and Rachel, died 1801, aged 73.

On a fourth stone,—the family of Thomas, just mentioned as dying in May 1796, who was son of the said David and Rachel.

In addition to the seven pages in the "Genealogist," the Leach pedigree gives the descent of Mary Coates and her husband Joshua Cowling of Brunthwaite, but I have not printed it there nor need do here, having no reference to Bingley, though the Rev. David Cowling, sometime of Riddlesden, was a descendant.

Two branches omitted are here inserted; Thomas Leach, b. 1672, who married Ellen Hoyle, had two sons, John, who married Grace Rawson of Laund House, and had issue Thomas of Riddlesden, Sarah and William; and Thomas, born 1700, married Ann Garth.

David, son of John and Mary (Hartley) Leach, was born in 1695, and died at Riddlesden 8 Aug. 1752, aged 56, having married Rachel Fenton of Hunslet, died 25 Aug. 1779, aged 89. Their issue were Rachel, Ann, Mary, Thomas, as given on gravestone record, and William of Morton, born 1732, married Mary Helliwell (b. 1733, d. 1805), leaving two daughters, Nancy married Samuel Cowling, and Rachel married Matthew Darbishire and their daughter Rachel Leach Darbishire married David Cowling. Their gravestone at Bingley bears this record,—

David Cowling, late of the City of York, d. 1817, aged 33.
Rachel Leach Cowling, relict, died at York, interred here 1833, aged 49.
David Coates, d. April 1738, aged 51.
David, son of John Coates, d. 1792, aged 45.
Elizabeth, wife of John Coates, of Bank House, d. 1799, 77.
John Coates, d. 1805, aged 85.

HORSFALL.—This family takes its name from the old homestead Horsfall, near Hebden Bridge, where they have been located for more than six centuries. Bishop Horsfall, of Kilkenny, and his son Sir Cyprian, of Inisnag Castle, bore the same arms, as may be seen in St. Canice Cathedral, and that branch is represented in the female line by Sir Robert Langridge. Before the Reformation a yeomanry branch were located at Haworth, where wills from 1536 to the present are preserved at York.

ANCIENT BINGLEY.

William Horsfall, will proved Aug. 1536, bur. at Haworth.
 ├── William, : not proved which :
 │   └── Richard, of Oxenhope.
 │   ├── Jonas,
 │   │   ├── Jonas
 │   │   └── Michael, of Denholme.
 │   │   └── Thomas, of Denholme.
 │   │   ├── Michael, of Rothwell
 │   │   ├── Thomas, of Cullingworth, in Bingley parish, tanner, bur. at Haworth, 1770, will proved Jan. 1771.
 │   │   │   ├── William, of Cullingworth, tanner, = Anne,
 │   │   │   │   ├── James, born 1791.
 │   │   │   │   ├── William, d. 1791.
 │   │   │   │   └── Sarah, d. 1801, bur. at Bingley.
 │   │   │   ├── Jonas, d. 1777, aged 20.
 │   │   │   ├── Lydia,
 │   │   │   └── Hannah.
 │   │   ├── Timothy, of Denholme, d. 1795, aged 72, will, 1796.
 │   │   │   ├── Timothy, of Goitstock, cotton spinner, b. 1764, d. 1811, buried at Bingley, =Sarah, dau. Jermh. Garnett, of Otley and Bowling Hall.
 │   │   │   │   ├── 1. John Garnett H.,
 │   │   │   │   ├── 2. Jeremiah.
 │   │   │   │   ├── 3. William,
 │   │   │   │   ├── 4. Timothy,
 │   │   │   │   ├── 5. Michael, bur. at Bingley, 1841.
 │   │   │   │   ├── 6. Charles, bur. at Bingley, 1822.
 │   │   │   │   ├── 7. Thomas, b. 1803, d. 1861, bur. at Burley.
 │   │   │   │   │   =Martha, dau. Rev. Jas. Charnock, Haworth.
 │   │   │   │   │   ├── Sophia=Henry Bliss, son of Sir Malby Crofton. Mrs. Crofton is Lady of the Manor of Burley.
 │   │   │   │   │   └── Emmeline, =John Gethin, Esq., =Rev. J. H. Hudleston, M.A. Ripley.
 │   │   │   │   ├── 8. Mary, b. 1786, d. 1858, bur. at Bingley.
 │   │   │   │   ├── 9. Martha, b. 1791, d. 1821.
 │   │   │   │   ├── 10. Sarah, b. 1800, = Rev. John Barber, Wilsden. She died s.p. 1879.
 │   │   │   │   └── 11. Anne, b. 1805, d. 1887, s.p. = Rev. Thomas Fairbank, Bramley. =Wm. Moxon, Esq., Shipston on Stour.
 │   │   │   └── others, including Thomas.
 │   │   └── others.
 │   └── William, of Whiteshaw, Thornton.
 ├── Richard,
 ├── Thomas,
 └── others.

ANCIENT BINGLEY.

1. John Garnett Horsfall, the eldest, of Goitstock and Bolton Royd, Bradford, born 1788, died 1848, married his cousin Mary, dau. of Thomas Horsfall of Denholme* above, and her brother Thomas Hill Horsfall owned lands in Micklethwaite, Bingley, Saltonstall, Denholme, Wilsden, &c., died unmarried. She was born in 1797, buried at Shipley in 1850 with her husband. Their children were—

John, Bolton Royd, and Gawthorpe Hall, bur. nr. Berlin, 1869.	Wm. of Manningham, bur. 1859, at Shipley.	Charles, of Thirsk, bur. at Shipley, 1854.	Anne, =Rev. W. T. Garrett, Bedale, lands at Micklethwaite.
Joseph John Mendelssohn, of Wimbledon and Denholme, b.1853.	Thomas M. ⵟ	Alex. M., James M., Charles M.	Mary, ⵟ

2. Jeremiah, of Addingham, born 1792,
= Anne, dau. John Tomlin, Esq., Clitheroe.

John Tomlin, b. 1821; Sarah Anne, Elizabeth, Martha, Mary Garnett.	Alfred, b. 1829. ⵟ	Esther, Samuel Tomlin, b. 1839.	Michael Edw. R., ⵟ	Jeremiah Garnett, of Dalbeattie.

3. William, of Calverley and Hornby Grange, J.P.
= Margaret, dau. Rev. N. T. Heineken, Bradford.

William Christian, d. in 1888, near Dublin.	Thomas Garnett, J.P., Hornby Grange, b. 1834.	Michael Heineken, J.P., of Little Smeaton. ⵟ	Emma Sarah Grace Margaretta Caroline Mary Edith

4. Timothy Horsfall, of Ryshworth Hall and Hawksworth Hall, J.P., born 1795, bur. at Otley, 1879.
= Mary Anne, dau. Thos. Moss, Esq., Liverpool.

Thomas Moss, of Burley, ⵟ b. 1829.	Jane Elizabeth ⵟ Isabella ⵟ Mary Ann and Martha bur. at Bingley, infants.

Opposite the altar in 1847, there was a stone bearing an incised cross on the left side, and an innovated inscription where the brass had been torn away, viz.,—Michael son of the Rev. Timothy Normanton of Rochdale, grandson of Mr. James Smith of Hill End in this parish, died July 27, 1765.

FEATHER. William Fether of the Ravenroyde in the parish of Byngley made his will dated Feb. 17, 1593. He directed that his body should be buried in the churchyard of Byngley. The rest of the lease of the messuage in which he then dwelt he gave to his son William. To Christopher, Mawde, William, and Ellen, children of William Laycocke, deceased, £6-13-4 equally to be divided among them. To John Laycocke another son of said William, gift. To William Fether the son aforesaid £10. To Ephan the wife of William Wood, and daughter of the testator £10. He appointed his son William and daughter Mawde Fether, executors. The will was proved March 19, 1593, at York.

William Feather of Ravenroyde in Bingley made his will March 7, 1618; directing his body to be buried in Bingley Churchyard. He mentions his wife Isabell and a daughter Elizabeth, then under age, but both to be executors. Proved Dec. 20, 1619, at York.

Thomas Fether of Hallowes in Bradford parish, bachelor, will dated Oct. 18, 1706, gave to his sister Sarah, wife of John Gawkeroger £10, to his nephew Nathan Dickson £10, to his nephew Richard Horsfall £5, to Mary Hartley £10, to Mr. James Roberts, late Vicar of Bingley £5, to his brother John Fether 20s., and to Thomas son of John 10s. To Martha wife of Thomas Mitchell of Haworth 5s. To Sarah Booth £5. To Nathan Fearnside 5s. To John Mitchell servant to Robert Ferrand, Esq., at Harden Grange, 20s. To Timothy son of Robert Clayton of Harden 5s. His nephew Thomas Horsfall of Denholme he appointed sole executor and residuary legatee.

John Feather of Westshaw, Haworth, yeoman, will dated April 5, proved Oct. 23, 1729, left his wife Sarah, and her father Jonas Horsfall, executors.

Edward Fether of the Villa of Byngley paid 4d. subsidy roll for Skyrack, 1524.

Mary Fether, widow, Bingley, and Edwd. Watson, clothier, were married at Kildwick in 1637.

LAMPLUGH—WICKHAM. A monument in Bingley church bears the words—

THE REV. WM. LAMPLUGH, OF COTTINGLEY, VICAR OF DEWSBURY, DIED MAY 7, 1776, AGED 72, HIS WIFE ELIZABETH, ONLY CHILD OF THOMAS DOBSON OF COTTINGLEY, DIED 21 NOV. 1778, AGED 70. ALSO, HENRY WICKHAM, ESQ., OF COTTINGLEY, DIED THERE 9 OCT., 1804, AGED 74. ALSO OF HIS WIFE ELIZABETH, ONLY CHILD OF THE SAID REV. WM. AND ELIZABETH LAMPLUGH, DIED AT YORK 23 APRIL, 1815, aged 77; ALSO THREE OF THEIR CHILDREN ELIZABETH AND HENRY, INFANTS, AND ANNABELLA, DIED 14 NOV. 1797, AGED 28.

The following sketch pedigree (a full account will be found in the *Yorkshire Genealogist*, Vol. 2), will indicate the local relationship of this ancient family.

Bishop Wm. Wickham, Winchester, died 1595.
⊤ Anthonina, dau. of Bishop Barlow.
Henry, Archdeacon of York, bur. in York Minster, 1641.
⊤ Annabella, dau. Sir Henry Cholmeley.
Tobias, Dean of York, bur. in York Minster, 1697.
⊤Elizabeth, dau. of Wm. Wye, Esq.

Henry, bur. in York Minster, 1735,   William, Clerk of Peace, Wakefield, father of Rev. Tobias W. of Keighley.

⊤Margaret Archer, of Barbadoes.
Henry, D.D., Guiseley, bur. in Bath Abbey Church, 1772.
⊤Anne, dau. Wm. Calverley, Esq., bur. at Guiseley.
In the chancel, North-wall, Guiseley Church, marble monument—

Arms. — Ermine on a bordure engrailed gules, 8 mullets or, (Wickham), impaling Sable, an escutcheon between eight owls. Juxta | Quiescit olim præmiis beata | ANNA HENRICI WICKHAM | Ecclesiæ hujus Rectoris Conjux | .... obiit Aprilis xi., 1736, ætat suæ 27.

She was daughter of Wm. Calverley, of Leeds. Rev. Hy. Wickham, M.A., Fell. Trin. Coll., Camb., Chaplain to the Princess of Wales, was buried at Bath Abbey, June 2, 1772, aged 73.

Henry, of Cottingley, born Sep. 7, 1731, J.P., Lieut.-Col., died Oct. 9, 1804, mar. at Bingley, bur. at Bingley.
⊤Elizabeth, dau., heiress of Wm. Lamplugh, of Cottingley, Vicar of Dewsbury, and of Elizabeth, dau. of Thomas Dobson, of Cottingley. Mrs. W. died in 1815.

CALVERLEY ARMS.

HON. WILLIAM WICKHAM.

H. L. WICKHAM, ESQ.

LUCY WICKHAM.

WILLIAM WICKHAM, ESQ., M.P.

COL. HENRY WICKHAM.

ELIZABETH WICKHAM.

William, b. Dec. 1761, D.C.L., Sec. of State, P.C., of Cottingley and Binsted-Wyck, d. at Brighton, Mon. in York Minster. Life published in 1840. ⹀Eleonore, dau. Prof. Bertrand. Henry Louis, b. at Cottingley, May 19, 1789, M.A., Oxon, d. at Binsted, Oct. 1864. ⹀Lucy, grandr. Abp. Markham.	Lamplugh, b. 1768, M.A., Oxon, J.P., D.L., Vicar of Paul, East Riding, d. 1842. ⹀Sarah Elizth., d. Ric. Hird, Esq., Rawdon, and took name Hird. She d. 1812. = Hannah Frances, d. Rev. L. S. Lascelles.	Anne, d. 1857, aged 93. Harriet, d. 1847, aged 80. Annabella, d. 1795. Elizabeth, inf. Henry, inf.
	Henry Wickham, M.P., Bradford.	Lamplugh Wickham, J.P., Low Moor.	others.
William, b. July 10, 1831, M.A., Oxford, J.P., M.P., of Binsted-Wyck. ⹀Sophia, dau. co-h. H. F. Shaw-Lefevre, Esq.	Henry Lamplugh, Capt., J.P. ⹀Hon. Theresa Mary, dau. of Baron Arundell.	Leonora Emma, ⹀H. C. Herries, Esq., eld. son of Sir W.L.H.

I have to acknowledge the very great kindness of Mrs. Wickham in supplying photographs of her late esteemed husband, William Wickham, Esq., M.P., recently deceased, (who published in 1876, his grandfather's "Correspondence," in two volumes), and I reproduce the most recent one. To her generosity the reader and author are indebted for supplying photographic copies of the following paintings, from which I have obtained plates:

(1) Henry Louis Wickham, father of the late M.P., from a very dark painting.

(2) Lucy, daughter of William Markham, Esq., mother of the late M.P., a beautiful Yorkshire lady. The painting was made by Sir Charles Eastlake, R.A., about 1837. I have no need to indicate that the lady with the curls and fur is referred to.

(3) The late Member's grandfather, the Hon. William Wickham, Secretary of State, &c., reading a document.

(4) and (5) The Secretary's parents, Col. Henry Wickham, of Cottingley, and his wife Elizabeth Lamplugh, the Cottingley heiress.

MORVELL. Amongst the oldest Bingley families we find the Morvells, of whom William Morvell of Beckfoot had four daughters, Mary who married in Feb. 1675, Joseph Priestley, of Whitewindows, Halifax, Isabel the wife of John Dixon of Sowerby, Sarah wife of Isaac Taylor of Bradford, and ―― wife of John Holdsworth of Beckfoot.

A John Morvell alias fidler, of Byngley, was buried at Leeds in July, 1592.

APPLEYARD. A full pedigree of the Appleyards of Halifax parish will be found in the *Yorkshire Genealogist*, pp. 118-138.

Richard Appleyard, Norwood Green, in Hipper-
| holme, bapt. at Halifax, 1540.
Jonas, bap. Sep. 21, 1573, at Halifax.
|
Richard, bap. 28 Nov., 1596, at Halifax, buried
| there, 1675.

APPLEYARD ARMS.

Joshua, of Hipper-holme, bap. 1637 at Halifax.

Jonas, of Harden Grange, bap. at Halifax, Sep. 1642, bur. at Bingley, 3 Dec., 1675. ⹀ at Bingley, May 1663, Mary Crawshaw. Elizabeth, bap. 1665, at Bingley, bur. there Dec. 1670.

Richard, of Ryshworth, d, 1708. ⹀ at Bingley, Nov. 1700, Martha Hardcastle.

Ann, bapt. at Bingley, June 1701.

Sarah⹀Wm.Skirrow, ⊥ *a quo* Skirrows of London.

Robert, bp. 1702, Great Yarmouth.

Jonas, Willes-
| den,
⊥ Herts.

Jonas Appleyard's will, proved at York, July 1676. gives £4 and the best cloth suit of apparell to his brother Richard. He signed with a cross, and the witnesses were Ben. Ferrant, Wm. X Smyth.

ANDERTON. It seems very probable that this family settled near Bradford about 1700. There was a John Anderton of Woodhouse at that time, but our positive information starts with Mr. John Anderton,* of the Hall House or Hallas, or Hallowes, born 1732, married Alice dau. of —— Bynns of Oxenhope; he died Jan. 10, 1803, and was buried in the aisle of Bingley Church. Will proved at York Feb. 1803. She died in 1801. Issue, (1) James, of Boldshay Hall, married Deborah Horsfall, (cousin, it is said, of Mr. Timothy Horsfall, Goit Stock,) had issue who died s.p. (2) Thomas, b. 1756. (3) John, b. 1758, of the Manor House, Cullingworth.

(4) William, Vicar of Denton, afterwards of Poole, b. 1761, died unmarried, March 1838, buried at Bingley.

(5) Jonathan, physician, Keighley and Bradford.

(6) George, b. 1762, buried at Bingley, 1836, of Haworth and Bingley.

(7) Joseph, b. 1767, of Whiteshaw, Denholme.

(8) Jonas, of Keighley, married, and had issue.

(9) Robert, born 1775, bur. at Bingley 1803.

(10) Richard married and had issue.

* His parentage and place of marriage I wish to discover.

(11) Alice married —— Emmot, of Halifax, had issue.

(3) John, b. 1758, d. 1819, married Elizabeth Smith of Sutton, and had issue, Jonathan, b. 1784, Mary (married John Horsfall, Esq.,) John, of The Bent, d. unm. 1867, Richard, b. 1789, d. young, Sarah d. 1817, William of Bingley, b. 1793, married Mary dau. —— Maude Esq,, (issue three daughters, wives of J. B. Greenwood, Esq., Wm. Marriner, Esq., and John Brigg, Esq., M.P.,) Susannah, d. 1826, Joseph, b. 1801, married Mary Smith, issue Benjamin and John, Bingley.

(5) Jonathan, physician, mar. Sarah, dau. Samuel Blakey, Esq., solicitor, Keighley, and had issue Samuel Blakey A., physician at Lancaster, d. s.p. 1839; William, bur. at Haworth, 1828; John, d. s.p., Swithin A., J.P., b. 1803, d. at Bradford, 1860, married in 1823, issue as below.

(6) George, b. 1762, bur. at Bingley, 1836, married Sarah Ellison, Cullingworth, had issue.

(7) Joseph, b. 1767, married Mary Smith of Sutton, had issue George, of Cleckheaton, and other children.

Swithin Anderton, Esq., J.P., Bradford, b. 1803, d. 1860.
=Anne, d. Rev. John Braithwaite, of Sunderland, in 1823.

Samuel Blakey, b. 1824, d. s.p. 1874, buried at Undercliffe.	John, b. 1826, d. s.p. 1852.	Emma, Georgina, b.1827, mar. Wm. Foster, Esq., Hornby Castle.	Alfd.Wm., Sarah, Charles, Alfred, d. in infancy.	Fredk. William, b.1831, d.1885, bur. at Undercliffe, married Ruth, dau. John Foster, Esq., J.P. 2ndly, Eliza, dau. and heiress of Wm. Townend,	Edwin of Leeds, d.1889 bur.at Undercliffe.

Esq.,J.P.,Cullingworth,issue by 1st wife, George Frederick, Herbert Foster, Francis Swithin, Fredk. William, Alfred Foster, Florence Ruth.

HULBERT. The Rev. James Rayner, curate of Guiseley, bur. at Guiseley, Sep. 1754, married Hannah dau. of Stephen Parkinson, Esq., Fewston, in Aug. 1745, and had issue James Rayner, bap. 1746, (kept a school at Bingley some years, and had descendants there,) William b. 1749, died 1754, and Mary Rayner, bap. 1752, married —— Smith, Esq., of Gilstead Hall, and had a daughter Hannah Smith who married Rev. John Parker, Vicar of Sinnington. Mrs. Rayner married 2ndly James Hulbert, Esq., in Nov. 1759, a London physician, then attending professionally on the Vavasours at Weston Hall, where Mrs. Rayner paid a casual visit. An engagement followed and Mr. Hulbert and Mrs. Rayner were married in London, at St. George the Martyr's, City. He was a native of Corsham, Wiltshire, where the Hulberts still reside. Mrs. Hulbert disliking London they

HULBERT ARMS.

returned to Yorkshire, first to Otley, afterwards to New Laiths (Newlay), and lastly to the Old Vicarage, Bingley. There he followed his profession till his death, and he was buried at Guiseley eight years after his wife.

In Guiseley Church, on a square marble monument, north side of the south aisle :

Sacred to the Memory of James Hulbert | of Vicarage near Bingley, gent. who departed | this Life 27th June, 1799, aged 69 years.

Arms, Sable, a cross or between four leopards' heads jessant de lis argent. *Crest*, From a ducal coronet or, a talbot's head issuant argent. *Motto*, Honor Premium Virtutis.

Their children were Hannah, died at 19 ; Millicent died Jan. 1826, aged 62, and Thomas, of the Vicarage, Bingley, who died June 25, 1818, aged 56, having married Dorothy Wood of Morton, who died in 1843 aged 69. Their children were—

John of the Old Vicarage, died June 15, 1860, aged 68.
Hannah died 1871, unmarried like her brother.
Margaret, died 1871, married —— Scott, had issue.
Millicent, died 1823, married Edw. Noble, of Bingley.
Ann, bap. 1799, died 1883, at Old Vicarage.
James, bap. 1801, died July 1867, unmarried.
Mary, bur. at Guiseley.
Elizabeth, d. in infancy, 1807.
Sarah Rebecca,   ,,   1808.
Eliza,   ,,
Emma Arnold d. 1844 unmarried.

The portraits of William Hulbert of Corsham and his sister, which their brother Dr. Hulbert preserved, were given to Canon Hulbert of Almondbury on the death of Miss Ann Hulbert, under the erroneous impression that he was descendant of that line of Hulberts. His son now has them.

BEANLANDS. This pedigree is given in *Ilkley, Ancient and Modern,* p, 225, and begins with the Morton branch in 1544, the main line being continued by Alan, d. 1564. Christophar his son, d. 1589, Alan. d. 1611, Christopher, d. 1622, Christopher b. 1620, d. 1684, William d. 1683, William d. 1757, William, John d. 1777, all of Morton, in succession from father to son. John married Mary dau. of John Pulleyn, gent., and four of his sons were Bingley townsmen. (1) William, b. 1761, became a Wool Merchant in Bradford, but happening a misfortune in financial matters he rambled about the North of England and part of Scotland to evade the unmerciful demands of the law as it existed at that time, and died at Altona in 1815. I have been shewn a copy of the interesting notes of his wanderings, lent me by his great-grandson now Canon and Rector of Christ Church, Victoria, West Canada. (2) Benjamin, a merchant with his brother William, died without issue, as did also John and Joseph, cornfactors, of Bingley, the remaining brothers. William had married Mary dau. of William Haigh, of Halifax, in 1784, and she survived him till 1843. Their family consisted of three daughters and a son, John Beanlands of Prospect House, Bingley, b. 1785, died Dec. 1862, having married Anne dau. of Mr. Wm. Garnett of Otley, and sister to Rev. Richd. Garnett of the British Museum. Their issue was William, Benjamin, attorney-at-law, Arthur, M.A., of Univ. College, Durham, and Charles, M.A., Brighton. The Rev. Arthur Beanlands married Jane dau. and coh. of Thomas Jowett by Mary dau. and coh. of William Briggs of Wilsden, and their son is Canon Arthur J. Beanlands, Vancouver Island.

NEVILE. Vicar Nevile was a member of an aristocratic family. Gervas Nevile, Esq., of Holbeck, Mayor of Leeds, was his father, and William Nevile, Esq., High Sheriff in 1710 was his brother. The latter married Bridgett widow of John Ramsden, Esq., daughter of Walter Calverley, Esq. The Vicar succeeded to the Holbeck and Chevet estates, but died s.p.

BROADLEY. One of the oldest Nonconformist families of Bingley bore this name, and their descent may be traced in the Parish Registers. It was occasionally spelt Bradley, and one of them Major William Bradley, of Cromwell's army, is traditionally said to have emigrated to New Haven, Conn. about 1643.

MURGATROYD. James Murgatroyd of the Hollins, accounted by his neighbours worth £2000 a year, bought Riddlesden Hall of the Rishworths, built great part of it anew. This was about 1645. He had three sons and one daughter, John, Henry, Thomas and Mary, or Grace.

(1) John the eldest son succeeded to the estate at Riddlesden. He was twice married, (*a*) to a daughter of Midgley of Headley, and (*b*) to a daughter of Thomas Naylor of Wadsworth. There was no issue

of the second marriage, but by the first he had five sons. He disinherited his eldest son, Thomas, for marrying Elizabeth, daughter of Robert Savile of Marley, but the four younger sons, who were placed before him in succession to the estate, dying early in life, and having no children, the estate came at last to Thomas, who enjoyed it for five years, but his brother William having borrowed money from Mr. Nathaniel Spencer of Leeds, he had to repay out of the estates great costs of suits at law.

(2) Henry, son of James, lived at Oates-Royd, and married Mary, daughter of Gilbert Lacy, and had issue who intermarried with Cockcrofts and Oldfields of Calder valley.

(3) Thomas, third son, of Kershaw House in Midgley, married Hannah Rawson, of Greenhill.

(4) Mary, or Grace, only daughter, married Nicholas Starkie of Huntroyd, who was killed at Hoghton Tower in 1642, at the beginning of the civil wars. Mr. Edmund Starkie, one of the sons, acquired a portion of Riddlesden Estate on the ruin of the eldest branch of the family.

There had been a family of this name here a century earlier, for John Murgatroyd of Bingley parish made his will in 1551, directing that his body should be buried at Haworth, and besides bequests to his wife Agnes, and their two children Richard and Isabel, he ordered a small gift to Isabel dau. of John Rishworth. The Murgatroyds originally sprang from a place in Calder-dale called Moor-gate-royd. It was a clearing near Warley moor, Halifax parish. I expected to be able to amplify the family notices in the Registers by notes from a bundle of deeds in the possession of the Rev. J. H. Carter, Weaste, but have as yet only secured two. (a) Omnibus Xpi fidelibus, &c., John Fairbanke, of Skircote, yeoman, in consideration of a sum of money paid by James Murgateroide, junior, of Murgateroide, in Warley, quit-claimed to M. the rent from a messuage, &c., in Ovenden Wood, dated 25 August, 1599. Seal (a nondescript goat) and signature of John ffairebank. Witnesses, Saml. King, Abraham Denton, Richard +Lome, Js. Midgley, W. Midgley. The Midgleys were the greatest conveyancers of these parts of Airedale and Calderdale for many years, and wrote a beautiful hand.

Indenture (1610, 27 Feb.,) between John Wright of Laycock, yeoman, of one part, and John Bairstowe of Brownestehurst, and James Murgatroyde of Murgatroyde in Warley, yeomen, of the other partie; Wright for £300 sold to Bairstowe and Murgatroyde the messuage in Kighley called Parkbanke, in Edward Wright's tenure, and the messuage in Laycock in Henry Ambler's tenure, and the houses, &c., in Kighley in Wm. Sugden's tenure, and the houses, &c., of John Wright's estate. Witnesses, John Cloughe, Robte Wright, John Hirde, Godfrey Walker. The first three make marks.

Mr. Carter, Birmingham, has supplied three later notes from wills.

Calendar LXXXI, No. 567. Mary Murgatroyd, of Bingley, co. York, spinster, bequeathes to

Francis, son of my brother James M., £40,
Mary, dau.   „   „   £40,
John, son of my brother Thomas M., £30,
James,   „   „   £30,
Mary, dau.   „   „   £30,

Edmund M., my brother, £4 a year, William Radclyffe, son of John R., of Seals, £40 at 21; my sisters my brothers' wives, each 21/-; Mary Hopkinson, 20/-, and some of my wearing clothes. Residue to James Murgatroyd of Greenhill, my nephew, and executor. Dated 28 July, 1720. Proved 7 Septr., 1730.

Calendar LXXXIV., No. 290, John Murgatroyd of Lees, otherwise, Hainworth, parish of Bingley, yeoman, mentions sons James and John, and various daughters; my lands, &c., in Bingley, to my son James, and he and John Shackleton to be executors. Dated 23 Mar., 1725. Proved 18 June, 1736.

Calendar LXIII., (?), No. 129. James Murgatroyd of Greenhill, Bingley, gentleman. Messuage and lands at Greenhill, and at Adwalton in parish of Burstal, to sister Mary M. for life, rem'r to Trustees to hold during minority of James, son of John M. of Lightcliff, and if he die before 21, rem'r to James M., son of Thomas M., of Leeds, dyer, and his right heirs—the said Thomas M. and Mary his wife are mentioned, also the sd. John M. of Lightcliff and his present wife—also Mauds and Brooksbanks. Dated 23 Feb., 1769. Proved 4 June, 1762.

Whilst referring to Greenhill, we may add three more notes from deeds just received.

Indenture 31 Mch. 35 Eliz., 1593, between Wm. Rawson of Greenhill, yeoman, Christr. Walters of Wooddehouse, in Craven, Anthony Rawson of the Beckefoote, yeoman, that Wm. Rawson granted to the two others named the messuage in Bingley called Lau^{r}ocke hall or the Height in the tenure of said Anthony, with all its belongings. Witnesses, Anthony Whitley, Wm. Rothery and John Baracloughe.

An indenture dated 26 March, 12th James I, 1619, between William Hall, of Greenhill in Bingley, yeoman, and John Drake, of Kippin in Thornton, yeoman, and John Rawson of Bingley, yeoman, reciting that William Hall and his heirs held two messuages in Kighley in the tenures of Christr. Bothamley, John Widdop and Robt. Tayler; the indenture witnessed that William Hall, for the cutting of former intailes, &c., agreed with Drake and Rawson. John Whitley, John Illingworth, Wm. Butterfield, Alexander Greave, witnesses, who all make marks.

Omnibus Xpi fidelibus ad quos hoc prsens scriptu' Indentatu' p ven^{r}it, Johes Oldfeld Senior de Bingley, yeom' salt'm in Dno' sempiternu' Sciatis (&c. in Latin,) that in consideration of a marriage to take place between one of his younger sons, Thomas Oldfeld and Agnes Leache of Gilsteade, widow, formerly wife of William Leache, deceased, he gave to John Rogers, junior, of Elum, and John Rawson of Beckfoote, in Cottingley, yeoman, the messuage &c. in Gilsteade,

with the Roydes, Smythiecroft, Shayclose, Shaywood, Oldroyd,
Dawleygappe, Walkerclose, Ealand, Lightfooteclose, with 1½ ac. in
Dawley, now in the tenure of his son John, brother of said Thomas
Oldfeld, with land 1 acre at the backside of Egid (Giles) Beane Lathe.
Signature of John Oldfield. Seal—a fleur de lis. Dated 16 ffebruary,
1597. Witnesses—Walter Woller, Wm. Myers, John Oldefelde,
junior, J. Midgley (with his fine hand-writing as usual). Counterpart
(in English); The true intent of thafforesaid dede of ffeoffment
&c., is that Rogers and Rawson hold the said properties in trust to
the use of John Oldfeld the elder, for his natural life, and then to the
use of his son Thomas and his future wife Agnes Leache, and during
her widowhood if she survived Thomas and did not marry again, and
finally to the heirs of said Thomas.

SHACKLETON. The Shackletons originally sprang from Shackleton near Heptonstall. Shackleton House in Harden, now demolished, was built or rebuilt in 1660. A gable stone bearing the letters S, RE, (standing for Roger and Elizabeth,) IP, 1660, has, with the old nail-studded oak front door, been removed to AnnaLiffey House, Lucan, Dublin, where a Shackleton descendant now lives. The old house was lighted by long low mullioned diamond paned windows.

RICHARD SHACKLETON, 1726-1792.

A substantial oak staircase led to the bedrooms, and as usual with
such houses there was a south aspect. Over the front porch was an
obliterated shield; and it is thought the Shackleton arms had once
been engraved thereon,—Or, on a fess gules, three arming buckles of
the field. In 1801, the house and lands were sold by Jane Shillito, a
descendant of Roger Shackleton, to Benjamin Ferrand, Esq. A John
Shackleton resided in the neighbourhood in 1532. The old home
became sub-divided into four cottages, early in this century.

1 John Shackleton of Shackleton House, wife named Jenet, was
father of

2 Roger, bapt. 1638, buried in 1677, married Elizabeth ———;
Richard, bapt. 1642; Elizabeth, bapt. 1645; Ann, bapt. 1651, married
John Jackson.

3 Richard, the son of Roger and Elizabeth, married 30, ix, 1682,
Sarah dau. Thomas Brigg of Calversike Hill, (she was born 17, xi,
1657, died 28, ii, 1703; he died 29, i, 1705,): issue

(a) Jeremiah, b. 30, viii, 1683, married at Bradford 10, vii., 1708,
Sarah Shiers, and had issue William, Roger (bapt. at Calverley 14
July, 1717, married Jane Kipping), Sarah married Nicholas Hague,
Mary married Howe.

(b) John b. 17, iii, 1686, (probably died in infancy, as he took no
part in the sale of shares in Shackleton House.)

(c) Richard b. 21, ix, 1688, d. 24, x, 1704.

(d) Roger, b. 8, v, 1691, married at York 19, iii, 1715, Jane dau.
Wm. and Ursula Readshaw of Beckwithshaw, (she was b. 23rd, ix.,
1692, died 7th, iii, 1727.) He died 6, iii, 1766, at York; will dated
3, iii, 1766. This Roger Shackleton, bought, 17th Jan. 1717, three-
quarter shares of Shackleton House and lands from his surviving
brothers Jeremiah and Abraham, and his sister Mary; issue Roger b.
6, v, 1724, d. 15, x, 1726; William b. 8, ii, 1725; Tabitha b. 13, v,
1720, (married at York 9, viii, 1739, Francis Thurman of Osberwick;
2ndly Edward Carbutt of Hull, and had issue, a son Edward); and
Patience b. 13, v, 1722, inherited Shackleton House from her father,
married John Webster of Selby; had issue, Saml. Webster, only son,
d. s.p. Jane Webster m. John Shillito, of Stainer Hall; she inherited
Shackleton House from her brother, and sold it in 1801 to Benjamin
Ferrand, Esq.

(e) Mary, b. 15, i, 1694, bapt. at Calverley Ch. Sept. 20, 1716, and
married the same day James Fletcher of Bolton, near Bradford.

4 (f) Abraham, b. 27, viii, 1696, of Ballytore, co. Kildare, married
in Autumn 1725, Margaret dau. Richard Wilkinson of Knowlbank in
Rilston, b. 1688, d. at Ballytore 4, iii, 1768; he died at Ballytore 24,
vi, 1771; issue *Elizabeth*, (b. at Ballytore 1732, married Maurice
Raynor and had a son William); and

5 *Richard*, b. at Ballytore 9, x, 1726, who married firstly, 2, ii, 1749,
Elizabeth dau. Henry Fuller of Ballytore, great grand-dr. of Major
Barcroft, Parliamentarian; she died at Ballytore, 19, v, 1754; secondly,
17, x, 1755, Elizabeth dau. Joshua Carleton, (b. 10, x, 1726; d. 23,
iii, 1804. He died 28th, viii, 1792. The issue of the two wives, all
of Ballytore, were Abraham, *postea*; Henry b. 1754, d. 1756; Deborah
b. 1749, married 26, x, 1780, Thomas Chandler of Athy; Margaret b.
1751, married in 1776 Samuel Grubb of Clonmel; Geo. Rooke;
Rachel; Mary b. 1758, married in 1791 Wm. Leadbeater; she d. 27,
vi, 1826. Sarah, b. 6, vi, 1790, d. at Ballytore 1847, an eminent
minister in the Society of Friends.

6 Abraham, eldest son of Richard and Elizabeth, born at Ballytore
8, xii, 1752, died there 2, viii, 1818, married at Dublin, 23, ii, 1779,
Lydia, (b. at Manchester, 3 April, 1749, d. 5, ii, 1829), dau. Ebenezer

Mellor, descendant of Judge Fell of Swarthmoor and Ann Askew the martyr. Abraham and Lydia had nine children,—Richard married but d. s.p. 1860, Abraham d. inf., Ebenezer, *as follows:* I; George *as follows:* II; Margaret d. young 1790, Elizabeth, d. unmar. 1848, Lydia, d. 1811, (marr. Jas. White, Ballytore, issue a daughter,) Mary d. 1869 unmarried, Margaret d. 1816 unmarried.

I. Ebenezer, of Ballytore, b. 21, v. 1784, d. 29 Mch., 1856, mar. Deb. Leadbeater, grandr. of Richard Shackleton; their issue died young. He married 2ndly Ellen d. Wm. Bell, Queen's Co., and had issue eight children,— *Richard Ebenezer*, M.A., Trin. Coll., Dublin, Gold Medalist, b. at Dublin, 1836, married at Cheltenham Elizth. Anne dau. Major Hy. Holland, grandr. of Wm. Bell, Queen's Co.;— issue Ebenezer, B.A., Trin. Coll. Dublin, Richard, b. 1866, twin with Ebenezer, died in 1871, Charles Dudley b. 1870, William, M.B., Trin. Coll. Dublin, b. 1872, Mary Eleanor b. 1868, Isabel, b. 1867, wife of Mr. Wm. Fennell and has issue.

Patrick Dudley S. b. 1837 at Moone, married Rebecca, dau. Thos. Jameson, issue two daughters, She died in 1891.

Theobald b. 1841, married Elizabeth Anne Jameson, sister of Rebecca.

Henry, B.A., M.D., M.R.C.S., Trin. Coll., Dublin, of Aberdeen House, Sydenham, b. 1847, mar. in 1872, Henrietta Letitia Sophia, d. and h. of H. J. Gavan, Esq., descendant of Fitzmaurice, Cary, Deering, &c., families; issue two sons and eight daughters.

Edmund, b. 1850, mar. Anna Maria, dau. Charles Leech; he died in Cape Colony having a son and a daughter.

Elizabeth, b. at Moone, 1832, mar. Philip Sydney Barrington, gr. grandson maternally of Richard and Elizabeth Shackleton.

Ellen Isabel, b. 1834, d. 1862, *Agnes Rose*, b. 1845.

II. George, of Ballytore, b. 21st, viii, 1785, mar. at Limerick in 1823, Hannah, dau. Josh. Fisher, issue thirteen children; *Abraham*, b. at Ballytore 1827, mar. Anna, dau. W. Webb, issue six children, b. at Ballytore. He married 2ndly in 1891, Anne Walpole née Harvey.

Joseph Fisher, s. of Lucan, b. 1832, mar. Jane Wigham, issue six children.

George Rookes, b. 1840, married Mary Rebecca, dau. Jas. Fisher.

Richard, b. 1841, married (1) Charlotte Elizabeth Milner, (2nd) Mary Elizabeth Walpole; issue—

Hannah Jane, b. 1824, mar. Arthur Thomas Palmer, Leeds. She died at Huddersfield in 1865; issue—

Lydia, b. 1828. *Deborah*, b. 1830, mar. John William Mullin; issue— *Elizabeth*, b. 1834, mar. Alfred Webb, M.P.

Sarah Edmundson, b. 1836. *Margaret Fell*, s. b. 1837, d. 1857.

Mary, b. 1838, mar. John Chandlee, Co. Tipperary.

Rebecca Harvey, b. 1842, mar. Richard Shackleton Chandlee, brother of John Chandlee.

Rachael, b. 1845, died at Ballytore, 1860.

Richard Shackleton, who married Sarah Brigg, became a Quaker, and the records of Asquith and Knaresborough Monthly Meetings, now deposited at Leeds, state that he, Adam and Abraham Bell, John Drake and his son John, Jonas Bottomley, John Milner and John Eastburn, were taken to the Wakefield Sessions, 2, xi. 1682, and refusing to take the Oath of Allegiance by swearing they were committed to prison by the Justices, Kay, Peebles, Blitheman and others, and remained in York Castle over three years, when they were released by order of James II., 15, i. 1686. For meeting together, 1683, Stephen Hudson, constable, and others of Bingley, took goods from Richard Shackleton's house in Harding during his incarceration in York Castle, as shewn above, to value of £11, by order of Henry Lord Fairfax, Thomas Fairfax and Walter Calverley, for being at a meeting at Stubbinhouse. This large sum was because the others present at the same meeting were too poor to be levied upon for fines. His wife and friends were allowed to stay at his prison lodgings. In 1696, John Hudson, constable, and Richard Ferrand, churchwardens, took from Richard Shackleton of Keighley meeting, by warrant from Henry Currer and Robert Ferrand, Esq., J.P., £2 demanded by James Roberts, priest of Bingley, and the same priest kept him two years in prison for refusing to pay 13s. 6d. for small tythes, and then seized goods under a new Act to the value of 18s. 6d. His house (at Harden) was licenced for meetings in 1696. He is described as a schoolmaster.

Roger Shackleton, of York, merchant, who married Jane Readshaw, was an influential Quaker there. In the British Museum, Add. MS. 32699, f. 51, there is a petition by him to the Duke of Newcastle, dated York 12. xii. 1741-2, called Feb., "The petitioner is ye person whom ye Duke favourably and effectually assisted some years ago in a suit commenced against him by the City of York, on his not qualifying himself to serve ye office of Sherriffe, because I conscientiously scrupled taking an oath, and what is called the Sacrament." The petitioner pleaded on behalf of "three of my honest friends, prisoners in ye Castle of York, who have been there nearly three years for non-payment of small tithes, viz., Richard Ward, B. Burne, and Wm. Bocock, ye whole £9 8s. 4d. and £57 3s. 4d. charges at Law. The prosecutor knows that these sums were recoverable in a summary way by Justice warrant, and that it was simply a scruple of conscience which induced 'em not to pay even if only one penny; all which he sleighted, and carried on an expensive suit at law, and at last imprisoned them; to their families great loss and almost ruine. If tradesmen and merchants should imitate his example we should destroy one another, but prudence and moderation governs more in civil than ecclesiastical affairs." Roger Shackleton was elected Sheriff of York in 1733, and paid £150 fine rather than take the Oath and Sacrament. Possibly it was refunded to him by the Duke's intervention. In the "Memoirs and Letters of Richard and Elizabeth Shackleton," by their daughter Mary Leadbeater, (b. 1758), we are told that Roger was a person of solid sense, great worth and benevolence, esteemed within and without the pale of his own society. The Archbishop valued his character and conversation, and was much influenced by him.

Abraham Shackleton founded the celebrated Quaker's School at Ballytore, co. Kildare. He was of weakly constitution but vigorous intellect. By application he became a good classical scholar. He was a teacher in David Hall's Quaker School at Skipton, and then became private tutor in Quaker families in Ireland. In 1725 he returned to marry Mary Wilkinson, of Rilston. Asquith meeting, certificate from Carloe meeting on Abraham Shackleton's removal is filed at Leeds, 29 v. 1725. Asquith meeting, Ann Andrew and Jane Shackleton to enquire into Margaret Wilkinson's clearness before marrying Abraham Shackleton, and similar enquiry as to Abraham Shackleton's clearness. Both reports favourable, this meeting gives them liberty to marry, and appoints John Bins and James Smith to see to ye orderly accomplishment, 23, vii. 1725. Asquith, 28, viii, 1725. The friends appointed to attend ye marriage certify itt was orderly, and Abraham Shackleton, having acquainted us att our last monthly meeting with his intention of returning back into Ireland with his wife, and requesting a certificate this meeting appoints David Hall and George Andrews to enquire into matters concerning this removal. Asquith, 25, ix. 1725, report being favourable, certificate therefore granted. Abraham Shackleton opened his school in 1726, and it soon became famous, and amongst the published list of scholars of all denominations, Catholic, Episcopalian and Dissenters, the most conspicuous is the name of Edmund Burke, 1741, afterwards of Beaconsfield, M.P. Mr. S. retired from school management in 1756, and spent some years in visiting and addressing Friends in the British Isles. When he died in 1771, Mr. Burke testified to his high qualities, and in 1780 in the House of Commons, said "I have been educated as a Protestant of the Church of England by a Dissenter, an honour to his sect, though that sect was one of the purest. Under his eye, I have read the Bible morning, noon and night, and have ever since been the happier and better man for such reading."

Richard Shackleton succeeded his father as master of the school at Ballytore. He was a friend of Burke's, and learned in the Hebrew and other languages. His "Memoir and Letters" by his daughter have been referred to. His portrait is here reproduced from an oil painting by Sesson. He died in 1792 having been succeeded by his son Abraham in 1779, as schoolmaster, who held it till 1803. His son-in-law, James White, re-opened it in 1806, but it was finally closed in 1836.

"I've read in foreign climes of Ballitore,"
He said, "and of its celebrated School."
Old Magazine.

Mary Leadbeater was of a poetical and literary turn, and wrote "The Beauties of Ballitore," sometimes ascribed to Burke. Besides the "Memoirs and Letters," she published "The Leadbeater Papers" or "Annals of Ballitore," and other volumes.

The Harden property of Roger Shackleton, the houses, barns, gardens, late inheritance of Edward Fournes, and the closes, the

Tenter-croft, Backside-close, Wheat-close or Fournes-field, Well-close, Robin-field, late Robert Illingworth's, with tithes thereon, passed to Richard his son and heir, (died 1705.) Roger, son of Richard, bought shares of his brothers and sister, (Jeremiah, of Bolton near Bradford, Abraham of York, and Mary Fletcher of Eccleshill,) 1717. The property passed to Roger's daughter, Patience Webster, whose daughter and heiress, Jane Shillito, sold it in 1801 to Benj. Ferrand, Esq.

"Surtees' Society," vol. 40, p. 100, we have—

1663—" Depositions from York Castle."

Thomas Shackleton, of Morton Banks, accuses Jonathan Shackleton before Sir John Armitage, of phenatticism," (probably Quakerism.) 'Thomas Shackleton,' of Morton Banks, par. Bingley, sayeth, 'that upon Sunday night last he heard Jonathan Shackleton of the same place say, 'Am I a phenattick? you shall know yet before March wind be blown, that we phenatticks will look all those in the face which now doe oppose us, for the king is a bloudy Papist, or else he would never give consent to the putting to death of soe many honest men as he hath.'

PARKER. John Parker, born about 1664, thought to have been a member of a branch from the Parkers of Browsholme and Marley, left Bingley about 1684 for Philadelphia, but returned to England in 1696 on a visit. He resided at Ravenroyd and joined the Society of Friends. About 1698 he went again to Philadelphia, and in 1699 Mary Doe, of London, followed him, and they were married. Her grandfather was named Vernon, and John Field, afterwards London printer, who joined the Friends in Yorkshire, was a kinsman of hers. John Parker and Jonas Parker, the latter married Isabel Feather of Micklethwaite in June, 1614, founded a family still located at West Chester, Pennsylvania. Abraham son of Jonas and Isabel, lived at Ravenroyd, his wife's name being Elizabeth. John Parker dealt in wild animals' skins till 1717 in Philadelphia.

PASLEW. *Arms:* Thoresby gives; Argent, a fesse between three mullets azure, pierced of the field. Instead of azure it is often given sable. Burke adds another for Yorkshire; Gules, a lion rampant argent crowned or. (J. A. Busfeild, Esq., confirms this from seals of John and Francis Paslew, of Riddlesden, 1572, with a lion only on the shield.) On the ceiling at East Riddlesden is the shield bearing engrailed, a lion rampant with a crescent indicating a second son. Dodsworth noticed at Keighley, 270 years ago, the arms of Paslew (mullets), Maude (lion rampant), Lacy? (Chevron three cross crosslets.) In "Whalley" are rhymes on "pass the water" as a play on the name.

The Paslews, from Wiswall in Lancashire, became lords of Newton and Riddlesden about the reign of Henry VIth. In 1540, Walter

ANCIENT BINGLEY.

Paslew received a grant of Harden Manor from the King Henry VIII, after it was taken from the priory of Drax. Being in debt to John Paslew of Wiswall, he sold the manor to him in 1572, but next year John Paslew conveyed Harden and Harden Grange to Martin Birkhead, Esq., of Grays Inn, London, and of Wakefield, for £105 13s. 4d. Robert Rishworth purchased from Francis Paslew, of Methley, the manor of Riddlesden, with Bank-houses, Marley, Thwaites, and other lands in Morton, Bingley, Keighley, &c., and John Rishworth, son of said Robert, in answer to the Court of Wards and Liveries, said that he held not of the King, but of the mesne lords and no title accrues to Queen Elizabeth on the death of Francis Paslew. (Edward Hailstone's MSS.)

Robert Paslew, of Riddlesden.
=Elizabeth, dau. and heiress of Simon Montalt
John, living 1425, had six oxgangs in Leeds, Woodhouse
=Amye Beckwith

Thomas=Jane, d. Sir John Nevile.   Elizabeth = Thomas Hawksworth
   Alexander=Maude, d. Thos.Lacy,Esq.   of Hawksworth.

Walter=Jane, dau. George=[Mary], Henry=Joyce, Stephen.
 d.1545 | Rich.   dau.Wm.   dau.   Jane = Walter
        | Clapham.   Arthington. Rich.Brown.   Hawks-
                                                  worth.

Francis,   Alex.   Isabel=(1) Robert Baildon, (2) John Brearey, of
 =Isabel, dau. Sir Wm. Calverley.   Menston.

Walter, d. Dec. 1573.   Stephen=Jane, dau. Michael Rawdon, of
 =Ellen, dau. John Lacy.   Rawdon.

Francis, died 1603, s.p.   Ellen = John   Rosamond = Henry
                                  Rishworth.   Milner.

Several discrepancies appear in this and the following pedigree, probably there are errors in both, and one amplifies the other, more or less.

From an Inquisition taken at Wakefield in 1637, on the death of Francis Paslew, of Glemham, we get a clear knowledge of the extent of the Paslew properties about Bingley, Morton, and Harden, and the names of the chief families of that time, and also full corroboration of many points in the following pedigree.

In 1392 there were two important branches of the Paslew family at Leeds. One of the name was Vicar of Leeds, 1408-18.

Robert Paslew, mentioned 13 Richard II., 7 Henry VI.
=Elizabeth, dau. & co-h. of Simon de Mahaut, Riddlesden.
John=Agnes.

    John=Johna Beckwith.   Edward.   Ralph.

ANCIENT BINGLEY.

Thomas, of Riddlesden, 1480.
⹀a daughter of ...... Metham.
Alexander, of Riddlesden, died 8 Henry VIII. Inquisition held at Ilkley.
⹀Maude, dau. Thomas Lacy, of Cromwellbottom, Elland, Esq.

Walter, Esquire, aged 11 at his father's death.
⹀Jane, dau. Richard Clapham, of Beamsley, Esq.

George, of Marley.
⹀[Bridget] Arthington.
Thomas, London, draper.
⹀
Stephen.

Stephen.

Jane = Walter Hawksworth.

Francis, of Riddlesden, Esq., (8 Eliz.) d. Sep. 1582.
⹀Isabel, dau. Sir Wm. Calverley.

Walter, d. father's lifetime, Dec. 1573.
⹀Ellen, dau. John Lacy, Esq., of Cromwellbottom & Leventhorpe, and Jane, dau. Sir Ric. Tempest, Bolton.

Richard, d. 1604.
Walter.
Thomas.

Edmund, d. 1595.
Alexr., d. 1571.
William, d. 1596.

Francis, of Glemham, ob. s.p.

Alexander, of Glemham.
⹀Margery, dau. Peter Smith, called Helen in Inquisition

Henry, of Glemham,
⹀Jane Brown.

Margaret.

Francis, of Methley, b. 1567-8 d. at Bordeaux 1603, s.p.

Helen = Henry Bannister.

Rosamond = (1) Milner, = (2) Adams.

Henry, of Glemham.

Alice, Margt.,

Elizth., Ann.

In 1282, William Paslew assisted in suppressing the Welsh rebellion, in which Roger de Clifford was surprised by the rebels in his castle of Hawarden, (now famous as the home of the Rt. Hon. W. E. Gladstone,) and carried prisoner by the Welsh, dying in captivity. Edmund Paslew served in parliament during the reign of Edward I.

Abbot John Paslew, who was executed in March 1536-7, was of this family. "Pendle," 329.

Wm. Paslew, of Bradford, will, 1450, *Bradford Antiq.* p. 202.

John Paslew, of Riddlesden, who died about 1467, directed that his body should be buried at Bingley. His mother(?) Amicia, in her will dated 1463, states "I leave all my vestments for the priest and the ornaments of the altar after my decease, to be given and appointed for the altar of St. John's church in Barnby," with her body, &c. I doubt whether it is correct to state that this lady was the mother of John Paslew of Riddlesden.

From wills, Dodsworth's MSS., &c.,—
1399. Administration granted to William Paslew on the death of his mother, Alice Paslew of Leeds.

1440. Will of Robert Paslew of Headingley.
1450. Will of William Paslew of Bradford.
1463. Will of Amicia Paslew of Barnby, proved Dec. 2.
John Paslew = Amicia de Riddlesden.

Richard, rector of Sandall.	John.	Johana=Wm.Wakefield	Edward, executor.	Ralph.

She bequeathed to her son John, one bed at Riddlesden. To her daughter Johana Wakefield, a girdle of red silk for life, and then to her granddaughter Elizabeth Wakefield. To her son Ralph, a bed and £7 13s. 4d., which was due from Thomas Beckwith. To Elizabeth Hawksworth a girdle of black silk. Bequest to a priest, to pray for the souls of her husband and herself. Her body was to be buried at Barnby church. [This accords in several points with the first part of the first pedigree.]

1467, May. John Paslew, of Riddlesden, directed that his body should be buried at All Saints, Bingley. To his son Thomas, after the decease of Joan his wife, a cup overlaid with silver and one mazer. Riddlesden he bequeathed to his wife for life, and remainder to Thomas their eldest son. John their son, to have 20s. out of Woodhouse, 8s. out of Haynworth, 13s. 4d. out of Piers close, 8s. out of Kighley and 8s. out of Smythfield yearly. John, the son, and William Beckwith to be executors. Proved in 1468.

1476. Administration of goods of Sir Richard Paslew, rector of Sandal, was granted.

1478, August. Edward Paslew, of Barnby on Don, gave to his brother Ralph two roods of hayland. He desired to be buried at Barnby. Agnes, his wife, executrix.

1513, July. Alexander Paslew, Esquire, directed that his body should be buried at Bingley. He appointed his wife Mawd and son Stephen executors; and Sir John Paslew, abbot, and John Lacy, supervisors. Possibly the abbot was his brother, as his wife's brother was a supervisor.

1543, March. "In the name of God, Amen. I, Walter Paslew, of Riddlesden [eldest son of last testator,] intend to take a journey against the Scots as directed by the king, make my will." Directions about his lands in Harden, Halton, Collingworth, Riecroft and Cowhouses. To Agnes, Julian, Mary and Jayne his daughters, £40 apiece. [These daughters are omitted in the pedigree given first.] Jane his wife and Francis their son, executors. [His wife was evidently *Jane* Clapham.] Francis to find George Paslew "my cousin" honestly meate and drink and clothes for life, or four marks yearly. [53s. 4d.; or 1s. a week was sufficient for his meat, drink and clothes!] Jane his wife to have the rewle (control) of the four younger sons and their lands till they reach 16. I bequeath the marriage of John Rawson, my ward, to Agnes, daughter of Dorothy Butler. Proved 1545.

1554. Feb. George Paslew desired to be buried in the quere of All Hallows, at Bingley. He refers to Janet his wife and their nine

children. [So both pedigrees give the wife's name wrongly.] The lease of Whitecote in Harden was given to son Thomas. Byngley Vicaredge and Priesthorpe lands on lease, and lands at Gersington to be appropriated to the education of the six sons. To my brother-in-law William Ardington, and brother Stephen Paslew, 40s. each, and make them, with Janet my wife, executors. The daughters Maude, Agnes and Ann, to be ordered by the executors in their marriage.

ELLAND.—Amongst the arms seen by Dodsworth in Bingley Church window, and figured on the accompanying plates of arms, those of Elland have been a puzzle to Antiquaries, but I think their presence here may be accounted for by the statement in the Hanson pedigree, (*Yorks. Geneal.*) that Roger of Rastrick, the head of the Hanson family, was son of William de Bingley who had a brother Henry de Ealand about 1290. There was a Gilbert de Bingley rector of Thornhill in 1310.

MAWDE. Gospatric. (Harl. MS. 6070.)

Adam, son of Gospatric, alias Adam de Monte Alto, or Mohaud, de Riddlesden.
= Richard M., of Riddlesden.

another son,
= Simon de Montalt, who conveyed lands to his uncle, Adam filius Gospatric,

William de Montalt de Riddlesden. (2, John.) He and his father witness an Arthington deed about 1186.
= Simon, 39 Henry III.,
= Adam de Mohaut, 28 Edw. I.
From Maude, Dodsworth's MSS., v. 127.

Henry de Montalt, a monk at Siningthwaite.

Sir Simon, 38 Henry III, = Lady Clarissa de Riddlesden, (Harl. MS., 2188.)
Richard, = Isabell = Wm. le Gentil, of Priesthorpe.

Richard Montalt, of Riddlesden, | Morton and Barnby.
Symon Mahaut,

Robert, of West Riddlesden,
|
Thomas, living 1320.

Elizabeth, co-h. = Rob. Paslew.

other daughters.

Constantine Monhault, of West Riddlesden, = a daughter of Keighley, of Newall,

ANCIENT BINGLEY. 251

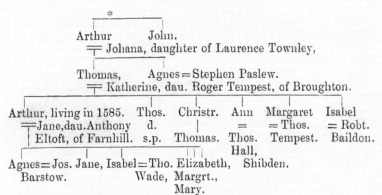

Arthur   John.
       ⊤ Johana, daughter of Laurence Townley,

Thomas,   Agnes = Stephen Paslew.
       ⊤ Katherine, dau. Roger Tempest, of Broughton.

Arthur, living in 1585. Thos. Christr. Ann   Margaret Isabel
⊤Jane, dau. Anthony   d.   =   = Thos.   = Robt.
  Eltoft, of Farnhill. s.p.   Thomas. Thos. Tempest. Baildon.
                                         Hall,
Agnes=Jos. Jane, Isabel=Tho. Elizabeth, Shibden.
Barstow.   Wade, Margrt.,
                     Mary.

The Mawds of the noble house of Hawarden are descendants of either the Airedale or Calderdale line. The arms, lion debruised, denoting according to tradition, that the head of the house captured William the Lion, king of Scotland, and conveyed him to the king, then in Normandy.

Thos. de Montalt was bailiff of Bingley, 1317.

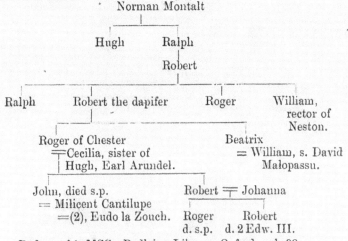

Norman Montalt

Hugh   Ralph
          Robert

Ralph   Robert the dapifer   Roger   William,
                                      rector of
                                      Neston.

Roger of Chester   Beatrix
⊤Cecilia, sister of   = William, s. David
  Hugh, Earl Arundel.   Malopassu.

John, died s.p.   Robert ⊤ Johanna
  = Milicent Cantilupe
  =(2), Eudo la Zouch.   Roger   Robert
                             d. s.p. d. 2 Edw. III.

Dodsworth's MSS., Bodleian Library, Oxford, vol. 99.

1534, May. Arthur Mawde of Bingley, desired to be buried at All Saints, Bingley. He gave 20s. to buy a bell for St. Andrew's, Keighley. He mentions his wife Johanna, his son Thomas, and his brother John. To Laurence Kighley and Thomas Maude, his son, forty marks owing by Stephen Tempest, which had to be used for Stephen Paslew. Walter Paslew of Riddlesden was a witness. Proved July, 1534.

1540, Robert Dyneley of Bramhop, gave to Ann and Janett, daughters of Anth. Mawd, a sylver spoon each.

1540. Laurence Kighley's will. Thomas Mawd and Stephen Paslew, witnesses.

1542, Feb. John Kighley of Newhall, gent., to Thomas, son of William Mawd, one sey doublet.

1561, June. Christopher Mawd, Ilkley, mentions Grace his wife, John, Arthur, Francis, sons; Isabel and Grace, daughters. Proved, Dec. 1561.

1320. Thos. Mohaud of Ridelesden, Ralph de Ikton, Thomas Vilayn de Eltoft and nine others were jury in a case of brawl at Leeds, when on a Sunday in June, after a game had been played about mid-day a quarrel ensued, but was settled by the on-lookers; after which they went to church carrying their swords and bucklers, and after Vespers had been sung Wm. le Wayt came out of church with Thomas his page, and quarrelled again with Roger, Robert, Thomas and Richard, sons of Roger de Northalle, alias Roger de Leedes, Knt., but Wm. was slain.

Richard of Montealto, lord of West Riddlesden, son of Simon who was living in 1160, died without issue, and gave his estates to Robert M. his cousin (which then meant a near relative); seal, a lion rampant. In a window at West Riddlesden are two shields, and remains of the name of Arthur Montalt in Old English letters. One shield bears a lion rampant with one bar, and the other a fess sable bearing crescent, three mullets in chief, one base.

As it would require a year's labour to gather the numerous fragments respecting this ancient family of Airedale and Calderdale, we must be content at present to leave these notes as they are, and refer to others in "Ilkley," "Yorkshire Genealogist," &c.

THORNTON.—From the last letter sent by Richard Thornton to Sir Roderick Murchison, lent to me by the Royal Geographical Society, and dated "Shupanza, Zambesi, Jan. 7, 1863, the facsimile autograph is taken.

Believe me to be
Yours gratefully
Richard Thornton

The letter consists of five pages, and has been printed in the Society Transactions, in which several of Thornton's papers appeared. The father of this promising young man and able geologist, was well known formerly in Bradford on account of his connection with the old "Court of Requests." Young Richard was born at Cottingley, near Bingley; and when a boy attended school at Bradford, riding on a pony

ANCIENT BINGLEY.

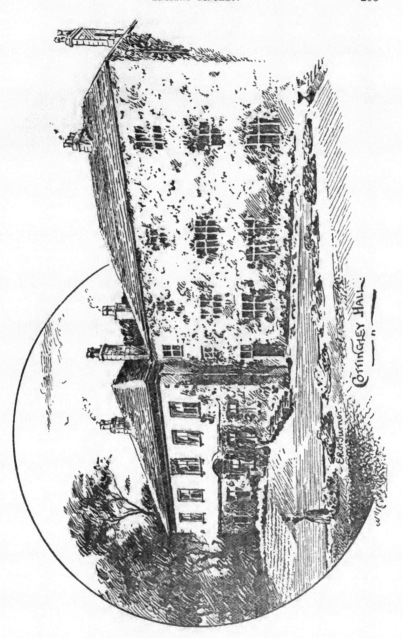

Cottingley Hall.

or donkey. As he grew up, he showed such an aptitude for studies of a scientific kind that his family, who had removed to Horton Road, Bradford, decided to send him to the School of Mines, in London; and when the great traveller, Dr. David Livingstone, proposed to revisit Africa in the year 1858, Sir R. I. Murchison recommended young Thornton to him, as an excellent geologist and geographer. Accordingly, in March, 1858, he left our shores with this prince of explorers, and after spending some time on the Zambesi, he detached himself from the party, and accompanied the great German traveller, the Baron C. von der Decken, in his first survey of the Kilimandjaro Mountains. These mountains, although in Africa, are covered on their tops or peaks with eternal snows. Here young Thornton drew the first contoured map of that wild and lofty country, took many observations of latitude and longitude, and kept an accurate diary. Copies of all these writings, as well as his original map, have been sent by his family to the Royal Geographical Society.

On the 23rd of May, 1864, the Founder's gold medal of the Royal Geographical Society was presented to Baron C. von der Decken, for his two surveys of Kilimandjaro, which he ascertained to have an altitude of 20,065 feet. In returning thanks he spoke as follows: "Happy and proud as I am to day there is still some sadness mingled with it. I miss here my poor friend, the late Richard Thornton, your countryman and my companion, during my first excursion to Kilimandjaro. We did not at that time reach so great an elevation as I did in my second journey, in which, with the aid of Dr. Karsten, I corrected the mistakes of the first. Thornton was, nevertheless, the first European besides myself who penetrated further than the low hills surrounding the great mountain, and settled by his testimony the question of snowy mountains in equatorial Africa. He was a good companion, and extremely useful during the expedition by taking observations, working very laboriously with the theodolite, and as a geologist in collecting and describing the rocks. If I ever come back to Europe and publish an account of my travels, I shall not omit to give due credit to my lamented companion."

On the same occasion, being the annual meeting of the society, Sir Roderick Impey Murchison, its distinguished president, spoke of him thus, and a more graceful compliment could not be imagined. He said (after giving some notices of others who had died during the year):

I have now to speak of a gifted and promising young man, Mr. Richard Thornton, of Bradford, who has lost his life by his zealous exertions to extend our acquaintance with the geography and geology of eastern Africa. I am proud to say that Richard Thornton received his scientific education in the Royal School of Mines, over which I preside, and that, being desirous of accompanying Livingstone in his last explorations, I confidently recommended him to the good will of the great traveller. When Livingstone last left our shores in March, 1858, young Thornton, then only nineteen years of age, accompanied him as geologist. Qualifying himself during the voyage, and at the Cape of Good Hope, in making astronomical calculations, and being also a good sketcher of ground and capable of constructing maps, he was as well adapted to lay down the physicial geography of the Zambesi river as to describe the various rocks which occupy its banks. In looking over his accurately kept diaries, in which he never failed to register every fact, I find that he made upwards of 7,000 observations, to fix relative geographical points, and to determine altitudes on the banks of the Zambesi. In leaving the tertiary rocks of the Delta behind him, and in ascending that river to the rapids, he described numerous rocks of former igneous origin; and, still further inland, various seams of thick and good coal (of which the Portuguese may very largely avail themselves); proving by the associated fossil remains, that the coal was of the old and best age of that mineral.

His health having failed, he was for awhile estranged from the Zambesi expedition, through a partial misunderstanding between his chief and himself. This having been completely done away with when my young friend returned to work out and complete his labours in the Zambesi region, I should not here have alluded to it, if not to recount the important services he rendered in the meantime to geographical and geological science, by becoming *ad interim* the scientific companion of Baron C. von der Decken, in his first survey of the Kilimandjaro Mountain, from Zanzibar and Mombas. Having recently examined the diary kept by Mr. Richard Thornton in that journey between Mombas and the highest point the travellers reached, and also on their return to Mombas, or between the last days of June and the 10th of October, I have no hesitation in saying that the labour is so graphically detailed, every movement so accurately recorded, the transactions with the various native tribes so clearly explained, and every hour of the 120 days' expedition so well accounted for, that, with the contoured map of the region which he prepared, together with many sketches of the form of the ground, I can really fancy myself, like his leader and himself, struggling to reach the snowy equatorial summits. The numerous obstacles opposed by the native chiefs, and the manner in which, after so many "showrys" or palavers, all difficulties were overcome; the perfect description of the habits and dresses of the natives—of the metamorphosed structure of the rocks—the vegetation of each zone of altitude—all these are given; whilst every moment of clear weather in that humid region was devoted to star and lunar observations, or to theodolite measurements of altitude, and the fixing of relative geographical points. All this, too, was scrupulously performed by Thornton, notwithstanding occasional attacks of fever, to which the Baron and himself were subjected. I cannot but hope that these diaries of an accurately minute philosopher, or at least large portions of them, will appear in print; for I have read few writings more instructive and characteristic. In fact, until Baron von der Decken and Thornton carried out this expedition no other African traveller has ever had presented to him such a vast variety of scenes of nature, within so limited a compass, as those which are seen in ascending from the eastern seaboard to the banana-groves on the skirts of the snow-clad peaks of Kilimandjaro.

As the account of this first ascent has been given to Continental Europe in German, so we may rejoice that our Thornton's English version of the same may soon appear; whilst Baron von der Decken, our Medallist of this year, unites with me in the expression of admiration of the undaunted efforts and able assistance of his companion. In truth, in his letters to myself, besides what is noted down in his diaries, Thornton correctly described (and for the first time) the nature of each rock in that region; by which I clearly learned that igneous rocks, whether syenites or porphyries, had penetrated micaceous slaty metamorphic strata, and that streams of vesicular lava, which occur on the flanks of the mountains, indicated clearly that the loftiest summits, now capped with snow, had been raised by the extrusion of a great subaërial volcano. If his life had been spared, this fine young man intended, as he wrote to me, to endeavour to traverse Africa, and compare its East and West coasts with each other, as well as with its vast lacustrine centre. Anxious, however, to finish off in the mean time those labours on the Zambesi which he had so far advanced, he rejoined his old chief Livingstone, and was on the point of completing the map of a mountainous tract on the north bank of the stream, when, in over-exerting himself, he fell a victim to that fever which has proved so fatal to our missionaries, to the devoted wife of Livingstone, and which, on more than one occasion, has nearly deprived of life that great traveller himself. One of his companions for a time on the Zambesi, the Rev. Henry Rowley, in writing to me of the never-flagging zeal and unconquerable energy, as well as of the generous nature and high character of Richard Thornton, adds: "Axe in hand, he would cut himself a path to the top of a thickly-wooded mountain, never leaving it till the setting sun made further observations impossible." In reviewing the journals and diaries of Richard Thornton, I am lost in admiration of his patient labours of registration, when combined with his vivacity of description. With such a delineator in words as Thornton, and such an artist as Mr. Baines—who has sent home such admirable coloured drawings of South-African scenes, particularly of the falls of the Zambesi—those of us who are destined never to be able to penetrate into the southern part of Africa, may quite realise to our mind's eye the true characters of that grand continent. Through the devotion of the brothers and sisters of the deceased traveller, the whole of his voluminous notes and observations have, I am happy to say, been carefully copied out and transmitted to us; and I am confident that every one who examines them will declare with myself, that Richard Thornton was so gifted and rising an explorer, that, had he lived, his indomitable zeal and his great acquirements would have surely placed him in the front rank of men of science. He died on the 21st April, 1863, at the early age of 25 years. There is a monument to Thornton in Shipley Church.

The following extract of a letter from Dr. Livingstone to Sir Roderick I. Murchison, contains a brief account of Thornton's last illness and death:—

Murchison Cataracts (on the Shire), April 25.

My dear Sir Roderick,—With sorrow I have to communicate the sad intelligence that Mr. Richard Thornton died on the 21st current. He performed a most fatiguing journey from this to Tette and back again, and that seemed to use up all his strength; for, thereafter, he could make no exertion without painful exhaustion. His object was to connect his bearings of the hills at Tette (on the Zambesi) with the mountains here. I knew nothing of his resolution till after he had left. He had resolved to go home after he had examined Zomba and the Melanje range, but on the 11th he was troubled with diarrhœa, which ran on to dysentery and fever. We hoped to the last that his youth and unimpaired constitution would carry him through, as he had suffered comparatively little from fever; but we were disappointed. An insidious delirium prevented us learning aught of his last wishes. All his papers, &c., were at once sealed up, and are sent home to his brother at Bradford. He is buried about 500 yards from the foot of the first cataract, and on the right bank of the Shire. * * * ."

WILLIAM BUSFEILD FERRAND, ESQ.—On page 199 will be found the portrait of this gentleman, but the brief sketch there given of his memoir is inadequate to convey the decided individualism of his character. As Mr. Busfeild, junior, with his stalwart proportions, emphatic utterance and dauntless courage, he was known far and wide. He was born April 26, 1809, and was educated at Bradford Grammar School. In 1837, when living at Milner Field, he became a candidate for Parliamentary honours at Bradford, but lost the election, Mr. Lister and Mr. Busfeild, senior, being returned. Having added the surname Ferrand, he became in 1841 M.P. for Knaresborough, which he retained nearly six years. He was a supporter of the Ten Hours' Factory Bill. His speech in Feb. 1842, on Sir Robert Peel's Corn Law Bill, was delivered with great force, and his exposure of the Truck system of paying wages in grocers' commodities and at public-houses was complete. He firmly adhered to the Young England party, to restore Squirearchy and its local government, and was one of the first to establish Field-garden allotments. This was accomplished, along with the institution of a Cricket Club, on Oct. 11, 1844, at Cottingley Bridge, a most successful undertaking and still flourishing. Amongst the visitors at the opening rejoicings were Mr. D'Israeli and Lord John Manners. D'Israeli, in Sybil, his novel, brings a little local colouring about the Druids' Altar from this visit. In 1851 Mr. Busfeild Ferrand was defeated at Aylesbury election. From 1863 to 1865, he sat as M.P. for Devonport. He was doggedly persevering in his undertakings, and strenuously supported the promotion of Agricultural interests, and as strongly opposed the Manufacturers who turned the pure River Aire into a filthy sewer.

He gave evidence at Leeds in 1866 before the Commission on the Pollution of Rivers. About 1840 the Bradford Beck and the Aire from Keighley were made the receptacles of all kinds of filth, and tippings, and the trout, graylings, eels and tench, were exterminated.

Mr. Ferrand died on the 31st March, 1889, and left a will dated Jan. 14, 1882, but Mrs. Hailstone his daughter, and her daughter Mrs. Ethel Carter, opposed the probate in March, 1890, on the ground that the testator was of unsound mind at the date of its alleged execution. William Busfeild, Esq., nephew of the testator, was executor and heir. The said ladies desired to set up a will dated 1847 instead. In the trial it was stated that Sarah Harriett, familiarly called Lilla, his daughter, was brought up by her grand-uncle, Walker Ferrand, Esq., who left her considerable property on his death in 1845. She went to her father's in 1846, but left some time after his second marriage in 1847, and a reconciliation was never effected, but complete alienation followed her marriage with Mr. Edward Hailstone, June 6, 1855, against her father's wish. The Duke of Rutland, who as Lord John Manners was intimate for many years with Mr. Ferrand, in his evidence stated that he had been asked by Mrs. Hailstone to intercede with her father, but could not do so unless she would apologise. This was done, but Mr. Ferrand declined to receive his daughter back to favour. The Duke had not referred to Mrs. Hailstone's dispute with her husband. The hearing of the case is reported at length in the papers of March 7 and 8, 1890, but the will was held to be valid.

ELM TREE HILL.

ALFRED SHARP, ESQ., J.P.

ALFRED SHARP, ESQ., J.P.—This gentleman was the third son of Mr. Jonas Sharp, founder of the celebrated firm of Worsted Spinners and Merchants of Bingley, Bradford, Glasgow, New York, &c. The business was established in a small way at Beckfoot, some time before the birth of Alfred, June 12th, 1823, at Elm Tree Hill. The family removed to the house in Chapel Lane now used as a store-room. At fifteen he commenced business training at the Chapel Lane mill, and soon afterwards became a Teacher at the Wesleyan Sunday School. In May, 1856, the family removed to Myrtle Grove, and in August following, Alfred married the daughter of Mr. James Walker, of Lindley, and six of their ten children reached maturity. His brothers William and James died in 1877, and Mr. John B. Sharp retired from the firm in 1892. Their only surviving sister the Countess Bagienski died in Warsaw in 1896. The family left Myrtle Grove in 1881, but

MYRTLE GROVE.

soon after removing to Carr Head, Crosshills, the Grove was sold by auction and Mr. Sharp became the purchaser, but did not return to occupy it until 1888. Mr. Alfred Sharp was one of the forty-two Commissioners who managed the town's affairs, joining the body in 1852. He retired as chairman in 1878, having accomplished many street improvements. In 1875 the Bingley School Board was formed and he became its first chairman. He was the Wesleyan Circuit Steward for over thirty years, and was a liberal contributor to all the Wesleyan funds. Towards the magnificent Wesleyan Chapel in Bingley, he and his brother William contributed about £7000, or half the cost. Mr. Alfred laid the foundation stone in November, 1871, and performed a similar function in April, 1860, for the Wesleyan

Day Schools, Hill Street, which cost £3000. Mr. Alfred Sharp was a leading worker in erecting and managing the Mechanics' Institute, which was founded in 1844 in Foresters' Court in York Street, and had three removals occasioned by additions to membership. In 1873 he was appointed a Co-optative Governor of the re-constituted Grammar School Board, and became chairman. In 1887 he initiated a movement to establish the Technical Institute, in Mornington Road, and subscribed £1000 towards the £4000 required. In 1878 he became a West Riding Magistrate and succeeded Mr. Busfeild Ferrand as chairman in March, 1891.

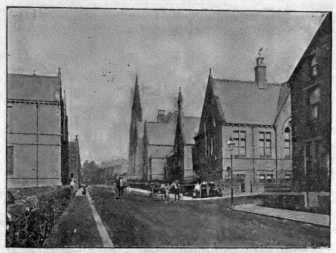

TECHNICAL SCHOOL.   WESLEYAN CHAPEL.   BOARD SCHOOLS.

At his suggestion the Free Libraries Act was adopted, and he gave £1000 towards founding a Free Library at the Mechanics' Institute. The Library was opened April 2, 1892, when great rejoicings took place, and his full-length portrait in oils, subscribed for publicly, was hung on the walls of the Institute; and a similar portrait given to the family. Mr. Sharp was a founder of the Liberal Club, and gained the decision that intoxicants should not be sold on the premises. The room now occupied by Mr. P. Astley in Main Street was first rented, then in 1880 the discarded Catholic Church in York Street was purchased. In 1885 when Bingley was included in a new Parliamentary Division under the name Otley Division, he assisted in returning Sir Andrew Fairbairn as the first Member. These are but a few of the prominent parts taken by Mr. Sharp in his public duties. He died June 1st, 1896, aged 72, and was buried in the public Cemetery, Bingley.

JOSHUA BRIGGS, of Baildon, was the author of "Vice Detected, and Virtue Recommended; Under the Influence of Sunday Schools." It was printed at Leeds, by J. Bowling, in 1788, and reprinted, along with the Account of the Centenary Celebration of the Baildon Sunday Schools in 1881, 64 pages. (Walker, printer, Shipley.) In 1764, the Rev. Theophilus Lindsay of Catterick, near Richmond, had a Sunday School of 100 boys, and in 1765 Miss Coppey established one at Bedale. George Brown, a Wesleyan at Mill Bank, Bradford, and some one else in Manningham started Sunday Schools five years before Raikes in July 1780 commenced the work in Gloucester, but Robert Raikes is justly regarded as the founder of the Sunday School system throughout the country. In 1784, the denominations in Bradford jointly established a Sunday School, as did those of the neighbouring villages, Baildon and Bingley included. The teachers were mainly paid ones, and much of the time was devoted to secular instruction. Books were scarce and, of course, dear; and few were able to read either print or writing. Friends had to lend a room either in a house or barn, or workshop, in which to hold the school. At Eldwick, a rickety table served for a desk, and woolcomber's benches brought from the cottages, served for stools. The result of the past century's labours has been most marvellous and beneficent. In the rudest garments, covered by a check pinafore, and shod in heavy clogs, lads and lasses trudged to these schools, and were told they were living in princely days. Many of them became useful local and travelling preachers amongst dissenters. Joshua Briggs was put parish apprentice at Baildon, but "turned over" to his master's brother at Beckwithshaw, and he got his first scholastic ideas by riding on horseback in front of his master's daughter, who conned her lessons as she sat on a pillion behind him, when going and returning from school. At the close of his apprenticeship he returned to Baildon, and then removed to Windhill, where he met with Ann Northrop, of Wrose, whom he married at Calverley Church in Feb., 1770. He was then under twenty-two. After 1780 he resided at Baildon, and whilst living near Baildon Green he issued the remarkably well-composed pamphlet above mentioned. He obtained work at Eldwick woollen mill (afterwards a corn-mill, and recently a kennel for Airedale harriers), and consequently removed there, conducting a school in his new home in or before 1796, at Mill Fold. He led the singing and played the violin. About 1800, he, with his wife and a large family, removed to Horncliffe, the old keeper's house on Rumbles Moor, where he kept a day school, his pupils lodging at the few farmhouses scattered on the moor edge, and amongst his scholars was John Nicholson, the Poet. Horncliffe is surrounded by wild, heathery moorland; and looks out upon moorclad hills in all directions. Its lofty altitude leaves it exposed to every storm. The whole scene is grand but weird, a solitude disturbed by no voice but that of the wild bird, and no sound but the whistling wind and the sportman's shot. Briggs and his family were employed also in besom making, disposing of their manufacture on Saturdays, at Bingley, Bradford and district around. No one who has seen the glorious sight of Rumbles Moor, with the ling in full bloom, can wonder at the inspiration John Nicholson received, coupled with the rustic but excellent scholastic training he got from the self-educated pedagogue.

BRIGGS' SCHOOL, RUMBLES MOOR.

At one time, for thirteen weeks, the Briggs family were cut off from outer communication by a terrible snow-storm. In 1806 or 1807, the home at Horncliffe was left for one at Baildon Moorside and thence to Tong Park, where he began another Day and Sunday School. As he became older, he trudged about from farm to farm, receiving a meal and a copper or two at his weekly call to instruct the youths, who were called from the loom, rough and ready, to receive lessons in writing and arithmetic. His appearance became very venerable, the flowing white hair matching with the old-world knee-breeches, thick stockings and buckled shoes. His heavy spectacles were thrust up to his brow when not needed. In his basket he carried a Bible, and an ordinary reading-book for younger pupils. He was prone to rhyming, another feature that he probably imparted to Nicholson. As many of the small tradesmen had to keep their books in self-invented hieroglyphics, Briggs found some employment in making up their accounts for them periodically. His wife was a very tiny body, jocosely named by Briggs as the Wrose Hill Strapper, but lived to reach the age of 77. He died the same year, 1827, aged 78, and is buried at Bethel Baptist Chapel, Shipley.

MILNER, OLDFIELD, FELL.—These families successively held Milner Field, which took its name from the Milners. In 1572, John Milner of Harden, held Milner Spring, now called St. Ives' Wood, and possessions in other parts of the parish. Milner Field passed from the family about this time to the Oldfields. In 1624, John O. settled it on Grace his daughter, who married Henry Johnson, of Gilstead, gent. He seems to have built or rebuilt it as shewn by an inscription | IO MO 1603. | In 1652, John Young devised it to Benjamin Young, who in 1674 conveyed it to Thomas Fell, of East Morton, gent., for £580. In 1697, he left it to his son David Fell, who was under sheriff in 1719, and dying leaving an only son Solomon, who sold it in 1721 to his uncle Thomas Fell, for £1000. This Thomas left an only son Thomas, who, dying in 1764 without issue, left it to his cousin Solomon Fell, junior, of Lincolns Inn and Milner Field, son of the Solomon who sold it before. Solomon, the younger, kept a pack of hounds, and his portrait with a favourite hound used to hang in the hall. In 1805 he died, leaving an only child, Harriet Pleasance, who married (1) James Ford, M.D., Southampton, and (2) in 1803, the Rev. W. Penny. Mrs. Penny died in 1812 leaving an only child, Elizabeth Harriet who married in 1840, the Rev. W. A. Weguelin. In 1834, Milner Field and Stubbing House were all that remained intact of their estate, and passed by purchase for £8000, to John Wilmer Field, Esq., of Heaton. He died about 1839 and left two daughters, one of whom, Mrs. Duncombe, got Milner Field in her portion, and about 1869, Admiral Duncombe sold it to Titus Salt, Esq., for about £21,000. He pulled the old house down, and built the present noble mansion, in which the Prince of Wales and other eminent persons have been entertained. The Fell arms are, Or, two bars sable on a white shield, two and one crosses pattee fitchée or.

FIELD ARMS.

Anthony Fell, Morton Banks, clothier, purchased lands from Arthur Maude, 1562, will 1595.
⹀ Margaret, buried June 1610.

Thomas, lands at Morton, Kilnsey, Arncliffe,
⹀ Agnes, d. 1639.

Anthony, b. 1582, = 1603, Ann Sagar.

Four daughters.

Anthony, b. 1598, Gilstead, settl. 1619,   Thomas, b. 1600, d. 1627,
     purch. Milner Wrose, Breary, &c.   = Isabella Ambler.
= Margaret, d. Myles Hall.
Thomas, bap. Jan. 10, 1629, gent., of Morton, purchased Milner Field,
     1674.
= Mary ———, (2) Elizabeth Crabtree, widow.

| Thomas, East Morton, gent., b. 1668, mar.settl.1713,held Stubbing-house, lands at Shipley, Eldwick, &c.; will 1724, devised estates at Bingley and Morton, with moiety of B. Quire to his eldest son; lands at Leeds, Halifax and Gildersome to son John; at Embsay, Skipton, Kildwick, Silsden to daughter Elizabeth.
= Elizabeth, d. Rowland Mitchell, who had £1000 at her marriage. | David, b. 1674, of Milner Field, d. 1719, Under Sheriff =
Solomon, d. 1770.
= Ann, | Joshua, b. 1682, d. 1697.
= Martha, b. 1685, d. 1699. |

| Thomas, d.1764, s.p. = Jane Leach. | John, d. s.p. | Elizabeth, s.p. = Thos. Perkins, | Solomon, of MilnerField, and Linc.Inn, Esq., d. Jan. 1805.
= Eliz. Hornby, | Numerous other children. |

Harriette Pleasance, d. April 1812,   Thomas,
  = (1) James Ford, M.D., s.p.   Solomon,
  = (2) Rev. W. Penny,   died in infancy.
Elizabeth Harriette = Rev. W. A. Weguelin.

In Bingley Church are monuments to Thomas Fell, Morton, gent., d. July 1, 1697, aged 67; and to Joshua Fell, d. 1697, aged 15; and Martha, d. 1699, aged 13.

The Builder of March 15, 1873, describes New Milner Field.

RIDDLESDEN.—This name is not an uncommon family name in West Yorkshire, and we find Thomas de Redilsden who resided at Mirfield in 1364, and held lands at Dalton near Huddersfield. Whether the name originated from Bingley parish I cannot prove.

PRIESTHORP.—Henry son of Nicholas de Priesthorp who held lands in Priesthorp in 1308, was probably known only as Henry Nichols or Nicholson.

FRANK.—No satisfactory pedigree of this family has yet been compiled, though they were well-to-do people at Cottingley from the days of the Reformation as proved by the Parish Registers, and William Frank, Esq., of Keighley, was buried in the Chancel at Keighley in

1578. Their arms are given,—Gules, a fesse sable, between three hawks proper. Also, Vert, a saltier ingrailed or. Stephen Frank of Cottingley, gent., was a juror at Leeds Sessions, 1597.

DOBSON.—We may hope also to get a pedigree of this family, represented by the Wickhams now, when the Registers are printed. Thomas Dobson of Priesthorpe was a man of local eminence in 1666, being also nephew and executor of the will of James Sagar, of Allerton and Wilsden, a local benefactor. The name is found here a century earlier.

SLATER.—The Wills at York and other MSS. shew this family to have been in influential standing for three centuries, at Cottingley, Eldwick, &c. Thomas Slater, 40th Queen Elizabeth, was charged by his Cottingley neighbours as a *barrectator*, or spy and tell-tale.

SAVILE.—A sketch of the Saviles of Howley, Thornhill, Elland, &c. would easily fill a book, and the short residence at Marley of a branch from Howley scarcely justifies fuller notice than already given. There are a few entries to be found in the Registers: 1647, July 23, John the sonne of Robert Savile of Marley was born at Howley Hall (Batley,) about —— in the night. Hee was bapt. att Howley the fift day of August in the same year by me Thos. Howgill, Vicar of Bingley.

1650, July 4, Robert son of Robert Savile of Marley gent., bapt. Buried Dec. 2, 1651.

We have no authentic records of the famous hal or fool kept by the Saviles known as Sil of Marley.

John Savile, who completed Howley in 1590, became Baron Savile and died about 1630.

PASLEW.—Arms, Gules a lion rampant argent, crowned, armed and langued sable. Much more genealogical matter requires gathering before the pedigree of the Leeds and Bingley Paslews can be properly compiled, including the numerous entries in Keighley Register, from 1564, Bingley 1579, and Wills before those dates at York.

CURRER.—We regret to leave the Bingley branch unrecorded in genealogical form, but the various branches were so prolific, Kildwick, Ilkley, Gilstead, Morton, Marley and Gawthorpe, that harm may be done at present by conjecture.

Bingley Bibliography.

JOHN NICHOLSON was and is emphatically the Airedale Poet. He was born at Weardley near Harewood, Nov. 29, 1790. His father, Thomas Nicholson, had married a farmer's daughter at Eldwick, and thither they removed when John was a few weeks old. After getting the rudiments of education from his father at the woolsorting board, John was sent to Briggs' school on Rumbles moor for a few years, as mentioned in the notice of that worthy, and 'finished off' at Bingley Grammar School by a year's course under the amiable and learned master, Dr. Hartley, who proved his friend afterwards in revising the proofs when he commenced printing his poems. John helped his father, a Worsted Manufacturer, in woolsorting, and in business he never rose higher than a sorter or comber. Pope's " Homer,"

John Nicholson.

"Shakespeare," and Young's "Night Thoughts," were Nicholson's great favourites. His thoughts were bent more on reading than woolsorting, so candles were withheld from him, but twisted cotton rag dipped in olive oil was within his reach, and he read and wrote, but his earliest effusions are lost. John James, his biographer, says that "there is no spot in Yorkshire better fitted to bring forth and nurture poetic ideas than Eldwick with its neighbourhood, for it embraces every variety of lowland and mountain scenery. The effect of pure mountain air in invigorating the intellect, and producing noble and exalted sentiments, is well established." From his schoolmaster, Briggs, he must have received directions and impulses that led him to court the Muses.

In early life he learnt, like many young people of that date, to play the hautboy, &c. This led him to riotous life, as musicians were invariably sought for wedding parties, and at one of these gatherings he met his lady-love, and married before he was twenty, but she died shortly after the birth of a child. He became very serious, and buried his hautboy on Rombalds moor where it probably still remains. He joined his parents at the Wesleyan Chapel and soon became a local preacher of great fluency, but severed his connection therewith for some reason or other. Whilst living in Bingley he had in 1813 married Martha Wild, who through the remainder of his life was most devoted to his interests. Soon after this second marriage he went to work for his father at Eldwick for three years. In 1818 he removed to Red Beck, and worked at Shipley Fields' mill for five years. Here he spent a happy time, with a small family and many literary friends.

He composed two successful plays for the Bradford Theatre;—"The Robber of the Alps," and "The Siege of Bradford." The latter was his first printed work, and ran through two editions. He got no money by it, but his fame was great, and he gave his whole mind after this to poetry. In 1820 he removed to Harden Beck, where he gained the practical friendship of J. G. Horsfall, Esq., who helped to support him, his wife making up the rest by working at the worsted mill, during the time he was composing "Airedale." He also composed after work hours when wandering on moonlight nights along the beck side, and especially near Goit Stock Waterfall; and in summer mornings by four o'clock, on a big flat rock overlooking Harden valley. He was then a steady, industrious workman. When "Airedale" was completed he removed to Hewenden mill, a mile away, and laboured three years for Mr. Stephen Skirrow as a woolsorter. There was a gang of poachers around the place, and Mr. Horsfall having suggested that he should write a poem called "The Poacher," he joined their company to get hints. By treating them, he got into dissipated habits himself. Jack Moore and Dan Ingham were two of their leaders, and are represented in the poem by Ignotus and Desparo.

In 1824 he issued his "Airedale" by subscription, and he roamed about the country supplying the subscribers and hawking to others. His taste for liquors gained upon him, and his life henceforth was full of calamities. The first edition of "Airedale" was sold at 6s. each, and he began to vend a second edition in 1825 all around the country. He became an inveterate drunkard by this loose life, and generally spent all he got in drink. Mr. Horsfall tried to restore him but of no avail. He next wrote, and printed in 1827, the "Lyre of Ebor." He then resided at Bingley, had a wife and six children, and no work.

BINGLEY IN 1830; FROM BAILEY HILL.

His drinking habits increased, but he had won the friendship of George Lane Fox, Esq., of Bramham, who gave him above £100 at various times, and continued his generosity to Nicholson's widow.

In Oct. 1827, leaving £4 at home, he departed to London to hawk his books, and was introduced to London Society by Mr. Richard

Nichols, brother-in-law to Mr. Stephen Skirrow. Nicholson was a conspicuous figure in the Metropolis, being dressed in a blue coat, corduroy breeches, grey yarn stockings; and his hair had not been combed for twelve months. Chantrey's workmen in London made a bust of the poet still in his family's possession. For a riotous affair in Drury Lane he was hauled off to Covent Garden Prison, and the amusing adventure was printed, with a few flourishes, in all the London papers. He arrived at Bingley penniless, having spent £17 and all the money he had received for books. He published a pamphlet comparing the healthy Rombalds moor with London, much to the advantage of the former. In it he deprecates the custom of pressing people to drink, especially those already enslaved. Soon after, he visited London again, but his wife insisted on accompanying him. Whilst there, they buried one of their children. He was six days of the week when at home encased in a woolsorter's checked brat, and from being the masher of early years became a great sloven. Dr. Birkbeck and James Montgomery were good friends to him, as were also Lords Harewood and Ribblesdale. His printer having failed, Nicholson lost a great quantity of his books, which were sold by auction, and the market was thus glutted, and he became a woolcomber.

In 1833 he left Bingley, and henceforward resided at Bradford, where for ten years (when not drinking) he worked for Mr., afterwards Sir Titus Salt. His family were partly workers, so they were in better circumstances. In 1836 he became an abstainer for 17 weeks, but fell back again. Recklessness from this time ruled him, yet he printed several good pieces, "Low Moor Iron Works," "A Walk from Knaresborough to Harrogate," "England's Lament for the Loss of her Constitution." He wrote against the socialists and chartists. On April 13th, 1843, as was his wont at holiday times, he set off to visit his aunt at Eldwick. It was near midnight when at Shipley, and he was worse for liquor. He went by the canal side to Dixon's Mill (now near Saltaire bridge), and was crossing the Aire by the stepping stones, as there was no bridge. It was a dark and stormy night, and the river was swollen. He lost his footing, but managed to catch a branch a few yards lower down and extricate himself. He was, however, so insensate that he remained on the bank all night, and was found by a farm labourer in the morning soon after he had ceased to breathe. On the 18th, his remains were conveyed from the Bay Horse Inn, Baildon, to Bingley Church-yard, on the north side of the church. There would be a thousand people at his funeral; there was a choral service, and a mourning peal was rung from the church bells. Two of his eight children were then of tender age. His vice of intemperance had no other vice following in its train.

My friend Abraham Holroyd was able to identify the cottage of "Mary of Marley":

AT Marley stood the rural cot,
In Bingley's sweet sequester'd dale,
The spreading oaks enclos'd the spot
Where dwelt the beauty of the vale.

* * * *

Her ebon locks were richer far
Than is the raven's glossy plume;
Her eyes outshone the ev'ning star;
Her lovely cheeks the rose's bloom.

* * * *

She milk'd beneath the beech tree's shade,
And there the turf was worn away,
Where cattle had for cent'ries laid,
To shun the summer's sultry ray.

* * * *

[Lysander, on] that fatal night,
His footsteps slipp'd—the cruel tide
Danc'd and exulted with its freight,
Then lifeless cast him on its side.
How chang'd is lovely Mary now!
How pale and frantic she appears!
Description fails to paint her woe,
And numbers to recount her tears.

"The Malt-kiln Fire" has an old-world strain in it, telling of the manner in which the long evenings were occasionally spent.

YE woods, in Rishworth's verdant vale,
Which oft have echoed to the horn!
Ye rocky hills, that blushed so deep
From hunters gay at early morn!
Weep till your tears in crystal rills
Make winding Aire with grief run o'er,
That on the brown-robed heathy hills,
The huntsman's shout is heard no more.

* * * *

Mourn o'er great Parker's ancient race;
Round Marley Hall in sorrow tread;
Where dwelt the glory of the chase,
Who oft the noble sportsmen led.
Then take the horn, the requiem blow,
O'er rural bliss that now is lost,
And sound the dirge o'er those laid low,
Who never sighed at hunting's cost!

The lines on the death of Thomas Cooper, Esq., Surgeon, Bingley, are unique and fitting memorials of his worth.

Gathering of the Craven Warriors, against the Scots:—

THEY answered the sounds, and the valley below
In the noblest echoes replied;
The Leaches and Starkeys, with quiver and bow,
Bade adieu to the new-married bride.
At Riddlesden Hall the banner is raised,
Which the warrior Parkers behold,
Then the sunbeams upon their armour blazed,
And their helmets glittered like gold.

On Bingley:—

    THY beauties, Bingley! never have been sung,
      By stranger-bard, or native poet's tongue.
         *   *   *   *   *

    Thy hanging woods, thy fountains, and thy bowers,
    Thy dashing floods, thy landscapes, and thy flowers,
    Thy bold grey rocks, thy heathy purple fells,
    Where silent solitude with beauty dwells;
    Thy homes where honest worth still finds a seat,
    And love and virtue a serene retreat.
         *   *   *   *   *

    We have the mountain breeze, the cold pure spring,
    The woods where ev'ry British bird doth sing;
    Wild plants and flowers, wild birds, and scenes as wild,
    Or soft as any on which nature smiled;
    The weeping birch, the great majestic oak.
    Where dark green ivy forms a winter's cloak;
    The purple heath, where dappled moorcocks crow;
    The sylvan vales, with limping hares below;
    The brooding pheasant, beauty of the wood,*
    And spotted trouts that cleave the amber flood.
    For finer walks, for more sequester'd bowers,
    For cooler grottos, and for richer flowers,
    For streams that wind more beautiful along,
    For birds with louder chorus to their song,
    For all that gen'rous Nature can bestow,
    All Yorkshire scenes to Bingley-vale must bow.

Airedale in Ancient Times, 198 pp. Two editions, 1825-6.

Lyre of Ebor, Genius of Intemperance, 218 pp. Bradford, 1827.

England's Lament for the Loss of her Constitution, a poem published in 1829 on the passing of the Roman Catholic Relief Bill. Re-published as being very applicable to the present time. Bradford, H. O. Mawson, 18 pages, 1850.

Lines on the Grand Musical Festival at York, Sept. 1825, iv, 16 pages. Preface dated, Hewenden, Sep. 30, 1825. Bradford, printed for the Author, by G. & E. Nicholson, 1825.

The Vale of Ilkley; and the Poet's Sick-bed, 16 pages. Bradford, E. Nicholson, 32 Kirkgate, 1831.

    "But the trumpet now is still,
    Not a rock from yonder hill,
    Echoes back the piercing blast,
    As when General Fairfax past."

The loneliness of the moors and the grandeur of a thunder-storm are vividly pictured by Bingley's great poet.

Life and Poems, by John James, 1844. Stansfield, Bradford.
    ,,   ,,   ,,   1854.
    ,,   ,,   ,,   Dearden's edition, published by Harrison & Son, Bingley, 268 pp., 4th edition, 1859.

    * The herons, at the Harden lakes, may be added.

Life and Poems, by John James, Harrison's verbatim edition., with preface by Abraham Holroyd, published by Thomas Harrison, Bingley, viii, 261 pp, 1876.
Low Moor Iron Works, 1829.
  ,,   ,,   12 pages, 1856.
Following Nicholson, the Prestons deserve priority.

THE PRESTONS OF GILSTEAD.—William Preston, of Bradford, soon after the birth of his son Benjamin, born August 10th, 1819, removed to Waterside, near Girlington, where his other eminent son, John, was born April 3rd, 1822. Ben Preston is supposed to have inherited his grandfather Preston's rhyming propensities. Ben was apprenticed for six years as a woolsorter, and during his apprenticeship he sent poetic effusions to a local paper. Our mutual friend, Abraham Holroyd, secured the publication of some of Ben's longer dialect poems in broad-sheets and pamphlets, which with others were issued in book form in 1872. Preston's health giving way, he at length realized his yearning for a country house. Mr. Alfred Harris, jun., having had 2½ acres awarded him from Bingley common lands, he sold the allotment to Benjamin Preston, who built a house thereon, and removed thereto in May, 1865. He had many visitors from Bradford, and to satisfy some of them he obtained a beer licence. Soon after his settlement here, I first made his acquaintance, and that of his brother John who had a house close by. A rich uncle was specially kind to the two brothers, and Ben built another house close to Eldwick Beck, which he named Hammondale, a name that gives a pun on his uncle's name, and trade of brewer. The public-house he left for some one with less antipathy to the twaddle indulged in there. He is pre-eminently the Burns of Bradford dialect, and whilst such pieces as "Natterin Nan,"

BENJAMIN PRESTON.

"T'Poor Weyver," "T'Creakin Gate," "T'Spicy Man," &c., will never be unwelcome to Yorkshire dialect readers, his other poems in Queen's English must eventually find a place in all collections of the best poets. Mr. Preston still lives, but never writes to the papers now. The broad, common sense embodied in his uncollected prose works, would justify their immediate publication in book form. Mr. Preston has been too indifferent in this matter, and others have had to collect and edit his poems.

His works include—*Poll Blossom*, &c. *A Poetical Sarmon*, preycht to't White Heathens o' Wibsa, i' ther native tongue. Be a Latter Day Saint. 8 pages, Parkinson, Bradford; 1854. Two other editions, Cooke, Bradford. *Natterin Nan*. 8 pages, J. M. Jowett, Bradford; 1856. Two editions by Cooke, Bradford. One edition by Abm. Holroyd, Bradford. *T"Spicy Man*. 8 pages, Holroyd, Bradford: 1859.

Poems and Songs in the Dialect of Bradford-Dale, be a Yorkshire Likenass Takker. 1864. Sewell for A. Holroyd, Bradford.

T'Creakin Gaat. 1859. Holroyd, Bradford. 8 pp.

T'Maister o't Hause. 8 pages. 1859.

"The Dialect Poems of Benjamin Preston, with notice of the Author by John Emanuel Preston. 1872. 64 pages, and portrait. Printed by Harrison, Bingley, for Abraham Holroyd of Saltaire.

Poems; published by Brear, Bradford. 1881.

JOHN PRESTON, his brother, had a fair schooling, and from his earliest years had a literary and philosophic cast of mind. He made Nature and Art his constant study. He owned a chemist's shop in Bradford, studied homeopathy, painted stage scenery at the theatre, practised photography, publicly acted and recited; and left the Baptist creed of his parents to become a student of Swedenborg's teachings. About 1852 he married Maria Marchbank, who had but one child, John Emanuel, whose paintings like those of his father, are eagerly purchased; and whose researches on Eldwick moor for prehistoric remains have added to our knowledge of primitive man in Airedale. In 1862, John Preston bought two allotments on Gilstead Moor where he built his home, Littlebeck Hall, then with a flat roof, but afterwards enlarged. On my first visit to father and son, (the mother had died in 1857), they were both engaged in painting local scenery. The rain found its way through the roof in two places, and we had to make a dash to enter the front door to avoid a shower bath. We mounted a ladder to the loft, to see a large and fine collection of china and antiquities. The uncomfortable surroundings were nothing to the philosophic father; Ruskin and Swedenborg had lifted him out of his environments; and they were happy as the day was long. A casual lady visitor from Cornwall was wooed and won by the son, and in a short time the impress of her hands was visible in every room. A third generation of artists and archæologists tenant the spot that scores of Bradfordians formerly visited for the sake of the genial and

JOHN PRESTON, GILSTEAD.

cultured Preston brothers. John became founder and president of the Swedenborgian Church at Saltaire; and he was their most regular speaker. On April 29th, 1888, he succumbed under an attack of bronchitis, and was buried in Bingley Cemetery. Instead of the usual black-edged funeral card, so common in Victoria's reign, a cheerful gold-edged card, with gold letters, records—In memory of John Preston, Artist, Theologian and Philosopher, who passed away from this Natural Life to the Spiritual, April 29, 1888, aged 66 years. His remains were interred at Bingley Cemetery, May 2nd. His last words:—"Amen. All right. Give me a light."

Further particulars may be found in "Sermons by An Artist. (John Preston). With Memoir by his brother Ben." Printed at Leeds for the Saltaire New Church Society, 1888, pp. xvi, 250; with splendid portrait from Gaskell's oil-painting. Also, a life, with list of his paintings, by Butler Wood, is in the *Bradford Antiquary*, accompanied by another portrait.

ABRAHAM HOLROYD.—Like his friends the Prestons, but several years afterwards, my very dear and old friend Abraham bought an acre of ground at Gilstead, and erected Harmony Cottage, but Mrs.

Holroyd was unable to brave the rigours of the moorland climate, and he and his wife took up their abode with their daughter near Shipley, where they died. Besides the Preston publications mentioned, he wrote and edited,—

Eldwick Glen: A Poem. 20 pages. [By Abraham Holroyd.] Bradford, Woodhead and Worsnop, for Abraham Holroyd, Westgate, 1854.

> "Workers in mill, and mine, and in the soil,
> Then seek repose from long, laborious toil;
> And in these woods, now so familiar grown,
> Forget awhile the noisy, busy town."
> "High overhead huge rocks on rocks are pil'd
> Of various forms, magnificently wild.
> In olden times, before the Romans came
> Here rose the Druids' sacrificial flame."

The Life of Joseph Lister, of Bradford, born 1627, died 1709. 48 pages, 3d. Shipley, J. Pratt for Abraham Holroyd, Westgate, Bradford, 1860.

[The Autobiography of Joseph Lister, with Defence of Bradford and Capture of Leeds in 1642, was edited by Thomas Wright, Esq., M.A., F.S.A. 1842, London, J. Russell Smith. Pp. x, 59, and index. Notes on Accepted Lister, and the Sieges of Bradford.]

Holroyd's Collectanea. Issued in parts. 184 pp. 1873. 3s. Reprints of papers on Bradford History.

A Garland of Poetry. Edited by A. H. 2s. pp. xi, 199, 1873. Printed at Pateley Bridge.

Dialect Poems of Ben Preston; with notice of the Author, by John Emanuel Preston (nephew). 1s.

Saltaire & its Founder: Sir Titus Salt. 3 editions; 1s. &c. n.d.; 1871, 40 pp.; 1873, 91 pp.; printed by Harrison, Bingley.

Holroyd's Collection of Yorkshire Ballads.

John James' Lecture on Lord Bacon. 1d.

Spice Islands in the Sea of Reading. 1s.

ABRAHAM HOLROYD.

The Bradfordian, in parts. 236 pp. 1860-62.

P. Brontë's Cottage in the Wood; prose only. Harrison, Bingley, 1865, 16 pp.

Holroyd's Bradford Historical Almanack, 1860 to 1865,

Welcome to the Prince and Princess of Wales to Milner Field, June 23, 1882.

Louis Miall's Physical Geography &c. of Bradford and Neighbourhood, 1863.

The Galaxy, 4 pp. only, 1867.

Holroyd Souvenir. Mrs. F. C. Galloway. A choice little Memoir, privately printed. 1893. 30 pp. 5 illustrations.

A. H. died Jan. 1, 1888, and was buried at Clayton.

The earliest bibliographical item I remember for Bingley is the following:—

The Traditions of the Church no way destructive of Religion.—A SERMON preach'd at *Bingley* Church, on *Sunday*, Sept. 12, 1731. By Is. Smith, Minister of *Haworth*, near *Kighley*, *Yorkshire*. London, Jer. Batley. 1731. 6d. pp. iv, 21, small 4to.

"To Richardson Ferrand, Esq.,—Sir, The great *Esteem* I always had for your *Merit*, both as a *Gentleman* and a *Scholar*, ever since I had the happiness of your Acquaintance, makes me lay hold on every Opportunity of shewing it: And as the following Sermon happen'd to be preach'd before you, I beg leave to Dedicate it to one who knows both how to *Approve* or *Censure* it according to the *Rules* of right Reason and Judgment."

I am, Sir, *Your most humble and devoted Servant*,

ISAAC SMITH.

Particulars respecting this eccentric Haworth Incumbent will be found in *Haworth Past and Present*, but Canon Hulbert sent me a pamphlet not noticed in that book, entitled, "A Letter to the *People of Haworth* Parish." By Isaac Smith, M.A., occasioned by His late Suspension. London, 1739; no printer's name: pp. viii, 56. Mr. Smith had offended the authorities by marrying couples who came beyond his chapelry.

The Rev. T. Lillie, Independent Minister at Bingley, published a Funeral Sermon on Mrs. Philipps, of Keighley, 52 pp., printed at Bradford in 1785.

Compassion the duty and dignity of man; and cruelty the disgrace of his nature.—A SERMON occasioned by that branch of British Commerce which extends to the Human Species, preached to a Congregation of Protestant Dissenters in Hull, Jan. 21, 1789. By John Beatson. Hull, printed for the Author. Price 1s. 64 pages. [See notice of him under the Baptists.]

Funeral Sermon on Joseph Lister of Kippin, late of Bingley. Leedes, 1709. 13 pp.

Joseph Lister, "Siege of Bradford," 1776. Leeds.
,, ,, ,, 1785. Bolton, Lanc.
,, ,, ,, 1790. Wakefield.
,, ,, ,, 1810. Knaresbro'.
,, ,, ,, no date. Wakefield.
,, ,, ,, 1821. Bradford.
,, ,, ,, 1842. London.
,, ,, ,, 1860. Holroyd.
,, ,, ,, 1894. Horsfall Turner.

The Rev. J. A. Busfeild, A.B., Curate of Skipton, was Author of *The Christian's Guide*, in six Lectures, &c., for use of Parishioners of Skipton. Dedicated to W. Wilberforce, Esq., M.P. Printed by J. Fawcett, Ewood, 1800, 157 pp.

Baldwin, of Bradford, Remarks on the Conduct of J. A. Busfeild, Esq., J.P., 1791.

Fragments on Bingley and its Families, collected by Johnson Atkinson Busfeild, Esq., 1847, &c. (3 Vols.), folio manuscript, original drawings, emblazoned arms, pictures inserted.

He printed privately (Gaskarth, Bradford, 1875,) a quarto volume, 167 pp., of the History of his family, and fragments relating to Bingley.

Leeds and Liverpool Canal; a letter on the proposed deviation, 20 pp. Bradford, G. Nicholson, no date.

List of Proprietors, L. and L. Canal, corrected to 1800. 23 pp. Ditto, 1806. Ditto, 1842, 21 pp.

J. Priestley's Letter to the Proprietors of L. and L. Canal, 20 pp., Bradford, G. Nicholson, 1793.

The following is only presented as an incomplete list issued from the Bingley Press; by John Harrison, Myrtle Place; then John Harrison & Son, York Place; afterwards Thomas Harrison, Queen Street; now Thomas Harrison & Sons, Queen Street. Firm established in 1827.

Poetry, original Hymns and Pieces, by W. R. Lund, Denholme, 12 pages.

An Acrostic, a Poem—"Improvement of the Times, and Horrors of Intemperance." By Silas Cryer, author of "Lines on the Panic," "Elegy on Job Senior," "The Death of R. C. Wildon," "The Better Country," "The Christian's Warfare," &c. Price 1d. 12 pages. 1862.

A Letter to the Heads of Families, by the Rev. T. Garbutt, Wesleyan Minister, with an Address on Family Religion. 14 pages. Price 1d.

Select Poems; Mathematical Geography; New Telegraphy, &c., &c., by Miles Atkinson, Silsden. 11 pages. 1860.

Directions for studying the Holy Scriptures, designed chiefly for religious young persons. By a late Author, enlarged by the Rev. Thomas Garbutt, Wesleyan Minister. 14 pages. 1842.

Sacred Dramas for Schools and Bands of Hope. Cave of Adullam, Song of Moses, Deborah and Barak. By Benson Bailey. 16 pages. 1867.

"Songs of Zion : Dialogues on Infidelity." By Benson Bailey. A series of small Books for Sunday Schools, Recitations, &c.

"Rosanus, and other Poems"; Odes, Songs and Sonnets. By W. C. Rushton. 64 pages. [Address on the Death of Lord F. Cavendish.] [Dialogue] 8 pages. "Nathan and Wife, and Frank Forethowt of Careful Lodge, i't City o' Bingley, 1850." [Refers to buying goods from Scotchmen, or travelling packmen ; buying beef in abundance for one feast and not paying for it till next, and to crowds of visitors coming to the "King of Feasts" to devour other people's beef and tarts. These three customs still obtain to a smaller degree.]

"The House that Jack Built :" a Lecture delivered by W. B. Affleck, in Bradford. Rev. H. J. Betts in the chair. 23 pages. Mr. Affleck was a born orator and temperance advocate.

"Home Thoughts," by W. B. Affleck, of Yeadon. Two editions. 132 pp. 1866.

"Fragments in Verse," by Wm. Harrison, Schoolmaster, Bradford, 144 pp., 1862.

Ward's "Methodism in Bingley," 1863.

Bailey's "Ilkley, Bolton Abbey and Pearls of Craven," 1852, several editions.

"Strive and Thrive, or A. McKechnie's New Reform Bill." 20 pages. J. Harrison and Son, *Courant* Office.

"Marriage Contrasted ; An Evening on the Brink of the Wharfe, near Bolton Abbey. By Miles Atkinson, Silsden. 1d. 16 pages.

"Joe Lupton, and His Wife Sarah, Keepers of the Fleece Inn, or a Smell of Roast Beef." By Miles Atkinson.

"A Dialogue between Mr. Gleaner and others," being a companion to "Joe Lupton." To which is added "The Drunkard's Will." 16 pages.

"A Stroll down Silsden on Feast Monday, and other Poems"; by Miles Atkinson. 16 pages.

"Old Three Laps," being incidents in the singular life of William Sharp, who, on being crossed in love, voluntarily went to bed in good health, and remained there for a period of forty-nine years, 16 pages.

"Interesting Incidents in the Singular Life of William Sharp, alias Old Three Laps"; also "A Sketch of the Life and Vagaries of Jack Lob." 16 pages.

[Old Three Laps' father was a maker of 'draw boys' worsted goods, which he sold at Halifax Market last century, and acquired a moderate fortune thereby. This he chiefly invested in two farms near Keighley,—Two Laws, and Worlds. The latter is near Rumbles Moor, and it was there that Three Laps performed his strange freak. He was interred in Keighley Churchyard in March, 1865, aged 79. Jack Lob, otherwise John Robinson, of Cottingley, was a parish wonder and half-wit.]

"Interesting, &c.," another edition. 16 pages.

The American Harp, first series. A Dialogue—"My Mansion in Heaven." By Thomas Lister, Esq. Poem, 26 pages.

"The Wandering Gentile," and "The Wanderer's Companion," each in prose and poetry. By Thomas Lister, Esq.

"Memoirs of T. and M. Lister."

Hymns for Holy Communion. 18 pages.

"Life of Old Job Senior, the Rumbolds Moor Hermit." With a full page portrait, suitable for framing. 1d.

"Old Job Senior," another edition, 14 pages. Another edition, 16 pages. Old Job was a familiar figure in Airedale, as well as Wharfedale.

"The Pig, how to breed and how to feed." 1853.

"A Dialogue, showing the result of Improvident Marriages, from real life," with a Yorkshire Ditty. 1d.

"Blind Jack, or the Life and surprising Adventures of John Metcalf, the blind Road-Surveyor, of Knaresborough." 16 pages.

"Incidents in the Life of Tom Lee, a notorious Robber, who was gibbetted in Grassington Wood for the murder of Dr. Petty." 16 pp.

"The Life-Story of Thomas Worsnop." Preface dated, Wilsden, Feb. 1867. 31 pages.

"Life and Sayings of Thomas Worsnop, Eccleshill; Apostle of Total Abstinence." 12 mo., 136 pp. 1870. The author was Francis Butterfield, of Wilsden. Tommy was a noted Teetotal Advocate, with a touch of the buffoon: a born orator nevertheless.

"New School Reciter." New Dialogues for Sabbath Schools. 2 parts. 2d. each.

Extensive variety of new Dialogues: packet. 6d.

"Elijah the Tishbite," a Dialogue. 1d.

"The Awakening," a Dialogue. 1d.

"The Cottage in the Wood," by the late Rev. P. Brontë. 1d. 1865.

"The Right Sort of Stuff to make a Woman." 4th ed. (100,000), by the Rev. A. McKechnie. 1d.

"The Right Sort of Stuff to make a Man." 4th ed. (100,000), by the Rev. A. McKechnie. 1d.

"Sugar Candy for Spoiled Husbands, or the Wife at Home." Rev. A. McKechnie. 1d.

"Sugar Plums for Big Babies." Rev. A. McKechnie. 1d.

"A Man with a Lump in his Head," announced.

Rev. E. Cossey, "A Brief Sketch of the Craven Baptist Mission Churches." 1d. 11 pp. "Telephone" Office, 1882.

"Neighbourliness," by the Saltaire Congregational Minister, 1874.

T. Bailey, "The Managers' and Overlookers' Assistant," 47 pp.

"Directions for Studying the Holy Scriptures," 12 pp. 1842.

"Age of Long Chimneys," 12mo.

"Airedale Courant," 1853.

"Bingley Telephone."

"Memorial Sermon" for the late Rev. R. S. Blackburn, Primitive Methodist Minister, Fernando Po, West Africa, April 1879, by Rev. T. Mitchell. 2d. 21 pages.

Bingley Cottage Hospital, Bazaar and Fancy Fair in the Drill Shed, Oct. 2-5, 1889. Opened by Wm. Busfeild, Esq., Morland Hall, Penrith, and St. Ives, Bingley. Programme, 48 pages; Bingley, T. Harrison & Sons, 1889.

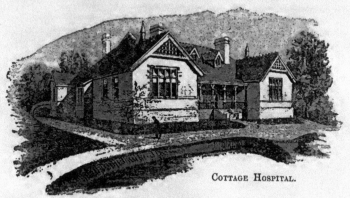

COTTAGE HOSPITAL.

"A Sermon" preached in the Parish Church of Bingley; Sunday, August 29th, 1830, (being Bingley-Tide), by the Rev. R. Hartley, D.D., Vicar of Bingley, and published for the benefit of the Church Sunday School. Bingley, J. Harrison, 1830. 26 pages.

BINGLEY PARISH CHURCH.

The Vicar states that he had a few months previously established a Church Sunday School in the Grammar School, where, as there were two storeys, the Girls and Boys had separate rooms. Twice a week there were evening writing classes at the National School free to the S. Scholars. There were 260 on the Sunday School Roll, half of whom attended the week-night writing classes.

Rev. W. Thoseby, Primitive Methodist Minister, was author of "Heavenly Dew Drops." 2nd edition. 127 pp. Bingley, T. Harrison, Main Street.

W. Scruton's "History of Bradford" was printed by Messrs. Harrison, 1890, pp. xvi, 262.

Most of the Antiquarian and Genealogical Works by J. Horsfall Turner, as given at the end of this volume, have been printed by Messrs. Harrison. Also, this volume in 1897; and also this year, "A Key to English Antiquities," by Mrs. Armitage, pp. xvii., 331, illustrated.

Mr. Dobson has issued a few books and pamphlets, amongst them being—

"Mahomet, Reviewed in his Physiological and Pathological Aspects." By W. A. Bowes, Wesleyan Teacher, Bingley. 2d. 30 pages. 1851.

This arose out of four lectures, delivered by Mr. W. Binns, in Sept. and Oct., 1851, before the Bingley Mechanics' Institution, by way of criticism.

R. C. Wildon's "Visit to Druids' Altar."

R. C. Wildon's "Poacher's Child," pp. iv., 76, 1853.

"A Voice from the Sycamore, on Elm Tree Hill, Bingley. By Robert Carrick Wildon. 20 pages. J. Dobson, Market-place, 1856.

> "To mar the calm no mortal walk'd abroad,
> Save watchful Varley pacing up and down,
> Who here and there with stately footsteps strode,
> To guard the peace and quiet of our Town."

The tree moaned—

> "In trying times of war and woe,
> I saw the sons of Bingley go,
> To aid their brethren and their king,
> When Buonaparte made Europe ring."

> "How oft from out the Elm Tree Inn
> I've heard the burst of jocund din."

The tree, or rather the poet, proceeds to describe the hunts which began and ended at the Elm Tree Inn, with Jerry Scott the head keeper of the fox-hounds at Harden, and Passavant and Outerside—three stout Nimrods.

> "Oh, I have heard old Glover tell—
> While from his eyes the big tears fell—
> How hard they rode, how fast they ran,
> Fox, horses, dogs, and every man,
> O'er marshes, ditches, gates and stiles.
> Full forty-five long weary miles.
> But sports like these we now have none,
> Old Bingley's proudest days are gone."

After naming the dogs, the tree mentions the hunters,—Butterfield, Foulds, and Greenwood.

> "Where, where is Hulbert? where is Wood?
> Who'd follow once through fire or flood—
> Where's Slicer? who such aid could lend,
> And Waddington? our staunchest friend!
> The founder of our gallant band,
> Supporting us with heart and hand,
> And oft I see him gaze on me,
> And speak of sports that used to be."

John Nicholson's Poem on Low Moor Iron Works. Dobson, 1856.

See p. 113 of Mr. Dickon's "Catalogue of Bradford Books" for a list of Nicholson's Works.

The Poetical Works of Wm. Dixon, Steeton; pp. viii, 192. Bingley, John Dobson, 1853.

Lines written on a Beautiful Glen situated between Bingley and Baildon. By R. West, Bard of the Vale, Prospect Street, Bingley. 8 pages. J. Dobson, near the Railway Station. 1851. Introduction dated March, 1849.

Eldwick or Shipley Glen had not then been fixed as the name of this favourite pic-nic place. Brackenhall Green was the general local name, but it was then becoming widely renowned:

> "BEHOLD how they flock to the Glen from each village.
> Sweet echo resounds from Baildon's high plain.
> Here Robin Hood's Chair is hewn out in the rock.
> The Larches and Poplars uplift their proud heads.
> But O what sweet melodies sound in the wood.
> The old Druid's Pulpit is seen in the Glen,
> And the Writing Desk foo, if tradition be true.
> From Bingley and Bradford, and Leeds they resort—
> Some have breathed the foul gas in the mill.
> Ye Cottingley friends and Wilsden likewise,
> And Harden that lies near the Grange,
> You may come to the Glen sweet pleasures to find,
> And your minds relieve with a change.
> And Cullingworth, too, where Odd-fellows unite,
> Considered intelligent men,
> If you choose, you may roam o'er the sweet fragrant bloom,
> You are welcome to visit the Glen."

Lines composed on Margaret, the Beauty of Craven. By R. West, Bard of the Vale, Bingley. 8 pages. 1857.

One verse will suffice as a specimen:—

> Skirrow was a blooming rustic, who wheeled himself round the room,
> While mirth resounded in loud laughs, with rosy cheeks in full bloom.

A Sermon by the Rev. R. Newton, D.D., Oct. 31, 1850, in the Wesleyan Chapel, Keighley, to improve the death of the late Rev. Theodore Dury, M.A., twenty-six years Rector. 16 pages. Bingley, J. Dobson, 1850.

We must now throw together a few Bingley bibliographical fragments.

SHIPLEY GLEN.—The following irregular Verses on Shipley Glen, are inscribed "to my friend Mr. John Dawson, Wood Cottage, Baildon Green, by the Author, J. Wilcock, Horton." 8 pages. Bradford, J. Parkinson, 1848.

"A turf-brown stream from Eldwick flows,—
The dews of Rom'lies' Moor,—
Headlong down the glen it goes
To Aire's more peaceful shore.
Awaken'd by its gurgling din,
The Aire looks up, *and takes it in.*"

John Watson's Account of two Trances of Eliz. Dickinson, with Funeral Sermon. Sandbeds, Bingley, 12 pp., 1832; printed at Bradford.

Rev. P. Garrett's Discourse on the death of the Rev. A. Clarke.

Rev. G. Mather, "Mother's Reward," 1860.

W. Watson's "Youthful Lyrics," 1856.

An Essay on Character; morally, &c. By Silas Cryer, Bingley, Author of "Leisure Musings," "The Better Country," "An Ode to Sobriety," "A Poem on the Evils of Intemperance," "The Christian's Warfare," "Lines on seeing a Sparrow in a Church," "To a Skylark," &c. 28 pages. Keighley, P. Gregson, 1865.

The Essay was read at the Christian Instruction Society, Independent Sunday School, Bingley, Nov. 1, 1864.

"The Abstainer's Companion," 3 parts. Part 1: St. Paul's Advice to Timothy, &c. Part 2: 14 Original Melodies, by Silas Cryer, returned from Halifax to Skirrow's Fold, Dubb, Bingley. 32 pp. Halifax, Baildon & Son.

Leisure Musings; consisting of Original Poems on Pleasant Subjects. By Silas Cryer, Author of "An Essay on Secular Literature." 72 pages. Keighley *Herald Office*, 1876.

On the Death of the Rev. A. Hudson, M.A,, Vicar of Holy Trinity Church, Bingley, d. 18 April, 1877. Memoir of Mr. R. H. Hodgson, Solicitor, a native of Bingley. "Acrostic on Bingley."

HOLY TRINITY CHURCH, BINGLEY.

"The Bingley Messenger," continued several years.

Holy Trinity Sunday School Hymn Book, compiled by Rev. Albert Hudson. 1872. 94 pp.

Rev. S. Clapham, vicar; (see *National Biogr. Dict.*), published a 4to. volume of Sermons, various dates, also Sermon preached at Knaresbro', 1794, and nine other works. He was born at Leeds in 1755, educated at Cambridge, M.A. in 1780, vicar of Great Ouseburn 1797-1830, Christchurch, Hants., 1802-30, Bingley 1792-7, and Knaresbro.' Curate of Yarm, 1790. Rector of Gussage, Dorset, 1806. His two daughters erected a monument to him in Christchurch Priory Church. He died at Sidmouth, June 1st, 1830.

J. Campkin published "Poor Joe," "Nobbut and Ne'er heed," "Ellen Archer," 1867. [Harrison.]

Robert Carrick Wildon was author of "The Poacher's Child." Bradford. He also issued 'Song on a Summer's Day.' Leeds, 127 pp., 1850.

"Bingley Chronicle," weekly newspaper.

James Hird, another of the fair crop of Bingley poets, must be placed in the bibliographical list. His portrait also appears in "Forshaw's Poets of Bingley, Keighley and Haworth."

William Atherton, Independent Minister, Bingley, was author of Sermons and Addresses, 1839.

Dr. Cheadle, son of the Vicar, along with Lord Milton, was author of a work on the "North West Passage by Land," published by Cassell & Co.

The Rev. Wm. Hudswell, a native of Bingley, son of the Independent Minister, was author of a 12 page tract, entitled—"Duties of Christians to their Churches."

"Bingley Independent Chapel Case." Pamphlets referred to in the Nonconformist chapter.

"A Letter to the Parishioners of Bingley on the Duty of Restoring their Parish Church, by a Member of the Yorkshire Architectural Society." London, 1842.

"Church Bells and Bell-ringing at Bingley." Leeds, 1875.

The Rev. John Hanson, Baptist Minister, previously of Idle and Huddersfield, was author of "Think Again, or Annihilationism." 1875. Huddersfield, 64 pp.

Bingley Charities, Government Report, 1894, 49 pages.

Bingley Free Grammar School Scheme, for Management, and of other Charities comprised in the Bingley School and Charity Estate Act, 1853. Folio 15 pp. Todd, Bingley, 1873.

Bingley. Railway Acts, 1845.

Technical Education. A Lecture on "Industry and Art," by Alfred Harris, Esq., delivered at the Technical College, Bradford, March 5, 1883. London, 24 pages. 1883.

"Rhymes for the Times." By a Bingley Tallow Chandler. 46 pages. 1s. R. Aked, Keighley, printer, 1849. Satire on Radicals.

The Trial of Teetotalism versus Temperance, being a report of Mr. B. Earnshaw's Speech in reply to Mr. Thos. Hardy, Teetotal Advocate,

Manchester, on the Subject "Does the Bible sanction the Moderate Use of Alcoholic Drinks?" Delivered in the Foresters' Hall, Denholme, May 7, 1867. 2d. 16 pages. J. Hebden, printer, Cullingworth.

"The New Church Herald," [Swedenborgian] (Vol. I. only pub.) 1886, in 6 Monthly parts, 228 pp., Demy 8vo. Pub. by J. E. Dawson, at Eldwick Grange.

"Knowledge of Salvation by the Dismission of Sins." By John Preston. 7 pp. J. E. Dawson, Bingley, 1886. 1d.

"The Garden of Eden," by Isaac Sanctuary. 2nd ed. 8 pp. Eldwick, 1886.

Of lesser known writers, Bairstow, who wrote the tune "The Last Wish," deserves to be mentioned. No tune has been more popular, especially when sung to the words "Saviour and Lord of all." T. R. Taylor. The tune is carved on his gravestone in Bingley Independent Chapel-yard. John Dawson Fox has issued many poems on local printed slips. One is "On the Departure of the Rev. R. S. Blackburn, Primitive Methodist Minister, Denholme, in Bingley Circuit, for Fernando Po; July, 1878." He wrote another in June, 1879, on the death of the said minister, April 22nd, 1879, at Fernando Po, West Africa. He has issued a pamphlet—"Seventh Annual Review of the Year." Dec. 1894. 21 pages.

In Forshaw's "Poets of Bingley," &c., two editions, are notices of Rev. John Beatson, of Cottingley, b. 1743, d. 1798, and a list of seven of his works. (2) Mr. J. Arthur Binns, born at Bingley, 1826, editor of "Hymns of Worship," 1854; "Bradford Examiner," 1854-5; "Year Book," 1862. (3) Robert Collyer, D.D. (4) Edward Collinson, on "Bingley Tide." (5) Silas Cryer. (6) William Dixon. (7) J. D. Fox. (8) James Hird, the Bradford poet, a native of Bingley parish. (9) Abraham Holroyd. (10) John Illingworth. (11) Thomas Ince. (12) J. Milligan, M.R.C.S. (13) John Nicholson. (14) Ben Preston. (15) Bingley Tallow-chandler. (16) Jane Shackleton, née Atkinson, of Cullingworth. (17) W. C. Rushton. (18) Abraham Wildman. (19) Robert Carrick Wildon. (20) Wm. Wright, of Hoyle House End, Hermit Hole, Bingley.

Mr. Halliwell Sutcliffe, and his father, the Grammar School Master at Bingley, are natives of Haworth, and Bingley residents. The son was was at King's College, Cambridge, from 1889 to 1893, where he took his degree as a senior Op. in the Mathematical Tripos. In 1895 he issued "A Tragedy in Grey:" a Novel; 144 pages; and in 1896 "The XIth Commandment;" 380 pages. He has two works just about to be issued from the press—"A Man of the Moors," and "An Episode in Arcady." There is no doubt that all four volumes will be specially interesting to Airedale readers because of the local colouring. "The XIth Commandment" has been a decided success, and "A Man of the Moors," touching as it does on Haworth and Bingley topics, will be equally popular. Colonial and American editions have also been issued.

Bingley Parish Charities and Grammar School.

A FOLIO PAMPHLET of 49 pages on the Charities of Bingley Parish, printed by Eyre and Spottiswoode, London, 1894, may be obtained from any local bookseller for about Sixpence, and therefore there is no necessity to reprint it here; at the same time, it is absolutely necessary as a supplement to this History of Bingley, and a copy should be found in every bookcase in the town, as should also a copy of the Charity Commissioners' Grammar School Scheme. The charities referred to are:—

MERCY SMITH'S, £100 to the poor, Bingley township, 1752.

REV. G. NEVILE'S, 15s. yearly in bread to the poor of the parish, 1726.

MRS. SARAH RHODES' cottages at Priesthorpe, 1785.

THOMAS BUSFEILD, ESQ., for clothing.

CULLINGWORTH SCHOOL.

LOST CHARITIES, reported 1827, Grace Keighley's, Isabella Hall's.

PRINCE OF WALES' PARK.

WESLEYAN CHAPEL AND SCHOOL, 1815.

INDEPENDENT CHAPEL, with Mrs. Hutton's Charity, wherein Bingley shares with Idle, Eastwood, Thornton, &c., 1720, 1773, &c. [Crabtree's *Halifax*, p. 524.]

CULLINGWORTH WESLEYAN CHAPEL.

MORTON BANKS WESLEYAN CHAPEL.

It may be worth noting here that the early Registers of the Wesleyan Chapel, Bingley, founded 1763, are preserved at Somerset House, London, and date from 1816 to 1837. Those of Cullingworth Wesleyans (founded 1806,) date from 1822-34; those of Harden Wesleyans (founded 1795,) from 1814-87.

SAMUEL SUNDERLAND'S GIFT to the Vicar.
,,   ,,   to the Poor.
,,   ,,   to the Grammar School.

WILLIAM WOOLLERS' GIFT to the School, &c.

MRS. STAVELEY'S GIFT supplementing Mrs. Rhodes'.

GILSTEAD ENCLOSURE ALLOTMENT AND SCHOOL.

MRS. HARRIET WOOD'S Hospital Charities, 1886.

THE COTTAGE HOSPITAL: Queen's Jubilee Memorial, 1887; foundation stone laid by Walter Dunlop, Esq., J. P., of the Grange.

THE MECHANICS' INSTITUTE, 1840, 1861.

FREE LIBRARY, 1889. Mr. Alfred Sharp was the prime mover in these latter movements.

ELYMAS WADSWORTH'S GIFT, 1890, to Cullingworth Baptist Chapel.

In this valuable report there is much interesting matter besides the long account of the Grammar School. In 1529 land was held in

Greenhill for the support of a Grammar School. The income is referred to under dates 1570, 1602, 1622, &c., and many other matters relating to the School and Charities are given in the old Churchwarden's Account Book, copied by Mr. Hartley Hartley and myself. A reference in the School deed of 1605 to a messuage called Lady House or Roodford is of interest as indicating a cross dedicated to the Virgin, probably at the river-ford. Abraham Bynnes and Sybill his wife, William Wooller (died about 1597), Michael Broadley, Nicholas Walker, Thomas Howgill, the vicar, Richard Sunderland and his son Samuel must ever be remembered as the public benefactors of the early Protestant centuries, and they notify their anti-popery spirit in the School Inquisition of 1623, &c. In these enquiries we learn the names of several fields belonging to the estate, Stackflat, Thompson wife-ing, Buredge close, Lightfoot close, Hanging acre, Mastall, Woodside in Micklethwaite, Louse pasture, Poticarhills, Dubb in Micklethwaite, (evidently a pond-field), Pinfold acre, Laythorpe, Greenhill and Crossbutts in Micklethwaite, Eight acres, &c. The value of the School estate in 1831 was estimated at £400 yearly. In 1816 a National School was established by voluntary subscription, and in 1820, when Dr. Hartley was Master, the Lord Chancellor decreed that the Free School should be conducted for teaching the children of the inhabitants the learned languages. It is a pity that no one connected with the school has taken the trouble to compile a list of its eminent masters and pupils.

To this object I contribute a few paragraphs:

Henry, son of Henry Johnson, attorney, Bingley, was admitted sizar at St. John's, Cambridge, June 30, 1645, aged 18. He was admitted in Oxford four years before, resided there one year, by the testimony of Thomas Watkins, of Bingley.

This Thomas Watkins was master of Bingley school before 1645, and was there in 1651, removing in that year to Bradford school, for Joseph son of Abraham Dawson, clothier, of Leeds, was under him at Bradford. Probably this Joseph Dawson, born about 1637, was the incumbent ejected from Thornton in 1662.

John son of John Midgley, gent., of Thornton, bred at Bingley under Mr. Leake, the Schoolmaster, was admitted pensioner at St. John's, Cambridge, April 16, 1647, aged 21.

Edmund Garforthe, son of William G., yeoman, of Steeton, bred at Bingley under Mr. Watkins, was admitted sizar at St. John's, Cambridge, May 8, 1648, aged 17. He became Vicar of Gargrave, 1660-73.

George son of William Crooke of Askwith, bred at Bingley under Mr. Watkins, was admitted pensioner at St. John's, June 23, 1648, aged 17.

Henry son of John Johnson, gent., of *Woodesworth*, Yorkshire, at Bingley under Mr. Watkins, admitted sizar Sept. 10, 1649, aged 15; St. John's, Cambridge.

William son of William Thornton, clothier, of Cottingley, born at Beckfoot, trained at Bingley school under Mr. Watkins, admitted sizar at St. John's, June 21, 1651, aged 17.

Thomas son of Richard Hudson, bailiff, born at Bingley, bred at Bingley under Mr. Ellison, schoolmaster, was admitted sizar at St. John's College, Cambridge, May 21, 1711, aged 18. I have no doubt this is the Thomas Hudson, page 225, who became Master of Bingley Grammar School, died in 1756, and was succeeded by his son Thomas as master, who died in 1785.

It will be seen that these are only a few of the names of schoolmasters and pupils of Bingley school, and a perusal of the Oxford and Cambridge University Registers is necessary to complete the story of the venerable school at Bingley.

Many names of notable men, some now living, may be added traditionally, but a safer way is to give documentary evidence.

The Rev. Dr. Stephen Parkinson, born near Keighley in 1823, became scholar under Mr. Cheadle at Bingley, entered St. John's, Cambridge. He became senior wrangler in 1845, and was author of works on Mechanics, Optics, &c. Lord Kelvin was his rival in 1845.

GREENHILL HALL.

Bingley Old Grammar School.

Methodism.

FROM the Life of Richard Burdsall it appears that the Methodists had a barn fitted up with seats and pulpit in Bingley for services, about 1753, Jan. 1st. On a visit to Eldwick he heard that the Rev. W. Grimshaw, of Haworth, was to preach in the barn at Bingley. A broad set, sharp-looking little man, habited as a layman, buttoned up from the storm, came in, gave out a hymn, prayed, and preached from "Glory to God in the highest." But Thomas Lee had preached at Harden in 1747. Amongst the Harden Methodists were William Waterhouse of Hill End, who reached the age of 95, and his mother Mary Waterhouse, died March 5, 1822, aged 103, as testified on the stone in Bingley churchyard. From meetings in cottage houses, they got a room over a stable in Harden Lane, and also held services at Hill End. In 1813 a chapel was built, enlarged in 1835, and enlarged again in 1896. The Reformers tried to seize the chapel, and a Chancery Trial followed but they lost. The Reformers met then in Matthew Wilkinson's lathe, &c., till their chapel was built in 1853.

FIRST WESLEYAN CHAPEL.   OLD MARKET PLACE.

In 1763, the Bingley Methodists had three classes in the Society and only thirty members owing to the Baptist secession. Thomas Middlesbrough, farmer, Castlefields, John Curtiss, stuff maker, Bingley, David Binns, weaver, Harden Brow, were the class leaders. Mr. Ward printed a list of the thirty members. The Society was so poor that the Conference sent pecuniary aid 1766-1775. Their first preaching room was in the blacksmith's shop on Elm Tree Hill, at a yearly rental of 30s. The second place was a large room (over buildings where the first chapel was afterwards built,) in 1770. About 1790, the first chapel was built near the first meeting room. Mr. Walker Waddington was seized with hydrophobia in the chapel, and died or was smothered Sep. 1, 1795, aged 31.

As the Methodists offered extempore prayers at the National Sunday School, built by subscription, they were warned that it was against the rule, so they left to form one of their own, and Mr. John Dean, one of the members, gave a piece of land for the purpose. It was decided to build a chapel thereon with a school-room underneath. This second chapel was erected in 1816 at a cost of £3839 10s., the trustees being Thomas Whitley, Joshua Briggs, Joseph Cooper, David Binns, Wm. Foulds, Matthew Foster, Joseph Barraclough, John Dean, Wm. Whitley, Thomas Nicholson (father of the poet), John Sharp, John Wilkinson, and Thomas Longbottom.

An amusing story is told of Dean who, in 1828, was superintending the erection of St. Paul's Church, Shipley. By announcing himself as Dean of St. Paul's, he got a front seat on the platform at the parliamentary election, York. Dean's wit was very serviceable at one of the opening services. A foolish creature cried out that the chapel was falling, but Dean commanded the people to "sit still, for it would not give way if it was crammed full of lead." Dr. Newton preached at the opening service, and the Rev. Theodore Dury, rector of Keighley was one of the hearers and dated his conversion from that sermon. Dr. Hartley, son of Wesley's friend, was, like his father, on friendly terms with the Wesleyans, and had a pew in the chapel, and the curate (afterwards Dr. Cartman, of Skipton,) frequently attended on Sunday evenings to hear Dr. Beaumont, 1817-8. The church was closed after the afternoon service. Almost all the northern Methodist notables preached in this old chapel, which was sold in 1874 to the Midland Railway Company, to build the railway station on the spot.

In 1828 Morton Wesleyan Chapel was opened, when the Rev. Philip Garrett preached. Amongst the fruits of a great revival under Dr. Beaumont, were William Longbottom and Thomas Cryer, notable missionaries. William Longbottom (son of Thomas, son of Matthew, both Wesleyans,) married a daughter of Mr. England, Bingley, and from 1835 they laboured at the Cape Colony. Being planned to Swan River, West Australia, they were shipwrecked at Encounter Bay, but reached Adelaide eventually, and successfully laboured there for some time. Mr. Longbottom died there in 1849, and his memoir appears in the *Wesleyan Magazine* for 1853, and a long account of his father as a soldier in Mr. Ward's *Bingley Methodism*.

Thomas Cryer, born at Bingley in 1800, married the daughter of Mr. Jeremiah White of Gilstead, and after a few months' ministry in England, they went to India and laboured there twenty-two years. His memoir appears in the same volume of the *Magazine* as his friend Longbottom's.

John Whitley of Toils Farm, Eldwick, was a convert under Mr. Skirrow, the founder of the Baptist cause in Bingley, but remained with the Methodists. Mr. Wesley is believed to have visited Toils

TOILS FARM.

Farm on his journeys to and from Otley, and he induced Mr. Whitley to become an itinerant preacher, but he relinquished it in five years. On a pane in the house-window is the portrait of Mr. Wesley and a

ELDWICK METHODIST CHAPEL.

verse believed to be written by him; but the date Oct. 1776, does not accord with his seventh visit, in May of that year.

> Man, thy years are ever sliding,
> Brightest hours have no abiding,
> Use the golden moments well.
> Life is wasting,
> Death is hasting,
> Death consigns to heaven or hell.

Francis Whitley, son of John, also became a local preacher, and travelled thousands of miles in his forty-eight years' experience. His memoir is given in the Magazine for 1823.

WESLEY WINDOW, TOILS FARM.

In Bingley Churchyard is a tombstone to the Whitleys:—
Martha wife of John, d. Feb. 20, 1776, aged 58. John, died in London, March 11, 1813, aged 90. Sarah, wife of Francis their son, d. Sept. 18, 1815, aged 73. Francis d. Nov. 27, 1821, aged 72.

For memoir of his son, Rev. John Whitley, see Methodist Magazine. Francis' daughter was mother of John Nicholson, the poet, who resided for some time at Toils Farm before and after his marriage. Young Nicholson was a local preacher, but his early marriage hindered his promotion to an itinerancy as designed by the Rev. Alex. Suter, and in 1815 his name disappeared from the plan. Greenhill Hall, the residence of Mr. Thomas Whitley, a trustee of Bingley Wesleyan Chapel, is closely connected with local Methodism.

Eldwick Methodists formed a society in 1766, and met in hired rooms till they erected a chapel in 1832, by boon labour, and about £9 in cash. The present neat edifice, from plans by Mr. John Bruce, cost £700. Memorial stones were laid March 30, 1888, by Miss White, Mr. H. Platts, and Mr. R. Fawcett.

The present Bingley Wesleyan Church cost over £13,000, towards which Messrs. Sharp contributed about half, and Mr. William Sharp gave also the organ (£1000) and the minister's house.

THOMAS MITCHELL, another Bingley man, became one of Wesley's preachers. He had been a soldier and served at the time of Prince Charles' Rebellion, 1745, with the English army. He joined the Wesleyans soon after the suppression of the Rebellion, and left Bingley for Bradford, being the only Methodist in that town for a short period. He kept brief diaries of his travels, one of which lies before me, but it gives only the names of the places he visited, the texts he took, and religious reflections. He refers in another book, to John Wesley's visit to Bradford in 1747, when Mr. Wesley formed a class, but all fell away except Mitchell. In 1748 he was appointed a travelling preacher or helper, in which service he spent nearly forty years. The minutes of 1785 record his death. His autobiography appeared in the *Magazine* for 1781. His sufferings (especially in 1751, at a place in Lincolnshire, where he was thrown into a pond, covered with white paint,) were incredible.

In 1790 the Rev. Isaac Lilly, a native of Bingley, became a travelling preacher. He reached the age of 85. In 1793, died at John Watson's, Sandbeds, aged 19, Elizabeth Dickinson, who had created great excitement by public preaching and trances. (See Bibliography.)

To the small book by Mr. Ward on "Methodism in Bingley," much may be added from the *Methodist Magazine*, thus:

1819, Memoir of Samuel Whitaker refers to the frequent horse-races on Harding moor.

1826, James Bentley of Bingley circuit, which then included Wilsden and Denholme, died, aged 81, a class-leader nearly 40 years.

1829. Joseph Pickles of Wilsden, born 1733, member for 65 years, left surviving, 7 children, 73 grand-children, 179 great grand-children,

50 great great grand-children; total 309, and 101 had died, giving 410.

August, 1839, death of Mrs. Weatherhead, Bingley, niece of Rev. J. Sugden, aged 33.

March, 1840, aged 78, Allen Edmondson, cousin of the Rev. Jonathan Edmondson, died with relatives at Bingley; he had erected cotton mills in England and Ireland.

Jan. 10, 1840, aged 74, Henry Sturk, an active Methodist, died.

John Patrick born at Bingley, Feb. 1757, died Feb. 1839.

In the *Arminian Magazine*, Vol. 3, are portraits of Mr. Lee and Mr. Mitchell, Methodist preachers of Keighley and Bingley.

The Rev. J. Needham, 1811, sent to the *Wesleyan Magazine* a notice of Wm. Hargreaves, native of Bingley parish, who died April 20, 1811, aged 69. His wife died two years before. Five of their seven sons who grew to maturity were soldiers, the oldest fell on the plains of Delhi, another died in the east, and a third fell at Rosetta Siege.

Mrs. Fell of Milner Field, a generous Methodist, died in 1811.

Feb. 1812, aged 84, died Eli Jowett, Riddlesden, fifty years a Methodist.

In the *Magazine* for May 1814, the great meeting of the Bingley Wesleyan Missionary Society (established Nov. 1813) is reported.

June, 1845. Mrs. Susanna Milner, of Cross Flatts, died. Methodist class held at her house. Her husband was killed by falling into a coalpit many years before this date on returning from his work in a snow-storm.

Dec. 1844, Mary Jane Warrener, dau. Rev. W. M'Kittrick, died at Bingley, aged 20.

The Yorkshire Circuit in 1746 included Lancashire and five other Southern counties. In 1749, Haworth was made the head of a Circuit, and in 1776 Keighley was substituted for the name Haworth. In 1808 Bingley was separated from Keighley Circuit, and included Yeadon until 1829, and Shipley until 1823, but Shipley was joined again 1828-30. Thornton was in Bingley Circuit for some years before 1843. A list of the Bingley ministers will be found in Mr. Ward's book.

The Rev. John Wesley visited Bingley on Saturday, May 21, 1757, "I had a little Conference with our preachers (at Keighley.) In the afternoon I preached at Bingley. I have not lately seen so genteel a congregation; yet the Word of God fell heavy upon them." The following morning he preached at five o'clock, and then took horse for Haworth. He notes in his journal that an earthquake was felt at Bingley and forwards to Lancashire. He had passed through Bingley several times previously.

July 7, 1761, he again preached at Bingley.

August 4, 1766, "Monday, at one I preached at Bingley, but with a heavy heart, finding so many of the Methodists here, as well as at Haworth, perverted by the Anabaptists."

1770, July, preached at Bingley.

Monday, July 6, 1772, at noon I preached at Bingley to a large congregation.

In 1776, on his seventh visit, the church is mentioned for the first time but possibly he had preached in it before. "Saturday, May 27, 1776, I preached in the church at Bingley, perhaps not so filled before for these hundred years." The Rev. Richard Hartley was vicar at that time.

See illustration, Toils Farm, 1776, Oct.?

Mr. Wesley usually lodged with Mr. Johnson Atkinson Busfeild at Myrtle Grove, which he had built where Springhead farm previously stood. Mr. Wesley notes in his journal, Monday, April 19, 1779, I preached at Bingley to a numerous congregation. I dined with Mr. Busfeild in his little paradise, but it can give no happiness unless God is there.

Sunday, April 23, 1780. Mr. Richardson being unwilling that I should preach any more in Haworth Church, Providence opened another, I preached at Bingley Church both morning and afternoon. Wet in the morning, but in the afternoon many were crowded out.

1782, May 28, Bingley Church was hot, but the heat was supportable both morning and afternoon.

1784, Sunday, July 18, I preached morning and afternoon in Bingley Church. Before service I stepped into the Sunday School, which contains 240 children, taught every Sunday by several masters and superintended by the curate . . . I find these schools springing up wherever I go . . . , Tuesday, 20th, though it rained hard all day, in the morning we had a good congregation at five. Wednesday, 21, I met the Society and found but one or two of the original members, most of them having gone to Abraham's bosom. I was a little surprised to find that only two or three of the rest had stood fast in the glorious liberty. Thursday, 22, although it rained yet I met the congregation, and most of these were athirst for salvation. Friday, 23, abundance of people were present at five in the morning, and such a company of children as I have hardly seen in England."

1786, May 23, Sunday, preached at Bingley Church in the afternoon, but as there were many hundreds that could not get in, Mr. Atmore preached abroad at the same time.

1788, Sunday, May 27, Bingley Church sufficiently crowded in the afternoon, but as many could not get in Mr. Wrigley preached in the street.

He is stated to have preached at the Market Cross and from steps near the Fleece Inn, and from the horse-steps at the White Horse Inn.

JONATHAN MASKEW, a native of Bingley parish, was one of Wesley's early converts. He joined the Methodists about 1744, and was a recognised preacher in 1752. Wesley said of him that ten such preachers would carry the world before them. The Bingley circuit book gives items of cost for shirts, stockings, cravats, &c., given to him. At Guiseley he was stripped nearly naked, rolled in the dirt and almost killed. His memoir appears in the *Methodist Magazine*,

296 ANCIENT BINGLEY.

1798. He died in 1793, aged 83, after nearly fifty years of diligent service in various parts of England. Notices of him appear in the *Lives* of Grimshaw, *Methodist Memorial* by Atmore, *Methodism in Manchester*, *Haworth Past and Present*, &c. He was popularly known as Grimshaw's Man.

OLD DEED IN BINGLEY CHURCH.—*See page 78.*

Modern Annals.

BINGLEY has taken its share in the development of the woollen trade ever since the origin of surnames, as the presence of the Walkers and Listers can testify, and as tradesmen began to prosper, taxation—from 1300—was placed on wool as well as land. After the Reformation very little wool was exported, and foreign refugees at various times have settled in Norwich, Halifax and other parts, and given a stimulus to the trade. Though the workpeople lived on common food, as rye, barley and oat-bread, with very little meat except bacon, and cheap home-brewed beer, or herb-teas; and wooden trenchers served for plates; the clothiers began to make wheat-bread, and build better houses.

Farmers generally were also small manufacturers and sold their super-produce to merchants who attended the markets, and canvassed the country. By 1750 the shalloon, calimanco, bombazine, and tammy makers had got a wide reputation in this neighbourhood, and in the registers and other lists of persons, we find from this time in Bingley, spinners, stuffmakers, weavers, woolcombers and tailors, and these necessitated concomitant trades, cordwainers, glaziers, plasterers, builders, besides husbandmen. The farmers adopted stuff manufacturing as that usurped the place of wool. The looms and the spinning-wheels were found at the majority of houses, and large market-halls were erected in many towns; Wakefield Tammy Hall, 1766; Bradford, 1773; Halifax Piece Hall, 1779. Keighley and Haworth were more directly connected then with the Halifax branch of the trade. Strings of pack-horses regularly went to both Halifax and Bradford from Bingley. Combers embezzled the wool and otherwise cheated the masters who got the Worsted Acts passed in 1777, and a committee with inspector was appointed. Great rejoicings followed the Act of 1788 forbidding the exportation of wool. The material was distributed for miles around and gathered back on fixed dates. This inconvenience suggested the establishment of mills at Addingham 1787, Leeming mill, Haworth, 1790, Hewenden worsted mill, 1792, Bradford, 1800. Providence mill, Bingley, was built in 1801 as a steam cotton mill by Hartleys. As there was exemption from soap duty called soap-drawback, we can compare the relative amount of work at various places.

Bingley—	Keighley—	Haworth—	Bradford—
1810, £159.	£199.	£382.	£851.

There were sixteen worsted manufacturers in Bingley, of whom Nicholls, Sharp and Hartley were the three doing largest trade. The Luddites did not affect the worsted trade of Airedale. Mr. John Holland of Brighouse introduced the moreen trade from Norwich in 1811, but Akroyd of Halifax pushed the trade most; and wildbores, plain-backs and plain and ribbed calimancoes were largely made.

In 1820 the drawback on the soap duty for Bingley was £333. From this time the trade went by leaps and bounds, and a full account may be found in James' *Worsted Manufacture*, wherein Bingley takes its due share, and the names of Robert Milligan of Bingley, and the Townends of Cullingworth were specially prominent in the Exhibition of 1851. Great changes for the better followed the labours of Richard Oastler and his party, and the 1833 Factory Act was the starting point in the moral, social and intellectual improvement of the labouring classes, who had hitherto enjoyed only the religious privileges of their forefathers.

In 1770, a general map in four sheets was issued by Joseph Priestley, Leedes, 4to, of the Leedes and Liverpool Canal. The Act for making this Canal, was passed in 1768. On March 21st, 1774, the portion

FIVE RISE LOCKS.

from Shipley to Bingley was completed. There were great rejoicings on witnessing the descent of the first boat down the Five Rise Lock. The Church bells were rung, and bands of music played, and a general holiday was observed. A view of the Five Locks by J. Ludewig Hogrew, "Prospect des 5 Locks," 1777, is in the King's MSS., British Museum.

At this period road-making became a science, but for a long time, down to the end of George III's days, deep ruts rendered dangerous even the best highways. Coach travelling, though very expensive, became frequent for those who could afford it. Amongst the most noted coaches passing through Bingley, we hear of The Packet, 1792 to 1800, on Monday, Wednesday and Friday from Leeds at 9 a.m. to Bradford and Bingley where the passengers and luggage were transferred to the canal packet boat to proceed to Skipton, Liverpool and America. The fare for inside the coach and the front boat cabin from Leeds to Skipton was 6s. 6d.; outside the coach and back cabin 3s. 6d. Mr. Maud of the Old Queen's Head managed the Bingley end; afterwards the Old King's Arms, and later still the Elm Tree Inn were starting places. In 1796 the coach ran between Bingley and Bradford, where the Leeds coach was joined.

In 1792 a coach passed through Bingley to Bradford at 2 p.m., on Tuesdays, Thursdays and Saturdays. The Leeds and Kendall Diligence 1789-1791, ran through Bradford, Bingley, Keighley and Settle, on Mondays, Thursdays and Saturdays. It left Leeds at 4 a.m., the inside fare for the full journey one way was 25s.

In 1817 the Anticipation Coach left Skipton daily at 5 a.m. passing through Bingley and Bradford to Leeds, returning thence at 3-30 p.m. The Britannia in 1818-1821 took its place, but returned at 5 p.m.

In 1820 the Alexander left Leeds daily at 4 a.m. in summer, later in winter, for Bradford, where another coach carried its freight, as required, to Skipton, via Bingley. This coach ran over twenty years. The Crown Union ran in 1828 from Keighley every Tuesday via Bingley, Shipley, Idle, Calverley to Leeds, returning at 5 p.m. The Invincible, 1824-1842, left Leeds daily at 7 a.m. via Bingley, Crosshills, Colne, Blackburn to Preston, to meet the 3-30 coach for Blackpool. The Mail Coach, 1841-3, left Leeds daily at 7-30, bearing the London letters and passengers, via Bradford, Bingley, Skipton, Settle to Lancaster, where it was due at 4 p.m.

In 1834 the Rockingham ran every afternoon to Skipton via Bingley.

The Sunday School of 240 children, visited by Mr. Wesley in 1784, was undenominational, and supported by public subscription. Mr. John White was upper master at 2s. 6d. per Sunday, and Mr. Jeremiah Briggs was under-master at 2s. per Sunday, and John Longbottom and Solomon Clark were assistants at 1s. per Sunday. The school hours were from 9 to 4 in winter, and 8 a.m. to 6 p.m., April to October. The first year's subscription came to £47 and the expenses to £39. It was founded in June, 1784, and one regulation was that children of Dissenters were to be allowed to attend their own places of worship.

1794, great rejoicings at Myrtle Grove when Mr. Wm. Busfeild attained his majority.

1795, James Crosland, of Eldwick, buried at Baildon, April, aged 5; died of canine madness.

1807. Poll for M.P's. for Yorkshire, May 20 to June 5. Candidates, Wilberforce, Milton and Lascelles: voting at York.

BINGLEY.			BINGLEY.	
Geo. Anderton, worsted manufacr.	W.L.		Chas. Hartley, cotton spinner	L.
John do. woolstapler	W.L.		Joshua Hill, mason	L.
Wm. Atkinson, farmer	W.L.		Joseph Hall, yeoman	M.
Joseph Beanlands, yeoman	M.		Thos. Hartley, cotton spinner	M.
John do. grocer	M.		Wm. do. do.	M.
James Brearey, woolcomber	W.L.		Joseph Heaton, gent.	L.M.
Johnson Atkinson Busfeild, Esq.	W.L.		Richd. Hodgson, gent.	M.
Jas. Barber, maltster	L.		Thos. Hulbert, gent.	M.
John Butterfield, cordwainer	M.		Tim. Horsfall, cottontwist spin.	W.L.
Francis do. yeoman	M.		Wm. Holdsworth. clerk	W.L.
Wm. Ellis, Esq., Castlefield	W.L.		Abm. Hudswell, dissent. minr.	M.
John Gott, carpenter	M.		Jonas Jowitt, blacksmith	W.L.
Richard Hartley, clerk	W.L.		John Kitchen, miller	M.

BINGLEY.

George Morville, maltster	M.
Tim. Mawd, butcher	M.
John Moorhouse, timber merchant	M.
Robt. Murgatroyd, yeoman	W.L.
Wm. Nicholls, farmer	W.L.
Wm. Oddy, yeoman	M.
Michael Pickles, farmer	W.L.
Henry do, do.	L.
John Pitts, clothsearcher	M.
Thos. Rushforth, yeoman	L.
Christr. Scott, maltster	L.
Wm. Smith, manufacturer	W.L.
Stephen Skirrow, clothier	M.
Timothy do. farmer	M.
Jonas Tetley, farmer	W.L.
Wm. Taylor, manufacturer	W.L.
David Whitley, grocer	M.
John Walley, woolcomber	W.L.
Jonath. Whitaker, yeoman	W.L.

COTTINGLEY.

John Burdett, gent.	M.
Jas. Goodall, labourer	W.
Abm. Knowles, farmer	W.L.
John Ramsbottom, farmer	W.
Michael Maud, yeoman	W.L.
Wm. Pulleyn, farmer	M.
John Stockdale, gent.	L.

GAWTHORPE HALL.

Joseph Heddon, gent.	L.

HARDING.

Joshua Anderson, carpenter	W.L.
John Bailey, yeoman	W.L.
John Holmes, shopkeeper	W.L.
Jonas Knowles, yeoman	W.L.
Wm. Leach, woolcomber	W.L.
Jas. Murgatroyd, yeoman	L.
Abm. Wilkinson, yeoman	L.

HELWICK.

Joseph Baldwin, clothier	M.
John Stead, yeoman	W.L.

MICKLETHWAITE.

Thos. Nicholls, gent.	W.L.

MORTON.

Jonath. Barker, cotton spinner	W.
Hill do. do.	L.
Wm. Busfeild, Esq.	M.
Abm. Briggs, paper maker	M.
Thos. Emmott, yeoman	M.
John Greenwood, yeoman	M.
Christr. do. do.	M.
Joseph Longbottom, yeoman	W.L.
Timothy Lister, yeoman	M.
James do. do.	M.
Thos. Leach, cotton spinner	M.
John Coates Phillips, gent.	M.
Thos. Rishworth, gent.	M.
Joseph Royston, yeoman	M.
George Walmsley, yeoman	M.
Joseph Wright, paper maker	M.
Joseph Wilkinson, yeoman	M.

RYCROFT.

John Wilkinson, yeoman, Harding,	M.

For BINGLEY and HARDING FREEHOLDS.

B Thos. Ellingthorp, yeo., Barcroft	W.L.
B Jacob Denby, yeoman, Foweather	M.
H Wm. Hodgson, wors. mfr., Hnw'th.	W.L.
H Thos. Rhodes, mason do.	W.L.
H Roger Shackleton, gent. do.	W L.
B Robt. Naylor, yeo., Hawkesworth	M.
B Jas. Mann, maltster, Holbeck	W.L.
B John Butler, ironmonger, Kirkstall Forge	W.L.

1811, Aug. 28. Testimonial presented by the Officers of Bingley Volunteer Infantry to Major Currer Fothergill Busfeild their Commanding Officer, in testimony of their regard.

1814. Bingley National Schools erected. Gen. Twiss gave £340. Dr. Hartley, £200. Edwd. Ferrand, Esq., £166. Walker Ferrand, Esq., £190. William Ellis, Esq., Castlefield Mill, £100. Capt. Staveley, £30. Rev. W. Penny, £25. Rev. G. Ferrand, £25. J. Lane Fox, Esq., £25. Walter Skirrow, Esq., London, £10 10s. 0d. Mrs. Ferrand, Cottingley, £10 10s. 0d. Miss Currer, £10. Diocesan Society, £50. National School Society, £300, &c. Total, £1541. Mr. Richardson the first schoolmaster, became postmaster in 1830 and held that office thirty years. He died in 1875, aged 84 years.

1822. Baines' Directory gives a list of tradespeople and chief inhabitants.

1825. Great Woolcombers' Strike; riots in Bradford.

1830, Jan. The Airedale heifer owned by Mr. Slingsby, of Riddlesden Hall, was killed, He had had 400 guineas offered for it and half the proceeds by exhibiting it in various towns. It weighed 41¾ stone per quarter, 16 Ibs. to stone, and measured from its nose to the stump of its tail 11 ft. 10 in. The Inn at Riddlesden is named after it, and drawings of it were eagerly purchased.

1830. The Gazetteer notices of Bingley consisted of a brief paragraph, that it was a parish, township and market-town in Craven deanery, Skyrack wapentake, with market on Tuesdays, and fairs on Jan. 25, and August 25-6-7 for horned cattle, sheep and linen. Bingley Tide—the King of Feasts—is held the first Sunday after Aug. 22. Air salubrious and water abundant. Church and Grammar School. Five Almshouses, each with £3 yearly and endowment, gift of Mrs. Sarah Rhodes. Newsroom. Trades—worsted, cotton, paper and malt. Built on a hill between the river and canal.

1836. Freemasons' Lodge, Sincerity, instituted. Duke of York's Lodge of Freemasons; seal given in Riley's work.

1837. Mr. Busfeild, Upwood, elected M.P. for Bradford, and again in 1851.

1837. Present Vicarage built: the ground had to be "piled," being swampy.

On the 26th April, 1841, a faculty was obtained from "Edward, Lord Archbishop of York, to our well-beloved in Christ, Sarah Ferrand of St. Ives, widow," for the said Sarah Ferrand and her family exclusively, to use a vault in the new burial ground called Kirk-ing, twenty-three feet square, fenced off.

1842. Plug-drawing at the Castlefield and other mills; Chartist riots then and in 1848. Great excitement prevailed in Bingley in the 1848 Chartist rising; many were fetched out of bed.

1844, Oct. 19, Bingley and Cottingley Allotment Gardens opened.

1847, March 16, the Midland Railway was opened, the first station being down Dean's yard near where the third has recently been erected. Great difficulties were experienced in finding a solid foundation for the line owing to the existence of an insatiable quagmire or bog. This morass was forty-five feet deep, composed of turf, bog-soil and swamp, which yielded to the pressure of the embankment so readily that the ground was rent into fissures, engulphing and capsizing the line. Amongst disembogued matter were remains of fishes, particularly the skins of eels, which were collected by the curious. It was evident that a deep and extensive lake formerly filled the valley. Thousands of people visited the site, and the Leeds papers of Sept. 1845 gave graphic accounts of the difficulties the workmen had in constructing the railway. "John Smith's father, about 1795, lost a cow in the ditch passing through the Ings, and it was never seen after falling in." Sixty tons of earth and stone were cast into the morass every hour from Nab wood on the east by steam-power and on the west by horse-power, notwithstanding next morning all were swallowed up, the lighter spongy matter rising at the sides and flowing over the mass again. It was questioned when the work could be completed, "but when finished it will be one of the finest rides in the

West Riding." Park Road, or Toad Lane, passes over it. By throwing whole trees into the slack, a remedy was found and the line to Bingley was finished about a month after the despairing newspaper accounts. In 1852 there were only seven trains daily each way, stopping at Bingley, and three on Sundays.

1847. Bingley Improvement Commissioners appointed, and afterwards a Local Board was formed for Bingley proper. Gas was supplied some years after this date by Messrs. Sharp, the price at one time being 8s. per thousand feet.

1848. The Tower-window of the Parish Church was restored by J. A. Busfeild, Esq.

1848, March 17. Public meeting of inhabitants of Bingley thanked Mrs. Ferrand and J. A. Busfeild, Esq., for their gifts towards the restoration and furnishing of the Parish Church. Rev. James Cheadle in the chair.

1851, March. Bingley Building Society established; it and the Co-operative Society are flourishing institutions.

1853. New Grammar School built, costing £1000, but being near the bog and showing signs of sinking, it was abandoned in 1863 for the present site.

1855. The Grange built, formerly called St. Ives.

Wesleyan Day School was held many years under the chapel, but in 1860, April 28, Mr. Alfred Sharp laid the foundation stone for the present Schools, costing £2,800. Opened August 14, 1861.

1863, March 10. First sod cut of "Prince of Wales' Park."

1864. Mechanics' Institute, Main street, opened: cost £3000.

1868. Great explosion of boiler near the National School, sixteen persons killed.

Holy Trinity Church, Bingley, was consecrated by Bishop Bickersteth, Oct. 23, 1868, when a population of 4,500 was assigned to it. It was valued at £200 per annum, seats for 700, and the Rev. Albert Hudson, M.A., was the vicar. Alfred Harris, Esq., gave £1000, one-fifth of the cost.

1870. The Ryshworth Chapel, north-chancel aisle rebuilt by J. A. Busfeild, Esq., and the rest of the church restored 1870-1, cost £3000.

1871. Cemetery opened on Bailey Hill, cost £8500. Consecrated in August, 1870.

1872, December. The sycamore tree on Elm Tree Hill fell. It had always been a favourite lounging resort. Wildon and Nicholson sang its praises. The hunters assembled around it before starting. The *Keighley News*, Nov.–Jan., 1887-8, has articles about it.

1874. Wesleyan Chapel built in Mornington road. Wellington street Chapel sold.

1874, June 20. Baptist Chapel, Park road, foundation stone laid by T. Aked. Formerly they had a chapel in Main street.

1874. Re-organization of Bingley Grammar School; the Rev. Mr. Dixon pensioned, and Mr. Sutcliffe, B.A., appointed.

1875. Bingley School Board formed.

1881. New font in parish church by Norman Shaw, R.A.

1882, August 22. The Improvement Commissioners purchased the Market Rights from Mr. Lane Fox, lord of the manor, for £800, and a Friday market has been established. Since that date, 1887 to 1895, the whole of the market buildings, &c., have been swept away and Main street is no longer like itself; whilst a magnificent railway station has been erected, and a public park and a cemetery laid out.

1887-8. The *Keighley News* of these and many other years, give interesting articles on current Bingley topics.

1888, Dec. Upper and lower stones of a Roman quern or millstone found in Bingley, deposited in the Free Library. Technical College erected.

1889, Oct. 2-5. W. Busfeild, Esq., of Moreland Hall, Penrith, opened the Bingley Cottage Hospital Bazaar.

1890, June. East Window in Parish Church, erected by Dr. Cheadle, son of vicar, to the memory of his wife, Anne, d. of Wm. Murgatroyd, Esq., of Bankfield.

1896, August 29. Castlefield mills burnt down. £17,000 damage.

1896. A prosperous Agricultural Show is held annually.

1896. Curfew bell and Shrovetide Pancake bell are still rung at the parish church; whilst Bingley Tide, held the first Sunday after Aug. 22, keeps up its reputation as the "King of Feasts."

Population returns—

In 1577, there were 41 baptisms and 30 burials.
   1686 ,, 54 ,, 44 ,,
   1741 ,, 77 ,, 75 ,,
   1778 ,, 115 ,, 95 ,,
   1802 ,, 133 ,, 88 ,,

Dr. Whitaker, in his hatred to mills, adds: "The cause of this sudden increase is that which every moralist and every lover of his country must deplore." Yet the first worsted factory was not erected here till about 1806.

	Township.	Parish.
Population: 1801—	4100.	
1811—		
1821—	6136.	7375.
1831—	8036.	9256.
1841—	10157.	11860.
1851—	13434.	
1861—	13249.	
1871—		18116 in 3784 houses.
1881—	18437.	
1891—	19284.	21418.

Topographical Notes.

BY way of conclusion, we draw together some topographical notes to amplify previous references.

EAST RIDDLESDEN. In 1320 the Bolton Priory compotus mentions the stagnum or fishpond at Riddlesden, possibly the pond shewn in the view. The enormous open fireplace in one of the cottages is worthy of inspection. It is a great pity this house has been divided into tenements, instead of being laid out as a mansion. A house that runs back to the Conquest in its descent from Gospatric the son of Archil, and from Simon de Montalt or Mawde, whose mother was sister of Adam filius Gospatric, is one of no ordinary interest. Before 1400 West Riddlesden estate was taken from it, and the Mawdes or Maudes resided there till it passed by marriage of the Maude heiress to the Leach family, and was purchased from the Leaches in 1809 by the Greenwoods of Keighley. East Riddlesden passed to the Paslews by a marriage which took place between Robert Paslew and Elizabeth Montalt in 1402. One of the *de Elands* held lands here in right of his wife Katherine Montalt, 1362. Walter Paslew joined in the Rising of the North with the Nortons of Rilston, and in the Tower of London are the words inscribed by him, "Walter Paslew, 1569. Extrema anchora Christus, 1570." His daughter Ellen married John Rishworth, Esq., Coley, whose son John and grandson Robert resided at Riddlesden until they mortgaged, and eventually sold it to James Murgatroyd of Warley, who restored the old hall about 1634. His son John was a very wealthy man, but he died in debt in 1662. The story of these Murgatroyds will be found in the *Bradford Antiquary*, April, 1892, in a paper by Mr. W. A. Brigg. East Riddlesden passed to the Starkies about 1688, who resided here for a century. Since the division by the marriage of Starkies heiresses, the mansion has been occupied as a farm and cottages. From the will of Alex. Paslew, 1513, we learn that the Riddlesden chantry at Bingley, in which he desired to be buried, was dedicated to St. Lawrence, and to the altar of St. Lawrence Qwere he gave a vestment of chamlett.

WEST RIDDLESDEN was retained by the Maudes much longer than East Riddlesden, and it passed by marriage to the Leaches, the heiress surviving her seven brothers. The Greenwoods of Keighley, were the next owners, by purchase from Leach. Mr. J. B. Sedgwick of Stone Gappe, became tenant in 1857. Stained glass in the staircase indicates Arthur Maude's ownership.

RIDDLESDEN OR MORTON BANKS VILLAGE. The incumbents of Riddlesden, Morton Banks, have been the Revs. Messrs. Fawcett, Fisher, Sandbergh, Colebach Share, David Cowling, H. A. Claxton; and the schoolmasters, Charles Boyce, Lambert, W. Wilkinson, James Smith. Besides the two old Halls, Riddlesden or Morton Banks has some substantial old straw-thatched houses and many new houses. The Keighley and Bingley Hospital is a notable structure. The Primitive Methodist Chapel, and the Wesleyan Chapel (memorial stones laid Sep. 23, 1882, by Robert Clough and John W. Laycock,) are the chief buildings of interest. The Primitive Chapel, built 1843, was enlarged in 1896, the stones bearing the names of Mrs. Waterhouse and Ald. Ira Ickringill, J.P., April 25, 1896. Elam, or eel-holme, near the ford where the Roman coins were found, is an old farm-house.

Probably Riddlesden is derived from the British Rhyd, a ford.

MORTON CHURCH, St. Luke's, was opened in 1851, the services before being held in the National School. Mr. Greenwood, the clerk for over fifty years, records the incumbents as follows: Rev. Wm. Fawcett, Sept. 1845 to 1876. Rev. Francis Marriner, Sept. 1876 to 1884. Rev. Joseph Weedow, 1884 to 1892, when he shot himself at Rhyl after some shameful proceedings. Rev. W. H. S. Hartley succeeded. The schoolmasters here have been Nicholas Barker, about 1845, first master, — Walker, Benj. Bartram, George Normington, Wm. Hartley, James Fortune, Charles Boyce, Edwin Cotton, 1860, Henry Young, 1864, Cotton again, Wm. Fitton Green, 1866, Wilkinson Greenwood, son of the clerk, since 1867. Robert Holmes, author of "Keighley, Past and Present," or so reputed, was schoolmaster at East Morton National School. At the British School in Morton the masters have included since 1829, Philpot, Narracott, Creighton, Hodgson, Wm. Gill, Chas. Boyce.

An old milestone near Blackpots, dated 1739, gives 3 m. to Keighley, 2 m. to Eighley (Ilkley), 6 m. to Skipton, 5 m. to Otley. There is another milestone in a field at the lodge, Upwood.

UPWOOD, formerly a shooting lodge, was the home of the Busfeild family until recently, when Captain Sparks became tenant.

In MORTON the public buildings include the Primitive Methodist Chapel, 1827; the Methodist Chapel, 1846, and School, 1875; the Independent Chapel, Bethel, 1845, the National School, 1845, the Busfeild Arms and other public-houses, a house dated I.L. 1700. The Independents have a minister's house, given by Mr. J. W. Wright, but since the removal of the Rev. John Mills to Frome, there has been no resident minister. An old Town's School is in existence. The ruined mill in the clough adds picturesqueness to the scenery, but the larger ones higher up are of more benefit. On May 28, 1849, a great flood happened at Sunnydale. Mr. Smith, a founder of the Independent Chapel, had dammed up three streams to run a new paper mill. A heavy thunderstorm caused the embankment to yield, and most of the dams in the valley were burst, houses damaged, furniture lost, but no lives sacrificed.

RYSHWORTH HALL lies in the valley. It is supposed to be named after the Rishworths of Riddlesden, but I think it is much older than their date, as a homestead. The surname *de Rishford* has been given

T

in our earlier pages. The Eltofts sold it in 1591 to Edward Bynns, and Abm. Binns, Esq., J.P., sold it in 1672, to W. Busfeild, Esq. These were the great families here before the Civil Wars, and a chantry chapel at Bingley is named after the estate. It passed to the Busfeild family. Mr. Alfred Harris, afterwards of Oxton Hall. Tadcaster, resided here some years ago; also Mr. C. Dunlop. Mr. C. E. Sugden is the present tenant.

GREENHILL HALL was the home of the old family of Whitley.

MYRTLE GROVE was formerly known as Springhead farm. It was built by J. A. Busfeild, Esq., and 'this paradise' was visited by the venerable Wesley. General Twiss was a tenant. It was purchased by Mr. Sharp as elsewhere stated.

MICKLETHWAITE. The Methodist Free Church foundation stone bears the name of J. W. Wright, Esq., April 3, 1875. The congregation formerly met in the square lower down. The Wesleyan Chapel bears date 1853; enlarged 1883; memorial stone laid July 28th, by Miss Butler (Mrs. Asquith). Here are several quaint old houses.

GAWTHORPE HALL has been the property of the Walkers, the Currers, Benson, Lord Bingley, and the Lane Fox family, but it passed in modern times by purchase to Mr. Horsfall, who restored it, and sold it to Major Salmond, and he disposed of it to Mr. Weatherhead. It is a fine old mansion, commanding beautiful and extensive prospects.

MARLEY. The home of the Marleys, and Saviles of olden times, is worthy a careful examination. It was rebuilt by John Savile, Esq., in 1627, as indicated by his arms and initials. His jester or hal, Sil o' Marley, had a reputation that survives to this day. The Maudes and Currers had lived here before the Saviles. Robert Savile, the spend-thrift, sold Marley to Samuel Sunderland, Esq., of Hill End, Harden, a native of Coley. Mr. Sunderland died in 1667, and bequeathed Marley to his nephew Robert Parker of Browsholme, who removed Joshua Walker, the tenant, as Heywood says, and Mr. Parker gathered many antiquarian treasures when residing here. He was a benefactor to the hospital at Waddington. Mrs. Ferrand became owner by purchase in 1842.

THE OLD VICARAGE was the property of the Monks of Drax, and undoubtedly the earlier vicars resided here. An ancient mound called the Monks' Tower, some venerable yews, a monster tithe barn, and a peculiar water-trough are objects of interest. Notices of the Hulberts of Old Vicarage, and of the Dobsons appear previously. Mr. H. W. Hardcastle, of Priesthorpe, is the present owner, but Mr. Orchardson is the tenant.

Near the Old Vicarage is the Spa Well, which with such holy-wells as St. Ives' and St. Anthony's at Harden, was formerly in much esteem.

LONGWOOD, near Marley, named after the wood, is the name of a mansion built in 1867 for Mr. Selwyn. It soon passed to Mr. Harris and then to Mr. John Taylor, and soon again to Mr. Albert Mitchell.

The public Cemetery, area 10 acres, is one of the most picturesque God's acres in the country, and we may say unique in having a marvellous variety of plants and trees.

The Grammar Schools, Technical College, Free Library, Town Hall, Court House, Cottage Hospital, Park of 18 acres, are but the chief town attractions, with the places of worship, of Bingley.

As a coaching-centre there is no reason to wonder why Bingley has such quaint old inns as the King's Head, (where the Court Leet was held,) the Brown Cow, (where the Petty Sessions and afterwards the Local Board met, in a room afterwards used as a school by Mr. Hogg,) the White Horse, (from whose horse-steps John Wesley is said to have preached,) the Old Queen's Head, the Old Elm Tree Inn, the Fleece, and the Ring of Bells.

ELDWICK HALL.

ELDWICK HALL bears date 1696, R.L., and on the end I.H.S. 1716. Benjamin Harboyne, a Lisbon banker, had the misfortune to see his home and family swallowed up in the earthquake of 1755, when most of Lisbon was ruined. The shock so affected his reason that he became a raving maniac, and was brought over to England and kept in chains by a keeper at Eldwick Hall, till he died. The story is told that a man was once murdered here by his brother, and Joseph Raistrick, who lived here last century, discovered about 1770, a quantity of human bones and a rusty blocker, under the barn floor. William Raistrick, son of Joseph, returning from Bingley church one Sunday morning, jumped into Eldwick mill dam to rescue a girl, and handed her out to people near, but he sank back and was not recovered. Henry Atkinson, who lived at Eldwick Hall about 1830, was so famous a marksman, that he shot through a wooden trencher held in his son's hand, at 150 yards' distance. As at Marley Hall, there is a tradition that a hal or fool was kept here in former times.

In the fields to the right, higher up the lane, is TOILS FARM (? the hole's farm), the home of John Whitley, who came here in 1759 from Hanshaw in Netherdale. Besides the Wesley portrait, and inscription dated 1776, there are glass markings in shorthand dated 1675, and the name T. Denton, 1802. James Whitley, of Harrogate, grandson of Francis, started the alpaca trade at Holy-land, Morton, now converted into four cottages, and did a large business in woolcombing, his workmen "(de)livering in" their work from all the villages around.

ELDWICK CHURCH.

Eldwick is a very quiet hamlet with a new Church, new Board School, new Wesleyan Chapel, three Inns and an old Mill, but Gilstead has increased largely in population during the past thirty years, whilst Eldwick itself has dwindled to half its population of last century. We have elsewhere shewn that the old name was Helwick.

In an undated deed, Robert de Villayn gave all his land in the common field of Helewyke and in the field of Faheder, or Faweather, with common pasture in Helewyke township to Rievaulx Priory.

MILNER FIELD has been previously described. The present mansion was erected in 1872.

BECKFOOT. On the house will be found the inscription **T B** 1617, with the cross of the Knights of St. John, and at the gable corners the carved stones usually called the Crusaders' Lanterns. The barn shews traces of ecclesiastical architecture, and it is not unlikely that a chapel existed here in Catholic times. The letters IR ER AR indicate the Rawson ownership in former times.

COTTINGLEY BRIDGE HOUSE was formerly the home of the Busfeilds.

COTTINGLEY was formerly on the main road, before the highway was made from the bridge to Bingley in 1825. An old home of the Hollings family, and the Sun Inn are noteworthy buildings. The Town Hall, opened in March, 1865, and costing £3000, took the place of a Day and Sunday School which had been conducted for sixty years in inconvenient extemporized buildings. An organ was added in 1869, and the management is undenominational.

The Mechanics' Institute, established 1852, removed to the Town Hall in October, 1865.

Stock House, near Goit Stock, was the home of Mr. Thomas Baines, manufacturer, son of the Rev. Samuel Baines, Wilsden.

A Church, dedicated to St. Michael and All Angels, was consecrated in Sept. 1886. There had previously been a Mission Church. Henry Mason, Esq., was the founder and patron.

BANKFIELD, built in 1848, was formerly the residence of Wm. Murgatroyd, Esq., Mayor of Bradford in 1854. It became the property of Henry Mason, Esq., and was enlarged in 1871. Here he made his special collection of paintings.

NAB-WOOD has its name from the knoll or nab, and not from the slang term for thieving.

HIRST WOOD is a redundancy, as both words mean the same. The scenery about Hirst Mill is specially fine, and artists often frequent the spot.

COTTINGLEY HOUSE was the seat of the Dobsons, and the Lamplugh-Wickhams. It passed to the Ferrands by purchase. Mr. Richard Thornton, father of the explorer, was a tenant here.

COTTINGLEY HALL, now demolished, bore date 1659, R.A.F. (Robert and Anne Ferrand), and the knights' double cross.

At HARDEN, we learn from the Bingley Register, one child and one monster of John Milner's was borne, Sep. 24, 1583, and viewed by somndry prsons; and in the burials, same date, one monster and one prfect child of John Mylner of Harden. Other curious extracts from these registers will be found in my pamphlet "A Day at Bingley," and references to Emmat, a Bingley centenarian, and to Thornton, an usher at Bingley School, who died on Rundles Moor in 1694, will be found in Heywood's *Diaries*.

The Whites of Harden deserve passing notice. The Rev. Mr. White of Northowram was a native of Harden, and his brother Thomas was master of Northowram "Bell" School.

The names of Milligan, Sharp, and Watmuff, are identified with the Harden Mill since 1800.

St. Ives, (the ancient Halton Grange and more recently Harden Grange), is the spot that would tempt the visitor to 'linger a bit longer.' It was built in 1616. In a summer-house may be seen a table bearing the inscription: "This table was at Harden Hall when the troops under General Fairfax were encamped at Harden Moor MDCXLII." Besides the Ferrand Arms as seen on our engraving, there is the quaint advice:

> If thou a house shall finde,
> Built to thy mynde,
>   And that without thy cost,
> Serve thou the more
> God and the poore
>   And then my labour is not loste.

HERON, St. Ives Lake.

The magnificent woods and moss-covered rocks afford hours of pleasure to the rambling naturalist, whilst the moor beyond is enchanting. St. Ives lake or Coppice pond is one of the Yorkshire haunts of the Heron. Near the lake are the Blantyre rocks which the late Hon. Mrs. Ferrand liked to visit, and near which is the obelisk to the memory of her husband, with a long inscription as previously recorded. The Soldiers' Graves, Fairfax Entrenchments, and Druids' Altar are beyond the park boundaries. The Cave, called Panhole, was explored in 1874, but no traces of human occupation were found.

On the terrace at St. Ives may be seen some fossil lizards and a stone coffin or bath found close by.

HARDEN GRANGE, the old St. Ives, was rebuilt in 1855, and has been for many years the residence of Walter Dunlop, Esq. A stone on the road entering Harden village is dated 1713, and bears the Ferrand crest and the statement that the road belonged to Benjamin Ferrand, Esq. The Cockrofts have given their name to a mill and fold.

WOODBANK bears the inscription S.F. 1635.

HILL-END, Harden, is memorable as the residence of Mr. Samuel Sunderland, when he was robbed. Over the mistal-door are his initials, S.S. 1650. One of the Waterhouses in more recent times reached 103 years of age in this healthy homestead.

RYECROFT is a hamlet with a Primitive Methodist Chapel. SHACKLETON HOUSE, the home of the Quaker family from 1669 at latest, has been previously described. THORN HOUSE, over two hundred years old, was the residence of the Knowles.

ANCIENT BINGLEY. 311

HAINWORTH, in Bingley parish, was joined with Ingrow in Keighley parish to form St. John's parish, in 1841. References to this place will be found in the Domesday chapter.

HALLAS or HALLOWES and HEWENDEN have been previously mentioned. GOIT-STOCK waterfall, and the home of the Horsfalls are worthy of a particular visit. Hallas Hall bears date 1737, but this is very modern compared with the antiquity of the name. The Wrights and the Andertons are the old residents.

GOIT-STOCK WATERFALL. *Photo. by H. England, Esq.*

MYTHOLM, possibly middle-holm or pasture, is a frequent place-name in Calder and Airedales. An old endowed School, dated 1680, served for Harden in former times, and for a village Sunday School. The Church of England, Wesleyans, Independents and Wesleyan Reformers have large places of worship in Harden, and there are several large mills.

CULLINGWORTH is a large and prosperous village, the principal land-owners being Sir Francis Sharp Powell, Bart., M.P., W. Ferrand, Esq., and Messrs. Townend. The Royd is a modern mansion built by Mr. Townend on a piece of cleared woodland as the name indicates. The pedigree of the family runs back here at least five generations, from William Townend, his son Simeon, his son George who died in 1837, who had several sons, Robert (father of Joseph, George and Frederick), Simeon, George, William, Edward, &c. Robert died in 1862, and William in 1844. One branch of the family resides at The Nook. Cullingworth has a church dedicated to St. John; the successive incumbents have been, Rev. G. Poyntz, Rev. T. Brayshaw, a native of Idle, afterwards of Keighley school, and author of a work on Mnemonics; Rev. J. H. Mitchell, who died in June, 1873, the Rev. Robert Stansfield, now of Keighley.

The Wesleyan cause is over 120 years old, but the chapel was not erected until 1806, the day school in 1844.

The Baptists originated in 1835.

The old village school of last century was demolished when the new church school was built.

The Oddfellows' Lodge was founded in 1832, and their hall was built in 1835.

The Enclosure Act of 1816 brought much of the moorland into cultivation; the section assigned to the lord of the manor is known as the Lord's Allotments.

Dolphin Lane, Flappit Springs, Castlestead Ring, Laverack Hall, Catstones cairn, and Mootham Stone are interesting places, as the names indicate: Of the first two, Dolphin may be derived from a personal name, and Flappit from a bird. Castlestead is an ancient encampment. Laverock is a frequent name for old houses around which the "gentle laverock," layrock or lark sang. Catstones or cat-steps are common near woods, and have no reference to cats, but, like *cote*, and Welsh *coyd*, indicate a footpath or steps on a woody brow. Mootham is a jutting rock, but whether it indicates a moot or place of assembly must be left to conjecture. Three becks, Ellar-car (named after the elder shrubbery at the rocks), Cow-house, and Many wells (which carries its watery explanation to all observers,) meet to form the Harden Beck.

Works by J. HORSFALL TURNER, Idel, Bradford.

YORKSHIRE COUNTY MAGAZINE, an Illustrated Monthly, 4 vols., in parts 20/-
YORKSHIRE NOTES & QUERIES, with the YORKSHIRE GENEALOGIST, YORKSHIRE BIBLIOGRAPHER, and YORKSHIRE FOLK-LORE JOURNAL. 22 parts, 1700 pages, 550 illustrations ... 30/-
[Emblazoned Arms, Steel plates, Woodcuts, &c.]
ILKLEY, ANCIENT & MODERN, 80 choice illustrations ... 14/-
Large Paper, very few remain 24/-
HISTORY OF BRIGHOUSE & HIPPERHOLME, 170 illus. 10/-
Large Paper 25/-
HAWORTH, PAST & PRESENT, 20 illus., only 10 copies remain, 3/-
REV. O. HEYWOOD'S DIARIES, 1630-1702, illustrating the General and Family History of Yorkshire and Lancashire, 4 vols., 380 pages each, illustrated 24/-
NONCONFORMIST REGISTER, Births, Marriages, Deaths, 1644-1750, by Heywood and Dickenson. Supplement to Y. & L. Parish Registers. 5 illustrations, 380 pages 6/-
NONCONFORMITY IN IDEL & HISTORY OF AIREDALE COLLEGE, 10 illustrations 3/-
INDEPENDENCY AT BRIGHOUSE, 4 illustrations ... 3/-
BIOGR. HALIFAX, a Biographical and Genealogical History, vol. I only ready, a re-print of half of Mr. Watson's "Halifax," 6/-
LIFE OF CAPT. HODGSON, Halifax, Ripon, 1640-83... 1/6.
WRIGHT'S ANTIQUITIES of Halifax ... ... 1/6.
TRIPLEX MEMORIALE, (York, 1650), by Ainsworth. Three quaint Sermons, from the only known copy 2/-
HALIFAX GIBBET BOOK, with additions 2/-
MORLEY AND TOPCLIFFE NONCONFORMIST REGISTERS, 1654-1888, 12 illus., historical sketches by W. Smith, F.S.A.S., 6/-
ELLAND TRAGEDIES; 1330-50 ... ... 2/-
BRADFORD SIEGES AND HISTORY (1776), ... 2/-
IDEL IN OLDEN TIMES ... ... 8d.
A DAY AT SKIPTON, 36 illustrations ... ... 6d.
A DAY IN NIDDERDALE, 7 illustrations ... ... 3d.
A DAY AT BOLTON PRIORY, 13 illustrations ... ... 3d.
A DAY AT BINGLEY 14 ,, ... 3d.
A DAY AT HAWORTH 14 ,, ... 3d.
CHARLOTTE BRONTË'S LETTERS. (All disposed of.)
REV. PATRICK BRONTË: His Life and Works, illustrated; 5/- to Subscribers. Large paper copies 10/-

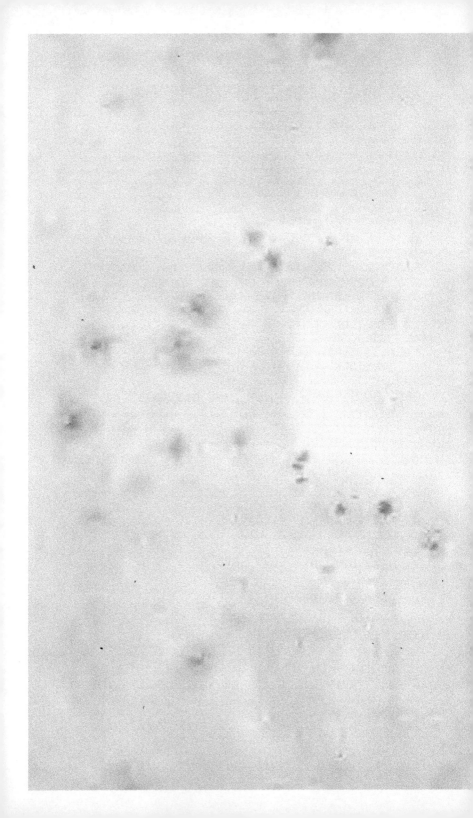

CPSIA information can be obtained
at www.ICGtesting.com
Printed in the USA
BVHW031146011221
622971BV00004B/106